SCIENCE TEACHING

Philosophy of Education Research Library

Series Editors
V. A. Howard and Israel Scheffler
Harvard Graduate School of Education

Recent decades have witnessed the decline of distinctively philosophical thinking about education. Practitioners and the public alike have increasingly turned rather to psychology, the social sciences and to technology in search of basic knowledge and direction. However, philosophical problems continue to surface at the center of educational concerns, confronting educators and citizens as well with inescapable questions of value, meaning, purpose, and justification.

PERL will publish works addressed to teachers, school administrators and researchers in every branch of education, as well as to philosophers and the reflective public. The series will illuminate the philosophical and historical bases of educational practice, and assess new educational trends as they emerge.

Already published

SCIENCE TEACHING

The Role of History and Philosophy of Science
Michael R. Matthews

ROUTLEDGE
New York • London

Published in 1994 by

Routledge
29 West 35 Street
New York, NY 10001

Published in Great Britain by

Routledge
11 New Fetter Lane
London EC4P 4EE

Library of Congress Cataloging-in-Publication Data

Matthews, Michael R.
    History, philosophy, and science teaching / Michael R. Matthews.
       p.   cm.—(Philosophy of education research library)
    Includes bibliographical references and index.
    ISBN 0-415-90282-7 (cloth)—ISBN 0-415-90899-X (pbk)
    1. Science—Study and teaching—History.   2. Science—Study and teach-
ing—Philosophy.   3. Science teachers—Training of.   I. Title.
    II. Series.
    Q181.M183   1994
    507'.1—dc20   93-32237
                                                       CIP

British Library Cataloguing-in-Publication Data also available.

For Clare and Alice

Contents

Acknowledgments

For the past five years the writing of this book has severely encroached upon my family time. My wife Julie House and daughters Clare and Alice deserve thanks for their forbearance. Julie House is owed a significant additional debt for copyediting and proofing numerous drafts of the book. She did her best to correct the worst of the expression, the most serious of the grammatical mistakes, and frequent misspellings. In addition she argued over most of the central points, and was persistent in trying to keep the text focused. All readers are indebted to her for making their job so much easier than it otherwise would have been.

I am grateful to Professor Israel Scheffler for the invitation to write this book for his, and Vernon Howard's, Philosophy of Education Research Library, and to Jayne Fargnoli, the Routledge education editor, for her patience.

I am indebted to the many members of the International History, Philosophy, and Science Teaching Group who have been generous over the past five years with ideas, hospitality and enthusiasm. Two major conferences organised by Ken Tobin and David Gruender (Tallahassee 1989) and Skip Hills and Brian McAndrews (Kingston 1992) stimulated much that has gone into this book. Editorship of the journal *Science & Education*, which is devoted to the theme of the book, has enabled me to read, and benefit from, the work of a wide range of authors from all over the globe. The advice and encouragement of Martin Eger and Fabio Bevilacqua have been of special importance. Others, too numerous to mention, are, I hope, aware of my gratitude.

I have a debt to my teachers who introduced me to the history and philosophy of science. I am particularly grateful to Professor Wallis A. Suchting, formerly of Sydney University, whose standards of scholarship and breadth of knowledge are a model for those who have had the good fortune to be his students. Professor Abner Shimony at Boston University introduced me to the writings of Galileo, and Professors Robert S. Cohen and Marx W. Wartofsky, also of Boston University, helpfully placed science and the philosophy of science in the broader social and historical context. I am also indebted to Dr Bill Andersen, formerly of Sydney University, my first teacher in philosophy of education, who encouraged, among others, a young, naive science student to identify and grapple with philosophical questions in education.

My employers, the University of New South Wales and the University of Auckland, have made this book possible. The former's library is a cornucopia of materials in science education and the history and philosophy of science. The University of Auckland was a generous and supportive employer during my two year period as the Foundation Professor of Science Education. This enabled me to complete the book.

Friends have been good enough to read the penultimate version of the manuscript and suggest corrections and offer valuable advice. To Drs. Michael Howard, Peter Slezak, Colin Gauld, Wallis Suchting, Richard Thorley, Fabio Bevilacqua, Harvey Siegel and James Wandersee I am very grateful. Their scholarship and attention to detail have saved readers from the worst of my errors. Jan Duncan has been of great assistance in proofreading, checking of references, and the preparation of figures.

Finally, I am grateful to Gill Kent, Routledge's copyeditor, for her meticulous attention to detail. The book is considerably more polished for her labors.

Preface

This book seeks to contribute to science teaching and science teacher education by bringing the history and philosophy of science (HPS) and science teaching into closer contact. My belief is that science teaching can be improved if it is infused with the historical and philosophical dimensions of science. Such contextual, or liberal, teaching of science in schools benefits both those students going on to further study of science, and those, the majority, for whom school science is their last contact with formal science instruction.

The conviction that the learning *of* science needs to be accompanied by learning *about* science is basic to liberal approaches to the teaching of science. This position has been eloquently argued by, amongst others, Ernst Mach, James Conant, Gerald Holton, Joseph Schwab and Martin Wagenschein. This book is a housekeeping effort in the liberal tradition: it attempts to survey the history of debate on the matter; to list the chief publications; to itemize contemporary relevant research, particularly in children's learning of science; to point to present-day practical and theoretical problems in science education to which the history and philosophy of science can contribute; to give an account of curriculum developments embodying the liberal spirit of science instruction; and to indicate ways in which the history and philosophy of science can be usefully included in teacher preparation programs.

This book is the work of a underlaborer in the garden, to use John Locke's expression. Some furrows have been made and some seeds planted. Hopefully other people will water the garden, straighten the furrows, plant other seeds, and remove some of the weeds. If the book stimulates science teachers at both schools and universities to be more interested in the history and philosophy of science, and encourages historians, philosophers and sociologists of science to become interested and involved with science education, then it will have achieved one purpose. If it contributes to the inclusion of HPS studies in science teacher-education programs, it will have achieved another purpose. If it promotes an interest in educational theory amongst science educators, it will have achieved still another.

The theme of this book is that science teachers need three competencies: first, knowledge and appreciation of science; second, some understanding of HPS in order to do justice to the subject they are teaching and to teach it well, and in order to make intelligent appraisals of the many theoretical and educational debates that rage around the science curriculum; third, some educational theory or vision that can inform their classroom activities and relations with students, and provide a rationale and purpose for their pedagogical efforts. Science teachers contribute to the overall education of students, thus they need some moderately well-formed view of what education is, and the goals it should be pursuing. Teachers need to keep their eyes on the educational prize, the more so when social pressures increasingly devalue the intellectual and critical traditions of education.

It is widely recognised that there is a crisis in Western science education. Levels of science literacy are disturbingly low. This is anomalous because science is one of the greatest achievements of human culture. It has a wonderfully interesting and complex past, it has revealed an enormous amount about ourselves and the world in which we live, it has directly and indirectly transformed the social and natural worlds, and the human and environmental problems requiring scientific understanding are pressing—yet, disturbingly, students and teachers are deserting science.

This flight from the science classroom by both teachers and students has been depressingly well documented. In the US in the mid-1980s it was estimated that each year 600 science graduates entered the teaching profession whilst 8,000 left it (Mayer 1987). In 1986, 7,100 US high schools had no course in physics, and 4,200 had no course in chemistry (Mayer 1987). In 1990 only four states required the three years of basic science recommended by the sobering 1983 report *A Nation at Risk*, the rest allowed high school graduation with only two years science (Beardsley 1992, p.80). Irrespective of years required, seventy percent of all school students drop science at the first available opportunity—which is one reason why in 1986 less than one in five high school graduates had studied any physics. In 1991 the Carnegie Commission on Science, Technology and Government warned that the failings of science education were so great that they posed a "chronic and serious threat to our nation's future" (Beardsley 1992, p.79). In the UK, recent reports of the National Commission on Education and the Royal Society have both documented similar trends. One commentator has said that "wherever you look, students are turning away from science. Those that do go to university are often of a frighteningly low calibre" (Bown 1993, p.12). In Australia in 1989 science education programmes had the lowest entrance requirement of all university degrees.

There are complex economic, social, cultural, and systemic reasons for this rejection of science. These are beyond the scope of teachers to rectify. But there are also educational reasons for the rejection of science that are within the power of teachers and administrators to change. In 1989, for example, a disturbing number of the very top Australian school science achievers gave "too boring" as the reason for not pursuing university science. It is these curriculum and pedagogical failings that the history and philosophy of science can help rectify.

One part of this contribution by HPS is to connect topics in particular scientific disciplines, to connect the disciplines of science with each other, to connect the sciences generally with mathematics, philosophy, literature, psychology, history, technology, commerce and theology, and finally, to display the interconnections of science and culture—the arts, ethics, religion, politics—more broadly. Science has developed in conjunction with other disciplines; there has been mutual interdependence. It has also developed, and is practiced, within a broader cultural and social milieu. These interconnections and interdependencies can be appropriately explored in science programs from elementary school through to graduate study. The result is far more satisfying for students than the unconnected topics that constitute most programs of school and university science. Courses in the sciences are too often, as one student remarked, "forced marches through unknown country without time to look sideways."

The defense of science in schools is important, if not necessary, to the intellectual health of society. Pseudoscientific and irrational world views already have a strong hold in Western culture; antiscience is on the rise. It is not just the ramparts of society that have been invaded—witness the checkout-counter tabloids with their "Elvis Lives" stories, Gallup polls showing that forty percent of the adult US population believe that human life began on earth just a couple of thousand years ago, and astrology columns in every newspaper. But the educational citadel has been compromised—a small, and hopefully not representative, 1988 survey of US biology teachers revealed that thirty percent rejected the theory of evolution, while twenty-two percent believed in ghosts (Martin 1994). For all its faults, the scientific tradition has promoted rationality, critical thinking and objectivity. It instills a concern for evidence, and for having ideas judged not by personal or social interest, but by how the world is; a sense of "Cosmic Piety," as Bertrand Russell called it. These values are under attack both inside and outside the academy. Some educationally-influential versions of postmodernism and constructivism turn their back on rationality and objectivity, saying that their pursuit is Quixotic. This is indeed a serious challenge to the profession of science teaching.

The vitality of the scientific tradition, and its positive impact on society, depends upon children being successfully introduced to its achievements, methods and thought processes, by teachers who understand and value science. The history and philosophy of science contributes to this understanding and valuation.

This book grows out of, and is a contribution to, the International History, Philosophy, and Science Teaching Group. This is a heterogenous group of teachers, scientists, educators, historians, mathematicians, philosophers of education and philosophers of science who over the past five years have staged two conferences[1] and have arranged the publication of many special issues of academic journals devoted to HPS and science teaching.[2] Some basic papers in the field have been gathered together and published in my *History, Philosophy, and Science Teaching: Select Readings* (OISE Press,

Toronto, and Teachers College Press, New York, 1990). These might be useful for further reading. The International History, Philosophy, and Science Teaching Group is also associated with a new journal devoted to the subject of this book—*Science & Education: Contributions from the History, Philosophy, and Sociology of Science and Mathematics.*[3]

CHAPTER 1

The Rapprochement Between History, Philosophy and Science Education

In 1985 a paper was published titled "Science Education and Philosophy of Science: Twenty-Five Years of Mutually Exclusive Development" (Duschl 1985). This was an account of the missed opportunities and shortsighted curricular projects that resulted from the development of science education largely separate from the disciplines of history and philosophy of science. Pleasingly, in recent times there has been some rapprochement between these fields. The well-documented crisis in science education and analyses of its causes and remedies are resulting in both the theory and, importantly, the practice of science education becoming more informed by the history and philosophy of science.

This book seeks to contribute to this rapprochement in a number of ways: by outlining the arguments for the role of HPS in science education; by reviewing the history of school science curricula in order to situate the claims of HPS-informed teaching against other approaches to science; by examining the successes and failures of previous efforts to bring HPS into closer connection with the science program; by elaborating some case studies where the contrast between HPS and "professional" approaches to science teaching and curricula development can be evaluated; by looking at some instances of prominent educational debates in science education— constructivism and multicultural science education—that can be clarified and informed by HPS; and finally, by outlining the contribution of HPS to science teacher education. It is hoped that the book will stimulate interest in educational matters among historians and philosophers of science, and encourage interest in historical and philosophical matters among science teachers and, particularly, the educators of science teachers.

The present rapprochement between HPS and science education represents in part a renaissance of the long-marginalised liberal, or contextual, tradition of science education, a tradition contributed to in the last hundred years by scientists and educators such as Ernst Mach, Pierre Duhem, Alfred North Whitehead, Percy Nunn, James Conant, Joseph Schwab, Martin Wagenschein and Gerald Holton. At its most general level the liberal tradition in education embraces Aristotle's delineation of truth, goodness, and beauty as the ideals that people ought to cultivate in their appropriate spheres of endeavor. That is, in intellectual matters truth should be sought, in moral matters goodness, and in artistic and creative matters beauty. Education is to contribute to these ends: it is to assist the development of a person's knowledge, moral outlook and behavior, and aesthetic sensibilities and capacities. For a liberal, education is more than the preparation for work.

The liberal tradition is characterized by a number of educational commitments.[1] One is that education entails the introduction of children to the best traditions of their culture, including the academic disciplines, in such a way that they both understand the subject discipline, and know something about the discipline—its methodology, assumptions, limitations, history and so forth. A second feature is that, as far as is possible and appropriate, the relations of particular subjects to each other, and their relation to the broader canvas of ethics, religion, culture, economics and politics should be acknowledged and investigated. The liberal tradition seeks to overcome intellectual fragmentation. Contributors to the liberal tradition believe that science taught from such a perspective, and informed by the history and philosophy of the subject, can engender understanding of nature, the appreciation of beauty in both nature and science, and the awareness of ethical issues unveiled by scientific knowledge and created by scientific practice.

Science has been one of the most significant contributors to the development of our culture and our understanding of the world. Food production, medicine, entertainment, war, industry, human reproduction, transportation, accommodation, religion, space exploration and people's self-understanding—their sense of place in the universe and in the world of nature—have all been profoundly affected by science. Of course science has not been without its critics,[2] but if education is to be an initiation into the best and most important achievements of our culture, then science deserves its place in the curriculum alongside literature, music, art, technology, history and social science. And all students ought to have some knowledge of, and hopefully appreciation and enthusiasm for, the subject. There are of course legitimate and important questions concerned with *who* decides *what* is best in *whose* culture. These are pressing questions in all societies: what is the appropriate voice to be given to children, teachers, teacher unions, university educationalists, discipline authorities, business leaders and politicians in deciding the curriculum? Should such questions, regardless of who decides them, be decided on a local level or on a regional or national level? And irrespective of who decides and where they decide, are there social and educational principles of any kind that should guide such deliberations? These are all important and long-debated issues of educational and political theory that inevitably confront science teachers.

The liberal tradition maintains that science education should not just be an education or training *in* science, although of course it must be this, but also an education *about* science. Students educated in science should have an appreciation of scientific methods, their diversity and their limitations. They should have a feeling for methodological issues, such as how scientific theories are evaluated and how competing theories are appraised, and a sense of the interrelated role of experiment, mathematics and religious and philosophical commitment in the development of science. All students, whether science majors or others, should have some knowledge of the great episodes in the development of science and consequently of culture: the ancient demythologizing of the world picture; the Copernican relocation of the earth from the centre of the solar system; the development of experimental and mathematical science associated with Galileo and Newton; Newton's demonstration that the terrestrial laws of attraction operated in the celestial realms; Darwin's epochal theory of evolution and his claims for a naturalistic understanding of life; Pasteur's discovery of the microbial basis of infection; Einstein's theories of gravitation and relativity; the discovery of the DNA code and research on the genetic basis of life. They should, depending upon their age, have an appreciation of the intellectual, technical, social and personal factors that contributed to these monumental achievements. Clearly all of these goals for general education, and for science education, point to the integration of history and philosophy into the science curriculum of schools and teacher education programmes. Teachers of science need to know something of the history and nature of the discipline they are teaching.

The rapprochement between HPS and science education is not only dependent upon the virtues of a liberal view of science education: a good technical science education also requires some integration of history and philosophy into the program. Knowledge *of* science entails knowledge of scientific facts, laws, theories—the *products* of science; it also entails knowledge of the *processes* of science—the technical and intellectual ways in which science develops and tests its knowledge claims. HPS is important for the understanding of these process skills. Technical—or "professional" as it is sometimes called—science education is enhanced if students know the meaning of terms that they are using and if they can think critically about texts, reports and their own scientific activity. Their abilities as scientists are enhanced if they have read examples of sustained inquiry, clever experimentation, and insightful hypotheses. Alfred North Whitehead expressed this view of good technical education when, just after World War Two, he said:

> The antithesis between a technical and a liberal education is fallacious. There can be no adequate technical education which is not liberal, and no liberal education which is not technical: that is, no education which does not impart both technique and intellectual vision. (Whitehead 1947, p. 73)

To teach Boyle's Law without reflection on what "law" means in science, without considering what constitutes evidence for a law in science, and without attention to who Boyle was, when he lived, and what he did, is to teach in a truncated way. More can be made of the educational moment than merely teaching, or assisting students to discover that for a given gas at a constant temperature, pressure times volume is a constant. Similarly, to teach evolution without considerations concerning theory and evidence, and Darwin's life, times and the religious, literary and philosophical controversies his theory occasioned, is also limited. Students doing and interpreting experiments need to know something of how data relies upon theory, how evidence relates to the support or falsification of hypotheses, how real cases relate to ideal cases in science, and a host of other matters which all involve philosophical or methodological concerns. Science has a rich and influential history, and it is replete with philosophical and cultural ramifications. An education in science should present students with something of this richness, and engage them in some of the big questions that have consumed scientists. Whether these questions are regarded as extrascientific or intrascientific is, pedagogically, not very important.

A common occurrence in science classrooms is a child asking: If no one has seen atoms, how come we are drawing pictures of them? Such a child is raising one of the most interesting questions in philosophy of science: the relationship of evidence to models, and of models to reality. Good science teachers should encourage such questions and be able to provide satisfactory answers, or suggestions for further questions. To reply "I do not know," or "because it is in the book" is to forego the opportunity of introducing students to the rich methodological dimensions of science. Einstein caught this philosophical dimension of science when he once described physicists as "philosophers in workmen's clothes." Science teachers, as well as being competent in science, psychology, pastoral care, crisis management and everything else demanded of them, need also to be philosophers. Students commonly ask: Why are we studying this? How do we know this is true? Does this make sense to anyone? Teachers should take advantage of such questions to widen the intellectual horizons of their students, to give them a sense that there are many big issues that deserve reflection and consideration.

Lee Shulman, a US educational researcher and policy analyst, has developed this feature of the teacher's role with his notion of Pedagogical Content Knowledge. Of this he has said:

> To think properly about content knowledge requires going beyond knowledge of the facts or concepts of a domain. It requires understanding the structures of the subject matter . . . Teachers must not only be capable of defining for students the accepted truths in a domain. They must also be able to explain why a particular proposition is deemed warranted, why it is worth knowing, and how it relates to other propositions, both within the discipline and without, both in theory and in practice. (Shulman 1986, p. 9)

The abilities sought by Shulman are enhanced if teachers are interested in and familiar with the history and philosophy of whatever subject they are teaching. The US National Standards in Science Education group is urging teachers to ask themselves and their students not just what do we know in science, but how do we know what we know. These are routine methodological questions that lead into and are answered by the philosophy of science. There are other factors promoting the present rapprochement between science education and HPS. The most significant is the failure of orthodox, technical, noncontextual science education to engage students or promote knowledge and appreciation of science in the population. There is a crisis in contemporary science education evidenced in the flight from the science classroom of both teachers and students, and in the appallingly high figures for science illiteracy in the Western world. Some of the details will be examined in Chapter 3, but the outlines are clear enough. In the US seventy percent of all school students drop science from their program at the first available opportunity. The American National Science Foundation charged that "the nation's undergraduate programs in science, mathematics and technology have declined in quality and scope to such an extent that they are no longer meeting national needs. A unique American resource has been eroded" (Heilbron 1987, p. 556). Teachers and administrators are receptive to different approaches, such as those proposed by advocates of liberal or contextual teaching, that might alleviate this problem.

Studies of scientific illiteracy reveal a situation that is culturally alarming, not just because they indicate that large percentages of the population do not know the meaning of basic scientific concepts,[3] and thus have little if any idea of how nature functions and how technology works, but because they suggest widespread antiscientific views, and illogical thought. Newspaper astrology columns are read by far more people than science columns; the tabloid press, with their Elvis sightings and Martian visits, adorn checkout counters and are consumed by millions worldwide each day. When thought becomes so free from rational constraints, then outpourings of racism, prejudice, hysteria and fanaticism of all kinds can be expected. For all its faults, science has been an important factor in combating superstition, prejudice and ignorance. It has provided, albeit falteringly, a counterinfluence to the natural inclinations of people to judge circumstances in terms of their own self-interest. When people *en masse* abandon science, or science education abandons them, then the world is at a critical juncture. At such a time the role of the science teacher is especially vital, and in need of all the intellectual and material support possible.

Integration of HPS and science education has been proposed recently by numerous government and educational bodies. Among these have been the American Association for the Advancement of Science in two of its very influential reports *Project 2061* (AAAS 1989) and *The Liberal Art of Science* (AAAS 1990); the British National Curriculum Council (NCC 1988); the Science Council of Canada (SCC 1984); the Danish Science and Technology curriculum, and in The Netherlands, the PLON curriculum materials.[4] In these cases HPS is not simply another item of subject matter

added to the science syllabus; what is proposed is the more general incorporation of HPS themes into the content of curricula. The American Association for the Advancement of Science has written that:

> Science courses should place science in its historical perspective. Liberally
> educated students—the science major and the non-major alike—should complete
> their science courses with an appreciation of science as part of an intellectual,
> social, and cultural tradition. . . . Science courses must convey these aspects
> of science by stressing its ethical, social, economic, and political dimensions.
> (AAAS 1989, p. 24)

Other indicators of a rapprochement include the significant increase in
academic activity and research pertaining to HPS and science teaching.
This is seen in the formation of the International History, Philosophy, and
Science Teaching Group and its staging of international conferences on
HPS and Science Teaching—the first at Florida State University in 1989,
the second at Queen's University, Kingston, Ontario in 1992, the third at
University of Minnesota in 1995;[5] also in the series of conferences sponsored by the European Physical Society on History of Physics and Physics
Teaching;[6] and in the activities of the Education Committees of the US
and British History of Science Societies.[7] In the last few years there have
been about three hundred scholarly papers published on the subject of
history, philosophy and science teaching, and the establishment of the
journal *Science & Education*, devoted to this subject.

The advocates of a contextual approach to science teaching are not just
educational dreamers. There has been a tradition of attempts to teach science
in an HPS-informed or liberal manner. The strengths and weaknesses of
these attempts can be examined. Perhaps the outstanding example was the
Harvard Project Physics course developed for schools in the early 1960s
by Gerald Holton, James Rutherford and Fletcher Watson.[8] Over sixty
studies of the effectiveness of the program were published (Welch 1973)
and these were all positive and encouraging. Measures such as retention
in science, participation of women, improvement on critical thinking tests
and understanding of subject matter all showed improvement where the
Project Physics curriculum was adopted. Another example of a widely
adopted HPS-influenced course was the Yellow Version of the BSCS
Biology course developed by John Moore and Joseph Schwab.[9]

One of the great drawbacks to the effectiveness of liberal approaches was
and still is inadequately prepared teachers. The liberal approach requires a
great deal from teachers; this needs to be recognised and provided for by
those who educate and employ teachers. Teachers have an important but
onerous social role. A scientist has to understand simply what he or she
is doing in a narrow field, a teacher has to understand a broad field of
science, and moreover understand it in a way that can be made intelligible

and interesting to students—without teachers there would be no scientists. In addition teachers need a philosophy of education which provides guidelines and objectives for their classroom and extraclassroom activity. Science teachers need to have a considered view of what they are attempting to accomplish in school; they need a philosophy of education that will inform all aspects of their professional life. Purposes dictate methods.

The inclusion of history and philosophy of science does not, of course, provide all the answers to the present science education crisis—ultimately these answers lie deep in the heart of culture and economics. But the history and philosophy of science has a contribution to make to the overall task of improving science teaching and learning. Aspects of this contribution might be itemized as follows:

● HPS can humanize the sciences and connect them to personal, ethical, cultural and political concerns. There is evidence that this makes science and engineering programs more attractive to many students, and particularly girls, who currently reject them.

● HPS, particularly basic logical and analytic exercises—Does this conclusion follow from the premises? and, What do you mean by such and such?—can make classrooms more challenging, and enhance reasoning and critical thinking skills.

● HPS can contribute to the fuller understanding of scientific subject matter—it can help to overcome the "sea of meaninglessness," as Joseph Novak once said, where formulae and equations are recited without knowledge of what they mean or to what they refer.

● HPS can improve teacher education by assisting teachers to develop a richer and more authentic understanding of science and its place in the intellectual and social scheme of things. This has a flow-on effect, as there is much evidence that teachers' epistemology, or views about the nature of science, affect how they teach and the scientific message they convey to students.

● HPS can assist teachers appreciate the learning difficulties of students, because it alerts them to the historic difficulties of scientific development and conceptual change. Galileo was forty years of age before he formulated the modern conception of acceleration; despite prolonged thought he never worked out a correct theory for the tides. By historical studies teachers can see what some of the intellectual and conceptual difficulties were in the early periods of scientific disciplines. This knowledge can assist with the organization of the curriculum and the teaching of lessons.

● HPS can contribute to the clearer appraisal of many contemporary educational debates that engage science teachers and curriculum planners. Many of these debates—about constructivist teaching methods, multicultural science education, feminist science, environmental science, inquiry learning, science-technology-society curricula and so forth—make claims and assumptions about the history and epistemology of science, or the nature of human knowledge and its production and validation. Without some grounding in HPS, teachers can be too easily carried along by fashionable ideas which later, sadly, "seemed good at the time."

One reason that HPS has such a multifaceted role is that historical and philosophical reflection on the development of science is basic to any understanding of human knowledge. And as all education is concerned with the promotion of knowledge and understanding in some form, it is not surprising that HPS has wide relevance to education. To think seriously about the promotion and validation of human knowledge without trying to understand the sciences is impossible. When Karl Popper, in the 1930s, asserted that the history and philosophy of science was central to epistemology he was merely continuing the tradition of the major Western philosophers, who since the sixteenth century have informed their epistemological views by their not always adequate understanding of the natural sciences. The questions of What do we know? and How do we know it? are basic to all disciplines. The second question is not just a question about the method used in an investigation, it is a question about what makes the method fruitful in knowledge production. It is a methodological question of the kind discussed in HPS. It is not just a method question about how to get results.

Finally, HPS has been discussed so far as if it is something uncontroversial and settled. This is far from the case, as any perusal of the professional journals will attest. Serious scholars disagree over many high-level topics in the history and philosophy of science. The writer has certain views on these disputes and these will be apparent in the text. However the overall argument of this book is basically unaffected by particular disagreements, and thankfully there is a reasonable consensus on many lower-level points. The overall argument is that HPS is *relevant* to, and *implied* by, much of the practice and theory of science education. Beyond that, readers need to come to their own decisions about the specific topics—Galileo's use of mathematics and his debate with the church, the function of thought experiments, the claims of realism against empiricism, how to appraise one theory against others, and so forth. Most advocates of a liberal approach to science education share Schwab's dismay with science being taught as a "rhetoric of conclusions," and wish to avoid teaching a rhetoric of conclusions about the history and philosophy of science. No matter how strongly a teacher holds particular views in the history and philosophy of science, a HPS education requires that students themselves come to hold their own reasoned opinions on the subject.

Science teachers need to be encouraged to come to their own conclusions about the big philosophical issues, but these conclusions will be based on certain intellectual procedures that are shared by opposing viewpoints: a concern with evidence, attention to sources and their reliability, forms of valid or probable argument, and willingness to listen to and value other opinions, and so forth. Science education needs to encourage students to exercise reason, and also to be reasonable. Teachers should try to interest students in the historical and philosophical questions that can be asked of particular subject matter, rather than try to give them definitive answers, or impose their own views. As Richard Peters (1966) observed, education is not so much the arriving as the travelling with a different view.

Knowledge of the historical and philosophical dimensions of science promotes a richer, more educationally valuable, view of science and of science education. There is not, of course, a single HPS-informed view of science or of science education. There are two broad camps discernible in the literature: those who appeal to HPS to support the teaching of science, and those who appeal to HPS to puncture the perceived arrogance and authority of science. The second group stress the human face of science, the fallibility of science, the impact of politics and special interests, including racial, class and sexual interests, on the pursuit of science; they argue for skepticism about scientific knowledge claims. For this group, HPS shows that science is one among a number of equally valid ways of looking at the world, it has no epistemic privilege; its supposed privilege derives merely from social considerations and technological success. This group includes those influenced by postmodernist philosophy, and certain sociologies of science.

This book whilst written from the standpoint of the first group, does embrace a number of the positions of the second group: science does have a human, cultural, and historical dimension, it is closely connected with philosophy, interests and values, and its knowledge claims are frequently tentative. This is just to say that science is more complex, and more interesting, than many simple-minded accounts might have us, and science students, believe. But none of these admissions need lead to skepticism about the cognitive claims of science.

The fact of different orientations towards science is not itself educationally unhealthy. When Peters spoke of education, as distinct from training or schooling, involving the travelling with a different view, he meant not so much travelling with a *particular* different view, but rather being prepared to look out the window, being prepared to reflect on the educational journey and the countryside, being aware of options, thinking about the purposes of the journey, checkintg how one's own view compares with that of others and being prepared to learn from them. HPS promoted these outlooks and dispositions in science teachers and students.

While the author sees and values a particular scientific landscape characterised by the three Rs—Reason, Realism and Rationality—the thesis of the book is just that, other things being equal, science teachers with HPS interests will make science more interesting and more supportive of students' educational development.

CHAPTER 2

Historical Debates About the Science Curriculum

Most advocating an increased role for the history and philosophy of science in science teaching value the cultural, social and philosophical dimensions of science, but they also want standard science subject matter taught and learnt better. This book will argue that HPS contributes to both goals.

A *minimal* view of the role of HPS is that historical and philosophical matters be elaborated as they occur in standard science programs: when Boyle's Law is mentioned, some time should be spent on the life, times and achievements of Boyle; when plate tectonic theory is studied, some time should be spent discussing what a scientific theory is, and how it differs from a model, hypothesis or a simple belief, and perhaps the process of theory change in a scientific community, and how nationalism and other extrascientific factors can impinge on the process; when nuclear power is studied, some time should be spent on the economics, politics and ethics of nuclear power, or perhaps the moral quandaries of scientists working in nuclear weapons research. This is an icing-on-the-cake position. A *maximal* view of the role of HPS is that the science curriculum ought to be fashioned in such a way that the historical, cultural and philosophical dimensions of science are explicitly dealt with, perhaps with the curriculum being organized on historical grounds. This is a full-fledged liberal approach to the teaching of science, and can be seen in programs like Harvard Project Physics, or the Harvard Case Studies in Experimental Science.

Just as science can learn from its own history, so also can science education learn from its history. In order to appraise the worth and practicality of HPS-informed science teaching, it is useful to be aware of the history and diversity of school science curricula, and of the major debates that have occurred in efforts to improve science instruction. Unfortunately historical perspective is often lacking in educational debate; educational wheels are frequently re-invented.[1] This and the following chapter will outline the development of school science with a view to understanding present claims for contextual or liberal approaches. The fact of diversity and change prompts questions about the justification of different curricular orientations, and about the degree to which change is driven by educational versus other considerations.[2]

Natural Philosophy in the Curriculum

Science, then called "natural philosophy," was introduced into schools, the few that there were, in the middle of the eighteenth century. Its introduction was not universally lauded. Theology, the classics and humanities were regarded as appropriate subjects for the elite, while basic literacy, numeracy and religion, along with simple trade and domestic skills, were thought appropriate for the masses.[3] In the nineteenth century Thomas Huxley, Henry Armstrong and T. P. Nunn in England, John Dewey in the United States, Ernst Mach and J. F. Herbert in Germany, and earlier, the mathematician de Condorcet in France were some who championed the place of science education.[4] No sooner was science included in the curriculum than debate began about its contents, objectives, teaching methods and clientele. The clientele debate revolved around whether science should be the same for all students, or whether there should be different programs depending upon whether students were proceeding with university studies or terminating their education at the end of school.

In Britain, a practical approach was widespread. Science was a servant of the industrial revolution. A noteworthy text was James Ferguson's *Natural Philosophy* (1750), which went through many editions, was revised in 1806 by Sir David Brewster, and published in America in 1806. Brewster's introduction says "The chief object of Mr. Ferguson's labours was to give a familiar view of physical science and to render it accessible to those who are not accustomed to mathematical investigation" (Woodhull, 1910, p. 18). Brewster went on to say that "No book upon the same subject has been so generally read, and so widely circulated, among all ranks of the community." Sixty-two pages of the text were devoted to machines, and forty pages to pumps. This applied, technical, everyday emphasis was repeated in other widely used texts, such as the twenty-two editions of R. G. Parker's *The School Compendium of Experimental Philosophy* (1837), the seventy-three editions of J. L. Comstock's *System of Natural Philosophy* (1846), and J. W. Draper's *Natural Philosophy for Schools* (1847).

Draper stated what was to be a long-standing dilemma in the teaching of science when he said: "There are two different methods in which Natural Philosophy is now taught: (1) as an experimental science; (2) as a branch of mathematics. I believe that the proper course is to teach physical science experimentally first" (Woodhull 1910, p. 21). US colleges and British universities did not agree. Natural Philosophy disappeared from American schools around 1872, to be replaced by high school physics, and texts which increasingly were filled with algebra and mathematical formulae, in which diagrams of common machines were replaced by abstract line drawings. Along with the new texts came the long-standing problem of the overstuffed curricula. The New York State Department of Education issued its *Topical Syllabus in Physics* in 1905. This contained 260 topics, which for a course of 120 hours meant a new topic each half hour of class time (Mann 1912, p. 66).

Not all agreed that the new science teaching was an improvement on the old, and at the end of the nineteenth century many, gathered under the banner of "The New Movement in Physics Teaching," advocated a return to the applied, experimental focus of the old natural philosophy courses and texts.[5] A part of this advocacy was for the teaching of the principles of science in science programs, and it was reasonably held that a topic each thirty minutes, discussed in essentially a foreign language, was not conducive to children learning the principles of science. An example of the sort of science that the new movement opposed was the setting of questions such as "A force of 5000 dynes acts for 10 seconds on a mass of 250 grams. What momentum is imparted to the body?" without students knowing experientially what a force of 5000 dynes meant in everyday life. Could such a force, for instance, knock an adult down? (Mann 1912, p. 89).

US Science Education to the 1950s

There have been three competing traditions in US science education up to the present time: theoretical, stressing the structure of the disciplines; applied, stressing the science and workings of everyday things; liberal or contextual, stressing the historical development and cultural implications of science. None of these traditions have, of course, been exclusive.

A significant trend in the development of science education up to the 1950s was the increasing recognition of the practical, vocational, social and humanitarian aspects of science, and the inclusion of these aspects in the curriculum. Biology teaching, for instance, became less theoretical over this period (Hurd 1961, Rosenthal 1985). One teacher in 1909 complained that school biology texts were so encyclopaedic and theoretical that they were more appropriate for doctoral exams. After observing a class, the teacher wondered what meaning "oogonia," "antheridia," and "oospore" conveyed to students (Rosenthal 1985). During the first half of this century, in response to a multitude of pressures—among them the Progressive Education Society, business and industrial demands, environmental problems, demographic changes, and health concerns—school biology increasingly diverged from university biology. Finley wrote a 1926 text which stressed the "practical, ecological, economic, human welfare aspects of biology." He observed that generally "the aim of biology teaching . . . changed from 'biology for the sake of biology' to 'biology in relation to human welfare'" (Rosenthal 1985, p. 105).[6]

World War Two gave further impetus to practical biology: disease prevention, hygiene, agriculture were all part of the practical applications that guided course design. Columbia Teachers College developed a curriculum that stressed the "content and methods of science in dealing with personal and social issues that have been raised largely as a result of advances in science." The aim was to give a "clearer understanding of society [and] of the social function of science" (Layton & Powers 1949). This concern with making science personally relevant can be seen in a report of the Consumer Education Society of the National Association of Secondary Principals. This report, *The Place of Science in the Education of the Consumer*, was published in 1945 by the National Science Teachers Association. It urged that science teaching should focus on knowledge which helps consumers purchase wisely and on procedures useful in the solution of consumer problems (Hurd 1961, p. 85).

It was not only biology that developed more practical concerns: physics texts up to the mid-fifties were also concerned with applied questions, and gave everyday illustrations of physical principles. As Roberts (1982) has pointed out, it was common for the chapters on electricity to discuss the workings of the telephone, the electric iron, home circuits and fuses, and everyday electrical appliances; the chapters on liquids dealt with town water systems, hydraulic brakes and other such matters.

There were predictable tensions in this applied science tradition. Some stressed applications at the personal level—hygiene, consumer decisions, planting gardens, hobbies, and so on; others responded to the demands of business for vocational skills and stressed social applications of science (Callahan 1962); still others stressed understanding the interaction of society and science. Present-day Science-Technology-Society programs are in the same tradition as these interwar applied science courses.

The applied tradition was criticized from two sides: on the one were advocates of teaching the theoretical, disciplinary structure of science, and on the other, advocates of the humanistic, cultural aspects of science. The Union of American Biological Societies criticized the tendency to teach biology not as a science but as "a way to pleasing hobbies, and a series of practical technologies" (Rosenthal 1985, p. 109). It championed specialist, disciplinary courses. This call was echoed in the 1947 report of the American Association for the Advancement of Science titled "The Present Effectiveness of our Schools in the Training of Scientists." It stated:

> The report is based on the premise that our people should take such steps as may be necessary to ensure (1) enough competent scientists to do whatever job may be ahead, and (2) a voting public that understands and supports the scientists' role in defense and in the design for better living. (In Klopfer & Champagne 1990, p. 137)

In contrast the Harvard Committee (1945) advocated a science program in which "the facts of science must be learned in another context, cultural, historical, and philosophical." The committee produced a manifesto for liberal science education. It claimed:

Science instruction in general education should be characterized mainly by broad integrative elements—the comparison of scientific with other modes of thought, the comparison and contrast of the individual sciences with one another, the relations of science with its own past and with general human history, and of science with problems of human society. These are areas in which science can make a lasting contribution to the general education of all students . . . Below the college level, virtually all science teaching should be devoted to general education. (Conant 1945, pp. 155–156)

In 1944 the National Educational Association issued a report, *Education for All American Youth*, that proposed a liberal approach to the sciences for precollege programs. In addition to knowledge of specific subject matters, science by the tenth grade should introduce students to the role of science in human progress, to the scientific view of the world and of man, to the history of science and an imaginative association with the great scientists and their major experiments (Hurd 1961, p. 83).

Clarence Faust, speaking at a 1958 national conference of presidential science advisers held at Yale university, stressed this contextual approach:

What American life most needs, is a new respect for intelligence, for intellectual achievement, for the life of the mind, for books and for learning, for basic science and for philosophic wisdom . . . education cannot realize its promise if it is viewed merely as a means to individual advancement, social achievement, and national power . . . we need wisdom, not merely power . . . a commitment to the basic function of education. (Elbers & Duncan 1959, p. 178)

Thus at the time of the *Sputnik* crisis at least three competing views about the nature, purposes, and emphases of school science can be identified:

1) A practical, technical, applied emphasis.
2) A liberal, generalist, humanistic emphasis.
3) A specialist, theoretical, disciplinary emphasis.

These are akin to what Eisner (1979) calls "curricular orientations." Roberts (1982), in his survey of numerous science curricula, identified seven "curriculum emphases." The above three correspond, approximately, with his "everyday coping," "the self as explainer," and "correct explanations." Neither Roberts's distinctions, nor the above tripartite divisions, are meant to be mutually exclusive. Curricula that stress one, usually include something of the others. What is in contention between the views is the general orientation of the science program, and the goals that it seeks to achieve.

1950s National Science Foundation Curricula

In the early 1950s American academics, scientists and professional associations, with physicists at the forefront, led agitation for the reform of

US science education. These groups were concerned about the decline of science and mathematics in schools. In the forty years between 1910 and 1950, the number of nonacademic subjects (cooking, typing, driving and so on) in US schools increased from eight to 215, separate physics and chemistry courses were amalgamated into general science, and algebra became part of general mathematics.[7]

In 1956 Jerrold Zacharias,[8] a physicist at MIT, used a small grant from the National Science Foundation to set up the Physical Science Study Committee (PSSC). This committee produced the PSSC *Physics* text which was eventually to be used by millions of students in the US and throughout the world. Its intention was to focus upon the conceptual structure of physics, and teach the subject as a discipline: applied material was almost totally absent from the text. Air pressure for instance is not mentioned in the index, it is discussed in the chapter on "The Nature of Gases," and the chapter proceeds entirely without mention of barometers or steam engines, the former making its first appearance in the notes to the chapter.[9]

On October 4th, 1957, the Soviet *Sputnik* went into orbit, and its shock waves swept across the US political and educational landscape. One commentator, Dianne Ravitch, has said:

> The Soviet launch . . . promptly ended the debate that had raged for several years about the quality of American education. Those who had argued since the late 1940s that American schools were not rigorous enough and that life adjustment education had cheapened intellectual values felt vindicated, and as one historian later wrote, "a shocked and humbled nation embarked on a bitter orgy of pedagogical soul-searching." (in DeBoer 1991, p. 146)

Sputnik brought the claims of reformers of science education into national prominence. The launch triggered a flurry of legislation, the principal being the 1957 National Defense Education Act, which gave $94 million for science education in the three years from 1958 to 1961, and a further $600 million in the years from 1961 to 1975. Conferences and meetings occurred across the country. A representative one was the above-mentioned Yale conference sponsored by the President's Committee on Scientists and Engineers (Elbers & Duncan 1959).

The National Science Foundation was instrumental in the transformation of school science into proto-university science, a process sometimes called the professionalization of school science. The NSF's first school curriculum grant was for $1,725 in 1954; its 1956 grant to PSSC was $300,000. The National Defense Act transformed this meagre level of funding, and subsequently transformed US science education. In 1957 the NSF said that its curriculum projects:

> seek to respond to the concern, often expressed by scientists and educators, over failure of instructional programs in primary and secondary schools to arouse

motivating interest in, and understanding of, the scientific disciplines. General agreement prevails that much of the science taught in schools today does not reflect the current state of knowledge nor does it necessarily represent the best possible choice of materials for instructional purposes. (Crane 1976, pp. 56–57)

The NSF put scientists firmly in the saddle of curriculum reform, teachers were at best stable-hands, and education faculty rarely got as far as the stable door. The PSSC project epitomized "top-down" curriculum development; its maxim was "Make physics teacher-proof." In a 1962 explanation of its policies, the NSF said that:

Projects are directed by college-level scientists, and grants are made to institutions of higher learning and professional scientific societies. Emphasis is placed on subject matter rather than pedagogy. (Klopfer & Champagne 1990, p. 139)

Testing did not always have the significance that the policy gave it. One teacher who participated said:

My own experience with that process suggests the results of classroom tryouts had little effect on subsequent versions. Scientists were usually hesitant to accept the criticism of their "science" from school teachers unless very convincing substantiating data were provided. (Welch 1979, p. 288)

The NSF supported the explosion of "alphabet curricula" in the late 1950s and early 1960s. The first curriculum to be widely used was that of the MIT's Physical Sciences Study Committee (PSSC). Then followed the Chemical Bond Approach (CBA), Biological Sciences Curriculum Study (BSCS), Chemical Education Materials (CHEMS), Earth Science Curriculum Project (ESCP), Introductory Physical Science (IPS), Project Physics and a host of others. By 1975 the NSF supported twenty-eight science curriculum reform projects. A number of these were directed at the elementary school: Elementary Science Study (ESS), Science Curriculum Improvement Study (SCIS) and Science—A Process Approach (SAPA).[10]

Most of the NSF-funded projects neglected practical and technological applications of science. One review said:

There is little or nothing of STS [Science-Technology-Society] in currently available textbooks. Our group reviewed a number of widely used textbooks . . . and found virtually no references to technology in general, or to our eight specific areas of concern. In fact, we found fewer references to technology than in textbooks of twenty years ago. The books have become more theoretical, more abstract with fewer practical applications. They appear to have evolved in a context where science education is considered the domain of an 'elite' group of students. (Piel 1981, p. 106 quoted in Bybee 1985)

The success of the Russian *Sputnik*, along with the vocal demands of science professionals, created enormous legislative and commercial pressure to use school science as a means of preparing students for tertiary science studies. In the thirty years between 1957 and 1987, the practical and the liberal curriculum emphases progressively gave way to the academic, or professional, model of curriculum design.

Two important exceptions to the general ahistorical, professional curricula supported by the NSF were the Harvard Project Physics course, and the Yellow Version of the BSCS High School Biology course. Another small-scale example of a historical-philosophical science program was the Klopfer and Cooley "Use of Case Histories in the Development of Student Understanding of Science and Scientists." These case histories were consciously aimed at replicating the well-established Harvard Case Studies in Experimental Science used successfully at the college level. One review of the utilization of the case-study approach said that "the method is definitely effective in increasing student understanding of science and scientists when used in biology, chemistry, and physics classes in high schools" (Klopfer & Cooley 1963, p. 46).[11]

Appraisal of the NSF Reforms

By the mid-1970s, after twenty years of energetic involvement, and $1.5 billion in financial support, the NSF withdrew from school curriculum development. In 1975 federal funding for the NSF's curriculum developments was below what it had been in 1959. The times had changed: the Soviet threat had receded, the US had its man on the moon, school enrollments were falling, and there was a state and local authority backlash against the *de facto* introduction of a national curriculum—such federal interference was (and still is) a matter of grave concern to the over 16,000 fiercely independent school boards in the US.

Numerous studies were done on the effectiveness of the massive federal intervention. Among the more prominent were those of Helgeson, Blosser and Howe, which reviewed all research appearing between 1955 and 1975 (Helgeson et al. 1977); Weiss (1978), which surveyed national teaching and curriculum practices; Stake and Easley (1978); and Project Synthesis, directed by Norris Harms, which scrutinized hundreds of studies (Harms & Yager 1981). These studies found that the curricular reforms were only partially successful in meeting their own objectives, and in fulfilling the hopes that government and society held for them.

After 1975, adoption of the NSF curricula was widespread but patchy. In 1976 only fifty percent of school districts were using any NSF-sponsored secondary curriculum, and only thirty percent of districts were using them in elementary school (Jackson 1983, p. 149). Introductory Physical Science was the most widely used NSF curriculum, at one stage being used in about twenty-five percent of school districts; most other curricula failed to reach a ten percent "penetration" level. Further, adoption of curricula, of course, did not necessarily mean adoption of their spirit, or of their recommended teaching methods. As one major study concluded, it was often a case of "new wine in old bottles" (Stake & Easley 1978). In 1979 the original director of the PSSC project lamented that the curriculum reform movement was suffering a "deadening sense of frustration and near defeat." To this proponent, it was a time of "despair and confusion" (Jackson 1983, p. 152).

Now, in the 1990s, when school science reform is once more on the agenda, it is timely to know how much of this failure and confusion was due to the curriculum materials, how much to teacher inadequacies, how much to implementation and logistic failures, how much to general anti-intellectual or antiscientific cultural factors and how much to a residue factor of faulty learning theory and inadequate views of scientific method that the schemes incorporated. It may be, however, that there are no overall answers to the question; perhaps the reasons for failure may be localized, varying from curriculum to curriculum, and from school district to school district.

One respected physics teacher, textbook writer and curriculum planner, Arnold Arons, has drawn attention to the fact that "curricular material, however skilful and imaginative, cannot 'teach themselves'" (Arons 1983, p. 117). He believes that "a substantial body of interesting, imaginative, and educationally sound material was developed" in the NSF-sponsored curricula. He attributes the failures to two causes: first, inadequate logistic support for school teachers; second, and more importantly, the inadequate training of teachers.

The first factor covers such commonplace things as the absence of laboratory assistants in schools and of money for equipment or films, little free time to set up experiments and maintain displays, and minimum study leave provisions. The second factor covers such things as lack of knowledge of subject matter, failure to appreciate the psychological requirements for science learning, particularly the need for experience and familiarity with reality to precede theory and concepts, poor in-service courses where teachers were "given more of the same rapidly paced, irrelevant, and unintelligible college courses that had had no visible intellectual effect in the past" (Arons 1983, p. 120), and the failure of science teachers to appreciate and convey the rich intellectual and cultural import of their subject. Science was taught as a rhetoric of conclusions, to use Schwab's term, and the fluid nature of scientific inquiry and conclusions was seldom apparent.

Other studies support Arons's reluctance to blame the NSF curricula. Welch concludes that "when compared to teacher effectiveness, student ability, time on task, and the many other things that influence learning, curriculum does not appear to be an important factor." He cites studies that show that only five percent of the variance in student achievement was due to curriculum/non-curriculum treatments. Welch reports that his Project Physics team "eventually concluded that 5% was an acceptable return on our investment since we could seldom find greater curricular impact on the students" (Welch 1979, p. 301).

One way of looking at these results is that although curriculum is important, it is not important *by itself*: the mere change of curriculum, without change of teacher education, assessment tasks, resources and support, is not going to have any dramatic effect on student engagement, interest and learning of science or of any other subject. It is of little use to set up high-powered curriculum committees that devise curricula which are then sent in the mail to schools. Curriculum without appropriate texts, examinations, teacher commitments and systematic support is like a car without petrol—it looks nice but doesn't go anywhere. What many have said is that results such as Welch's and analyses such as Arons's[12] point to the fundamental importance of teachers—their knowledge, enthusiasm, educational philosophy and attitudes—for successful teaching.

British Curricular Reform

Natural Philosophy entered British schools, such as they were, in the mid-eighteenth century.[13] By the middle of the nineteenth century the "science of everyday things" was common in primary schools (Jenkins 1979). The work of the Reverends Charles Mayo and Richard Dawes was influential. Not suprisingly, given the widespread enthusiasm for Paley's *The Evidences*, much of this science of everyday things, and nature study, was used to promote religious perspectives. However this effect did not save science from those who thought that the lower classes were being dangerously overeducated and becoming far too critical. The Revised Curriculum Code of 1862 basically removed all science from state-funded primary schools. The Clarendon Commission in 1864 supported the importance of classical studies, but it also lamented the absence of scientific studies in the education of the upper classes. In 1867 the British Association for the Advancement of Science threw its influence behind efforts to have science reinstated and reconstituted in the curriculum.[14] Thomas Huxley in his influential address, "A Liberal Education; and Where to Find it" (Huxley 1868), given at the opening of the South London Working Man's College, focused attention on the importance of science to education, and ridiculed contemporary curricula that excluded science.[15]

Armstrong and the Heuristic Method

At the turn of the century Henry Armstrong,[16] professor of chemistry at Imperial College, London, led a crusade against the dry, verbal, didactic pedagogy that then prevailed in science classrooms.[17] Armstrong said of this scholastic approach that:

I have no hesitation in saying that at the present day the so-called science taught in most schools, especially that which is demanded by examiners, is not only worthless, but positively detrimental. (Armstrong 1903, p. 170)

In contrast to these didactic methods, Armstrong advocated the heuristic method (or what might loosely be called the discovery method), which he characterized thus:

Heuristic methods of teaching are methods which involve our placing students as far as possible in the attitude of the discoverer—methods which involve their *finding out* instead of merely being told about things. It should not be necessary to justify such a policy in education . . . discovery and invention are divine prerogatives, in some sense granted to all, meant for daily usage and that it is consequently of importance that we be taught the rules of the game of discovery and learn to play it skilfully. (Armstrong 1903, p. 236)

Armstrong's views ought not to be identified with the extreme "discovery *ex nihilo*" view, or the "Robinson Crusoe" view, advocated by some enthusiasts of discovery learning. To place students as far as possible in the attitude of the discoverer does mean that students have to have some stock of concepts, of techniques, of instruments, of calculating abilities and so on—the things that the discoverer surely starts out with. Armstrong said:

It is needless to say that young scholars cannot be expected to find out everything themselves; but the facts must always be presented to them so that the process by which results are obtained is made sufficiently clear as well as the methods by which any conclusion based on the facts are deduced. (Armstrong 1903, p. 255)

As with Ernst Mach before him, Armstrong believed that experience should precede theory, that percept should precede concept. This was one way of saying that science learning should be practical; students should be familiar with the phenomena to which scientific theory is applied. Through Armstrong, this Machian empiricism pervaded a good deal of British science education up to and including the Nuffield Science schemes of the 1960s.

Armstrong also believed that the heuristic method should be historical. In this he acknowledges a 1884 paper of Meiklejohn, who had said:

This view has its historical side; and it will be found that the best way, the truest method, that the individual can follow is the path of research that has been taken and followed by whole races in past times. (Armstrong 1903, p. 237)

So, for Armstrong, the discovery method was something that stressed pupil activity and individual reasoning, but this was in a context created by the teacher, and this context was designed to follow the historical path of the development of science. Reflecting upon his life's work he said:

> Our primary object was to train the students to think and to solve problems—to ask questions and to secure answers—to teach them, in fact, to help themselves . . . the work was a great strain on the staff. (Richmond & Quraishi 1964, p. 519)

Armstrong's crusade had mixed results: some victories, many defeats, some converts, many unmoved. He started a tradition in British science education that has emphasized inquiry teaching, historical study, pupil activity and investigation. The fortunes of this tradition have fluctuated during this century. At different times and with different people, different aspects of Armstrong's ideas have been emphasized: inquiry learning can be ahistorical, practical work can be didactic and reduced merely to the following of cookbook recipes, historical study can be just a sweetener for technocratic science.

John Bradley, at the University of Hull, was one of the finest exponents of Armstrong's heurism.[18] He had a passionate commitment to teaching chemistry in a manner that allowed students to fall in love with it: "This falling in love with chemistry is the Real Right Thing about learning chemistry; and it is the only item of educational psychology which the teacher of chemistry needs to know" (Bradley 1964, 45, p. 364). He was an admirer of Ernst Mach[19] and endorsed Mach's instrumentalist view of theory, insisting that theoretical discussion be X-rated, and that children not be exposed to it at least until the final school years: "The young people of this country come hopefully to school asking for the bread of experience; we give them the stones of atomic models" (Bradley 1964, 45, p. 366).

Bradley built an introductory chemistry course around the celebrated "copper problem" (oxidation), where students begin with heating copper and noticing that it puts on two coats, a scarlet inner one and a black outer one. From there the course takes off, with students suggesting reasons for this, testing them, asking whether copper gains or loses weight on heating and why, devising ways to heat copper without air, the investigation of oxygen, reduction problems and so on. All of this is very low-technology teaching:

> By returning from the far country [US] with its painted Jezebels of atomic models to the homeland and pure gospel of Armstrong, the teaching of chemistry could be immensely improved without the expenditure of a penny. Indeed money could be saved, because sulphuric acid is cheaper than models of models of models. (Bradley 1964, 45, p. 366)

Nuffield Science

By the 1960s disquiet was being expressed at English science achievement levels and participation rates. The major response to this was the

Nuffield Science Courses. Like the NSF courses, a number of the Nuffield courses advocated discovery learning and the inquiry method of teaching. The Nuffield schemes were developed at the time of the *Plowden Report* (1967) which recommended child-centered teaching for British primary schools. The Nuffield schemes resurrected the inquiry portion of the Armstrong tradition while largely neglecting the historical dimension. As with the NSF courses, the Nuffield courses held an inductivist view of scientific method (Stevens 1978). This is seen in the Physics Year 4 Teachers Guide when, discussing Newton's Second Law, the advice is given that:

> Students should be left on their own to draw conclusions from their graphs. It is much less valuable, though much quicker for the teacher to impose a well-taught conclusion. What the pupils find out for themselves from the slopes of these graphs (without ever being told to look at the slopes) will remain in their minds as one of their great discoveries in physics—particularly if we can tell them that they are finding out part of the story of Newton's great Laws of Motion. (In Harris & Taylor 1983, p. 285)

The Physics Year 3 Guide says: "what [students] need are simple general instructions, where to look but not what to look at" (in Harris & Taylor 1983, p. 278).

The Nuffield Courses dominated British school science teaching in the 1960s and 1970s. As in the US the idea was to produce "little scientists" by having students engage in scientific discovery. Some of the problems with the approach surfaced very early.[20] The British Association for Science Education (ASE) in its 1963 *Training of Graduate Science Teachers* stressed the obvious problem of teachers who did not understand, or have an interest in, the nature of science itself. Of graduate teachers it said: "Many behave and think scientifically as a result of their training but they lack an understanding of the basic nature and aims of science" (ASE 1963, p.13).

Contextual Science

In the decade after its adoption, voices were increasingly raised against the Nuffield approach. The sociologist Michael Young observed in 1976 that: "Despite a decade of unprecedented investment in curriculum innovation, school science displays many of the manifestations of a continuing 'crisis'" (Young 1976, p. 47). The ASE in its 1979 report, *Alternatives for Science Education*, advocated a science education for all students to the age of sixteen years, saying that such a curriculum should "incorporate a reasonable balance between the specialist and generalist aspects of science" and should reflect science as a "cultural activity." In a later report,

Education through Science (1981), the teaching of science as a cultural activity was spelt out as:

> the more generalized pursuit of scientific knowledge and culture that takes account of the history, philosophy and social implications of scientific activities, and therefore leads to an understanding of the contribution science and technology make to society and the world of ideas.

The ASE recognised the importance of the history and philosophy of science in its own "Science in Society" project that includes a reader on the subject (Ramage 1983).

In support of the wider, contextual view of science education, the ASE funded two curriculum projects, the 1981 "Science and Society" course (ASE 1981), and the 1983 "Science in its Social Context" (SISCON) course (Solomon 1985). The latter course was influenced by successful university Science-Technology-Society programs, of which an exemplary textbook was John Ziman's *Teaching and Learning About Science and Society* (1980).

Joan Solomon has outlined the two views that surfaced in the ASE on how to teach social issues in science. On the one hand there was the mainstream group which, recognizing the benefit and necessity of making science more socially responsive, proposed adding social issues to the existing science syllabus. This has been the standard approach: after dealing with combustion and hydrocarbons, then raise questions about motor cars, pollution, public transport and government policy; after dealing with genetics, coding of DNA, and cloning, then raise moral questions about genetic engineering, eugenics, acceptable and unacceptable medical interventions and social priorities, and so on. This "add on" approach has its obvious advantages and disadvantages.

On the other hand, a group on the committee advocated teaching science *through* social issues. They claimed that such an approach increased interest and motivation, broke boundaries between subjects, provided opportunities for free writing, developed discussion and library skills, provided exposure to Third World and multiethnic studies, and made possible individual and pupil choice of topics (Solomon 1985, p. 154).

This argument between "add-on" and "integral" approaches to Science-Technology-Society education has occurred in the US and Canada. Against the add-on view, for example, Hurd warned that most "STS instructional materials are being shoehorned into obsolete curriculum structures and taught by traditional methods that achieve at best outmoded objectives" (Hurd 1985, p. 95).

Another argument concerns the place of history in STS programs. History is integral to the SISCON course, where all the topics include a historical review. Solomon supports the historical dimension in STS courses, saying that "incidents from the past allow sufficient perspective for us to reflect upon social and technological factors; present crises are sometimes too charged with feeling for us to see them clearly." Further, "as an introduction to social history such materials are clearly excellent in their own right, but as sources from which we can begin to demonstrate the benefits and risks of the social interactions of science and technology they are invaluable" (Solomon 1989b, p. 48). This historical dimension is, unfortunately, less evident in US and Canadian STS courses.

Inquiry Learning and the Need for HPS

The US and British curricular reforms of the 1960s aimed at more than just specifying content areas or laying down topics to be taught; they were also concerned to develop scientific attitudes and methods among students. Reformers wanted students to become scientific, not just learn science. To this end, "inquiry" or "discovery learning" was a prominent feature of the NSF and Nuffield reforms, one advocate saying "All of modern science curriculum developments stress teaching science as inquiry" (Sund & Trowbridge 1967, p. 22). The appraisal of inquiry learning is interesting for the light that it sheds on a number of important educational matters—concept acquisition, social dependence of learning and so forth—but it is especially interesting for those promoting HPS in science education. The arguments for, and the fate of, inquiry learning illustrate a case where HPS can contribute to theoretical debates about science education that have widespread practical implications.

The inquiry or discovery approach to teaching and learning was separately advocated by two very prominent theorists—Joseph Schwab, a University of Chicago educationalist involved with the BSCS project, and Jerome S. Bruner, a Harvard cognitive psychologist. Schwab's first publication on the subject was in 1958; he elaborated upon it in 1960 in what was to become a classic of inquiry theory. Bruner was director of a working party of thirty-five that the National Academy of Sciences convened in the summer of 1959 at Woods Hole on Cape Cod, Massachusetts, to investigate the rash of new curricula and to see whether basic principles of learning and curriculum construction could be elucidated.[21]

Bruner's main contribution was to bring to the discussion the "cognitive turn" that was taking place in psychology.[22] He also brought a concern with classrooms, teachers and educational practices at a time when educational psychologists preferred to think of "learning theory" in terms of rats, pigeons, stimulii and reinforcement schedules. In this context he introduced the cognitive, human-centered ideas of Jean Piaget to the group. He also stressed the importance of "structure" for learning. This was connected with his idea of the "generativeness" of knowledge:

"Learning" is, most often, figuring out how to use what you already know in order to go beyond what you currently think. There are many ways of doing that. Some are more intuitive; others are formally derivative. But they all depend on knowing something "structural" about what you are contemplating—how it is put together. Knowing how something is put together is worth a thousand facts about it. It permits you to go beyond it. (Bruner 1983, p. 183)

There is an ambiguity here, as will be emphasized in Chapter 6, between the material object of knowledge and the theoretical object of knowledge. The structure of disciplines that Bruner and Schwab elevate to the forefront of science learning are structures in the theoretical objects of science: the structure of interrelating definitions and concepts contained in Newton's *Principia*, the structure of geometry as contained in Euclid's *Elements*, the structure of evolutionary theory in Darwin's *Origin*, the structure of Brönsted's acid/base theory or of plate tectonic theory. Once these structures are grasped, then distant theorems can be derived from axioms, and predictions can be made about likely intervening species or the acidity of new chlorides and so on. But these are not the objects contemplated by the neophyte: they contemplate material objects such as falling stones, triangles, or a range of flora. There are two very different senses of "structure" being used here: the structure of objects and the structure of disciplines. The structure of a leaf is one thing, the structure of photosynthesis theory is quite another. And two very different modes of contemplation and manipulation are required for the different objects; one is turned around in the hand, the other is turned over in the mind.

Bruner's 1961 *Harvard Educational Review* article, "The Act of Discovery," popularized discovery learning. With its popularization came its distortion. In 1966 Bruner wrote a follow-up essay, "Some Elements of Discovery," distancing himself from the educational excesses touted in the name of discovery learning. He confided that, "I am not sure any more what discovery is" (Bruner 1974, p. 84), and complained that, "Discovery was being treated by some educators as if it were valuable in and of itself, no matter what it was a discovery of or in whose service" (Bruner 1974, p. 15).

Discovery learning aimed to promote thinking and reasoning skills and independent research. In the words of one advocate:

it gives students more opportunities to think and learn how to think critically. As inquirers, students learn to be independent, to compare, to analyze, to synthesize knowledge, and to develop their mental and creative faculties. (Sund & Trowbridge 1967, p. 22)

More specifically, discovery learning was welcomed as a way for students to grasp the nature of scientific inquiry. Students would learn about the nature of scientific discovery and reasoning by themselves participating in inquiry. In the words of the PSSC text, students were to be "scientists for a day"; they were to learn about science by being scientific, by conducting scientific investigations.

James Rutherford (a major figure in the Harvard Project Physics Course of the mid-sixties and director of the AAAS Project 2061 of the early 1990s) stated the 1960s progressive view thus:

> When it comes to the teaching of science it is perfectly clear where we, as science teachers, science educators, or scientists, stand; we are unalterably opposed to the rote memorization of the mere facts and minutiae of science. By contrast, we stand foursquare for the teaching of the scientific method, critical thinking, the scientific attitude, the problem-solving approach, the discovery method, and, of special interest here, the inquiry method. (Rutherford 1964, p. 80)

Much was written on the theory and practice of discovery learning.[23] At one level the inquiry approach was very attractive. For students to discover by experiment and manipulation what materials are attracted to a magnet and what materials are not, rather than being told this by a teacher, is an advance on rote learning. Bruner said that discovery methods were preferable because they promoted an increase in intellectual potency, they involved a shift from extrinsic to intrinsic rewards, they taught the heuristics of discovering, and they were an aid to memory processing (Bruner 1961).

But the theoretical promise of inquiry teaching was not always fulfilled. One extensive review of the American inquiry-based programs and curricula of the 1960s concluded:

> In spite of new curricula, better trained teachers, and improved facilities and equipment, the optimistic expectations for students becoming inquirers have seldom been fulfilled. (Welch et al. 1981, p. 33)

The reviewers said that the problem lay in large part with teachers:

> Science was something teachers took in college, but it was not something they experienced as a process of inquiry. . . . The values associated with speculative, critical thinking were often ignored and sometimes ridiculed. (Welch et al. 1981, pp. 38–39)

Another critic advanced a similar consideration, locating the flaw with discovery learning in the image of science, or the epistemology of science, that infused the curriculum.

> A basic flaw in the process is the apparent assumption that science is a sort of commonsensical activity, and that the appropriate "skills" are the primary ingredients in doing productive work. There seems to be no explicit recognition of the powerful role of the conceptual frames of reference within which scientists

and children operate and to which they are firmly bound. These general views of the physical world demand careful nurture . . . by a variety of means. (J. Myron Atkin, in Glass 1970, p. 20)

Conclusion

James Rutherford, early in the 1960s, made a prescient observation that went largely unheeded:

Science teachers must come to know just how inquiry is in fact conducted in the sciences. Until science teachers have acquired a rather thorough grounding in the history and philosophy of the sciences they teach, this kind of understanding will elude them, in which event not much progress toward the teaching of science as inquiry can be expected. (Rutherford 1964, p. 84)

This book endorses Rutherford's claim that teachers' familiarity with the history and philosophy of science is essential for the improvement of science teaching. It will be argued later that such a familiarity would have enabled teachers to avoid much of the naiveté associated with the claims of discovery learning—naive and false views such as: that scientific method is inductive, that observation does not depend upon conceptual understanding, and that messing about with real objects can reveal the structure of the scientific theories that apply to those objects.

People's ideas and ways of thinking derive from, and can be tested in, three separate but intersecting domains: firstly, their immediate sensory experience of the world, secondly, their participation in everyday life with its conversations, newspapers, television etc., and thirdly, their formal instruction which takes part mostly in school. A constant problem for science education has been to keep these domains in some sort of harmony (see the useful discussion in Terry Russell's contribution to Black & Lucas (1993)).

Scientific thinking is not natural thinking. Feral children do not develop scientific thought even though they might be successful in coping with their environment. Nor does mere participation in everyday life lead to science. Many developed cultures—India and China come to mind—existed for centuries, or millennia, without science developing. Rich philosophic, poetic, and technical achievements did not result in scientific habits of thought. Science is a peculiar way of thinking about, and investigating, the world; the procedures of science need to be learnt as much as its findings. Scientific thinking and knowledge depends upon the third domain; it depends upon formal instruction in science and initiation into a way of thinking which is "unnatural" (Wolpe 1992), and is characterised by "uncommon sense" (Cromer 1993). HPS assists teachers and students to understand how the three domains interact.

CHAPTER 3

Contemporary Curricular Developments

By the early 1980s it was apparent to all that there was a second-generation crisis in Western, and particularly US, science education: it was labeled "the science literacy crisis." Despite all the money and effort that had been expended since *Sputnik*, the bulk of American high school graduates and citizens had minimal scientific understanding. A few knew a great deal; the vast majority knew very little. This state of affairs had been documented in countless research articles, and government reports. But what brought it to popular attention in the US, and galvanized the government to action, was the publication in 1983 of *A Nation at Risk* (National Commission on Excellence in Education, 1983). Its conclusion was stark: "the educational foundations of our society are presently being eroded by a rising tide of mediocrity that threatens our very future as a nation and as a people." It expressed a particular concern about the abysmal state of scientific and mathematical knowledge of high school graduates.[1] In the five years after the publication of *A Nation At Risk*, over three hundred reports documented the sorry state of US education. In 1983 twenty bills were put before Congress designed to offer solutions to the national crisis of science education. These bills and reports all urged the adoption of "scientific and technology literacy for all" as the goal of school science instruction. "Science for all" has been adopted as a goal for science education not just in the US, but in the UK, Canada, Australia, New Zealand and most other countries.

This chapter will first convey the dimensions of the 1980s scientific literacy crisis, it will comment on the definitions of literacy proffered, and then examine two major curricular projects—Project 2061 in the US and the British National Curriculum—that are responses to this crisis. These are noteworthy for the importance they place on the contextual, or liberal, teaching of science. Their effective teaching will require HPS-informed teachers.

Science Literacy and the 1980s Crisis

The facts of the matter were not disputed: school graduates had not undertaken many science courses, they did not know much science, and cared little about learning science. The National Assessment of Educational Progress (NAEP)—a Congress-mandated four-yearly nationwide assessment involving twenty thousand students—has monitored the scientific knowledge of nine-, thirteen-, and seventeen-year-olds since 1969. Scores for all groups declined in the 1970s, improved somewhat in the 1980s, but in 1990 the test scores of nine- and thirteen-year-olds were the same as in 1970, whilst the performance of seventeen-year-olds was lower than in 1970.[2] Various researchers suggest that only forty-five percent of adult Americans know that the earth goes around the sun once each year. A third believe that boiling radioactive milk makes it safe to drink. Some forty percent believe that aliens from outer space have visited Earth, and fifty-four percent reject the idea that humans evolved from earlier species (Fisher 1992a, p. 62). Equally alarming were the results of the large-scale international comparative studies on mathematics and science achievement. These studies involving fifteen to twenty countries are conducted each four to six years by the International Education Assessment Association. US students are at the lowest end of the distribution for all age groups tested.[3]

Jon Miller, at the University of Northern Illinois, was funded by the NSF to conduct a longitudinal study of American adult scientific understanding (Miller 1983, 1987 and 1992). Among statements to which he asked a representative sample of two thousand adults to answer true or false were "The earliest human beings lived at the same time as the dinosaurs" and "Antibiotics kill viruses as well as bacteria." Only thirty-seven percent of the sample answered the first question correctly, and twenty-six percent the second. Reflecting on his own and other comparable studies he concluded that between five and nine percent of US citizens were scientifically literate (Miller 1992, p. 14).

Of course it should not be thought that the crisis is entirely one of instruction, or that the schools are able to counteract major cultural, social or economic forces. The fact that the US has five hundred lawyers for each engineer, whilst Japan has five hundred engineers for each lawyer is not something that schools can control; nor can schools influence the massive disparity in salaries paid to lawyers and accountants in contrast to science teachers or engineers. Further, schools have little effect on a mass culture that is anti-intellectual and operates at the sound-bite level of analysis. Boyer, in his influential 1983 report *High School*, drew attention to this:

> After visiting schools from coast to coast, we are left with the distinct impression that high schools lack a clear and vital mission. They are unable to find common purposes or establish educational priorities that are widely shared. They seem unable to put it all together. The institution is adrift. (Boyer 1983, p. 63)

Stevenson's study of Asian and Chicago schools included a question "Let's say there is a wizard who will let you make a wish about anything you want. What would you wish?" Almost seventy percent of Chinese students wished for educational improvement or abilities, fewer than ten percent of Chicago children did so, preferring money and playthings. The

National Science Foundation commented upon the context of curriculum development and reform in a 1980 statement. It said that a persistent criticism of school science reform has been the lack of:

> a sense of direction and a theory and philosophy which should provide guidance to curriculum development and instruction . . . It seems doubtful that there ever had been a time in which there has been so much uncertainty about the purposes of education. (NSF 1980, p. 67)

A deeper appreciation of science, its history and philosophy, and its cultural significance is the beginning of the type of overall educational philosophy that the NSF is seeking from science teachers. Teachers need to value their subject and be able to convey to students the reason they value their subject. HPS can contribute to the sense of value that science ought to convey. The current efforts by the National Research Council to formulate national standards for school science in the US will focus upon some of these matters.[4] The present US science education reforms, and their relationship, or lack of, to the reform movements of the 1960s are well analyzed by Senta Raizen (1991) and by Leo Klopfer and Audrey Champagne (1990).

Definition of Scientific Literacy

The authors of *A Nation At Risk* called for the promotion of scientific literacy for all students, saying that:

> The teaching of science in high school should provide graduates with an introduction to: (a) the concepts, laws, and processes of the physical and biological sciences; (b) the methods of scientific inquiry and reasoning; (c) the applications of scientific knowledge to everyday life, and (d) the social and environmental implications of scientific and technological development. (NCEE 1983, p. 25)

There are many ways to define science literacy: from a narrow definition where literacy is the ability to recognise formulae and give correct definitions, to a more expansive or liberal definition which includes understanding of concepts and some degree of understanding about the nature of science and its historical and social dimensions.[5] There is no one correct definition of science literacy; it is a matter of different conceptions proving their worth for the promotion of particular ends. For schoolchildren, the overarching end is their educational development. The contention of this book is that an expansive or liberal definition of literacy is more conducive to this end than restricted definitions. This argument, as with so many matters confronting science teachers, requires a vision of good education, a philosophy of education. The liberal view of education underpinning this book holds that education generally, and science education in particular, is not just a means of developing "human resources" so that countries can overcome their balance of payments deficit, or stay competitive with other economies. The latter, economistic view of education, promotes a narrow conception of scientific literacy.

Paul Dehart Hurd, at the end of the 1950s, advocated a broad conception of literacy that entailed students knowing something of the interrelationship between science and society (Hurd 1958). He has continued to emphasise this theme in publications over the past three decades. In lamenting the failure of the NSF discipline-based reforms of the 1960s to give students a sense of the broader canvas of science, he said in 1987—in words that HPS advocates can endorse—that:

> A measure of scientific literacy is a measure of cultural awareness. The traditional science curriculum leaves students foreigners in their own culture. A problem in bringing about the essential reform of science teaching is that there are too many scientists who are scientifically illiterate and too few philosophers, sociologists, and historians of science and technology who are interested in precollege science education. (Hurd 1987, p. 136)

A still more expansive definition was proposed by the National Science Teachers Association in 1982. It defined a scientifically literate person as one who understands that society controls science and technology through the allocation of resources; who uses scientific concepts, process skills and values in making everyday decisions; who recognizes the limitations as well as the usefulness of science and technology in advancing human welfare; who knows the major concepts, hypotheses and theories of science and is able to use them; who distinguishes between scientific evidence and personal opinion; who has a richer view of the world as the result of science education; and who knows reliable sources of scientific and technological information and uses these sources in the process of decision-making (NSTA 1982).

Liberal accounts of scientific literacy are more expansive than professional ones. Liberal accounts contain technical, social and cultural elements. A scientifically literate person should know some science (its content and processes), something about science, and they should have internalized something of scientific procedures and attitudes. Thus we might expect a scientifically literate person to, among other things:

1) Understand fundamental concepts, laws, principles and facts in the basic sciences.
2) Appreciate the variety of scientific methodologies, attitudes and dispositions, and appropriately utilize them.
3) Connect scientific theory to everyday life and recognize chemical, physical and biological processes in the world around them.
4) Recognize the manifold ways that science and its related technology interact with the economics, culture and politics of society.

5) Understand parts of the history of science, and the ways in which it has shaped, and in turn has been shaped by, cultural, moral and religious forces.

The above account of literacy is still very formal, and it does not spell out what a scientific method is, or what a scientific attitude is, or what is the interaction between science and culture. In subsequent chapters this book will indicate ways that the formalisms can be given substance. The definition of literacy offered here is not particularly controversial. Most would agree that students learning science should also learn about science, and become scientific in outlook and habits of mind. Problems arise when these generalities are spelt out for particular age groups in particular circumstances. This is what curriculum implementation is about.

The Responsibility of Schools

There are many societal and systematic factors undermining education that teachers, schools and administrators cannot affect. The bleak funds- and equipment-starved schools portrayed in Jonathan Kozol's *Savage Inequalities* (1991) largely defy the best efforts of teachers. But the Western educational crisis is deeper than funds and equipment. In Europe after World War Two schools had few books, but children learned writing and arithmetic often by tracing letters and numbers in sandboxes. Indo-Chinese refugee children attend the most crowded and poorly funded Australian and US schools, yet their educational performance is overall far better than children in more privileged schools. Despite the massive increase in numbers of schools, and in the years of attendance at school, Western culture is becoming increasingly hostile to education. The staggering amount of television watched is both a cause and an effect of this antieducational culture. Recent research indicates that the average eighteen-year-old in the US has spent twenty thousand hours watching TV compared to eleven thousand in school, and that families spend, on average, 7.5 hours per day watching television (Hamburg 1992).[6] Neil Postman, in his recent critique of television culture, has warned that:

> When a population becomes distracted by trivia, when cultural life is redefined as a perpetual round of entertainments, when serious public conversation becomes a form of baby-talk, when, in short, a people become an audience and their public business a vaudeville act, then a nation finds itself at risk; culture-death is a clear possibility. (Postman 1985, p. 161)

But there are also many antieducational factors that are within schools' competence and influence to affect. One disturbing finding in many of the reports is that the more science students do, the less they like it (Yager & Bonstetter 1984, Brunkhorst & Yager 1986). The National Assessment of Educational Progress data shows that traditional science instruction tends to negate natural interest, and cause some of the best students to pursue other disciplines. In a 1991 report of the National Science Board, *Science and Engineering Indicators*, nearly thirty percent of all seventh-graders express a preference for a career in science or engineering. This percentage steadily drops through high school, and by the end of high school less than twenty-five percent of boys and, dramatically, less than ten percent of girls express such a career interest (National Science Board, 1991). By the end of the 1980s fully seventy percent of US school students took no more science and mathematics than the minimum required to graduate from high school.

Also of concern is the degree to which even successful science education has failed to transform students' intellectual outlook. One study found that belief in astrology was largely unaffected by completion of a US science degree: students who commenced the degree program believing in astrology finished the program believing in it. Forty percent of the US population, despite all their years at school, believe that astrology is scientific; astrology columns are more widely read in newspapers than science columns.

The educational system contributes to the flight from scientific understanding by promoting encyclopedic curricula. The American Council on Education's 1940 report, *What the High School Ought to Teach*, lamented that "courses in the natural sciences are now far too often mere encyclopedic lists of the findings of scientific research. They often fill the memory with facts rather than stimulate pupils to scientific thinking" (Hurd 1961, p. 74). The 1905 New York State physics syllabus, which required a new topic to be covered each half hour, has previously been mentioned; eighty years later the same state's biology syllabus required students to learn 1440 scientific terms and concepts in one year (Swift 1988). One commentator remarked that in school science "students learn more technical words in a one-year course than they would encounter studying a foreign language for two or more years" (Yager 1984, p. 51). A typical school text of 300 to 350 pages can contain 2,400 to 3,000 new terms. This translates as twenty new concepts per lesson, or one every two minutes. Mary Budd Rowe of Stanford relates how one student gave up on his earth science text, declaring that "Its a damn dictionary! Who reads dictionaries?" Rowe comments that "Science books have turned into fantastic dictionaries . . . the plot, the story line—the way in which ideas interact—have disappeared" (Fisher 1992b, p. 53). Ernst Mach in the last century warned against this tendency to overstuff curricula: "How can the mind thrive when matter is heaped upon matter, and new materials piled constantly on old, undigested materials" (Mach 1895/1986, p. 368). In his view there was a clear choice: a student could be taught a lot and thus understand a little, or taught a little and understand a lot. Mach favored the latter.[7]

The argument of this book is that some of these shortcomings of science instruction can be mitigated if the historical and philosophical dimensions of science are more routinely infused in the science classroom: critical and reflective questions can be encouraged; some storyline or narrative can be developed; examples of the interactions of science with worldviews can be displayed; moral and political dilemmas can be relived and debated; and a sense of participation in a tradition can be fostered. This will involve teaching fewer topics, but teaching them better, and teaching them in such a way that the larger scientific picture emerges.

As a partial response to the flight from science classrooms, particularly by women and minority groups, and the staggering rates of scientific illiteracy, governments and educational authorities in the Western world had in the 1980s put into train a number of science curriculum reforms. A noteworthy feature of most of the contemporary curriculum reform proposals is that they advocate the teaching of science more contextually; the curricula incorporate the rich historical, philosophical, ethical, technical and social dimensions of science, presenting science as a more liberal enterprise than was the case in the professional and technical curricula developed in the 1960s.

Two outstanding examples of the contemporary convergence between HPS and science education are the new British National Curriculum, and the American AAAS Project 2061 curriculum. Other examples are the Biological Sciences Curriculum Study "Curriculum Framework" proposal, the AAAS "Science as a Liberal Art" project, and the various STS curricula developed in Canada and parts of the US. Beyond these there have been curricular developments in Denmark, the Netherlands, and Italy that have also been constructed on historical principles, and that attempt to introduce some elementary philosophical considerations into school science courses (Bevilacqua & Kennedy 1983, Thomsen 1986, Blondel & Brouzeng 1988, Nielsen & Thomsen 1990).

Project 2061

In 1985 the AAAS established an extensive national study called *Project 2061*, (2061 being the return date of Halley's Comet), to stimulate and promote an overhaul of science education in schools (its brief included mathematics, technology and social science, along with the natural sciences).[8] The project recognizes that in America "quick fixes always fail in education" (AAAS 1989, p. 154). There is no national lever that can be pulled to transform education. A national curriculum is not politically or legally possible. Even state curricula (such as can be put in place in Canada and Australia, where national curricula are also prohibited) are not an option. There are three million people employed in American education, nearly two hundred billion dollars a year is expended, and fifty million students attend eighty thousand schools in fifty states. Educational decisions are made by thousands of different entities, including sixteen thousand separate school districts; and federal and state courts constantly mandate, and reverse, major programs. Given this diversity, the project realistically says of itself that, "Project 2061 constitutes, of course, only one of many efforts to chart new directions in science, mathematics, and technology education" (AAAS 1989, p. 155). It can only advise, inform and hope to influence curricular policy, philosophy and content.

Five discipline-based panels of academics, teachers and administrators met over a period of three years. They were asked "Out of all the possibilities, what knowledge, skills, and habits of mind associated with science should all Americans have by the time they leave school?" They were asked to make their selections based not only on scientific significance but also on human significance. More particularly the panels were asked to select material considering its:

> *Utility*: would the content be useful for employment and making personal decisions?
> *Social Responsibility*: would it help citizens participate intelligently in making social and political decisions on matters involving science and technology?
> *Intrinsic Value*: would it present aspects of science, mathematics and technology that are so important in human history or so pervasive in our culture that a general education would be incomplete without them?
> *Philosophical Value*: would the content contribute to the ability of people to ponder the enduring questions of human meaning, such as life and death, perception and reality, the individual good versus the collective welfare, certainty and doubt?
> *Childhood Enrichment*: would the content enhance childhood? (Stein 1989, p. 340)

Their first report, *Science for All Americans*, was published in 1989 (AAAS 1989, Rutherford & Ahlgren 1990). It advocates the achievement of scientific literacy by all American high school students. Its proposals are based on the belief that:

> the scientifically literate person is one who is aware that science, mathematics, and technology are interdependent human enterprises with strengths and limitations; understands key concepts and principles of science; is familiar with the natural world and recognises both its diversity and unity; and uses scientific knowledge and scientific ways of thinking for individual and social purposes. (AAAS 1989, p. 4)

The early pages establish its distinctive orientation, saying:

> To ensure the scientific literacy of all students, curricula must be changed to reduce the sheer amount of material covered; to weaken or eliminate rigid subject-matter boundaries; to pay more attention to the connections among science, mathematics, and technology; to present the scientific endeavor as a social enterprise that strongly influences—and is influenced by—human thought and action; and to foster scientific ways of thinking. (AAAS 1989, p. 5)

The report has a chapter on philosophy of science, and another on history of science. These are among twelve chapters that range over topics such as mathematics, technology, the physical world, the living environment, the human organism, human society and the designed world. The history and philosophy chapters are encouraging to those who advocate the inclusion of HPS in the school science curricula.

Philosophical Commitments

All science curricula contain views about the nature of science: images of science that influence what is included in the curriculum, how material is taught and how the curriculum is assessed. The image of science held by curriculum framers sets the tone of the curriculum, and the image of science held by teachers influences how the curriculum is taught and assessed. When spelled out, these images of science become statements about the nature of science, or about the epistemology of science. An inductive-empiricist view of science, for instance, dominated the curricula reforms of the 1960s.[9]

Project 2061's view of the nature of science can be found in its Chapter 1, titled "The Nature of Science," where there are discussions of objectivity, the mutability of science, the demarcation dispute about how science is distinguished from nonscience, evidence and how it relates to theory appraisal, scientific method as logic and as imagination, explanation and prediction, ethics, social policy, and the social organization of science. These themes are intended to be developed in science courses; it stresses that the themes are to be developed within the subject matter of science, and not treated as "add-ons."

The following philosophical theses are advocated in Chapter 1 of *Science for All Americans*.

1) *Realism.* There is an existing material world apart from, and independent of, human experiences and knowledge. This ontological position is in contrast to varieties of idealism which maintain that either there is no world outside of human experience, or that such a world, and human experience, is all ideational. The report says that "Science assumes that the universe is . . . a vast single system in which the basic rules are everywhere the same" (p. 25). Realism is only committed to the existence of an external world. The claim that its laws are everywhere the same is an elaboration of the basic realist position. To what extent the "basic rules" are assumed to be everywhere the same, and to what extent they are discovered to be the same, is a moot point even among realists.

2) *Fallibilism.* Humans can have knowledge of the world even though such knowledge is imperfect, and reliable comparisons can be made between competing theories or opinions. Fallibilism is an epistemological position that is opposed, on the one hand to relativism, which holds that no reliable comparison can be made between competing views, and, on the other

hand, to absolutism, which holds that current theory constitutes absolute, unimprovable, knowledge. The report says that "Scientists assume that even if there is no way to secure complete and absolute truth, increasingly accurate approximations can be made to account for the world and how it works" (p. 26). The notion of "approximate truth" is much debated, with many philosophers preferring to simply speak of better, or more progressive, theories.

3) *Durability*. Science characteristically does not just abandon its central ideas. The simple falsificationist picture of scientists examining and rejecting ideas in some sort of quality control process does not hold up. The report says "The modification of ideas, rather than their outright rejection, is the norm in science, as powerful constructs tend to survive and grow more precise" (p. 26). The philosopher Otto Neurath first gave picturesque expression to this view when he spoke of the correction of scientific theory as the fixing of a leaking boat at sea: the entire hull is not taken out, rather planks are examined and replaced one at a time. Willard van Orman Quine gave wide currency to the image (Quine 1960, p. 3). Imre Lakatos formalised this conception with his idea of science as a series of research programs with hard core commitments that were very resistant to change, and protective belt commitments that changed to accommodate discordant or falsifying data (Lakatos 1970).

4) *Rationalism*. The report holds to a modified form of rationalism, saying that "sooner or later scientific arguments must conform to the principles of logical reasoning—that is, to testing the validity of arguments by applying certain criteria of inference, demonstration, and common sense" (p. 27).

There has been much debate about what actually does, and what should, settle scientific disagreement (Engelhardt & Caplan 1987), and some discussion about the productive use that can be made of scientific controversy in the science classroom (Silverman 1992). The old view was that science was always rational in its deliberations among competing views, theories or research programs. As a result of some research in history, philosophy and sociology of science, this old view has been modified—certainly concerning what actually happens in the history of science; some even modify it concerning what should happen in scientific investigation.

5) *Antimethodism*. Although rationalist in its justification of scientific theory, the report rejects the idea that there is a single method of scientific discovery, saying that "There simply is no fixed set of steps that scientists always follow, no one path that leads them unerringly to scientific knowledge" (p. 26). The report stresses the creative dimension of science, saying "Scientific concepts do not emerge automatically from data or from any amount of analysis alone. This aspect is often overlooked in schools. Inventing hypotheses or theories about how the world works and then figuring out how they can be put to the test of reality is as creative as writing poetry, composing music, or designing sky-scrapers" (p. 27).

6) *Demarcationism*. Science can nevertheless be separated from nonscientific endeavors. This is a contentious and debated matter. It lay at the heart of the 1981 creationist trial when creation scientists were arguing that their activity was every bit as scientific as mainstream science and so they ought to have a place in the school science curriculum. Whether creation science

falls inside or outside the divide is one question, that there is a divide is another, and the report is unambiguous about it, saying: "There are, however, certain features of science that give it a distinctive character as a mode of inquiry" (p. 26).

7) *Predictability*. The report says: "it is not enough for scientific theories to fit only the observations that are already known. Theories should also fit additional observations that were not used in formulating the theories in the first place; that is, theories should have predictive power . . . predictions may be about evidence from the past that has not yet been found or studied" (p. 28). A part of the distinctiveness of science is its concern with predicting phenomena and having the results count. There are problems with this idea, and it is known that testing is not a simple matter; yet there is reasonable agreement on one aspect, namely that good scientific theories should uncover phenomena not currently known. They cannot merely keep accounting for what other theories bring to light, or what common sense has already ascertained.

8) *Objectivity*. It is recognised that science is a far more human activity than it was once conceived to be. We know that Francis Bacon's Idols of the Mind have persisted long after he urged their eradication in 1620. But the report, while recognising this human face of science, nevertheless maintains that science at its best tries to correct for, and rise above, subjective interests in the determination of truth. It says, "scientific evidence can be biased in how the data are interpreted, in the recording or reporting of the data, or even in the choice of what data to consider in the first place. Scientists' nationality, sex, ethnic origin, age, political convictions, and so on may incline them to look for or emphasize one or another kind of evidence or interpretation. . . . but scientists want to know the possible sources of bias and how bias is likely to influence evidence" (p. 28). The possibility of objectivity in science has been challenged by some feminists, some constructivists, and by most philosophical postmodernists. The issue is discussed in subsequent chapters.

9) *Moderate Externalism*. The attempt to eliminate subjectivity and interest from the realm of the determination of truth claims is not the same as saying that various interests should not influence what spheres of knowledge science should investigate. Whether research is conducted on space travel or cheapened public transport, on nuclear energy or solar energy, on chemical insecticide development or biological controls, will be a function of personal and social interests. Science does not proceed in a political vacuum; most countries draw up lists of national priority areas and will only release public funds for scientific research in these areas. Being on or off the list is a political matter.

The report recognizes that "As a social activity, science inevitably reflects social values and viewpoints. . . . The direction of scientific research is affected by informal influences within the culture of science itself, such as prevailing opinion on what questions are most interesting or what methods of investigation are most likely to be fruitful. . . . Funding agencies influence the direction of science by virtue of the decisions they make on which research to support" (p. 29). When decisions about truth or otherwise are made in order to serve the interests of funding or political bodies, then science has moved from moderate to complete externalism. While some sociologists of science argue the latter view, it is rejected in the report.

10) *Ethics.* There are two ethical contexts affecting science. One is the external context where ethics can determine the questions to research or to avoid; the other is the internal context where ethical considerations affect the conduct of research itself. Medical research is a prime example where ethics directly affects what is and in not researched—heart transplant research is conducted, but euthanasia research generally is not. More generally certain areas are researched because society and scientists think it is morally good to do so, where there are human needs that the research can fulfill. But ethics also affects the actual conduct of research. Some things are not done because they infringe general ethical norms, other things are not done because they infringe specifically scientific norms. As the report puts the matter, "Most scientists conduct themselves according to the ethical norms of science [these are] the strongly held traditions of accurate record keeping, openness, and replication, buttressed by the critical review of one's work by peers. . . . Another domain of scientific ethics relates to possible harm that could result from scientific experiments . . . due regard must be given to the health, comfort, and well-being of animal subjects. . . . Whether a scientist chooses to work on research of great potential risk to humanity, such as nuclear weapons or germ warfare, is considered by many scientists to be a matter of personal ethics, not one of professional ethics" (p. 30).

The report recognizes that scientists do not determine the ethical values of society; it rejects a triumphal "leave it all to the scientists" view, but it does show how scientific work is crucial to informed ethical deliberations. It says, "Nor do scientists have the means to settle issues concerning good and evil, although they can sometimes contribute to the discussion of such issues by identifying the likely consequences of particular actions" (p. 26).

From the foregoing sketch it is clear that Project 2061's image of science is clearly informed by current history, philosophy and sociology. As the document is meant to be a curriculum framework and not an academic treatise, it does not contain detailed arguments for the theses advanced. But as the project intends that local bodies will reflect on and respond to the document, then these theses will have to be more fully developed at that level. On just about every point listed above, philosophers, historians and sociologists of science will be aware of a body of contending literature. For instance, the claims of the "strong program" in sociology of science— the Edinburgh sociologists' contention that the history of theory change in science can be accounted for by sociological factors—are recognized but dealt with inconclusively. The demarcation statement is underdeveloped and very contentious. The impact of economics and national interests on scientific research might be understated. The gradualist account of the reform of theory could well be expanded to take more seriously the occurrence of scientific revolutions. Nevertheless, the document is a valuable starting point for reflection, and it clearly requires that teachers and decision makers be comfortable with philosophizing about science. It is not intended that the above list be a sort of Ten Epistemological Commandments carried forth from Washington. The list expresses the views of those framing the curriculum proposals. It is up to teachers and students to evaluate them in the light of their own reading and experience.[10]

History of Science

Curriculum proposals usually do say something about the nature of science, although not as explicitly as Project 2061. This proposal is, however, distinctive in the place it gives to the history of science in school science teaching. In introducing Chapter 10, on "Historical Perspectives," the report says:

> The emphasis here is on ten accounts of significant discoveries and changes that exemplify the evolution and impact of scientific knowledge: the planetary earth, universal gravitation, relativity, geologic time, plate tectonics, the conservation of matter, radioactivity and nuclear fission, the evolution of species, the nature of disease, and the Industrial Revolution. (AAAS 1989, p. 111)

Project 2061 says of these that "although other choices may be equally valid, these clearly fit our dual criteria of exemplifying historical themes and having cultural significance."

Project 2061 advances two types of arguments for bringing history into school science, both of which are of interest to philosophers of science and to educators. The first is that:

> generalizations about how the scientific enterprise operates would be empty without concrete examples. Consider for example, the proposition that new ideas are limited by the context in which they are conceived; are often rejected by the scientific establishment; sometimes spring from unexpected findings; and usually grow slowly, through contributions from many different investigators. Without historical examples, these generalizations would be no more than slogans, however well they might be remembered. (AAAS 1989, p. 111)

There is some ambiguity in the wording of this argument. It says that "generalizations . . . would be empty without concrete examples." This is consistent with the generalizations coming from nonhistorical sources (classical positivism). But the context of the statement and, more importantly, the content of the generalizations it advances, suggest that they could only arise by taking history seriously as a guide to philosophy. The assumption here is that the philosophy of science needs to be cognisant of the history of science: "Philosophy of science without history of science is empty; history of science without philosophy of science is blind," as Imre Lakatos expressed the matter (Lakatos 1978, p. 102). This is a contentious view in philosophy of science. For instance, it contradicts one of the central claims of positivism: namely that philosophy of science can be conducted quite independently of the history of science. For positivism, reason and logic dictate what the scientific method should be, the history of science being only of illustrative value—when scientists get the method right they are used as exemplars. Reichenbach expressed this in his classic distinction between the contexts of discovery and the contexts of justification, with philosophy being concerned only with the context of justification; history, sociology and psychology are concerned with the context of discovery (Reichenbach 1938).

There are, of course, a lot of well-known problems with this historical turn in the philosophy of science, a turn characteristic of what has been called "postpositivist" philosophy of science. The proper relation between the history and philosophy of science is much debated, and experts disagree on just how necessary history of science is for the development of a cogent philosophy of science. Hilary Putnam at one point exclaimed that the history of science is "irrelevant" to the philosophy of science (Suppe 1977, p. 437). The very influential positivist philosopher of science, Rudolf Carnap, has said of himself that he "was as unhistorically minded a person as one could imagine" (Suppe 1977, p. 310). No less a figure than Willard van Orman Quine has said the same thing; his influential epistemological corpus is almost devoid of any historical reference.

Beyond illustrating already arrived-at philosophical positions—something which both sides might agree to—the sticking point in the debate over the philosophical role of history is the extent to which the history of science can and should contribute to the formulation of doctrines in the philosophy of science. Questions arise such as: How do we identify the history of science without some philosophical presuppositions? How do we separate useful history of science from useless history of science without some prior conception of proper method? It seems that we need to know in advance of writing a history of science what will count as science; if we do not have such a view then we could presumably set off researching astrology, numerology and stamp collecting, rather than chemistry or geology. As with many either/or questions, the answer lies in the middle. The relationship between history of science and philosophy of science has to be interactive. There is ample evidence of history of science written in the service of a philosophical commitment. It is notorious that Galileo has become a "man for all philosophical seasons" (Crombie 1981). But there is also ample evidence that the history of science can change the philosophical commitments of those pursuing it. Thomas Kuhn's story of his philosophical transformation, occasioned by having to teach a Harvard General Education course on the history of science, is a well-known recent example. Philosophy is required to begin writing history, but it should be capable of being transformed by historical study.[11]

This debate about the place of history is characteristic of many issues in philosophy of science—it would be a rash person who said that the contentious matters of realism, empiricism, causation, explanation, idealization, falsification and rationality have been settled. But some things regarding the interplay of philosophy and history are agreed upon. Clearly the history of science should be used to *illustrate* positions arrived at in philosophy of science. An exposition of the nature of science, of theory evaluation or the ontological commitments of science which did not make mention of Darwin, Galileo, Newton, Kepler, Mach or Einstein would be very odd. It is particularly odd in educational settings where children have heard of the famous names and might expect to see them figure in any discussion of the nature of science. Project 2061's central point about the need to illustrate claims concerning the nature of science by reference to the history of science is an extremely important one for science education, and also for teaching the history and philosophy of science.[12]

Science For All Americans advances a second reason for bringing the history of science into science classrooms:

> some episodes in the history of the scientific endeavor are of surpassing significance to our cultural heritage. Such episodes certainly include Galileo's role in changing our perception of our place in the universe; Newton's demonstration that the same laws apply to motion in the heavens and on earth; Darwin's long observations of the variety and relatedness of life forms that led to his postulating a mechanism for how they came about; Lyell's careful documentation of the unbelievable age of the earth; and Pasteur's identification of infectious disease with tiny organisms that could be seen only with a microscope. These stories stand among the milestones of the development of all thought in Western civilization. (AAAS 1989, p. 111)

These comments underline the unfortunate fact that the history of science has fallen between academic stools. Arguably the greatest achievement of Western civilization, and that which has undoubtedly been responsible in large part for the shape of Western history, is usually not dealt with in school (or university) history departments because it is thought too technical or difficult; and it is not dealt with in science departments because it is thought irrelevant. Bringing HPS into science programs can in part rectify this situation. It can spur cooperation between school history and science departments. It can assist the integrative goals of education.

Project 2061 devotes one and a half pages to Galileo and his achievement in physics—"Displacing the Earth from the Center of the Universe." It is an informed treatment of the complexities of astronomical evidence at the time, the role of sense perception in Aristotelian science, the status of mathematical models in ancient astronomy, the tradition of realist versus instrumentalist interpretations of scientific theory, the interplay of metaphysics and physics at the beginning of the scientific revolution, the function of technology in the establishment of the new science, Galileo's use of rhetorical argument to establish his position, and the complex role of theological considerations in the evaluation of Galilean science. It deals with other historical episodes, providing material for teachers, programmers and curriculum developers to consider.

There are philosophical and educational problems with these recommendations. As in its first chapter on philosophy, it could be asked: Whose nature of science is going to be taught? so with its historical chapter it could be asked: Whose history of science is to be taught? Whigs, internalists, externalists, idealists, materialists—all have different accounts of the major episodes that Project 2061 commends to teachers. There is a great deal of unresolved controversy in the history of science: after nearly four hundred years some of the intellectual dust has still not settled on the trial of Galileo—as can be evidenced in the recent Vatican collection on the matter (Poupard 1987). The report does recognize that it deals with milestones in the development of Western civilization, but in multicultural classrooms there may be need for other milestones to be recognized and investigated. Some other specifically educational problems created by the inclusion of history of science in the science curriculum will be discussed in the following chapter.

There are many problems to be faced in the implementation of the Project 2061 recommendations. A major step forward has been the publication in 1993 of the project's *Benchmarks for Science Literacy* (AAAS 1993). For each of the ten areas of scientific literacy, including the nature of science and the history of science, subgoals have been identified, and these have been broken down into expected competencies for each school grade from kindergarten through to grade 12. Thus literacy goal 10K is "The Industrial Revolution," and second graders are expected to know something of tools and their relation to ease of work, fifth graders are expected to know something of energy sources for a variety of tools, eighth graders something about the steam engine, twelfth graders something about politics and geography of the Industrial Revolution and about the associated clash of interests between owners of the new technology and workers.

The *Benchmark* document includes a final chapter on "Habits of Mind" that deals with values, attitudes, communication, reasoning, manipulation skills and so on. This chapter moves discussion towards a very old question, namely: What are the qualities of an educated person? Education is far more than instruction in science, or even the sum of instruction in various disciplines. Teachers need to provide or facilitate such instruction, but they need to recognize that the goal of education is far wider, and they have to contribute to these wider goals within the teaching of their own subjects. HPS-informed science programs encourage this contribution by science teachers to the larger educational goals of understanding, critical thought, ethical development, and so on.

British National Curriculum

The British Education Reform Act (1988) provided for the establishment in England and Wales of a national school curriculum to replace the variety of university entrance curricula, Local Education Authority curricula and other courses of study and examinations that had characterized British secondary education. The National Curriculum Council recommended that science constitute twenty percent of the curriculum for all students aged from five to sixteen years. Its first report, *Science in the National Curriculum*, was produced in 1988 (NCC 1988), and revised in 1991 (NCC 1991).[13] A significant feature of the science curriculum is that about five percent of it is devoted to the history and philosophy of science. This was the last of seventeen "Attainment Targets" in the first report. The NCC in the beginning of its first report draws attention to this field. It says that the curriculum:

> is concerned with the nature of science, its history and the nature of scientific evidence. Council recognises that this aspect has not enjoyed a traditional place in science education in schools. . . . Since this target may be relatively unfamiliar to teachers, several examples have been given for each level to illustrate the area of study. (NCC 1988, p. 21)

The committee elaborates its intentions when it says of Attainment Target 17 that:

> pupils should develop their knowledge and understanding of the ways in which scientific ideas change through time and how the nature of these ideas and the uses to which they are put are affected by the social, moral, spiritual and cultural contexts in which they are developed. (NCC 1988, p. 113)

Although in the first report the history and philosophy of science is singled out as a separate attainment target, the expectation is that the themes identified will be taught as they arise in the context of the other attainment targets; this is made explicit in the second report.

Concerning the program of study for eleven- to fourteen-year-olds, the first report says that students should, through their investigations of the life of a famous scientist and/or the development of an important idea in science, be given the opportunity to:

- study the ideas and theories used in other times to explain natural phenomena;
- relate these ideas and theories to present scientific and technological understanding and knowledge;
- compare these ideas and theories with their own emerging understanding and relate them to available evidence.

For fourteen- to sixteen-year-olds, the committee recommends that pupils continue the course of study outlined above, but in addition they should also:

- distinguish between claims and arguments based on scientific data and evidence and those which are not;
- consider how the development of a particular scientific idea or theory relates to its historical and cultural, including the spiritual and moral, context;
- study examples of scientific controversies and the ways in which scientific ideas have changed. (NCC 1988, p. 113)

Beyond providing a program of study, the NCC report also itemizes expected competence levels. The report says pupils should at:

- Level 4, be able to describe the story of some scientific advance, for example, in the context of medicine, agriculture, industry or engineering, describing the new ideas and investigation or invention and the life and times of the principal scientist involved.
- Level 7, be able to give an historical account of a change in accepted theory or explanation and demonstrate an understanding of its effects on people's lives—physically, socially, spiritually, morally. For example, understanding the ecological balance and the greater concern for our environment; or the observations of the motion of Jupiter's moons and Galileo's dispute with the Church.
- Level 10, be able to demonstrate an understanding of the differences in scientific opinion on some topic, either from the past or the present, drawn from studying the relevant literature. (NCC 1988, pp. 114–115)

The NCC says of these levels of attainment that they are "pitched both to be realistic and challenging across the whole ability range" (NCC 1988, p. 117). There is no doubt that they are challenging; how realistic they are will in large part depend upon the ability and competence of teachers, and the ability of students. In the original 1988 document the importance given to HPS, and the detail with which HPS goals are spelled out, is exemplary. The revised report (1991) is less prescriptive about these HPS attainments, in part because they were thought to be too demanding.

Science-Technology-Society Curricula

Science-Technology-Society (STS) programs have been widely adopted as one way of making science teaching contextual and avoiding the abstractness of orthodox science courses. They continue the tradition of the science of everyday life that was common in the US between the world wars, and the science of common things that was prevalent in the UK between the wars. The NSTA Yearbooks of 1984 (Bybee et al. 1984), and 1985 (Bybee 1985) deal with the rationale and content of such STS programs. The NSTA publication *The Science, Technology, Society Movement* (Yager 1993) has reviewed their implementation. Currently six US states require, nine recommend, and nineteen encourage STS material in their science programs (Kumar & Berlin 1993). A 1990 Alberta, Canada, departmental guide to STS education, *Unifying the Goals of Science Education*, makes explicit a commitment to teaching about the nature of science, insisting that this "includes teaching the concepts that philosophers of science have developed to describe the nature of the scientific endeavour and the origins, limits and nature of scientific knowledge."

STS education had its origins in the failures of the discipline-based curricular reforms of the 1960s. Many saw the flight from science as a demand for more useful and relevant science courses, courses which would capture the attention of students and maintain their interest. In this regard STS courses are repeating one of the chief tenets of the progressivism of the 1930s—personal and social relevance. Roger Bybee, a leading STS advocate in the US, maintains that "Schooling in science ought to enhance the personal development of students and contribute to their lives as citizens. Achieving this purpose requires us to reinstate the personal and social goals that were eliminated in the curriculum reform movement of the 1960s and 1970s" (McFadden 1989, p. 261). The US National Science Teachers Association (NSTA) endorsed the STS orientation to science in its 1971 statement *School Science Education for the 1970s* (NSTA 1971). This view was repeated in its 1984 and 1985 yearbooks. See Solomon (1993) for UK.

Conclusion

With lessons learned from the curriculum reforms of the 1960s and the science education crisis of the 1980s, and with better comprehension of how children learn science, curricular projects are at present attempting to embody the following ideas:

- Less content should be taught, but it should be taught and evaluated in a way that encourages understanding and comprehension rather than memorization and rote leaning.
- Some of the connections between science, technology and society need to be appreciated. This is independent of whether full STS programs are taught.
- The cultural dimensions of science, its history and philosophy, its moral and religious implications, need to be appreciated; a science course should entail some learning about science, as well as learning of science.
- Curriculum change will only be effective if it is accompanied by widespread systematic changes involving teacher education or reeducation programs, funding, assessment schemes and texts.

These ideas are not without their problems and internal tensions.[14] It is probably the case that the curriculum documents overestimate the amount and sophistication of HPS material that can be conveyed in a school program that is devoted principally to the teaching of science. The topics mentioned in Project 2061, and in the first version of the British National Curriculum, are very complex, and teachers and students need to realize that there are few simple answers. It may be that an interest in the questions and some appreciation of the complexity are as much as can realistically be conveyed to most students, given the demands of the syllabus and of other subjects. Although a modest ambition, it is nevertheless an important one.

Curriculum development and classroom teaching needs to be cognizant of the psychological preparedness of students. Mature scientific thinking requires formal thought processes in the Piagetian scheme of sensorimotor, preoperational, concrete operational and formal operational modes of thinking. These thought processes are late in developing. In the US it is estimated that most first-year college students have not reached the stage of formal operational thought. One recent US study showed that less than six percent of seventeen-year-olds can solve simple algebra problems (Cromer 1993, p. 26). In the UK it is estimated that less than twenty percent of sixteen-year-olds in comprehensive schools are in the formal stage of reasoning (Black & Lucas 1993, p. 34). This is a powerful reason for science teaching to initially be as phenomonological and concrete as possible, and for explicit attention to be paid to the promotion of formal and abstract reasoning.

Teachers concerned with the HPS dimensions of science need also to be sensitive to the realities of psychological development. Teachers and curriculum framers need to seek in the HPS sphere the equivalent of phenomonological material. Things should be kept simple, concrete, and focused. The big questions—What is the nature of science? How does science relate to religion? Is knowledge of the world truly possible? Is science just a social product?—should be approached very slowly and with due reverence. Meaningful discussion of these questions requires sophisticated thinking, and a good stock of basic information about particular parts of the history of science and the philosophy of science.

Premature attention to the big questions in HPS can cheapen and devalue intellectual activity. This happens enough in society with the sound-bite level of analyses of complex economic, political and ethical questions the norm. Depressingly it happens enough in schools where children are encouraged to give opinions about all sorts of issues independently of any knowledge of them. This educational practice systematically devalues knowledge acquisition and sustained thought. Good HPS-informed science teaching can counteract these narcissistic practices by showing that things are more complex than meets the eye.

CHAPTER 4

History of Science in the Curriculum

In the middle of the nineteenth century, the Duke of Argyll, in his presidential address to the British Association for the Advancement of Science, stated that "what we want in the teaching of the young, is, not so much mere results, as the *methods* and above all, the *history* of science" (Jenkins 1990, p. 274). The Duke's exhortation has been more ignored than followed, but there has been a minority tradition in science education that has attempted to bring something of the history of science into science instruction. Leo Klopfer, long active in the task of bringing the history of science into US science teaching, has made the following melancholy observation about this tradition:

> Proposals for weaving the history and nature of science into the teaching of science in schools and colleges have a history of more than sixty years. Over this long period, various kinds of instructional materials which entwine science and the history of science were produced. The historical accounts, lessons, or units usually served to convey a philosophy of science in which educators believed at the time. Their philosophy of science identified ideas about the nature of science which they wished students to understand or appreciate. These ideas anchored a web, and the strands of science content and science history formed the web's pattern. Yet each of these webs was fragile; they rarely persisted for very long and left little trace on the science education landscape. (Klopfer 1992, p. 105)

This chapter will outline the changing fortune of the history of science in science curricula. It will illustrate some of the arguments for the inclusion of history in science programs. To illustrate these arguments, it will contrast historical with "professional" approaches to the teaching of air pressure. Finally, it will consider and reject some arguments that have been raised by scientists and historians against the inclusion of history in the science curriculum.

Reasons for History

At different times and places there have been appeals to the following reasons for including a historical component in science programs:[1]

1) History promotes the better comprehension of scientific concepts and methods.
2) Historical approaches connect the development of individual thinking with the development of scientific ideas.
3) History of science is intrinsically worthwhile. Important episodes in the history of science and culture—the Scientific Revolution, Darwinism, the discovery of penicillin and so on—should be familiar to all students.
4) History is necessary to understand the nature of science.
5) History counteracts the scientism and dogmatism that are commonly found in science texts and classes.
6) History, by examing the life and times of individual scientists, humanizes the subject matter of science, making it less abstract and more engaging for students.
7) History allows connections to be made within topics and disciplines of science, as well as with other academic disciplines; history displays the integrative and interdependent nature of human achievements.

Underlying the first argument is the belief that well-founded understanding is necessarily historical. The importance of history for the proper understanding of social institutions, such as political parties and churches, or of social customs and mores, such as marriage rites and associated laws, is widely appreciated. It is less well recognized that the same considerations apply to understanding the intellectual products of science. Ernst Mach's view was that: "Historical investigation not only promotes the understanding of that which now is, but also brings new possibilities before us" (Mach 1883/1960, p. 316). For Mach, the perspective of history allows people generally, and scientists in particular, to locate themselves in a tradition of thought, and to see how their concepts and the intellectual frameworks which give them meaning are historically conditioned. Thus the historical perspective encourages the having of new ideas, and novel conceptualizations. Albert Einstein speaks in his autobiographical essay about the grip that the mechanical world view had upon all scientists of his generation, including Maxwell and Hertz. He says that "It was Ernst Mach who, in his *History of Mechanics*, shook this dogmatic faith; this book exercised a profound influence upon me in this regard" (Schilpp 1951, p. 21).

The importance of a historical perspective for understanding has generally been more widely recognized in Continental thought than it has in British and American writing. Ludwik Fleck,[2] in a book which was instrumental in the development of Thomas Kuhn's philosophy of science (Kuhn 1970, p. vi), succinctly states this view as follows:

There can be no ahistorical understanding, that is to say an understanding separated from history, just as there can be no asocial act of understanding performed by an isolated researcher. (Fleck 1935/1979. In Sibum 1988, p. 139)

More recently Ernst Mayr, in the opening pages of his *The Growth of Biological Thought*, commends historical study to scientists in these terms:

I feel that the study of the history of a field is the best way of acquiring an understanding of its concepts. Only by going over the hard way by which these concepts were worked out—by learning all the earlier wrong assumptions that had to be refuted one by one, in other words by learning all past mistakes— can one hope to acquire a really thorough and sound understanding. In science one learns not only by one's own mistakes but by the history of the mistakes of others. (Mayr 1982, p. 20)

The second argument holds that not only does a historical perspective allow students to situate their concepts and conceptual schemes on the larger canvas of intellectual systems and the history of scientific ideas, but historical presentation also has a psychological role to play in the development of understanding. Ernst Mach was a strong advocate of this Genetic Method. This argument claims that the development of individual cognition in some way naturally mirrors the development of species cognition. Hegel was perhaps the first to enunciate this idea, Herbert Spencer followed him, and in this century it has been given its most influential voice in Piaget's system.[3] The latter has said:

The fundamental hypothesis of Genetic Epistemology is that there is a parallelism between the progress made in logical and rational organisation of knowledge and the corresponding formative psychological processes. (Piaget 1970, p. 13)

At a gross level the principle of parallelism is easy enough to understand: children begin with concrete thinking, their concepts are tied to sensation of different kinds; they slowly develop, under the influence of education, more refined or abstract concepts. At this level teachers have long made use of the parallelism doctrine. The chemist Hogg had said in his 1938 text that:

The historic development is a logical approach. The slow progress of the early centuries was owing to a lack of knowledge, to poor technique and to unmethodical attack. But these are precisely the difficulties of the beginner in chemistry. There is a bond of sympathy between the beginner and the pioneer. (Hogg 1938, p. vii; in Klopfer 1969)

James Wandersee (1985) has suggested ways in which knowledge of the historical development of a discipline can assist teachers in anticipating and understanding the difficulties that contemporary students have with learning subjects. The history can also suggest questions and experiments that promote appropriate conceptual change in students. There are approximately twenty-five hundred published studies on children's misconceptions in science; the information on the resistance of science learning to science instruction is overwhelming (Duit 1995). Knowledge of the slow and difficult path traversed in the historical development of particular sciences can assist teachers planning the organization of a program, the choice of experiments and activities, and their responses to classroom questions and puzzles.[4]

The third argument, that the history of science is intrinsically important, has not been advanced as much as it needs to be. To its credit, Project 2061 does advance the argument. Unfortunately most countries allow students to complete history courses without any knowledge of major scientific, mathematical and technical achievements, which constitute some of the most important episodes in the development of civilization. If as much history time were devoted to the scientific revolution as to political revolutions, to Mendel and genetics as to generals, to the development of time-keeping as to the development of constitutions—then the overall education of society would be considerably advanced, and the "two-cultures gap" lamented by C. P. Snow would be less apparent (Snow 1963).

The fourth argument, that history is necessary to understand the nature of science, has also been advocated by Project 2061 and discussed in the previous chapter.

The fifth argument, that history counteracts "scientism," was stated by Mach, who saw that recognition of the historicity of cognition promoted independence of mind, which for him was a cardinal virtue. He recognized that the same disposition could be developed by classical studies:

> A person who has read and understood the Greek and Roman authors has felt and experienced more than one who is restricted to the impressions of the present. He sees how men placed in different circumstances judge quite differently of the same things from what we do today. His own judgments will be rendered thus more independent. (Mach 1886/1943, p. 347)

The sixth argument, that history humanizes the sciences, has often been advanced in reaction to widespread abuse of science, and in reaction to authoritarian teaching practices associated with "scientism." Some historical study can counteract the revulsion for science and technology felt by many witnesses of high-tech wars, sonar-guided whale kills and so on. The lives and times of the great and not-so-great scientists are usually full of interesting and appealing incidents and issues that students can read about, debate and reenact. James Wandersee has successfully incorporated historical vignettes into science programs. These can be made as sophisticated as the class and resources allow (Wandersee 1990). History is a way of putting a face on Boyle's Law, Ohm's Law, Curie's discoveries, Mach bands, Planck's Constant and so on.

The seventh argument, that history integrates the sciences and other disciplines, has been the backbone of liberal approaches to the teaching of science. The integrative function of history was recognized by Percy Nunn, James Conant, Gerald Holton and others. It was one of the planks of the Harvard Committee Report, *General Education in a Free Society* (Conant 1945), and was prominent in the Harvard Project Physics program.

Science has developed in conjunction with mathematics, philosophy, technology, theology and commerce. In turn it has affected each of these fields, as well as literature and culture more generally. History allows science programs to reveal to students something of this rich tapestry and engender their appreciation of the interconnectiveness of human intellectual and practical endeavors.

Galileo's physics was dependent upon Euclidean geometry and the then just translated mechanical analyses of Archimedes (brought to Italy by those fleeing the Turkish invasion of Constantinople). It was also dependent upon technological advances, lens-grinding and the telescope being the most obvious. His philosophy allowed him to first understand, and then to break from, central Aristotelian concepts that constrained the physics of those around him. His theological views also freed him to investigate the heavens and to experiment with falling objects. Even music had a role to play, as in the timing of rolling bodies. And of course patronage, commerce and communications all contributed to Galileo's achievements. In turn, his new, mathematical, experimental physics had an enormous effect on further physics, philosophy, technology, commerce, mathematics and theology. The same rich pattern of influence and effect can be seen in the achievements of Newton, Darwin and Einstein, to name just the most obvious.[5] A historical approach to science allows students to connect the learning of specific scientific topics with their learning of mathematics, literature, political history, theology, geography, philosophy and so on. When the richness of science's history is appreciated, then collaboration between science, drama, mathematics, history and religious studies teachers in schools can fruitfully be encouraged.

The above arguments for the history of science are silent on *what* kind of history of science should be included. Historians of science notoriously take different approaches to their subject. There are *internalist* historians of science who concentrate upon the development of scientific concepts and understandings wholly from within the world of scientific ideas, largely ignoring the social and cultural milieu in which the ideas develop, and certainly denying any causative role to social factors on the development of scientific ideas. Alastair Crombie (1952) and A. R. Hall (1962) are representative internalist studies of the Scientific Revolution. There are also *externalist* historians of science who are concerned to connect the growth of science to its social circumstances—either the immediate personal and work circumstances of scientists (proximal externalists and sociologists of science such as Shapin (1982)), or the more general economic and political circumstances of the scientists' times (distal externalists such as Bernal (1939), and historians in the Marxist tradition, such as Hessen's (1931) dramatic, and for many notorious, study of Newton).

The difference between internal and external factors is not as clear-cut as it might first appear. Commerce and politics might be clear external factors, but what about mathematics, logic, methodology, metaphysics, technology, theology, ethics and even aesthetics? These are all spheres that determine a scientist's choice of research programs and research decisions. To say that they are external to science, as for instance the positivists and their critic Karl Popper did, requires a very circumscribed definition of science, and one that has unfortunate unintended consequences. Avoiding the internal/external categories and concentrating on the good/ bad, or progressive/retrogressive science demarcation might be more advantageous.

Again, some history of science is "scientific" history in the sense that it is written by scientists with an eye to the elucidation of contemporary science. This is sometimes called "Whiggish" history (following Butterfield 1949); other history of science is "historians" history, where the byways as well as the highways are travelled, where complexity, false paths and failures are as much respected as simplicity, truth and success.

These are all complex and much debated matters. Hopefully, science teachers will be aware of the divisions of scholarly opinion, and be conscious of what side of the various arguments they are adopting. To repeat, the purpose of historical and philosophical dimensions in science teaching is not just to provide still more things to know, it is to promote an awareness of interesting and important questions and a concern with their resolution.

History in US Science Curricula

In the United States the history of science has been less significant in schools than in Britain.[6] In the 1920s some chemists, following Holmyard, advocated a historical approach in science instruction, and a number of historically oriented texts were written.[7]

After World War Two the generalist or contextual approach to science teaching gained momentum. The dominant influence here was the president of Harvard University, James B. Conant, whose case-study approach to science education was widely adopted. He developed this while in charge of undergraduate general education at Harvard, and popularized it in a series of government reports (Harvard Committee 1945), and paperback best-sellers (Conant 1947, 1951). His two-volume *Harvard Case Histories in Experimental Science* (Conant 1957) became a popular university textbook. Conant's generalist credo was embodied in the 1945 Harvard University report *General Education in a Free Society* (Conant 1945). It proposed that:

> Science instruction in general education should be characterized mainly by broad integrative elements—the comparison of scientific with other modes of thought, the comparison and contrast of the individual sciences with one another, the relations of science with its own past and with general human history, and of science with problems of human society.

It then identifies a crucial feature of science, its abstractness and tradition-dependence, that make learning difficult and that, as Mach noted, history can render more intelligible:

> The facts of science and the experience of the laboratory no longer can stand by themselves; they no longer represent simple, spontaneous, and practical elements directly related to the everyday life of the student. As they become further removed from his experience, more subtle, more abstract, the facts must be learned in another context, cultural, historical and philosophical. Only such broader perspectives can give point and lasting value to scientific information and experience for the general student. (Conant 1945, p. 155)

Conant's influence cannot be overestimated. Thomas Kuhn, in the Preface of his first book, *The Copernican Revolution*, that arose from his lectures in Harvard's General Education program, says that: "Work with him [Conant] first persuaded me that historical study could yield a new sort of understanding of the structure and function of scientific research. Without my own Copernican revolution, which he fathered, neither this book nor my other essays in the history of science would have been written" (Kuhn 1957, p. xi).[8] Gerald Holton makes a similiar admission.[9] The then-young physics graduate, I. Bernard Cohen, worked with Conant on his Yale Invitation Lectures, subsequently published as *On Understanding Science: An Historical Approach* (Conant 1947). This bestseller argued, among other things, that the history of science was indispensible for the understanding of science. Cohen then worked with Conant's Harvard Committee, which produced the above-mentioned 1945 Report, the famous "red book." Additionally, Cohen in 1950 wrote a substantial essay on the importance of history for the teaching of science.[10] After the war, Conant organized a series of conferences of teachers of chemistry and physics, plus historians of science. One outcome of these conferences was the collection *Science in General Education* (McGrath 1948).

The success of Conant's Harvard Case Studies in college courses, and the example of Joseph Schwab's historical text-based science course at the University of Chicago (Schwab 1950) prompted Leo Klopfer, then at the University of Chicago, to emulate the approach in the teaching of secondary science. His rationale was presented in articles with Fletcher Watson, who was later to work on Harvard Project Physics (Klopfer & Watson 1957). One of Klopfer's and Watson's major concerns was to increase students' understanding of the scientific enterprise and of its interactions with society. Their disquiet concerned students' poor grasp of what would shortly be labelled "scientific literacy"—a term introduced by Fitzpatrick (1960). They saw historical studies as a way of expanding and enriching students' understanding of science.[11]

They produced a course of History of Science Cases for Schools [HOSC] (Klopfer 1960).[12] Each of eight cases was presented in a separate booklet containing the historical narrative, quotations from scientists' original papers, pertinent student experiments and exercises, marginal notes and questions, and space for students to write answers to questions. Teachers' guides and supplementary material were also produced. The experimental version was tested and evaluated in 108 classes with encouraging results:[13]

> the [HOSC] method is definitely effective in increasing student understanding of science and scientists when used in biology, chemistry, and physics classes in high schools . . . moreover . . . they achieve these significant gains in understanding of science and scientists with little or no concomitant loss of achievement in the usual content of high school science courses. (Klopfer & Cooley 1963, p. 46)

After this success the individual case studies were produced over a number of years and published by Science Research Associates in Chicago (Klopfer 1964–66); a version was also published by Wadsworth, San Francisco (Klopfer 1969). Despite their initial success they seem to have been one of the webs of which Klopfer said they "rarely persisted for very long and left little trace on the science education landscape."

The liberal or generalist program was endorsed by the National Society for the Study of Education in its 59th Yearbook (1960). This advised that:

> A student should learn something about the character of scientific knowledge, how it has developed, and how it is used. He must see that knowledge has a certain dynamic quality and that it is quite likely to shift in meaning and status with time.

However, as the yearbook was being written, the curricular and social times were changing. The National Science Foundation was formed in 1950, and made its first grant for the development of a high school science curriculum in 1956. This was to the Physical Science Study Committee (PSSC) at the Massachusetts Institute of Technology, whose draft text was published at the same time that the Soviet *Sputnik* was launched. There quickly followed the spate of NSF-funded curricular projects previously discussed, in which historical, technological and cultural matters were ignored. The emphasis was upon the mastery of science content in its most theoretical form. The NSF had a *professional* approach to school science, in contrast to the generalist or *contextual* approach of the NSSE yearbook. Its credo is stated in *Policies for Science Education*, prepared in 1960 by the Science Manpower Project at Teachers College, Columbia University:

> Let us note that [education] is the basic factor upon which an adequate science manpower supply depends. We must have improved science-education programs in the schools. . . . Then and only then, will we secure a flow of new scientific and technological personnel adequate to meet the present and projected needs of our culture. (Fitzpatrick 1960, p. 195; quoted in Klopfer & Champagne 1990)

These science curriculum reforms of the early 1960s proceeded without the participation of either historians or philosophers of science. There were two prominent exceptions, the Harvard Project Physics course, and the Yellow Version of the BSCS *High School Biology*. Less prominent were the Klopfer and Cooley Case Studies for High School developed in the period from 1956 to 1960.

The BSCS text was informed by the ideas of the University of Chicago biologist-philosopher-educationalist J. J. Schwab, who wrote an influential essay on "The Nature of Scientific Knowledge as Related to Liberal Education" (Schwab 1945), and who vigorously promoted the Deweyean idea of "science as enquiry."[14] Schwab wrote the *Teachers' Handbook* for the BSCS curriculum, in which he advocated the historical approach, saying that "the essence of teaching of science as enquiry would be to show some of the conclusions of science in the framework of the way they arise and are tested . . . [it] would also include a fair treatment of the doubts and incompleteness of science" (Schwab 1963, p. 41). History is also advocated because it "concerns man and events rather than conceptions in themselves. There is a human side to enquiry" (Schwab 1963, p. 42).

In the 1970s the American Physical Society established a section on the History of Physics. At the same time the History of Science Society established an Education Committee. Both have continued to be active in educational matters.

The history of chemistry in the US has always been more marginal to pedagogy than the history of physics or biology. In part this is because, as Stephen Brush remarks, "Chemists, compared with other scientists, have relatively little interest in the history of their own subject. This situation is reflected, and perpetuated, by the antihistorical character of most chemical education" (in Kauffman 1989, p. 81). There have been many calls for the inclusion of history of chemistry into chemistry education. Those of Bent (1977), Bohning (1984), Ihde (1971), Kauffman (1989) and Wicken (1976) are notable. The history of this endeavor has been documented by George Kauffman (1989). The American Chemical Society's guidelines for undergraduate education in chemistry recommend that "beginning and subsequent courses in chemistry incorporate historical perspective as well as reference to current developments in chemistry." The guidelines, like most guidelines, are more often ignored than followed.

History in British Science Curricula

In Britain there has been a long, if weak and uneven, tradition of incorporating the history of science in science education.[15] The British Association for the Advancement of Science (BAAS) at its 1917 conference repeated the call made by the Duke of Argyll at its 1855 conference. The association said that the history of science "supplied a solvent of that artificial barrier between literary studies and science which the school timetable sets up" (Jenkins 1990, p. 274). The influential government report of 1918 (*Natural Science in Education*, known as the Thompson Report, after its chair, J. J. Thompson) also saw a creative role for history:

> It is desirable . . . to introduce into the teaching some account of the main achievements of science and of the methods by which they have been obtained. There should be more of the spirit, and less of the valley of dry bones . . . One way of doing this is by lessons on the history of science. (Brock 1989, p. 31)

The report went on to say that:

> some knowledge of the history and philosophy of science should form part of the intellectual equipment of every science teacher in a secondary school.

These recommendations were included in the "Science for All" curriculum that was developed in the immediate postwar years (Mansell 1976).

Percy Nunn, the philosopher of science, Richard Gregory and other historically minded educationalists argued the case for history in the interwar years. They were influenced by the Hegelian, Spencerian and Herbartian idea that the development of individual thinking in some sense replicates the historical development of human thinking, a view later popularized by Piaget's genetic epistemology. Popular science textbooks incorporating these ideas were written by E. J. Holmyard, J. A. Cochrane and J. R. Partington. Holmyard's *Elementary Chemistry* sold over half a million copies between 1925 and 1960. He argued for an historical approach not just on motivational or instrumentalist grounds, but on cognitive grounds: teaching a topic historically was the only way that the nature of scientific truth could be conveyed. In the introduction to his influential text he said:

> The historical method is not, I believe, one of several equally good alternative schemes of teaching chemistry in schools: It is the only method which will effectively produce all the results which it is at once our privilege and our duty to aim. (Holmyard 1924; quoted in Klopfer 1990)

The British *School Science Review* welcomed the founding of the first professional journals in the history of science—*Annals of Science* (1936) and *Ambix* (1937)—with the comment that school teachers "knew from experience the value of historical details in arousing and maintaining interest and in meeting the criticism that science is unhuman . . . [the journal] ought to be placed in every school library" (Sherratt 1983, p. 421). In the 1920s and 1930s special courses on the history of science were offered to science teachers in Teacher Training Colleges, and beginning in 1921 a master's degree on the subject was offered at University College, London.

After the World War Two history gradually diminished in importance. It was a small part of the Nuffield O-level course, but generally the experiential Nuffield courses ignored the historical, social and cultural dimensions of science. A number of examining boards ran separate courses in the history of science, but by the 1980s the number of candidates presenting had dwindled dramatically. Prior to the National Curriculum the history of science found some place in the Nuffield programs, and in the SISCON (Science in a Social Context) and SaTiS (Science and Technology in Society) courses introduced in the early 1980s.

This decline in the contextual dimension of school science was of concern to the British Association for Science Education which, in a number of its reports, *Alternatives for Science Education* (1979), and *Education through Science* (1981), urged the incorporation of more historical and philosophical material into the science curriculum. Its 1979 *Alternatives for Science Education* maps three approaches to science education, all of which emphasize the history and philosophy of science. Its 1981 report advocated:

> teaching science as a cultural activity: the more generalised pursuit of scientific knowledge and culture that takes account of the history, philosophy and social implications of scientific activities, and therefore leads to an understanding of the contribution science and technology make to society and the world of ideas.

The previous chapter has discussed something of the incorporation of history into the current British National Curriculum in Science. These efforts, and their prospects, are reviewed by Stephen Pumfrey (1992). The ASE, as early as its 1963 report, *Training of Graduate Science Teachers*, recognized that teachers were not adequately prepared to teach this contextual science. Then, as now, specific efforts need to be made to incorporate HPS into preservice and in-service programs for teachers.

History in Continental Science Curricula

In Europe teaching the history of science in school science programs has been equally erratic.[16] Jürgen Teichmann at the Deutsches Museum in Munich has put effort into replicating historical experiments and provided notes and instruction for teachers (Teichmann 1986b), as has Heinz Sibum at Oldenburg University (Sibum 1988). Fabio Bevilacqua at the University of Pavia has developed sophisticated computer software for enhancing the historical teaching of science, which makes widely available the rich resources of the Pavia library, and makes available experiments performed with original instruments. The large-circulation Spanish science teachers' journal *Enseñanza de las Ciencias* carries a regular page on historical and philosophical matters of interest to teachers.

The Danish physics curriculum has incorporated history, technology and philosophy into the teaching of physics. Research carried out by Nielsen and Thomsen (1990) has shown that Danish students studying traditional, professional, science curricula had similar problems as their peers in the rest of the world: "they found physics difficult, unrelated to other school subjects, and with very little connection to real life." At the same time there has been a large increase in the number of students going into the final three years of high school. Both factors created demands for curriculum reform. The Danish Parliament proposed a bill for the creation of a new national physics curriculum in which five dimensions were to be incorporated:

1) Physics and the world around us.
2) The physicist's worldview.
3) Examples of modern technology.
4) Physics-technology-society relationships.
5) History and philosophy of physics.

The group of teachers, physicists, historians and philosophers who had responsibility for implementing the last dimension recognized that their task was formidable:

> Firstly, we had to convince the average physics teacher that history of physics is interesting and that students really may benefit from it; secondly, we had to teach him/her some interesting examples from the history of physics along with suggestions for actual use in the classroom; and thirdly, we had to convince the teacher that he/she would be able to teach the students on the historical-philosophical dimension without any problems (Nielsen & Thomsen 1990, p. 310).

The group produced a teachers' guide with one chapter on the historical-philosophical dimension in physics, a second chapter on dealing with primary sources, and five other chapters dealing with separate case studies. An extensive series of in-service workshops was held, and finally, books were produced for students on different aspects of the history of physics. Initial results suggest that the curriculum has been well received by both teachers and students. A comparable new course on technology has also been produced.[17]

Teaching About Air Pressure: The Contrast Between Historical and Professional Approaches

The best way to appreciate the contrasts between professional and contextual approaches to teaching science is to look at the different ways that specific topics are taught. Air pressure, a central topic in most elementary and high school science courses, will serve here as an example.

Historical Approaches

There have been good historical treatments of air pressure in science programs. Air pressure and Boyle's vacuum pump were the subject of the first of Conant's 1957 Harvard Case Studies. One of three physics units in the nine Klopfer Case Studies (Klopfer 1969a) is on air pressure (Case 6). This unit is comprised of a collection of texts, extracts, activities, slides, hardware and experiments. The case study

> combines the story of the overthrow in the 17th century of the ancient Aristotelian doctrine that nature abhors a vacuum with the application of hydrostatic principles to explain the phenomena associated with atmospheric pressure. The pioneer work of Torricelli with the barometer included the idea that the mercury column standing at a height of about 30 inches above the level of mercury in a dish was balanced by the weight of the "sea of air" pressing on the surface of the mercury. (Klopfer & Cooley 1961, p. 10)

Case 6 contains material on Galileo's incorrect account of why the lift pump can only bring water up thirty-four feet—his idea was that if any longer than this, the column would break under its own weight. The case asks students to hold up a length of chewed gum and see what its critical (nonbreaking) length is; and asks them whether by analogy it is possible that a similar situation will occur in a long column of water. The case also has material on Pascal's Law, and recommends the building of a simple hydraulic press to illustrate the principles. Among other benefits, the case allows students to see that great scientists such as Galileo get things wrong, and persist in erroneous beliefs. This is even more apparent in Galileo's commitment to a completely false account of the tides, a subject with which he occupied the final day of his 1633 *Dialogue*, and which he believed provided the best argument for the Copernican worldview.[18] History shows the fallibility of science and scientists, as well as the the triumphs.

Each of Klopfer's Case Studies has objectives listed under three headings:

1) Information about science subject matter and the narrative of the case.
2) Understanding of science concepts and principles.
3) Understanding of ideas concerning science and scientists.

The objectives that it lists under (3) for the unit on air pressure are instructive. It is said that after studying the unit, students should understand the following ideas concerning science and scientists:

- The meanings and functions of scientific hypotheses, principles and theories, and their interconnections.
- The difference between science and applied science or technology.
- The dynamic interaction between ideas and experiments, between thinking and doing, in scientific work.

- That a chain of reasoning, which often involves many assumptions, connects a theory with hypotheses that can actually be tested by experiments and observations.
- That factors involved in the establishment of a scientific theory or concept include experimental evidence, the personal convictions of participating scientists and the theory's usefulness.
- That scientific explanations of natural phenomena are given in terms of accepted laws and principles.
- That scientists are individuals possessing a wide range of personal characteristics and abilities.
- That science is an international activity.
- The nature and functions of scientific societies.
- That progress in science is, in part, dependent upon the existing state of technology and on other factors outside of science itself.
- That free communication among scientists through journals, books, meetings and personal correspondence is essential to the development of science.
- That new observations have a trigger effect: they shake up established concepts and lead to new hypotheses and new experiments.
- That new apparatus and new techniques are important in making possible new experiments and the exploration of new ideas.

This list could double as a suitable statement of the objectives of any course in the history and philosophy of science, as well as any program of study in science. (It is of some minor note that this characterization of science was first written in 1961, that is, *prior* to the publication of Thomas Kuhn's *Structure of Scientific Revolutions*, which gave wide exposure to similar views.)

The HOSC materials aimed at providing an education *about* science as well as an education *in* science, and with what are often called "intangible" outcomes. Of forty-seven teachers participating in one review of the HOSC materials, sixty-four percent said that their students gained intangible benefits that were not measured by tests. Some teachers' commented as follows:

- The students obtained a new feeling for the meaning of science.
- Discussion and opinions of class members played a larger part than normal . . . critical evaluation of science and scientists in our society was encouraged.
- Students gained a feeling of being part of a great adventure. (Klopfer & Cooley 1961, p. 128)

Air pressure is a ready-made field for integrating history of science into science teaching. There is a natural progression and parallelism between the evolving ideas and investigations of students and the historical story. Thirty years after the Klopfer Case Study, Joan Solomon in the UK, also wishing to incorporate historical and social themes into school science, wrote a booklet on the same subject titled *The Big Squeeze* for the British Association for Science Education (Solomon 1989a). It promotes understanding of air pressure by traversing the ancient Egyptians and Greeks, medieval pumps and bagpipes, Galileo's ideas, his student Torricelli's famous experiment with a tube of water to create a vacuum and the diverse interpretations advanced to account for the "space" above the water column, Torricelli's mercury barometer, Pascal's experiment of taking a barometer up a mountain and recording the changes in height of mercury supported and thus suggesting that air pressure is the result of the weight of air above the mercury, von Guericke's Magdeburg hemispheres, and finally, Boyle's vacuum pump and his speculations about the "springiness of air."

With good teaching, students can easily be led through this sequence of concepts and experiments.[19] Firstly, students can conjecture about whether there is anything in air or whether it is essentially empty. After thinking about tests of their conjectures they can be shown that air is difficult to compress—an empty test tube pushed into water shows this. If the same test tube is filled with water and then raised out of the beaker, we see the barometer situation. Secondly, students can be asked whether there would be a limit to the length of the water column supported in the test tube, and why the column is supported. Holding a clear plastic garden hose clamped at one end and placing the other end in a bucket of water, and then suspending it from a building provides an answer to this question. Thirdly, students can conjecture whether a heavier liquid would have a less high column supported, and what the predicted height of a mercury column would be. Finally, the creation of a vacuum in a cylinder and the subsequent pulling of a piston into it can be shown, and thus the basis of Newcomen's steam engine demonstrated.

With judicious use of assignments, experiments and essays a great many of the objectives of the HOSC unit on air pressure and the more general objectives of a contextual science program can be met. The interplay of science with philosophy on the one hand, and with technology on the other, can be beautifully seen: the Aristotelian doctrine of "nature abhors a vacuum" can be appreciated; the influence of this on scientists as prominent as Galileo can be seen; the efforts to support this philosophical and scientific doctrine in the light of Pascal's and Torricelli's demonstrations of its seeming falsity can be outlined; and by students making their own primitive steam engines (versions of Newcomen's cooling-induced vacuum engine), or just pistons and cylinders, the technical difficulties in the advancement of the science of air pressure can be appreciated.

A Professional Approach

A standard professional approach to the topic of air pressure can be found in the PSSC *Physics* text (1960), which was the first NSF-funded high school science program, and has been used by millions of students throughout the world. It contrasts markedly with the above historical treatment found in the Harvard Case Studies, the HOSC, Project Physics, and British materials. It is noteworthy that in the thirty-four chapters of the text not one is devoted to air pressure, nor is it mentioned in the index of approximately one thousand entries. Without mentioning air pressure, its treatment begins with Boyle's Law and a model of colliding molecules in a chamber. The discussion of this law assumes the existence of air pressure; however, all developments up to Boyle are ignored. There is no mention of Torricelli nor of Pascal, much less are Aristotle and the *horror vacui* doctrine mentioned. Boyle's Law is explained using the mole concept, and it is stated as:

> At a given temperature the pressure exerted by a gas is proportional to the number of molecules divided by the volume they occupy.
> $P = K \times N/V$, where K is the proportionality factor.

Notably absent from the PSSC discussion is any mention of technology. Although the expected change in the P-V relation is discussed for rarefied atmospheres, there is no mention of a barometer in the chapter; barometers are relegated to end-of-chapter exercises. Children can study the gas laws in the PSSC physics program without their connections to barometers and weather changes being mentioned or explained. Similarly water pumps, steam engines and all other technological uses of air pressure are omitted. The momentous connection of science with technology, and its dramatic effect on the transformation of economic and social life, is entirely omitted from PSSC physics. Not just PSSC but many of the other reforms projects of the early 1960s removed applied aspects of science from their programs. One reviewer of the 1960s reforms has said:

> The first major changes in all the NSF supported curriculum reform of the '60s was removing all technology and presenting pure science "in a way it is known to the scientist." It is only recently that many are proclaiming the fallacy of such efforts. (Yager & Penick 1987, p. 53)

Metaphysics and Physics in the Science of Air Pressure

A teacher's interest in history will influence how much a class learns from discussing and reenacting the historical progression that led to the contemporary understanding of air pressure. Aristotle was one of the earliest contributors to the philosophical/scientific debates about what constitutes air, and more particularly whether or not a void or vacuum is possible in nature. For many philosophical and scientific reasons he denied that a vacuum could exist in nature. He advanced his arguments for the *horror vacui* against the atomists, for whom the existence of a void between atoms was philosophically fundamental. The chief arguments against the possibility of a void are contained in Aristotle's *Physics* Book IV (reproduced in Matthews 1989). The historian Ernest Moody says of this text that:

It was, in a very definite sense, the cradle of mediaeval mechanics. And for Galileo . . . this text was a constant point of departure. Not only in this Pisan dialogue, but in the great *Discorsi* of Galileo's maturity, it was as a criticism of this Aristotelian text that he developed his dynamic theory of the motion of heavy bodies. (Moody 1951, p. 175)

Aristotle argued, reasonably enough given everyday experience, that the velocity (*V*) of a moving body varied directly as the force applied (*F*) and inversely as the resistance of the medium (*R*) through which it moved. (Think of pushing a car along a smooth road and then through sand.) That is:

$$V = K \times F/R$$

In a vacuum *R* would be zero, and a body once pushed would move with infinite speed. Thus its time of movement between two points *A* and *B* would be zero seconds, and thus it could not be said to move but would dissolve at *A* and be recreated instanteously at *B*. Thus Aristotle's conclusion was that in a vacuum there could be no motion. But as motion can be seen everywhere, then a vacuum is impossible. This basic belief that in nature there could be no vacuum dominated and constrained physics for over a thousand years, and Galileo struggled with it at the beginning of his philosophical/scientific investigations.

One enduring lesson from the consideration of these early Greek speculations on air pressure is the awareness of the way in which Aristotelian science and philosophy is rooted in the experience of the everyday world.[20] The ancient world was familiar with all the phenomena that introductory students can see and experience. The siphon was used to drain fluid, the pipette or clepsydra was used to transfer fluid, and the drinking straw was of course used. The move from all of this familiar experience to the belief that nature abhors a vacuum was very easy. Aristotle appealed to this common experience, and then added certain logical arguments about motion and place, and the outcome was the long-lasting and powerful doctrine of *horror vacui*.

A similar train of argument was used in discussing another aspect of the question: Does air have weight? The ancients, through observation of windmills, sails, balloons made of animal bladders and so on, realized that air contained something; it was not empty. Yet it did not appear to weigh anything; indeed it seemed to have a negative weight—it did not press down, but rather it seemed to go upwards. Aristotle held that things in their proper place had no weight or *gravitas* (as the Latins would say). Stones and matter had *gravitas* because they were trying to press down into the centre of the earth, their natural home; air had no *gravitas* but in contrast had *levitas* because its natural tendency was to go upwards to the sky, its natural place. Thus the claim that air had weight, in the sense that stones had weight, would invalidate an important plank in Aristotle's philosophy.

This same move from everyday experience to scientific and philosophical doctrines can be seen in Aristotelian theories of motion, astronomy, biology and much else. If this point can be appreciated, then students are in a position to grasp the most important feature of the scientific revolution of Galileo and Newton—the reinterpretation of everyday experience and certainties in the formulation of their new sciences; the move from Aristotle's explanation of the unfamiliar in terms of the familiar, to Newton's explanation of the familiar (falling bodies) in terms of the unfamiliar (inertia).

Torricelli's 1643 experiment (repeated in France in 1646 by Pascal) with an inverted closed tube of mercury placed in an open dish of mercury, where the mercury fell a distance from the top of the tube but always stayed at about thirty inches or seventy-six centimeters above the level of mercury in the dish, concentrated the minds of philosophers and scientists (to use an anachronistic distinction): the long-standing philosophical dispute about a vacuum seemed to be settled by a simple experiment. This same experiment can also engage the minds of contemporary students.

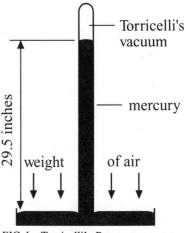

FIG.1   Torricelli's Barometer

Students can be shown Torricelli's apparatus—or now in mercury-free laboratories, some variant of it—and with or without prompting can see that there are two questions that need an answer:

1) What holds the column of mercury up?
2) Is there anything in the space above the mercury in the column?

These are separate questions although they are often merged. At the time of Pascal and Torricelli, many said the answer to the first question was that air pressure was forcing down on the surface of the mercury in the dish. Others, denying that air had weight, had other accounts of how the column of mercury was supported. In answer to the second question, many said that there was no vacuum, fewer said that there was a vacuum. In the middle of the seventeenth century all four possible answers had adherents.

The above questions can be reformulated in the following matrix (following Dijksterhuis 1986, p. 445) with representative adherents to different answers included.

	YES	**NO**
Does air pressure hold the mercury up?	Descartes Pascal	Aristotelians Roberval
Is there a vacuum above the mercury?	Pascal Roberval Boyle	Descartes Aristotelians Galileo Hobbes

Table 1 Seventeenth-century Opinions on Air Pressure and the Vacuum

The resolution of these competing views depended upon logical, technical and experimental considerations. Some, who denied air pressure and the vacuum, said that what caused the column to sink was the generation of vapors or spirits from the liquid. To test this view, Pascal took wine and water and asked his opponents what would sink further in Torricelli's tube. His audience reasoned that as wine was more volatile, it would vaporize more, and thus sink further down the tube than water. When the experiment was done, it was water that sank further. Pascal knew this would happen because it was heavier than wine. So the spirits hypothesis had either to be abandoned or reworked. Others who denied the vacuum said that a small amount of air had been left behind in the tube. Pascal took tubes of different diameters and established that what was constant was the height of the column, not the volume of the space, as the rival hypothesis would have it. Again the rival hypothesis had to be abandoned or reworked. Students can be led through these debates—by questions, by debates, by reading source materials—and can thus learn something of the process of scientific argument at the same time as they learn about air pressure.

This sequence illustrates the difference between simple observation and scientific experiment, the relationship of theory to the construction of experiments, and the less than straightforward reassessment of theory in the light of disconfirming experimental results. For instance, the *horror vacui* doctrine could be reconciled with the aberrant experimental results by a simple twist: it could have been said that the varying degrees of fall of the mercury column established the degree to which nature abhors a vacuum. Nature's abhorrence is not absolute, but relative to the substance at hand. Nature is prepared to pull mercury up a certain amount, and other liquids up differing amounts in its effort to avoid a vacuum. So the column height, rather than a measure of the pressure of air forcing down on the dish, was a measure of the degree to which nature abhors a vacuum. To combat this move requires that purely *ad hoc* hypotheses be ignored in science.

Pascal, in his best-known experiment, had a barometer taken up the Puy-de-Dome mountain in 1648, confirming that the height of the column decreased the higher it was taken. He thought that this was because the higher up the mountain the less air was pushing down on the surface of the mercury. Students can be encouraged to imagine this experimental test, and may in places have the opportunity to conduct it. Pascal's brother-in-law conducted the experiment and the results were as predicted. (He left a barometer at the base of the mountain to see that its level did not change during the day, a control that students might be encouraged to think of.) The results were wonderfully consistent with the air-pressure hypothesis, and indeed Pascal looked upon it as a *experimentum crucis* between the two doctrines.

It would seem that, against fundamental tenets of Aristotelian philosophy, the existence of a vacuum had been demonstrated, and at the same time it had been demonstrated that air has weight. But as in life, so also in science and philosophy, things were not always simple. The antivacuum theory could easily say that Pascal's experiment simply showed that, as we go higher towards the heavens, nature's abhorrence of a vacuum diminishes. Hobbes and Descartes, who were both firm opponents of Aristotelianism, acknowledged all the experimental evidence presented by Pascal and Roberval, yet denied their conclusion that it established the existence of a vacuum. Thomas Hobbes, for instance, said of Torricelli's supposedly definitive proof of the vacuum that:

> if the force with which the quicksilver descends be great enough . . . it will make the air penetrate the quicksilver in the vessel, and go up into the cylinder to fill the place which they [vacuists] thought was left empty. (Shapin & Schaffer 1985, p. 89)

Hobbes and Descartes respectively thought that the void was filled with aetherial substance, and with subtle matter.[21] When students are reminded that a vacuum entails zero or very low pressure, and further that liquids vaporize and then boil at low pressures, they might see that the subtle-matter view of the space above the mercury is not entirely without merit.

At just about every stage in the foregoing development, the basic scientific move from phenomenal evidence to invisible mechanisms has to be made. Students can easily repeat this process of evidence—conjecture—testing, and thus appreciate the nature of scientific hypotheses and their appraisal.

The complexity of testing hypotheses, problems of experimental design, the refutation of hypotheses given contrary evidence and the rescuing of hypotheses despite this evidence, are all evident in the history of understanding of air pressure. Discussion of this history can lead to such central, and much-written upon, philosophical questions as the possibility of crucial experiments (*vide* the Duhem-Quine thesis), the difference between *ad hoc* and justified alteration of theories in the light of contradictory evidence (*vide* Popper and Lakatos), and the role of metaphysics in the maintenance of scientific theories (*vide* Burtt and Buchdahl). Issues in the sociology of science can also be canvassed in this style of instruction. The dependence of one researcher on another can be seen—Torricelli upon Galileo, Boyle upon von Guericke—and then the consequent importance of open communication and truthfulness for science can be appreciated.

Most student's initial understanding of the testing of a scientific theory is given as follows:

> Theory (T) implies Observation (O)
> O occurs
> therefore T is confirmed
>
> or, O does not occur
> therefore T is false

The foregoing has shown that this simple view needs to be elaborated to take into account that it is the theory along with statements of initial conditions (C) that constitute the test situation. Thus we have:

> T and C together imply O
> if not O,
> then, not T, or not C

But this is still too simple because the test also embodies assumptions about the reliability and validity of the test apparatus and measuring instruments (I). Thus we have:

> T and C and I together imply O
> if not O,
> then, not T, or not C, or not I

When metaphysics (M) is assumed in a scientific experiment, we have this situation:

> M and T and C and I together imply O
> if not O,
> then, not M, or not T, or not C, or not I

The educational objective of critical thinking and careful reasoning can be realized with this historical approach because it engages the student's mind. A teacher well versed in the history of the topic can identify when children are making the same intellectual moves as previous scientists, and can encourage the reconsideration of earlier debates. This allows an appreciation of both the achievements and mistakes of earlier scientists, and perhaps some empathy with them.[22]

How to Introduce History

There have been two ways in which the history of science has been included in science programs: one has been the "add-on" approach, the other has been the integrated approach. In the first a standard, nonhistorical, science course is completed, and then a unit or units on the history of science are added on. These units may or may not be compulsory. This is the situation in a number of Australian states, and it was the situation in the UK until the advent of the National Curriculum. In the second approach the history of science is integrated into the study of science content. For instance, mechanics will cover not just equations and practical work, but how these equations were developed and how the concepts embodied in them were formed and changed. Evolution will treat not just the contemporary theory, but how the idea was present before Darwin, and how Darwin and Wallace transformed it, what the scientific, philosophical and theological arguments were when Darwin initially published his theory, what turned out to be problems with the initial formulation of the theory, how some of these were resolved with the "grand synthesis" of evolution and genetics and so on. The topic on continental drift will not just deal with the theory as it currently is accepted, but with its controversial origins as well. The Harvard Project Physics Course exemplified this integrated approach to the history of science, as do texts such as Gerald Holton's *Introduction to Concepts and Theories in Physical Science* (1952). Project 2061 and the British National Curriculum both recommend this approach. In biology the ongoing project of the Education Committee of the American Society of Zoologists, *Science as a Way of Knowing*, exemplifies this integrated approach to the use of history in science.[23]

There are many methods that are available to teachers wishing to introduce history into science classrooms: lectures, reproduction of historical experiments (Teichmann 1986b, Achilles 1986, Sibum 1988), dramatic reenactments and role-plays of historical debates and episodes (Solomon 1989b, Lochhead & Dufresne 1989, Gauld 1992), writing pen portraits of major characters (Wandersee 1990), essays, individual and group projects, or reading and interpretation of original papers. Projects and life-stories are well suited to elementary school children—Archimedes' bath, air pressure, the germ hunters, Copernicus are all topics that young children can be enthused about.

There is a difference between introducing history into a science course, and organizing a science course on historical grounds. The former, minimalist approach may well be all that can be done in many circumstances;

it is the approach recommended in the British National Curriculum. This minimalist approach might include giving historical background to contemporary topics and providing brief biographies of scientists whose names are mentioned—Darwin, Mendel, Crick, Pasteur and so on. The latter, maximalist, approach is that taken by Harvard Project Physics and the Danish Technology Curriculum.

An interesting bridging approach between the two methods is the use of history in order to create a story line for the science content; intellectual, personal and social history provides the framework onto which a science topic or whole course can be placed in a developing narrative. This approach presents information in a coherent and linked manner. Kieran Egan has argued for such teaching in his book *Teaching as Story Telling* (Egan 1986). Arnold Arons (1989) has argued for the use of historically inspired story lines to organise science courses, and did so in his 1965 and 1977 texts. Kenealy (1989), Stinner and Williams (1993) and Wandersee (1990) have recently argued for this story-line approach to science instruction. Kenealy characterizes the worst science texts as ones which "attempt to spraypaint their readers with an enormous amount of 'scientific facts,' and then test the readers' memory recall." He goes on to observe that:

> Reading such a book is much like confronting a psychology experiment which is testing recall of a random list of nonsense words. In fact, the experience is often worse than that, because the book is a presentation that purports to make sense, but is missing so many key elements needed to understand how human beings could ever reason to such bizarre things, that the reader often blames herself or himself and feels "stupid," and that science is only for special people who can think "that way" . . . such books and courses have lost a sense of coherence, a sense of plot, a sense of building to a climax, a sense of resolution. (Kenealy 1989, p. 215)

Teachers introducing the history of science to classes should also be sensitive to the philosophical issues that the history raises. This is because the historical development of science is intertwined with philosophy, and presenting the development of science independently of its philosophical context is to present a much-diminished account of science. And philosophy also suggests many interesting questions to address to the historical record. For instance, questions about theory confirmation, *ad hoc* hypotheses and types of explanation being used can all be asked of particular historical episodes. These questions can enrich and expand student discussion of the topics being dealt with, and can have a flow-over effect to other issues both inside and outside of science.

Opposition to History

The inclusion of history in science programs has been opposed from two sides: from historians who see history in science lessons either as poor history or as downright fabrication of history in support of current scientific ideology, and from scientists who see it as taking up valuable time that could be devoted to science proper, and who see it as possibly eroding the student's conviction that their hard effort is uncovering the truth about the world. In 1970, at an MIT conference sponsored by the International Commission on Physics Education (Brush & King 1972) arguments from both sides were advanced. The first case was argued by Martin Klein (1972), a research physicist turned historian; the second case made use of the same considerations that lay behind Kuhn's argument concerning the importance of the initiation of scientists into the dominant paradigm of the period, and his apprenticeship view of the education of a scientist.

Pseudo-history

Klein's argument was basically that teachers of science who select and use historical materials do so to further contemporary scientific or pedagogical purposes, that such selection is contrary to the canons of good history, and thus "in trying to teach physics by means of its history, or at least with the help of its history, we run a real risk of doing an injustice to the physics or to its history—or to both" (Klein 1972, p. 12). He quotes approvingly Arthur O. Lovejoy's caution that "The more a historian has his eye on the problems which history has generated in the present, or has his inquiry shaped by the philosophic or scientific conceptual material of the period in which he writes, the worse historian he is likely to be" (p. 13). The result of this partial or selective approach "is almost inevitably bad history, in the sense that the student gets no idea of the problems that really concerned past physicists, the contexts within which they worked, or the arguments that did or did not convince their contemporaries to accept new ideas" (p. 13).

Further, Klein suggested that there was a basic difference in the very enterprise of science and history that makes their marriage most improbable, and where it does occur, makes the union short and stormy:

> One reason it is difficult to make the history of physics serve the needs of physics teaching is an essential difference in the outlooks of physicist and historian . . . it is so hard to imagine combining the rich complexity of fact, which the historian strives for, with the sharply defined simple insight that the physicist seeks. (Klein 1972, p. 16)

In support of this view of the historical enterprise, he repeats Herbert Butterfield's injunction that "When he describes the past the historian had to recapture the richness of the moments . . . and far from sweeping them away, he piles up the concrete, the particular, the personal" (p. 16); and he mentions Otto Neugebauer, the historian of classical science, who, like

Butterfield, believed that the historian's role was to recover the complexity of the past.[24] His conclusion is that if good science teaching is historically informed, then it will be informed by bad history. He prefers no history to bad history.

Whitaker pushed these claims further in a two-part article titled "History and Quasi-history in Physics Education" (Whitaker 1979). Like Klein, his concern was to identify the prevalent fabrication of history to suit not just pedagogical ends, but the ends of scientific ideology, or the view of science held by the writer. These cases abound in textbooks.

One that has been much discussed is the widespread account of Einstein's postulation of the photon, following the perceived contradiction between the photoelectric effect and the wave theory of light. The photoelectric effect is apparent in the creation of current between plates in a vacuum when light shines upon one plate. According to the standard textbook account (PSSC 1960, p. 596), anomalous aspects of the photoelectric effect—such as the energy of the emitted electrons not depending upon the intensity of the light and the threshold frequency levels for producing the effect independently of the intensity of the light—were known by the end of the nineteenth century to be a problem for the orthodox wave theory of light. In the orthodox theory the intensity of light was a measure of the energy of light, so that light of any frequency, provided it was intense enough, should be able to produce the photoelectric effect. This does not happen.

The standard account says that Einstein's 1905 photon theory of light, with its Planck-inspired formula of $E = hf$ (energy of a photon equals a constant times the frequency of the light ray), was put forward as a brilliant solution to the anomalies and the harbinger of a new period in the physics of radiation. The old battle between particle and wave theories of light had been resolved in favour of a compromise view that saw light waves as coming in packages, and hence being particle-like. This account reinforces the public and scientific image of Einstein, it accords with the hypothetico-deductive model of scientific theory, it emphasizes the rationality of science, and it demonstrates the progressiveness of scientific work. In other words there is nothing in the standard account to disturb the rational, methodical and inevitable picture of scientific progress commonly held both by scientists and the public. The only problem with the account is that the actual history was nowhere near as straightforward as this.

For many years respectable scientists such as Lenard, Thomson and Lorentz put forward accounts of the photoelectric effect that focused on within-the-atom structures and behavior (resonance effects triggered by the light) rather than properties of the light beam.[25] These could account for the effect just as well as Einstein's peculiar hypothesis. Planck, the originator of the quantum theory, rejected Einstein's "wave package" or photon interpretation in his 1912 book on heat radiation. Robert Millikan, who was to receive a Nobel Prize for his confirmation of Einstein's 1905 hypothesis, says in his autobiography: "I think it is correct to say that the Einstein view of light pulses, or as we now call them, photons, had practically no convinced adherents prior to about 1915. . . . Nor in those earlier stages was even Einstein's advocacy vigorous or definite" (Millikan 1950, p. 67).

The mixed, indeed lukewarm reception accorded Einstein's hypothesis is evidenced by the fact that he did not receive the Nobel Prize for his paper until 1921, some sixteen years after its original publication. This suggests some slowness in the process of rational conversion of the scientific community. Even when adherents began to appear, they were adherents to Einstein's equation, not to his physical interpretation of the equation—a big difference. Millikan had written in 1916 that "Despite . . . the apparently complete success of the Einstein equation, the physical theory on which it was designed . . . is found so untenable that Einstein himself, I believe, no longer holds to it" (Pais 1982, p. 380). Indeed, as Jung notes (1983, p. 50), in his original 1905 paper Einstein spoke of his interpretation in very tentative terms: it was always prefaced by an "as if" statement—"as if light were to consist of energy quanta," "as if it consists of mutually independent energy," and similar statements.

The extremely popular Halliday and Resnick physics text makes much of Millikan's 1916 experimental confirmation of Einstein's photon theory, saying that his experiments "verified Einstein's ideas in every detail." But again the experiments did not confirm Einstein's theory, only his equation. And even the confirmation of his equation (linking the energy of the emitted electron to the frequency of bombarding light) was far from unequivocal. A series of experimental physicists interpreted Einstein's data as showing that the energy varied as frequency squared, or as frequency to the two-thirds power, or even that it had no connection with frequency (Kragh 1986, p. 74). Millikan's data was open to a variety of mathematical interpretations apart from the one he chose—energy varied as frequency. And this mathematical equation did not carry its physical interpretation upon its sleeve; it did not prove that light travelled in little bundles.

The foregoing example is not exceptional: science textbooks abound with pseudo- and quasi-history. Boyle is frequently credited with plotting pressure against the inverse of volume and concluding that P varies as $1/V$ with temperature constant. As Berg (1990) has shown, nowhere did Boyle plot such a graph. Among countless other examples is one presented on the first few pages of the PSSC *Physics* text, about how Galileo discovered the law of isochrony of the pendulum by timing the swings of the chandelier in the church at Pisa. The questionable nature of this claim will be discussed in Chapter 6.

Klein's and Whitaker's charges about the inaccuracy and bias of a good deal of history in science texts is certainly proven. The reason for these inaccuracies is an interesting question, and its answer would reveal much about the ideology of science education and the function of textbooks. Whitaker says of quasi-history that it is the "result of the large numbers of books by authors who have felt the need to enliven their account of [these episodes] with a little historical background, but have in fact rewritten the history so that it fits in step by step with the physics" (Whitaker 1979, p. 109). He does not see such history as arising from a conscious effort to support an author's vision of science: "I do not assume that writers of quasi-history necessarily have any philosophical intent, even subconsciously. I see quasi-history more often merely as a result of a rather misguided desire for order and logic, as a convenience in teaching and learning" (Whitaker 1979, p. 239). Whitaker traces the mistakes of quasi-history to a neglect of the "public and social nature of science."

Quasi-history is not just Klein's pseudo-history, or simplified history, where mistakes of omission are likely to occur, or where the story might fall short of the lofty standard of "the truth, the whole truth, and nothing but the truth"; rather, in quasi-history we have manufactured history masquerading as genuine history. This is akin to Lakatos's "rational reconstructions" of history (Lakatos 1971). Historical figures are painted in the hues of the current methodological orthodoxy. Galileo has been a fine example of the treatment: he appears as an experimentalist in empiricist texts, an instrumentalist in other texts, and a rationalist in still others. He has become a man for all philosophical seasons.[26] Where quasi-history is substituted for history, the power of history to inform the present is nullified. If the historian rigidly selects and interprets his material according to a prior philosophical position, it is difficult, if not impossible, for this reconstructed data to feed back into the proper assessment of the philosophical position.

History Versus Science

The second type of criticism brought at the MIT conference against history of science in science courses was that it sapped the neophyte scientific spirit. The historian Harold Burstyn elaborated Klein's problem in terms of the different outlooks of students rather than the different outlooks of teachers or professional historians and scientists. Burstyn cautions that:

> There is lot of evidence (including my own experience in teaching history of science to science students) that science students and students of other subjects have different outlooks on the world. To phrase it pejoratively, the science students are looking for the "right" answers, they are "convergent" rather than "divergent" thinkers. The problem Klein is getting at is this: Can you in fact use the historical materials, whose hallmark is their complexity, their diffuseness and imprecision, in the teaching of people who are interested in getting right answers, and who, if they are successful, can't be diverted from this quest as we historians might want to divert them? Isn't history therefore somewhat subversive of the aims of physics pedagogy? (Brush & King 1972, p. 26)

This charge was earlier made by Thomas Kuhn in a 1959 address to a conference on scientific creativity (Kuhn 1959). Kuhn repeated the charge in the first (1962) and second (1970) editions of his immensely popular *The Structure of Scientific Revolutions.* In his conference address he drew attention to the fact that:

> The single most striking feature of this [science] education is that, to an extent wholly unknown in other fields, it is conducted entirely through textbooks. Typically, undergraduate and graduate students of chemistry, physics, astronomy, geology, or biology acquire the substance of their fields from books written especially for students. (Kuhn 1959, p. 228)

He noted that science students are not encouraged to read the historical classics of their fields, "works in which they might discover other ways of regarding the problems discussed in their textbooks" (p. 229). All of this produces a rigorous training in convergent thought, and Kuhn maintains that the sciences "could not have achieved their present state or status without it" (p. 228). Kuhn justifies this training by its results: not just the production of good convergent thinkers, but also the production of a smaller group of innovators and creative scientists who would not have been able to be innovative unless they were throughly steeped in the orthodox thought of their discipline. These ideas provided the title both for his conference address and his subsequent book, *The Essential Tension* (1977). Kuhn elaborated these ideas in his *The Structure of Scientific Revolutions,* where he says that in a science classroom the history of science should be distorted, and earlier scientists should be portrayed as working upon the same set of problems that modern scientists work upon in order that the apprentice scientist should feel himself part of a successful truth-seeking tradition (Kuhn 1970, p. 138).

Kuhn's view of the importance of dogma and conviction in science education was earlier expressed, at the turn of the century, by those who feared the practical consequences of Poincaré's instrumentalist account of science. The President of the British Association for the Advancement of Science in 1901 warned of the danger of Poincaré's theory of science, saying that "If the confidence that his methods are weapons with which he can fight his way to the truth were taken from the scientific explorer, the paralysis of those engaged in a hopeless task would fall upon him" (Heilbron 1983, p. 178). Another reviewer of Poincaré's *Science and Hypothesis* warned that, though the message was right and a relief, indeed a revelation, it could "lead to mental disaster." The great empiricist, and historian of science, Oliver Lodge, thought that the book was "mischievous."

Stephen Brush developed the Kuhn charge further in his "Should the History of Science be Rated X?" (Brush 1974).[27] Here it was suggested, tongue-in-cheek, that history of science could be a bad influence on students because it undercuts the certainties of scientistic dogma seen as necessary for maintaining the enthusiasm of apprentices on a difficult task. He warned teachers that "the teacher who wants to indoctrinate his students in the traditional role of the scientist as a neutral fact finder should not use historical materials of the kind now being prepared by historians of science: they will not serve his purposes."

A Defense of History

The Klein-Kuhn charges are serious but not fatal; their main concerns can be addressed without ejecting history from science courses. The charges will be briefly restated and then commented upon.

Charge I: *Science and history are very different intellectual enterprises because the former looks for simplicity and ignores extraneous circumstances, whereas the latter celebrates and seeks complexity, thus there are two antagonistic mental outlooks to be cultivated if history is brought into the the science classroom.*

First, if this charge is true, is it such an unfortunate thing? The cultivation of different mental outlooks may be educationally proper. It is generally thought that a good school curriculum is one that encourages a range of perspectives and ways of dealing with problems; thus students are required to study mathematics, literature, art, history, science, and perhaps morals, civics and religion. The problem seems to be that there are different habits of mind being cultivated within the one classroom. But even this should not be a problem. The English teacher at different times encourages creativity and free expression, at other times rote learning and disciplined thought, at still other times empathic understanding and moral reasoning. These different outlooks are not regarded as disruptive to the overall task of developing a literate person. The science teacher should be no more worried than the English teacher by such heterogenity. Further, we have myriad examples of successful cross-disciplinary programs that avoid the putative pitfalls and achieve some of the objectives of a liberal education (Dick 1983, Leacock & Sharlin 1977, Lerner & Gosselin 1975, Patterson 1980).

It is not just history that brings intellectual schizophrenia to the science classroom. Increasingly morals and politics are regarded as legitimate and indeed necessary components of science education. This is most clear in the numerous Science-Technology-Society courses, where moral/political issues such as pollution, alternative energy sources, conservation and so on are used as themes around which the science course is developed. Such courses require that students think in moral and political as well as scientific ways within the one class. But apart from STS courses, the British National Curriculum, Project 2061 and other mainstream curriculum developments also require of the science student that they consider their subject from a variety of perspectives. The argument proffered against history would also rule out of the science classroom these other considerations. But there seem to be no empirical grounds for so doing, apart from lack of time in a crowded syllabus, and there are good pedagogical grounds for including the wider considerations.

Second, are the differences between a scientific and a historical approach as great as claimed? At one level, Klein's account of history as seeking complexity and putting nothing aside is simply wrong: all historical writing has to be selective. It is true that Klein's empiricist, fact-finding account of history has often been proposed. The eminent nineteenth-century historian, Ranke, proposed that the task of history was "simply to show how it was." Following this injunction, a recent book on Australian history titled *The Second Year* purported to recount everything that happened in Australia in 1789. The Preface directs those readers wanting to know what happened in the first year, 1788, to the author's earlier book, *The First Year*.

However, such empiricist accounts of history have been roundly criticized. In the foregoing example, apart from the assumption that Australian history began in 1788 with the arrival of the first British fleet, it is clearly ludicrous to think that everything that happened can be listed; each event is capable of being described in myriad ways. E. H. Carr's (1964) criticism of empiricism in history is perhaps the best known, another is Jones (1972). Without going into details, the simple point is that history cannot tell everything; it has to be selective. A history of railway development in England will legitimately ignore developments in the theatre; it will focus upon matters related to railways. But there is a superabundance of such matters—arrival and departures of trains, architecture of platforms, the work force, railway meals, orders for steel and so on—and selection needs to occur. A historian is not an archivist: the latter's job may be to file away all the timetables, meal menus, order books and so on (even this has to involve a sense of what is likely to be useful). The historian is supposed to select, and further, make something of the historical record. To say this, and to oppose simple empiricist views of history, is not to endorse extreme postmodernist accounts that maintain that history is just all construction, that there are no facts of the matter to ascertain.

Detail of correct dates, a concern with uncovering all the relevant correspondence, examining changes between editions, and other such scholarly endeavor can be of the utmost importance provided some objective is in mind, and provided some principle of inclusion/exclusion is operative. The scientist does leave aside the color, texture and composition of a falling ball, and replaces all this richness with a simple point mass; historians also have to leave aside some of the richness of historical episodes and seek for some essentials which are pertinent to the story they wish to tell. In this sense their discipline is not so different from science. A scholarly article might concentrate upon the trees, but in classrooms and student texts there should not be such attention paid to trees that the forest can no longer been seen.

Charge II: *Inevitably the history used in science courses is pseudo-history in virtue of it being in the service of science instruction.*

This claim is a variant of the first, and need not deter a science teacher. Its apparent strength lies in a confusion between writing history and using history in science classes. A science teacher is not engaged in the former task. There may be problems with writing history in order to serve ulterior ends if this results in the distortion of history. Writing for a purpose need not result in pseudo-history. Be this as it may, a science teacher is explicitly using history for pedagogical purposes and his or her use of history is to be judged on criteria different from that of a practising historian: the two activities are very different.

Charge III: *It is likely that the history used in science courses will be quasi-history because of the purposes and limitations of the science teacher.*

First, as has been said, there is a great deal of truth in this claim, and as such it serves as a timely caution to those advocating the use of history. The problem of "revisionist" histories is notorious in the political realm and often destroys the mind-expanding purpose of school history. We know that official Soviet histories of the Communist Party are historically worthless, the official history itself changing with each change in party leadership. After August 1991, all such histories are being consigned to the dustheap, and the entire Soviet school history curriculum is being rewritten. Much to the outrage of their Asian neighbors, and despite law suits brought by the courageous historian Saburo Ienaga, the official Japanese school history texts have rewritten the history of the Pacific War: the period is largely omitted, and where it is mentioned, it is in terms of Japan's efforts to encourage Asian economic growth. Many American histories of the "Opening of the West," of the conquest of Mexican territories, of the 1905 Spanish-US war, of the Vietnam War, of labor history and so forth, are themselves driven by ideology, and distort the historical record.

Given the importance and status of science and its accomplishments, it is not suprising that various political and ideological groups should write histories of science showing their own group as the champions. The Nazis wrote Aryan histories of science that demonstrated that Jewish scientists either did poor research or stole good ideas from Germans (Beyerchen 1977). The Soviet Union produced its own ideological version of the history of science (Graham 1972, Sheehan 1985). In the history of warfare between the church and science, both sides produced histories appropriate to their case. These histories are more or less conscious revisions of the historical record. But such revisions need not be conscious. Many have claimed that the monumental histories of science of Duhem, and the case studies of Poincaré, are both influenced and, some would say, compromised by their

Catholicism (Nye 1975, Paul 1979, 1985). Undoubtedly myths and ideologies abound in histories of science, just as they do in political, social, and religious histories.[28]

All of the foregoing are cases where things external to science affect the writing of its history. What Klein and Whitaker have warned against are cases where things internal to science, the methodological views of the scientist or historian, affect and distort its history, and where the conception of science held by the teacher affects his or her portrayal of history. This simply has to be acknowledged as a potential problem and efforts made to minimize its occurrence.

Second, it needs to be remembered that science teaching is not history research: they are different activities with different purposes and different criteria of success and authenticity. Standards of sophistication required for historical research are misplaced when applied to science pedagogy. In pedagogy the subject matter needs to be simplified. This is as true of history of science as it is of economics or of science itself. The pedagogical task is to produce a simplified history that illuminates the subject matter and promotes student interest in it, yet is not a caricature of the historical events. The simplification will be relevant to the age group being taught, and the overall curriculum being presented. The history can become more complex as the educational situation demands. To criticize elementary school teachers for hagiography is to misunderstand what they are doing, namely trying to interest students in important figures in the history of science; to criticize secondary school teachers for simplifying the history of genetics is again to misunderstand what they are doing, namely trying to teach about genetics in a way that is interesting and comprehensible to adolescents. The pedagogical art is to simplify stories in such a way that the inevitable distortion is educationally benign, not pernicious.

Charge IV: *That good historical study is corrosive of scientific commitment.*

This is an empirical claim for which the evidence is slight. The author has taught "History and Philosophy for Science Teachers" courses for many years without seeing any such deleterious results. In fact, comments such as "teachers are hungry for this information," "I never realised that Galileo did such things," "this makes me want to teach science better" are commonplace. The experience of Einstein, when given Mach's *The Science of Mechanics* by his friend Besso, might be more typical: exposure to history enlivened Einstein's commitment to science. Certainly for the history to make sense, a body of scientific knowledge and technique has to be mastered, but there is no evidence that this mastery is impeded or threatened by historical study. On the contrary, the extensive research done on the subject matter mastery of the hundreds of thousands of students who studied the Harvard Project Physics materials in the 1970s is impressive, and contradicts the pessimistic claim of Kuhn. Likewise the much more restricted evidence from the Klopfer and Cooley High School Case Studies suggest that history enlivens student interest in, and understanding of, science. Independently of the effectiveness claim, there are serious educational issues involved in trading putative student commitment to science for historical truthfulness about science (Siegel 1979b). This merges very quickly into the issue of indoctrination in education.

Conclusion

Science has been enormously influential in shaping the material, technical, religious and cultural dimensions of the modern world, and in turn it has been shaped by these societal aspects. Modern science is one of the major accomplishments of the human race. Although perhaps still through a glass darkly, we are nevertheless seeing something of the constitution of the the largest and smallest bodies in the world around us, and understanding more and more about our own bodies, brains, health, and more about our environment and the other species with which we share it. The professional purpose of science education is to introduce students into the conceptual and procedural realms of science. It has been argued that history of science facilitates this introduction. But science education also has a wider purpose which is to help students learn *about* science—its changing methods, its forms of organization, it methods of proof, its interrelationships with the rest of culture and so forth. It has been argued that this requires contextual and historical approaches to science teaching.

The integrative function of history is perhaps its fundamental value to science education. History allows seemingly unrelated topics within a science discipline to be connected to each other—Einstein's analysis of Brownian motion to confirm the atomic hypothesis, with Brown's attempts to prove Vitalism in biology, and maybe even Brown's botanical work in the early exploration of Australia. History also connects topics across the scientific disciplines—unravelling of the DNA code connected geology, crystallography, chemistry and molecular biology. Historical study shows the interconnections between different realms of knowledge—mathematics, philosophy, theology and physics all had parts to play in the development of, for instance, Newtonian mechanics, and the conservation laws. Finally, history allows some appreciation of the interconnections of realms of academic knowledge with economic, societal and cultural factors. Darwinian evolutionary theory was affected by, and in turn affected, religion, literature, political theory and educational practice. Historical presentation can weave all sorts of seemingly separate topics into strands within disciplines, and connect the strands into an intellectual tapestry. Students having some such picture is a central concern of liberal education. The cultural significance of science education is in part fulfilled to the extent that it contributes to students having a picture of the interconnectedness of things (Suchting 1994).

As with most educational matters, teachers are the key to successful historical teaching. Teachers need to be interested and trained in history. If they are so prepared and resourced, then in numerous formal and informal, planned and unplanned ways, history will contribute to the professional and cultural tasks of science education; if they are not, then merely legislating for history, or including it in the curriculum, will have little effect. As has often been said, good teachers can rescue the worst curriculum, and bad teachers can kill the best.

CHAPTER 5

Philosophy in the Curriculum

Some years ago, Robert Ennis opened a comprehensive review of the literature on philosophy of science and science teaching with the melancholy observation that: "With some exceptions philosophers of science have not shown much explicit interest in the problems of science education" (Ennis 1979, p. 138).[1] Happily there are some signs that this situation is changing; there are certainly signs that science educators are showing interest in utilizing the work of philosophers of science.[2]

Ennis had listed six questions that science teachers constantly encounter in their classrooms and staffrooms, questions that the deliberations and researches of philosophers of science could illuminate. These questions were: What characterizes the scientific method? What constitutes critical thinking about empirical statements? What is the structure of scientific disciplines? What is a scientific explanation? What role do value judgments play in the work of scientists? And what constitute good tests of scientific understanding? These questions are of perennial concern to science teachers, and science teacher education programs should initiate the exploration of them. But more contemporary questions can be identified to which philosophers can contribute—feminism and science, multiculturalism and science, constructivist theory, environmental ethics and so on. One of the theses of this book is that these are not extracurricular or add-on questions for science teachers: philosophy of science is part of the fabric of science teaching. The issue is just how clearly this is recognized and how explicitly the philosophical questions are dealt with.

Whenever science is taught, philosophy, to some degree, is also taught. Minimally, the teacher's own epistemology, or conception of science, is conveyed to students and contributes to the image of science that they develop in class. In this chapter, ways in which philosophy's presence in science education has been and can be made more explicit will be examined. It will be argued that by making philosophy more explicit the goals of good technical science education can be advanced—children will understand the subject better—and at the same time something of the more general cultural and epistemological dimension of science can be conveyed. This consideration can be extended to the teaching of history, mathematics, geography and most school subjects.

Science and Philosophy

The separation of science education from philosophy results in a distorted science education. From the ancient Greeks to the present, science has been interwoven with philosophy: science, metaphysics, logic and epistemology have been inseparable. Most of the great scientists—Democritus, Aristotle, Copernicus, Galileo, Descartes, Newton, Leibnitz, Boyle, Faraday, Darwin, Mach, Einstein, Planck, Heisenberg, Schrödinger—were at the same time philosophers. Scientists were called "natural philosophers" through to the end of the nineteenth century. Einstein spoke of the theoretical physicist as "a philosopher in workingman's clothes" (Bergmann 1949, p. v). Charles Sanders Peirce said, in his "Notes on Scientific Philosophy," "Find a scientific man who proposes to get along without any metaphysics . . . and you have found one whose doctrines are thoroughly vitiated by the crude and uncriticised metaphysics with which they are packed."

Metaphysical issues naturally emerge from the subject matter of science. Historical studies portray the interdependence of science and metaphysics. The Galilean/Aristotelian controversy over final causation, the Galilean/Keplerian controversy over the lunar theory of tides, the Newtonian/Cartesian argument over action at a distance, the Newtonian/Berkelian argument over the existence of absolute space and time, the Newtonian/Fresnelian argument over the particulate theory of light, the Darwinian/Paleyian argument over design and natural selection, the Mach/Planck argument over the realistic interpretation of atomic theory, the Einstein/Copenhagen dispute over the deterministic interpretation of quantum theory—all bring to the fore metaphysical issues. Metaphysics is pervasive in science.[3]

Galileo is an outstanding example of the scientist/philosopher. He made substantial philosophical contributions in a variety of areas: in ontology, with his distinction of primary and secondary qualities; in epistemology, both with his criticism of authority as an arbiter of knowledge claims and with his subordination of sensory evidence to mathematical reason; in methodology, with his development of the mathematical-experimental method; and in metaphysics, with his critique of the Aristotelian causal categories and rejection of teleology as an explanatory principle.[4] It is thus unfortunate that, despite his important contributions to the subject, and despite his acknowledged influence on just about all philosophers of the seventeenth century and such subsequent philosophers as Kant and Husserl, Galileo makes scant appearence in most histories of philosophy, and most science texts ignore his philosophical interests and contributions.[5]

Science has always been conducted within the context of the philosophical ideas of the time. This is to be expected. Scientists think, write and talk with the language and conceptual tools available to them; more generally, people who form opinions, are themselves formed in specific intellectual circumstances, and their opinions are constrained by these circumstances. Newton said that he was able to see further than others because he stood upon the shoulders of giants: without Copernicus, Kepler and Galileo, not to mention Euclid's geometry, there would not have been a unified theory of terrestrial and celestial mechanics. A scientist's understanding and approach to the world is formed by his or her education and milieu; and this milieu is pervaded by the philosophies of the period. From an objectivist point of view, what these claims are pointing to is the fact that science as a system of concepts, definitions, methodologies, results, instruments and professional organizations, predates the individual who comes to work upon and within it. Inasmuch as the former embodies philosophical suppositions, then the work of the scientist will be shaped by philosophy.

The connection of science with philosophy, broadly understood, is promoted in much present-day popular scientific literature. Books such as *God and the New Physics* (Davies 1983), *A Brief History of Time* (Hawking 1988), *On Human Nature* (Wilson 1978), *The Tao of Physics* (Capra 1975), and *The Dancing Wu Li Masters* (Zukav 1979) have been best-sellers and have conveyed, with sometimes more and other times less understanding, the basic idea that science affects, and is affected by, other disciplines— philosophy, psychology, theology, biology—and more generally the worldviews of a culture. The widespread impact of these books is comparable to that enjoyed in the interwar period by Arthur Eddington's *The Nature of the Physical World* (1928), James Jeans' *Physics and Philosophy* (1943), and J. D. Bernal's *The Social Function of Science* (1939). Jeans in the preface to his book said:

> The aim of the present book is very simply stated; it is to discuss . . . that borderland territory between physics and philosophy which used to seem so dull, but suddenly became so interesting and important through recent developments of theoretical physics. . . . The new interest extends far beyond the technical problems of physics and philosophy to questions which touch human life very closely. (Jeans 1943/1981, p. i)

The popular literature can provide an occasion for teachers to discuss the borderline territory between science and philosophy, and to connect laboratory life with cultural debates. Popular authors often neglect details, and sometimes seriously misunderstand important issues.[6] Along with good popular expositions there are numerous shoddy, but still popular, works that warp public appreciation of the issues. Teachers informed by the history and philosophy of science are in a better position to evaluate the worth of these competing orientations. By introducing students to the speculative, metaphysical and ethical questions that science throughout its history has considered, the chances of them being seduced by the first guru they meet offering worldviews a little out of the ordinary will be reduced.

Students without prior exposure to such debates can be a little like a country child on his or her first visit to the big city.

The role of religious belief in the motivation and conceptualizations of scientists is usually ignored in the science syllabus. Students learn often enough that Newton discovered three laws, and the formulae for them; they learn less often that Newton said, when he wrote his *Principia*, "I had an eye upon such principles as might work with considering men for the belief of a Deity; and nothing can rejoice me more than to find it useful for that purpose" (Thayer 1953, p. 46). They also learn that Boyle formulated the important law connecting pressure and volume of gases; they learn less often that he left a provision in his will for a set of public lectures "for proving the Christian religion against notorious infidels" and that he believed his own mechanical philosophy admirably suited for proving the existence of a Designer of the universe.

Despite the fact that, historically, the major Western scientists regarded their work as proclaiming the majesty of God, little is heard of this in the typical science classroom. There are engaging psychological, cultural and philosophical stories that are worth telling and exploring. No one expects that the long-running issue of science and religion will be solved in the science classroom, but surely it can be raised, and some outline of its components and history be given. Senior students, in particular, can benefit from familiarity with this issue, as it often bears upon their own personal affairs, and it bears upon discussions in their literature and history courses.[7]

The considerable literature generated by the Philosophy for Children movement suggests that children are both capable of, and interested in, pursuing elementary philosophical questions (Davson-Galle 1990, Lipman 1991, Lipman & Sharp 1978). The science classroom provides opportunities to do this. The science must come first, but there is the opportunity for children to encounter basic philosophical questions, and to acquire some basic philosophical skills of an analytic and reasoning kind.

Philosophy in the Science Curriculum

Science education is enriched, and is more faithful to its subject, if aspects of the interesting and complex interplay of science and philosophy can be conveyed in the classroom. The American Association for the Advancement of Science, in its proposal for the reform of college science teaching, *The Liberal Art of Science*, recognises this:

> The teaching of science must explore the interplay between science and the intellectual and cultural traditions in which it is firmly embedded. Science has a history that can demonstrate the relationship between science and the wider world of ideas and can illuminate contemporary issues. (AAAS 1990, p. xiv)

The British National Curriculum Council, the Canadian Science Council and other political and educational bodies have made comparable proposals.

There are various ways in which the interplay between science and philosophy can be conveyed: reading of selections from original sources; joint projects with history, social science, divinity or literature classes; dramatic reenactments of significant episodes in the history of science; essays on selected themes; debates on topical matters; or low-level philosophical questioning about scientific topics being studied or practical work being conducted. All philosophy of science begins with analytical and logical matters: What does a particular concept mean? How do we know the truth of a proposition? Does a conclusion follow from the premises adduced? These analytic and logical questions and habits of thought can be introduced as early as preschool—as Matthew Lipman and the Philosophy for Children programs attest—and they can be refined as children mature (Lipman & Sharp 1978). Susan Johnson and Jim Stewart (1991) provide a nice example of the incorporation of philosophy of science into a high school genetics course. They focus on the "three Ps" of science: problem posing, problem solving, and persuasion of peers.

Philosophy is not far below the surface in any scientific investigation. At a most basic level any text or scientific discussion will contain terms such as "law," "theory," "model," "explanation," "cause," "truth," "knowledge," "hypothesis," "confirmation," "observation," "evidence," "idealization," "time," "space," "fields," "species." Philosophy begins when students and teachers slow down the science lesson and ask what these terms mean and what the conditions are for their correct use. All of these concepts contribute to, and in part arise from, philosophical deliberation on issues of epistemology and metaphysics: questions about what things can be known and how we can know them, and about what things actually exist in the world and the relations possible between them. Students and teachers can be encouraged to ask the philosopher's standard questions: What do you mean by ———— ? and How do you know ———— ? of all these concepts. Such introductory philosophical analysis allows greater appreciation of the distinct empirical and conceptual issues involved when, for instance, Boyle's Law, Dalton's model or Darwin's theory is discussed. It also promotes critical and reflective thinking more generally.

School courses in Science-Technology-Society (STS) are another area in which science courses connect with philosophy, particularly ethical and political philosophy. A 1990 Department of Education guide to STS education issued by the provincial government of Alberta, Canada—*Unifying the Goals of Science Education*—gives prominence to teaching about the nature of science. Its reading list includes the work of Hawking, Einstein, Holton, Kuhn, Latour, Polanyi and Ravetz. A recent list of common STS topics includes: abortion, AIDS, endangered species, genetic engineering, organ transplants, nuclear war, space exploration, and waste management (Rubba et al.1991). These STS courses in England,[8] Holland,[9] Canada[10] and the US[11] deal explicitly with political and ethical issues involving notions such as justice, equality, the fair distribution of goods, responsibility and the like—all of which are clarified by philosophical analysis, and by reference to the history of these ideas. Without philosophical input, STS courses run the risk of just repeating fashionable and shallow ideology about pollution, nuclear energy, conservation and so on. This was seen in the 1940s Science for Consumers courses. Shallow views on these vital matters tend to be blown away at the first gust of national or self-interest that the student encounters upon leaving school.

Thus there are many opportunities in science teaching—whether in discipline-centred curricula, or in STS-inspired curricula, or in science-in-culture curricula—for raising philosophical questions and getting children into the habit of thinking philosophically. These opportunites need to be recognized and good use made of them.

Logic and Scientific Reasoning

The last chapter illustrated the advantages of a historical dimension in science education. In addition, history of science provides a vehicle to introduce some basic logic to students. Consider, for instance, debates over the photoelectric effect that have previously been discussed. The photoelectric effect and even Millikan's experiment can easily be shown in the classroom. Instead of imposing Einstein's photon theory and his equation as the scientific "royal highway" linking the two famous experiments, something else can be made of the occasion. The historical approach shows the hesitancy with which even great scientists propose their ideas; it illustrates the variety of sensible and rational interpretations of data possible at any time; and, finally, it allows the crucial distinction between mathematical equations or models and their physical interpretation to be portrayed.

History shows the variety of relations that were postulated in the early years of this century between emitted photoelectron energy and incoming light frequency. Philosophy can raise the question of whether and how data can prove a particular theory. Many different theories, or equations, can imply the same set of data points. These points do not *uniquely* determine a particular curve, or equation, much less a particular physical interpretation of the equation. If students can be led to appreciate this they are recognizing what Aristotle recognized in the fourth century BC: the fallacy of affirming the consequent, as he called it. Aristotle, and of course others before him, showed that an argument of the following form is invalid:

T implies O (a theory T implies an observation O)
O (the observation O is made)
Therefore T (the theory T is true)

The conclusion does not follow because as well as T implying O, any number of other either known or unknown theories (Ts) can also imply the same observation. The hypothesis that it rained last night implies that the road will be wet; but equally the hypotheses that the sanitation truck went past, that a water main broke, or that a lawn hose was turned on, also imply the same thing. Thus the mere observation that the road is wet does not prove any particular hypothesis.

This simple point of logic was a stumbling block for empiricist approaches to natural science from the time of Aristotle to the present. We do feel that confirmed predictions provide some warrant for belief in a theory; the logical point is that they cannot establish the truth of the theory, so we need to reconsider the type of truth that confirmed predictions imply. In the Middle Ages it was known as the problem of "saving the appearances."[12] Thomas Aquinas, in the thirteenth century, followed Aristotle in maintaining there were two degrees of certainty possible about the natural world. Aquinas said that:

> We can account for a thing in two different ways. The first way consists in establishing by a sufficient demonstration that a principle from which the thing follows is correct. Thus, in physics we supply a reason which is sufficient to prove the uniformity of the motion of the heavens. The second way of accounting for a thing consists, not in demonstrating its principles by a sufficient proof, but in showing which effects agree with a principle laid down beforehand. Thus, in astronomy we account for eccentrics and epicycles by the fact that we can save the sensible appearances of the heavenly motions by this hypothesis. But this is not a really probative reason, since the apparent movements can, perhaps, be saved by means of some other hypothesis. (*Summa Theologica*, Ia. xxxii, I, ad2, in Duhem 1908/1969, p. 42)

The basic point that facts are open to a variety of interpretations is commonly referred to as the "Duhem-Quine Thesis," which states that a scientific theory is underdetermined by its evidence. Pierre Duhem highlighted this logical point in his 1906 *The Aim and Structure of Physical Theory*; Karl Popper elaborated some of its consequences for science in his 1934 *Logic of Scientific Discovery*; and Willard van Orman Quine further developed it in his 1953 *From a Logical Point of View*. There are two forms of the thesis. One is stated by Aquinas, in which positive outcomes of a prediction cannot be used to establish the truth of a theory; the other is stated by Duhem, in which the failure of predictions to be borne out does not allow us to conclude that the theory is false, because the prediction results not just from the theory under consideration, but from that theory plus statements of background information.[13]

The fact that many students frequently commit the mistakes of reasoning to which Aristotle and Aquinas drew attention is a powerful argument for pausing over these philosophical matters in the course of science instruction. A small Australian study by Gordon Cochaud (1989) is suggestive of the problem that students have with this common form of scientific reasoning. He gave a brief, ten-item, logic test to first-year science students at an

Australian university. Among the items was this one where students had to fill in the conclusion:

> If one adds chloride ions to a silver solution then a white precipitate is produced.
> Addition of chloride ions to solution K produced a white precipitate.
> Therefore. . . .

In his group of sixty-five students, forty-eight concluded that solution K contained silver. Thus nearly three-quarters of a group of high-achieving high school graduates who had studied science for at least six years went along with fundamentally flawed reasoning. Little wonder that as citizens they are easily swayed by arguments such as:

> Communists support unionism.
> Fred supports unionism.
> Therefore Fred is a Communist.

The results on another item were staggering. Students were asked to complete the following syllogism:

> If an element has a low electronegativity then it is a metal.
> Element sodium is a metal.
> Therefore. . . .

Fifty-nine of the sixty-five students concluded, supposedly on the basis just of the information provided, that sodium has low electronegativity. Their answer happens to be correct, but it does not follow on the basis of the information given. It would only follow if the first premise were "If and only if an element. . . ." Thus fully ninety percent of the cream of high school graduates are prone to making basic logical errors. It is little wonder that arguments of the form:

> If people are cunning and deceitful they can obtain welfare payments.
> Fred obtains welfare payments.
> Therefore Fred is cunning and deceitful.

are very common and persuasive—a particular worry for jury trials!

The reasoning dimension of science competence has been recognised in curriculum documents. Ehud Jungwirth (1987), in a comprehensive study of the issue, lists a number of curriculum statements that make reference to critical-logical-analytical thinking skills. Among them are:

● To enable pupils to grasp the scientific method of approach and to cultivate *habits of logical and systematic thinking* in them. (Senior Biology, Cape of Good Hope, South Africa, 1977)

- To look for and *identify logical fallacies in arguments and invalid conclusions.* (Queensland Board of Secondary School Studies, Australia, 1983)
- The scientifically literate person has a substantial knowledge base . . . and *process skills,* which enable the individual . . . to *think logically.* (National Science Teachers Association, USA, 1982)

Jungwirth studied the reasoning processes of six hundred school students and four hundred trainee teachers (science graduates) and university science students in three countries. He used curriculum and extracurricular (life) test items that embodied the following kinds of faulty reasoning:

1) Assuming that events which follow others are caused by them.
2) Drawing conclusions on the basis of an insufficient number of instances.
3) Drawing conclusions on the basis of nonrepresentative instances.
4) Assuming that something that is true in specific circumstances is true in general.
5) Imputing causal significance to correlations.
6) Tautological reasoning.

His results were less than encouraging, given the importance of reasoning not just to science, but to social and personal functioning more generally— voting in an election, buying a car, deciding a school-board policy, determining what went wrong with the baked cake and so on. His results can be rounded out and summarized in the following table, where the percentages refer to percentages of the appropriate population who make mistakes of the above kind (1 to 4).

TYPE OF FAULTY REASONING	SCHOOL GRADES 9–12		UNIVERSITY STUDENTS	
	CURRICULUM	LIFE	CURRICULUM	LIFE
1)	40%	50%	30%	25%
2)	30%	40%	30%	40%
3)	15%	50%	60%	60%
4)	35%	50%	30%	60%

Table 2   Percentage of Erroneous Answers for Types of Invalid Reasoning

Jungwirth reports that the results on 5) and 6) tests were comparable to the above, and aggregating all the test results he provides the following summary of his findings. For adults, only the postgraduates performed above the 50% level, with the other postsecondary groups below, to very much below, that level. On the life-items none of the adult groups averaged at more than the two-thirds level. For schools on the curriculum-items none of the groups averaged at more than slightly above the twenty-five percent level; on the life-items, the scores were roughly twice as high (p. 51). Not unreasonably, Jungwirth concludes that time should be spent in science lessons on the rudiments of correct reasoning and that "Teachers' pre- and in-service training should convey the message that the 'covering of a large corpus of information' does *not* constitute the only, and not even the major component of science-*education*" (p. 57).

Jungwirth draws attention to the fact that in this reasoning domain the blind are leading the blind. Or as Marx said, "who will educate the educators?" He surveys the research on teachers' thinking skills, none of which is any more encouraging than the findings above on student thinking skills. Arnold Arons has pointed out that "we force a large fraction of students into blind memorisation by imposing on them . . . materials requiring abstract reasoning capacities they have not yet attained—and of which *many of their teachers are themselves incapable*" (Arons 1974). Garnett and Tobin (1984) concluded after administering the *Test On Logical Thinking* that "many of these teachers do not possess the reasoning patterns, which activity centred science curriculum seek to develop."

What Cochaud's and Jungwirth's studies suggest is that good formal and informal reasoning should be taught as part of a science course. Students can be given examples of the following formal logical fallacies, which are common in everyday publications as well as in scholarly texts, and they can be trained in recognizing and avoiding these fallacies.

The fallacy of affirming the consequent,	if P then Q
	Q
	therefore P
The fallacy of denying the antecedent,	if P then Q
	not P
	therefore not Q
The fallacy of asserting an alternative	P or Q
	P
	therefore not Q

Historical studies provide one context in which the elements of good reasoning can be illuminated. Often the same historical examples can also exhibit for students the "extralogical" dimension of science: the place that commitment to metaphysics plays in the determination of theory and research programs. Simple student experiments, "black-box" exercises and other activities where students guess unseen connections from the behavior of seen variables can highlight most of the logical fallacies and illustrate different interpretations of events, but these activities do not raise the important question of how science actually progresses and settles upon the best of rival theories.

History does place thinking skills into the broader scientific context; good scientific reasoning is not reducible to, or captured by, the rules of formal logic, nor even by the "rules" of informal logic. But the ability to discern interesting *departures* from logical thinking on the part of great scientists is dependent upon being able to recognize what formally correct and logical thinking is in the first place. The study of basic logic also assists with the promotion of critical thinking and reasoning skills in school programs.[14] Contributors to the Linda Crow (1989) volume, *Enhancing Critical Thinking in the Sciences*, discuss specific strategies for promoting the amalgm of problem solving, decision-making, creative thinking and critical thinking skills in the science classroom.

Rationality in Science and in Science Classrooms

Rationality is a central topic in philosophy of science, and it is important to science education. The long-standing view has been that science represents, perhaps preeminently, a sphere of rational inquiry and rational appraisal of competing beliefs; and that where there are departures from rational thinking in science, such departures are criticized as regrettable aberrations. This commitment to rationalism in science typifies the Enlightenment, or more generally the modern view of science. However in the past few decades, this rationalist understanding has come under attack: from within the philosophy of science, from certain sociologists of science, and from postmodernist French philosophers and others inspired by them.

These attacks on rationality are of consequence to science educators because they would alter the image of science; and further they challenge, if not undermine, one of the central justifications for the teaching of science, namely, that science teaching introduces children into a sphere of rational thought and debate that has laudable "carryover" effects in the rest of their studies and in life. If the adjudication of scientific dispute is truly a matter of "mob psychology," and if scientific advances are just whatever a community decrees them to be, independently of their epistemic worth, then the rationale for the inclusion of science in the curriculum is greatly diminished.

Rationalist philosophers of science were awoken from their slumber by Thomas Kuhn's 1962 *The Structure of Scientific Revolutions*, which was widely interpreted as saying that scientific transformations often depend as much upon mob psychology and the mortality of the aged as they do upon rational persuasion, and that progress in science need not be construed as advancement towards a fixed goal of the truth about nature. Paul Feyerabend extended this thesis in his *Against Method* (1975). Many of these irrationalist charges were answered by philosophers of science.[15] But no sooner had this been done than the Edinburgh school of sociologists of science—David Bloor, Barry Barnes, Steven Shapin, Michael Mulkay and others—further criticized rationalism in their externalist account of scientific change, the so-called "strong program" in the sociology of knowledge.[16]

Alongside these currents, French postmodernist philosophy, particularly the work of Michel Foucault, was asserting that all systems of ideas, science included, were the consequence of the distribution of power in society, and that changes in ideas were not to be accounted for by epistemological factors, but by sociological ones. Foucault inverts Francis Bacon's maxim that "Knowledge is power," and asserts that "Power is knowledge."[17]

Science teachers and teacher educators need to be aware of this multi-fronted assault on the rational assumptions of science. There is much in it that is informative, and which enlarges our understanding of how decision-making and theory change actually occur in science. The role of elites in a scientific community and their control over organs of publication, the function of rhetoric in scientific argument, the influence that economic power and interests have in the funding of research, and the determination of which problems to investigate and which to avoid—these are all matters which need to be taken into account, and which provide a richer and more realistic view of the scientific enterprise. Furthermore, it is correct to point out that conceptions of rationality have changed over time: the Aristotelian ideal is different from that of the British Empiricists, which is different from that of modern falsificationists or Bayesian probabilists. There is an historical dimension to rationality. But there is also much that is fundamentally mistaken, and educationally deleterious, in these attacks on scientific rationality.

At the highest level there is a confusion between ascertaining what actually happens in some specific instances, and pronouncements about what should generally happen in the conduct of science. Francis Bacon, in the early seventeenth century, alerted his readers to the operation of what he called "The Idols of the Mind." These were the various ways in which the effort to understand the world can be thwarted: by the inadequate language available to think and write in, by the corrosive effects of self-interest whereby people more readily believe what they want to believe, by the direct exercise of social power wielded by dominant groups. Much contemporary sociology of science is an extension of this early Baconian investigation. But Bacon took pains to identify the operation of "Idols" precisely in order to overcome or compensate for their effects. That is, he distinguished between what sometimes happens and what should happen in the pursuit of knowledge. Whenever sociologists point to the operation of contemporary idols, or old ones in new dress, it is possible to ask: Are such mechanisms, procedures or influences desirable in science? This latter normative question is the one asked by philosophers of science, and it is one that students can be encouraged to ask. Then if the effects of class, sex, race, power, self-interest and so on are identified as pernicious and contrary to the scientific endeavor, it is reasonable to delineate what the ideal is against which these failings are judged.

Now it certainly would be an embarrassment to the rational cause if no instances of scientific change could be found in which epistemological or evidential considerations were determinant, but there is no embarrassment to the rational cause if some instances of nonepistemological determination are uncovered. Indeed a good many of these have been documented: the long history of intelligence testing and its associated theory is now seen to be almost entirely driven by class, race and sex interests;[18] and the decades of Lysenkoist genetics, or more correctly antigenetics, in the USSR is now seen to have been in part driven by Communist Party interests, and in part by a mistaken metaphysics. But these cases can be identified, and they command our attention, because we have some sense that they are departures from proper scientific procedure.

Further, without such normative convictions, we would be in no position to complain about the above aberrations: if power is knowledge, then the white ruling class and the Communist Party certainly had power, and consequently the operation of this power must, by definition, result in knowledge. Few people, least of all minorities and those without power, would want to accept this conclusion.

Enough has been said to indicate that argument about the rationality of science is pertinent to science teaching. Siegel (1989b, 1993) defends rationality and the giving of reasons as the hallmark of science education. Eger (1988, 1989b) addresses the question of how such a conception can allow for the role of commitment, or faith, that has been so important to the development of science. Faith, or philosophical commitment, need not be irrational. Such commitments can be tested by evaluation of their scientific or experimental achievements or implications. Siegel (1993) addresses the quest for a naturalized philosophy of science, and how such a quest, if successful, would impact on our understanding of the rationality of science, and on the classroom teaching of science. These debates, and others, should find a place in teacher education programs, and can inform school science teaching.

Ernst Mach: Philosopher, Scientist and Educator

The first person to deal systematically with the contribution that philosophy can make to science education was Ernst Mach (1838–1916). Unfortunately his contribution to science education has been almost entirely ignored in the English-speaking world.[19] This is a pity, because current trends in the practice and theory of science education are in many respects repeating Mach's century-old arguments concerning the purposes and aims of science teaching, the nature of understanding and the optimum conditions for children's learning. This section will do what one obituary writer for Mach proposed:

> It is Mach the *educationalist* whom we must here bring to the attention of our readers, particularly the younger ones, and not as someone who has passed on, but as a man whose seed is destined to put down ever further roots in physics

teaching, and, with that, in all teaching about real things, and to fructify the whole spirit of this teaching. (Höfler 1916, W. A. Suchting trans.)

Mach was one of the great philosopher-scientists of the turn of the century. He was fluent in most European languages, an enthusiast of Greek and Latin classics, a physicist who made significant contributions to such diverse fields as electricity, gas dynamics, thermodynamics, optics, energy theory and mechanics; a historian and philosopher of science, a psychologist, Rector of Prague German University, a member of the Upper House in the Austrian Parliament and a writer of lucid prose.[20] He was a person of strong character and convictions, a socialist and outspoken liberal-humanist in the centre of the archconservative Catholic Austro-Hungarian Empire. Einstein said of him that "he peered into the world with the inquisitive eyes of a carefree child taking delight in the understanding of relationships" (Hiebert 1976, p. xxi).

The first of Mach's five hundred publications was in 1859, the year of Darwin's *The Origin of Species*; his last work was pubished five years after his death in 1921, the year of Einstein's *Relativity: The Special and General Theory*. His own contributions to physics are recognized in such terms as Mach bands, Mach principle, Mach angle, and Mach number. He contributed to the intellectual accomplishments of Boltzmann, Maxwell, Einstein, Planck, Poincaré, Heisenberg and indeed most of the leading physicists who were preparing the ground for the revolution of modern physics.[21] Mach's contribution to philosophy was also enormous, both through his influence on philosophical scientists, and on professional philosophers. Prominent among the latter were the founders of the Vienna Circle—Rudolf Carnap, Phillip Frank, Moritz Schlick and Otto Neurath. Mach was responsible for B.F. Steiner's behaviorist theory (Holton 1993a).

Mach's Educational Contributions

Mach's understanding of science and philosophy bore upon his educational ideas. Mach was influenced by the ideas of the German philosopher-psychologist-educationalist Johann Friedrich Herbart. He applied Herbart's ideas in his first teaching assignment, "Physics for Medical Students," and in the text he wrote arising from this course (*Compendium of Physics for Medical Students* 1863). Mach's concern here was with "economy of thought," with getting across the general outline of the conceptual modes of physics, and with overcoming the compartmentalism of physics.

Psychology was a long-standing interest of Mach's. At fifteen years of age Mach had read Kant's *Prologomena* and signaled his subsequent positivist commitments—"The superfluity of the role of the 'thing-in-itself' suddenly dawned upon me" (Blackmore 1972, p. 11). His teaching was the occasion to unite pedagogical, psychological and scientific concerns.

The first of his many science textbooks for school students, published in 1886, was widely used and went through several editions. Indeed most of the major figures in European physics at the beginning of this century learnt science from Mach's school texts. These texts provided a logical and historical introduction to science, they sought to present students with the "most naive, simple, and classical observations and thoughts from which great scientists have built physics" (Pyenson 1983, p. 34). Whilst at Prague German University he taught courses on "School Physics Teaching." In 1887 Mach founded and coedited what is probably the first science education journal published—*Zeitschrift für den Physikalischen und Chemischen Unterricht* (*Journal of Instruction in Physics and Chemistry*). He contributed regularly to this journal until a stroke forced his retirement in 1898.

Mach did not write any systematic work on educational theory or practice; his ideas are scattered throughout his texts and journal articles. However, there are three lectures where he addressed pedagogical issues. One of these is perhaps his most systematic treatment of education in general and science education in particular—"On Instruction in the Classics and the Mathematico-Physical Sciences" (1886), translated in his *Popular Scientific Lectures* (1893/1986). His other chief pedagogical papers are "On Instruction in Heat Theory" (1887), and "On the Psychological and Logical Moment in Scientific Instruction" (1890), in volumes one and four respectively of his *Zeitschrift*.

As well as intellectual and practical interests in education, Mach had a notable political involvement in educational reform. He addressed teacher organizations, spoke in the Austrian Parliament on the need for school curricular change, and was active in the struggles to transform the entrenched German gymnasium pattern of separating language and classics studies into separate schools from those for science and mathematics. Mach championed the creation of the new *Einheitsschule* where integrated education in the humanities and the sciences could occur. There have been few scientists who have displayed such a wide-ranging interest in education. This makes Mach's relative neglect by English-speaking science educators the more unfortunate.

Well-founded curricular and pedagogical proposals in school science are based upon two foundations: views about the nature and scope of science, and views about the nature and practice of education. There are of course other matters to be considered in drawing up curricula—political, social and psychological, to name just the obvious ones. But what one thinks, explicitly or implicitly, about the philosophy of science and about the philosophy of education will largely determine the form of the science curriculum. Mach's suggestions for the conduct of science education stem in part from his theory of science and his Herbartian theory of education. Some of the major themes of Mach's philosophy of science, his view of the nature of science, are the following:

- Scientific theory is an intellectual construction for economizing thought and thereby conjoining experiences.
- Science is fallible; it does not provide absolute truths.
- Science is a historically conditioned intellectual activity.
- Scientific theory can only be understood if its historical development is understood.

Mach's educational ideas are fairly simple, and relatively uncontroversial:

- Begin instruction with concrete materials and thoroughly familiarize students with the phenomena discussed.
- Aim for understanding and comprehension of the subject matter.
- Teach a little, but teach it well.
- Follow the historical order of development of a subject.
- Tailor teaching to the intellectual level and capacity of students.
- Address the philosophical questions that science entails and which gave rise to science.
- Show that just as individual ideas can be improved, so also scientific ideas have constantly been, and will continue to be, overhauled and improved.
- Engage the mind of the learner.

Although a preeminent theorist, and concerned with economy of thought in education, Mach firmly believed that abstractions in the science classroom should, as Hegel said of philosophy, take flight only at dusk. "Young students should not be spoiled by premature abstraction, but should be made acquainted with their material from living pictures of it before before they are made to work with it by purely ratiocinative methods" (Mach 1886/1986, p. 4). A simple point, usually observed in its breach, as Arnold Arons has lamented:

> As physics teaching now stands, there is a serious imbalance in which there is an overabundance of numerical problems using formulae in canned and inflexible examples and a very great lack of phenomenological thinking and reasoning. (Arons 1988, p. 18)

Another of Mach's concerns was the tendency to overfill the curriculum. For him the principal aims of education were to develop understanding, strengthen reason and promote imagination. A bloated curriculum counteracted these aims:

> I know nothing more terrible than the poor creatures who have learned too much. What they have acquired is a spider's web of thoughts too weak to furnish sure supports, but complicated enough to produce confusion. (Mach 1895/1986, p. 367)

Mach believed in presenting science historically, or as he put it, teaching should follow the genetic approach:

every young student could come into living contact with and pursue to their ultimate logical consequences merely a *few* mathematical or scientific discoveries. Such selections would be mainly and naturally associated with selections from the great scientific classics. A few powerful and lucid ideas could thus be made to take root in the mind and receive thorough elaboration. (Mach 1895/ 1986, p. 368).

Mach's major textbooks on mechanics (1883), heat (1869) and optics (1922) all follow the genetic method of exposition. Mach realised that the logic of a subject was not necessarily the logic of its presentation—a point known to most school teachers. The logic of a discipline and the logic of its pedagogy are not identical, as Duhem, who also preferred the genetic method, often said.[22]

Thought Experiments

A special feature of Mach's view of science education was his advocacy of thought experimentation (*Gedankenexperimente*). He said of thought experiments that "Experimenting in thought is important not only for the professional inquirer, but also for mental development as such"; not only the student but "the teacher gains immeasurably by this method" (Mach 1896/1976, p. 143). Thought experiments enabled the teacher to know what grasp students had on the fundamental concepts of a discipline.

Each edition of his *Zeitschrift* carried thought experiments for his readers to perform. For instance, he asks, what is expected to happen to a beaker of water in equilibrium on a balance when a suspended mass is lowered into it? Or in another issue, what happens when a stoppered bottle with a fly on its base is in equilibrium on a balance and then the fly takes off? These examples are of thought experiments of an anticipatory type—the actual experiment can be performed. They engage the mind, and they reveal what a student believes about the relevant concepts being investigated. However some thought experiments are not anticipatory but idealized, because the circumstances postulated cannot be produced—Newton's bucket experiment, Galileo's well through the centre of the earth and so on. Mach encouraged such exercises, believing that the exercise of imagination and creativity was another way of bridging the gap between humanities and the sciences: "The planner, the builder of castles in the air, the novelist, the author of social and technological utopias is experimenting with thought" (Mach 1896/1976, p. 136).

Mach's advocacy of thought experiment did not gain many adherents among science teachers of his day. Imagination, hypothesizing and creative thought were not characteristic of late-nineteenth-century science pedagogy. Einstein, who was to place thought experiments upon the centre stage of modern physics, made the oft-quoted remark about his own schooling that: "after I passed the final examination, I found the consideration of any scientific problems distasteful to me for an entire year," and "It is, in fact, nothing short of a miracle that the modern methods of instruction have not entirely strangled the holy curiosity of inquiry" (Schilpp 1951, p. 17).

Thought Experiments in Science

Thought experiments have had an important role in the history of science—witness their use by Galileo, Leibniz, Newton, Carnot and, in this century, by Einstein, Schrödinger and Heisenberg. Newton's thought experiment of the rotating bucket of water in an empty universe, which he believed established the existence of absolute space and motion, is one of the most influential conceptual experiments in the history of science.[23] Einstein, in his "Autobiographical Essay," states how as a teenager he felt ill at ease about the then-dominant physical interpretation of Maxwell's equations for electromagnetism. This feeling was vanquished, as was the mechanical interpretation of Maxwell's equations, by a thought experiment: Einstein imagined himself running along in front of a light beam and looking back at it. He says:

> I should observe such a beam of light as a spatially oscillatory electromagnetic field at rest. However, there seems to be no such thing, whether on the basis of experience or according to Maxwell's equations. (Schilpp 1951, p. 53)

He says that "in this paradox the germ of the special relativity theory is already contained." He goes on to say:

> The type of critical reasoning which was required for the discovery of this central point was decisively furthered, in my case, especially by the reading of . . . Ernst Mach's philosophical writings. (Schilpp 1951, p. 53)

Mach, in his *Mechanics*, draws attention to one of the great thought experiments in the history of science, the thought experiment in Day One of Galileo's 1638 *Discourses Concerning Two New Sciences*, which is directed at disproving the Aristotelian thesis that bodies in free-fall descend with a speed that is proportional to their weight. In Galileo's text the Aristotelian, Simplicio, stated the received view[24] that "bodies of different weight move in one and the same medium with different speeds which stand to one another in the same ratio as the weights" (Galileo 1638/1954, p. 60). There follows inconclusive talk about dropping cannonballs and musket balls from great heights and the claimed differences in time between when they hit the ground. The dialogue continues as follows, with Salviatti the spokesperson for Galileo.

SALV: But, even without further experiment, it is possible to prove clearly, by means of a short and conclusive argument, that a heavier body does not move more rapidly than a lighter one provided both bodies are of the same material and in short such as those mentioned by Aristotle. But tell me, Simplicio, whether you admit that each falling body acquires a definite speed fixed by nature, a velocity which cannot be increased or diminished except by the use of force [*violenza*] or resistance.

SIMP: There can be no doubt that one and the same body moving in a single medium has a fixed velocity which is determined by nature and which cannot be increased except by the addition of momentum [*impeto*] or diminished except by some resistance which retards it.

SALV: If then we take two bodies whose natural speeds are different, it is clear that on uniting the two, the more rapid one will be partly retarded by the slower, and the slower will be somewhat hastened by the swifter. Do you not agree with me in this opinion?

SIMP: You are unquestionably right.

SALV: But if this is true, and if a large stone moves with a speed of, say, eight while a smaller moves with a speed of four, then when they are united, the system will move with a speed less than eight; but the two stones when tied together make a stone larger than that which before moved with a speed of eight. Hence the heavier body moves with less speed than the lighter, an effect which is contrary to your supposition. Thus you see how, from your assumption that the heavier body moves more rapidly than the lighter one, I infer that the heavier body moves more slowly.

SIMP: I am all at sea because it appears to me that the smaller stone when added to the larger increases its weight and by adding weight I do not see how it can fail to increase its speed or, at least, not to diminish it.

Galileo's argument is short, it is conclusive and it is extremely elegant. Karl Popper described it as:

One of the most important imaginary experiments in the history of natural philosophy, and one of the simplest and most ingenious arguments in the history of rational thought about our universe. (Popper 1934/1959, p. 442)

This, and other such thought experiments, led Alexandre Koyré to claim, for Galileo somewhat exaggeratedly, "the glory and the merit of having known how to dispense with experiments" (Koyré 1968, p. 75).

Gottfried Leibniz's 1686 refutation of the Cartesian doctrine that momentum was the measure of "force of motion," or energy, is another influential thought experiment in the history of science.

When Leibniz formulated his thought experiment, the important conservation laws of classical physics had begun to be formulated. On theological and philosophical grounds it was held that the amount of matter in the world was constant—God had just once created the world and all in it. In addition it was held that the amount of motion in the world was also constant—God created matter and put it in motion, and a Perfect Creator should not have to return to His creation to keep "winding it up." But how was this amount of motion to be measured? Descartes proposed momentum, or the product of mass and velocity, as its measure. This made mathematical sense, it was elegant, and it was in accord with all practical demonstrations. In the five common machines being used at the time—the lever, windlass, pulley, wedge and screw—mass and velocity did compensate for each other (subject to experimental errors and inefficiencies). Leibniz comfortably disproved Descartes' proposition by a thought experiment (Leibniz 1686/1969).

Leibniz asked for two propositions to be assumed: one, that at its terminus a falling body acquires an amount of motion (or force of motion) sufficent to return it to its starting point; two, that the force of motion required to raise a unit body four units in height is the same as that required to raise a four-unit body one unit in height. Both propositions were assented to by Cartesians.

Leibniz went on to point out that a body of one unit mass falling four units of distance will have the same force of motion as a body of four units mass falling one unit of distance. But Galileo had proved that a body falling four units has twice the velocity as a body falling one unit. Thus on the Cartesian assumption that force of motion is measured by the product of the mass and velocity, the force of the first body is one times two, or two; the force of the second is four times one, or four. But by assumption, the forces of motion in the two cases are equal, thus its measure cannot be mass times velocity (momentum). The measure of the force that is conserved must be mass times velocity squared (kinetic energy).

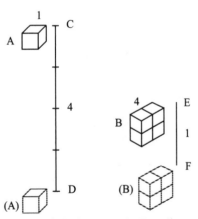

FIG.2 Leibniz's Thought Experiment

Once more we see that a thought experiment was able to establish a proposition that, in the historical context, actual experiments were unable or unlikely to do. It was accidental that the momentum measure was vindicated in the operation of then common machines; but any experimental test of the momentum-conservation hypothesis, any Hempelian "collection of empirical data by actual experimental or observational procedures" would have involved these machines.

Gaileo offers a model of thought experiment for the classroom. He begins with familiar circumstances, he conceptualizes these in the old theory, in thought he extends the familiar circumstances, and then he sees whether the old conceptualizations are adequate to the new situation: where they are not, he proposes new conceptualizations and new theories. This is also a model of philosophical investigation, which some maintain is one, large, ongoing thought experiment. Think, for instance, of philosophical investigation of the adequacy of ethical distinctions and their application. We commonly ask students to conjecture the meaning of right conduct with respect to, say, theft, and then propose circumstances where their understanding has to be modified or abandoned. This philosophical experimenting in thought is as old as the Socratic dialogues. Thought experiments can be divided into those that are *destructive* of accepted conceptual schemes or theories and those that are *constructive* or supportive of new or accepted theories. Some maintain that thought experiments tell us about the properties of the world, others maintain that they tell us only about the properties of thought, or more correctly, of concepts—see the references in Note 23 above.

Thought Experiments And Science Education

Science teachers and textbooks have generally neglected thought experiments. We have seen how Galileo disproved what was commonly regarded as the Aristotelian theorem that bodies fall with a velocity dependent upon their weight. Most science textbooks recall this achievement of Galileo's. However, they fabricate his method. The story repeatedly told is of how Galileo climbed the Leaning Tower of Pisa and dropped a cannonball and a stone and "with their simultaneous thud on the ground the Scientific Revolution was born." Lane Cooper (1935), a professor of language and literature, was in the early 1930s intrigued that the great Aristotle could believe something which was so "obviously false" and so easily disproved. His researches established first that Galileo had put words into Aristotle's mouth, and second that this supposed position was not disproved by dropping balls from the Tower of Pisa. That the textbook story has continued to function as such a powerful myth testifies to the grip of empiricism on science education.

The area of conceptual change is an obvious one for the utilization of thought experiments. This is the area of which Mach said that experimenting in thought enables teachers to learn how well students understand concepts. Consider, for instance, the distinction between natural and violent motions that was firmly embedded in Aristotelian physics—where natural motion occurs when bodies move toward their "natural" places, and violent motion when they move away from these places. Circular motion was natural for planets, motion towards the centre of the earth was natural for terrestrial heavy bodies. Galileo conjectured an experiment in which a well was bored through the centre of the earth to the other side. He asked Aristotelians to envisage what would happen when a stone was dropped down the well. Clearly it would travel "naturally" at increasing speed to the centre of the earth. But what happens when it gets there? Does it stop? Does it keep going and so "naturally" travel away from the earth's centre? Does it somehow turn naturally into violent motion? The thought experiment was used to investigate the inadequacy of the fundamental Aristotelian distinction. The actual experiment of course could never be performed, but its power to illuminate conceptual problems in the old physics was not compromised by that fact.

Some physics textbooks have made use of thought experiments for extending old or everyday conceptualizations to new areas, and thought experiments have been discussed in a few science education articles.[25] One text uses the historical approach to investigate and test the everyday notion that heat is a substance, fluid or entity that can be transferred from one object to another. It asks students to imagine a large insulated container in which there are two beakers of water, each with a thermometer that protrudes beyond the container. One beaker has a Bunsen burner under it, the other has Joule's apparatus of a paddlewheel and a falling mass attached (Wenham et al. 1972). Questions are raised about what temperature changes are seen, conjectures are invited about what implications there would be if the temperature rises in both systems and so on.

The use of computers and computer assisted instruction is a boon for thought experimentation in classrooms. Computers overcome one of the standard problems with routine laboratory work and pupil experimentation: namely that teachers have to do all the experimental design and planning (Hodson 1988). Problems of time, equipment, safety and so on have meant that students are often reduced to executing a teacher's preplanned experiment. Pupils learn manipulative skills which are important, but not the conceptual, creative skills that are the hallmark of good science. Computers remove practical obstacles to the generation and testing of hypotheses, and allow extrapolation to the idealized test situations characteristic of noteworthy thought experiments.

In Ontario some school courses have used thought experimentation in conjunction with science fiction themes—if the Bionic Man accelerated at a certain rate would his feet melt down? (Stinner 1990). These types of "thinking physics" problems allow teachers and students to determine what they mean by fundamental concepts such as gravity, force, pressure and so on, and to think about the correct conditions for the applicability of concepts.

A textbook that exemplifies this approach to physics is L. C. Epstein's *Thinking Physics* (1979), which contains numerous exercises such as the following:

- *Sputnik* I, the first artificial earth satellite, fell back to earth because friction with the outer part of the earth's atmosphere slowed it down. As *Sputnik* spiralled closer and closer to the earth its speed was observed to: decrease, remain constant, increase? (p. 157)
- Over a century ago, J. C. Maxwell calculated that if Saturn's rings were cut from a piece of sheet metal they would not be strong enough to withstand the tidal tension or gravitational gradient tension that Saturn would put on them and would, therefore, rip apart. But suppose the rings were cut from a piece of thick-plate, rather than thin-sheet iron. Might the thick-plate: fail as easily as the thin-sheet, fail more easily than the thin-sheet, not fail as easily as the thin-sheet? (p. 161)

These exercises require students to think about the meaning of concepts used in describing phenomena. They are thought experiments in the tradition of Mach's *Gedankenexperimente*. They engage the mind of the learner in ways that mere calculations, or "recipe book" carrying out of an empirical experiment fail to do. They support Mach's claim that: "Experimenting in thought is important not only for the professional inquirer, but also for mental development as such."

Ethics and Science Education

Ethical questions increasingly arise in the science classroom. The greenhouse effect, pollution, extinction of species, genetic engineering, military technology and the employment of scientists in the defense industries, the cost and direction of scientific research, nuclear energy and nuclear war, and so on—are all matters that are raised by students, and appear in new science curricula. Most major universities have ethics committees that regulate research in science and social science. The once straightforward and unreflective use of animals for scientific experiments and laboratory dissections is now questioned, and in many places strictly controlled—an aim of the New Zealand science syllabus is "the care of animals" and recognition of their rights. At the same time, in philosophy these questions are being dealt with in applied ethics and environmental ethics courses. Hitherto, partly under the influence of belief in value-free science, these questions have largely been ignored in science education—rats and mice have been routinely killed in front of classes, the chemistry of fusion and fission discussed without attention to the bomb or the ethics of nuclear energy use, the science of extractive industries discussed without attention to the sociopolitical-environmental issues involved.

John Ziman and numerous others have pointed out that orthodox science education has long promulgated naive materialism, primitive positivism and complacent technocracy (Ziman 1980). These positions are now in intellectual retreat. The PLON project in the Netherlands, the SISCON project in the UK, various Canadian projects (Aikenhead 1980), STS courses and the Project 2061 proposals in the US are educational responses to the recognition that science and values are more interwoven than previously acknowledged.

The interconnection of science and ethics is particularly clear in contemporary human genetics programs. The Human Genome Project has three percent (ninety million dollars) of its three-billion-dollar budget allocated to ethical and legal ramifications. In the US there are at least three state and national genetic education programs that explicitly address the ethical and religious dimensions of the Genome Project.[26] The Biological Sciences Curriculum Study (BSCS) program is outlined in a ninety-four page document sent to all US biology teachers. In addition to the science of the Genome Project, it has students engaging in analysis and debate over the ethical and policy issues generated by genetic screening and other techniques occasioned by the Genome Project. Should employers be allowed to screen prospective employees for the Huntington's chorea gene? Should those identified as genetically disposed to alcoholism be forbidden to drink? It says of these situations that:

> Individuals, institutions (schools, businesses, and other organizations), and society will have to deal with situations in which some interests are advanced and others are impaired. When the interests of everyone cannot be advanced, and when some interests are advanced at the expense of others, whose interests ought to receive priority? Questions about "oughts" properly are addressed by ethics and public policy. (BSCS 1992, p. 15)

One hopes that teachers will strive to make the ethical discussion as sophisticated as the scientific discussion. This requires that teachers be familiar with the history of ethical debate and the its major arguments. Something, but not much, is served by simply rehashing or asserting popular nostrums. Teachers can benefit, and their classes be enriched, by serious grappling with these ethical and social questions.[27]

Feminism and Science Education

In the last three decades there has been concern about the low participation rate of women in science. "Women and Science" research has focused on practical and pedagogical barriers to girls performing well in science. Matters raised have included teachers paying more attention to boys than girls, the lack of female role models and pursuits in textbooks, and so on. But beyond these practical or empirical matters, there have also developed feminist arguments about bias in the very nature of science and its practice.

This bias is held by some feminists to be responsible for girls shunning science or underachieving in it.

The writings of Ruth Bleier (1984), Evelyn Fox Keller (1985), Sandra Harding (1986), Helen Longino (1989) Jane Roland Martin (1989), and other feminist philosophers of science, have been influential in philosophy and education. Some feminists reject the quest for objectivity or universalism; others, such as Sandra Harding, seek a better version of objectivity, one that takes into account the cognitive perspectives of women and other groups. For Harding, this improved scientific knowledge:

> seeks a unity of knowledge combining moral and political with empirical understanding. And it seeks to unify knowledge of and by the heart with that which is gained by and about the brain and hand. It sees inquiry as comprising not just the mechanical observation of nature and others but the intervention of political and moral illumination "without which the secrets of nature cannot be uncovered." (Harding 1986, p. 241)

Some of the feminist criticisms are of specific scientific research programs. These criticisms need to be dealt with on a case-by-case basis to see whether the claims about bias are correct; and whether such bias, if it is there, has compromised the knowledge claims of the research (not all bias is detrimental to truth). Some fundamental questions, such as Martin's challenge of the putatively masculine bias in mainstream epistemology of science, require a more general and complex response. But there is an immediate issue raised in feminist literature with which science educators need to grapple.

Some feminists see girls' reluctance to pursue science as the result of science "being commonly portrayed as a discipline promoting objective, rational and analytic behaviour" (Bell 1988, p. 159). This argument may have some initial appeal, but it is fraught with problems. It does not explain why in many countries women are well represented in science. We are seldom told why objectivity, rationality and analytic thinking are bad. One might have thought that such traits were desirable, and sorely needed in the social and political arena. There are, of course, times when it is better to be reasonable than rational, and education should strive to promote reasonableness as a character trait (Burbules 1992). But reasonableness is parasitic upon being rational; that is, reasonableness can be seen as knowing when to put rationality aside in favor of other considerations (Siegel 1992).

Furthermore, many women reject the claim that objectivity, rationality and analytic thinking are alien to them. Norette Koertge, a prominent philosopher of science and one of the few to write on science education (Koertge 1969), maintains that science needs more unorthodox ideas, and a greater plurality of approaches. This is a standard Popperian position which does not in itself constitute an argument for a new epistemology of science. Against certain feminists, Koertge warns that:

If it really could be shown that patriarchal thinking not only played a crucial role in the Scientific Revolution but is also necessary for carrying out scientific inquiry as we now know it, that would constitute the strongest argument for patriarchy that I can think of. (Koertge 1981, p. 354)

And she goes on to say:

I continue to believe that science—even white, upperclass, male-dominated science—is one of the most important allies of oppressed people. (Koertge 1981, p. 354)

Conclusion

This chapter has discussed the interconnection of science and philosophy, and has suggested that aspects of this interaction be introduced to students in science classrooms. This is part of learning about the nature of science, a topic in all science curricula. It is not just a matter of learning *about* philosophy, although this is important, but also the opportunity can be provided to *do* philosophy. Philosophy begins with the questions such as "What do you mean by?" and "How do you know?" Students can be encouraged to ask these questions at each stage of their education in science. Such questions lead naturally into the sphere of logic and the appraisal of arguments, and there is a good deal of evidence that students' naive thinking in these areas needs to be trained and informed. The questions listed by Robert Ennis in 1979—concerning explanation, structure of disciplines, values, theory and observation, scientific method—are of perennial interest to the science teacher, and can be made interesting to students. This chapter has indicated a number of areas in contemporary curricula where philosophy has an explicit role to play.

Beyond curricular content there are lively areas of theoretical debate amongst science educators to which philosophy of science can contribute. Argument over constructivism, particularly its epistemological claims, is an obvious area, and will be dealt with in Chapter 7. Argument about appropriate multicultural science education is another area to which philosophy can contribute, as will be seen in Chapter 9. Feminist critiques of science, and consequent proposals for the reshaping of science education, are other obvious areas where knowledge of the history and philosophy of science is important. These critiques are complex and much debated, and justice cannot be done to them here. But by no means is the matter settled in favour of those feminists who reject the pursuit of objectivity, rationality, and analytic thinking: A great many women scientists endorse just such goals. Science educators have a great responsibility to be informed, and correct, in their weighing up of these arguments. This is impossible without knowledge of the history and philosophy of science.

CHAPTER 6

History and Philosophy in the Classroom: The Case of Pendulum Motion

In this chapter the teaching of a single topic, pendulum motion, will be discussed in order to illustrate the claims being made about the benefits of a liberal or contextual approach to science education. This topic is chosen in part because it has a place in nearly all science programs, and also because it is a relatively pedestrian topic. In "hot" topics such as evolution, genetic engineering or acid rain, historical and philosophical considerations are obviously useful. If the case for HPS can be made with a "boring" topic, then the usefulness of HPS for science teaching is better established. Furthermore, the science of pendulum motion illustrates important general topics alluded to in this book, including:

- The interplay of mathematics, observation and experiment in the development of modern science.
- The interactions of philosophy and science.
- The distinction between material objects and these objects as treated by science.
- The ambiguous role of empirical evidence in the justification or falsification of scientific claims.
- The contrast between modern scientific conceptualizations and those of common sense.

This case study can illustrate what Ernest Boyer was recommending in his influential book, *High School* (1983), where he identified some of the well-known problems with science education and suggested, as Conant had forty years earlier, that:

> These courses should be taught in a way that gives students an understanding of the principles of science that transcend the disciplines. The search for general principles of science can be, if not properly done, a superficial exercise. But if carefully designed, an interdisciplinary view will give all students—both specialists and non-specialists—a greater understanding of the meaning of science and the scientific process. (Boyer 1983, p. 107)

The Pendulum and the Science of Motion

In a letter of 1632, ten years before his death, Galileo surveyed his achievements in physics and recorded his debt to the pendulum for enabling him to measure the time of free-fall, which, he said, "we shall obtain from the marvellous property of the pendulum, which is that it makes all its vibrations, large or small, in equal times" (Drake 1978, p. 399). To use pendulum motion as a measure of the passage of time was a momentous enough achievement, but the pendulum is also central to Galileo's treatment of freefall, the motion of bodies through a resisting medium, the conservation of momentum, and the rate of fall of heavy and light bodies. His analysis of pendulum motion is thus central to his overthrow of Aristotelian physics and the development of the modern science of motion, a development about which the historian Herbert Butterfield has said:

> Of all the intellectual hurdles which the human mind has confronted and has overcome in the last fifteen hundred years, the one which seems to me to have been the most amazing in character and the most stupendous in the scope of its consequences is the one relating to the problem of motion. (Butterfield 1949, p. 3)

The pendulum played a major role in the scientific revolution. Christiaan Huygens patented a pendulum clock in 1657 and used it not only for an accurate measure of time, but also to determine to a remarkable degree of precision the gravitational constant g, (9.82m/s^2). Newton, in his *Principia*, used this value to establish that acceleration due to gravity on the surface of the earth was the same type of acceleration as the moon's centripetal acceleration towards the earth. Newton also used the pendulum to analyze wave motion, and subsequently to ascertain the speed of sound in air. Pendulum motion figured in Newton's major metaphysical dispute with the Cartesians, namely the dispute concerning the existence of the aether (Westfall 1980, p. 376). The importance of the pendulum in science and philosophy was exceeded only by its importance to commerce, navigation, exploration and Western expansion. A convenient and accurate measure of the passage of time was crucial for the pressing commercial problem of determining longitude at sea, as well as for everyday economic and social affairs. The pendulum was the answer to these problems.

Galileo and the Textbook

The standard textbook treatment of pendulum motion features the story of Galileo's discovery of the isochronic movement of the pendulum. One representative such account is the following:

> When he [Galileo] was barely seventeen years old, he made a passive observation of a chandelier swinging like a pendulum in the church at Pisa where he grew up. He noticed that it swung in the gentle breeze coming through the half-opened church door. Bored with the sermon, he watched the chandelier carefully, then placed his fingertips on his wrist, and felt his pulse. He noticed an amazing thing. . . . Sometimes the chandelier swings widely and sometimes it hardly swings at all . . . [yet] it made the same number of swings every sixty pulse beats. (Wolf 1981, p. 33)

This same story appears in the opening pages of the most widely used high school physics text in the world—the Physical Science Study Committee's *Physics* (PSSC 1960).

If the textbook account is to be believed, then a basic question is why it was that the supposed isochronism of the pendulum was only seen in the sixteenth century, when thousands of people of genius and with acute powers of observation had for thousands of years been pushing children on swings, and looking at swinging lamps and swinging weights, and using suspended bobs in tuning musical instruments, without seeing their isochronism. For centuries people had been concerned to find a reliable measure of time, both for scientific purposes and also in everyday life to determine the duration of activities and events, and the vital navigational matter of determining longitude at sea. As the isochronic pendulum was the answer to all these questions, the widespread failure to recognize something so apparently obvious is informative. It suggests that there is not just a problem of perception, but a deeper problem, a problem of epistemology, involved.

Nicole Oresme, in the fourteenth century, discussed pendulum motion. In his *On the Book of the Heavens and the World of Aristotle* he entertained the thought experiment of a body dropped into a well that had been drilled from one side of the earth, through the centre, and out the other side (a thought experiment repeated by Galileo in his 1635 *Dialogues Concerning the Two Chief World Systems*). Oresme likens this imaginary situation to that of a weight which hangs on a long cord and swings back and forth, each time nearly regaining its initial position (Clagett 1959, p. 570). Albert of Saxony, Tartaglia and Benedetti all discussed the same problem in the context of impetus theory. Leonardo da Vinci, a most acute observer, dealt on many occasions with pendulum motion and in the late 1490s sketched two pendulums, one on a reciprocating pump, the other on what appears to be a clock. He recognized that the descent along the arc of a circle is quicker than that along the shorter corresponding chord, an anticipation of Galileo's later Law of Chords. In 1569 Jacques Besson published a book in Lyon detailing the use of the pendulum in regulating mechanical saws, bellows, pumps and polishing machines.[1]

If the discovery of isochronic pendulum motion was as straightforward as the textbook story, we have the problem of explaining why Oresme, Leonardo, Buridan, Benedetti and all the other students of motion and observers of swinging pendulums in the Western and non-Western worlds did not see what Galileo is claimed to have seen. The question of how Galileo came to recognize and prove the laws of pendulum motion is germane to the teaching of the topic. Teachers want students to recognize and prove the properties of pendulum motion—period being independent of mass and amplitude, and varying inversely as the square root of length. How these properties were initially discovered can throw light on current attempts to teach and learn the topic.

Galileo's Account of Pendulum Motion

Galileo at different stages makes four claims about pendulum motion:

1) Period varies only with length; the Law of Length.
2) Period is independent of amplitude; the Law of Amplitude Independence.
3) Period is independent of weight; the Law of Weight Independence.
4) For a given length all periods are the same; the Law of Isochrony.

Contrary to the textbooks, it was not observation but mathematics, and experiment guided by mathematics, that played the major role in Galileo's discovery and proof of the properties of pendulum motion.

After his appointment to a lectureship in mathematics at the University of Pisa in 1588 Galileo quickly became immersed in the mathematics and mechanics of the "Superhuman Archimedes," whom he never mentions "without a feeling of awe" (Galileo 1590/1960, p. 67). Archimedes, above all else, utilized Euclidean geometry in the service of mechanics. He gave geometrical solutions to practical problems in the utilization of the then common machines—the lever, pulley, wheel and axle, wedge and screw.

Galileo's major Pisan work is his *On Motion* (1590/1960).[2] In it he deals with the full range of problems then being discussed among natural philosophers—free-fall, motion on balances, motion on inclined planes and circular motions. In these discussions the physical circumstances are depicted geometrically, and mathematical reasoning is used to establish various conclusions. Galileo's genius was to see that all of the above motions could be dealt with in one geometrical construction, and that further, this construction depicted the case of pendulum motion. That is, motions which appeared so different in the world could all be depicted and dealt with in a common manner.

In Chapter 14 of *On Motion* Galileo addresses the problem of "why the same heavy body, moving downward in natural motion over various planes . . . moves more readily and swiftly on those planes that make angles nearer a right angle with the horizon." Galileo says that, in order to answer these questions, we must first take into consideration that a "heavy body tends to move downwards with as much force as is necessary to lift it up," the problem then becomes "if we can then find how much greater force is needed to draw the body upward on line *bd* than on line *be*, we will then have found with how much greater force the body will descend on *bd* than on *be*." To answer this question Galileo then asks the reader to:

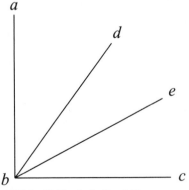

FIG.3 Galileo's Inclined Plane

consider a balance *cd*, with center *a*, having at point *c* a weight equal to another weight at point *d*. Now, if we suppose that line *ad* moves toward *s*, pivoting about the fixed point *a*, then the descent of the body at the initial point *d*, will be as if on the line *ef*.

He next says that "If, then, we can show that the body is less heavy at point *s* than at point *d*, clearly its motion on line *gh* will be slower than on *ef*." By utilizing the theory of moments, Galileo concludes that:

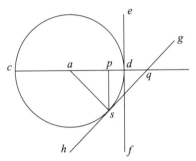

Therefore the speed on *ef* will bear to the speed on *gh* the same ratio as line *da* to line *pa*. . . . Consequently the same heavy body will descend vertically with greater force than on an inclined plane in proportion as the length of the descent on the incline is greater than the vertical fall. (Galileo 1590, p. 64)

FIG.4 Galileo's Inclined Plane Construction

Galileo is still enmeshed in parts of Aristotelian physics, as indicated by his assumption that speed of descent is proportional to weight—the transition from one conceptual scheme to another is usually not clear-cut, even for great thinkers. The above diagram also represents a pendulum suspended at *a*, having a length *ad*, and a bob which moves through *d*, *s*. Galileo makes use of this diagram to prove properties of pendulum motion. It is important to note that Galileo then qualifies this proof, saying:

But this proof must be understood on the assumption that there is no accidental resistance (occasioned by roughness of the moving body or of the inclined plane, or by the shape of the body). We must assume that the plane is, so to speak, incorporeal or, at least, that it is very carefully smoothed and perfectly hard . . . and that the moving body must be perfectly smooth . . . and of the hardest material.

Galileo has here introduced crucial idealizing conditions. His new science is not going to be simply about how the world behaves, but rather how it should behave. Or to put it another way, his science will be about how the world would behave if various conditions were fulfilled; for the pendulum, if the string were weightless, if the bob occasioned no air resistance, if the fulcrum were frictionless and so on. In controlled experiments some of these conditions can be fulfilled, but other conditions are incapable of being fulfilled, yet they were crucial to Galileo's science.[3]

Galileo's persistent opponent over the analysis of pendulum motion was the Aristotelian Guidobaldo del Monte, who was one of the great mathematicians of the sixteenth century, the director of the Venice arsenal and a patron of Galileo.[4] In 1602 Galileo wrote to del Monte of descent along a circular arc, the movement of the pendulum bob. In the letter Galileo outlined his theorem that "the time of descent along any chord of a vertical circle to its lowest point remains the same, regardless of the length and slope of the plane." He elaborated this to include the conjecture that descents along arcs of the lowest quadrant should be completed in the same time regardless of the length of the arc (Drake 1978, p. 68). This was a description of the isochronic pendulum. Galileo's proof of this theorem proceeded as follows. He said:

Let *BA* be the diameter of circle *BDA* erect to the horizontal, and from point *A* out to the circumference draw any lines *AF*, *AE*, *AD*, and *AC*. I show that equal moveables fall in equal times, whether along the vertical *BA* or through the inclined planes along lines *CA*, *DA*, *EA* and *FA*. Thus leaving at the same moment from points *B*, *C*, *D*, *E*, and *F*, they arrive at the same moment at terminus A; and line FA may be as short as you please.

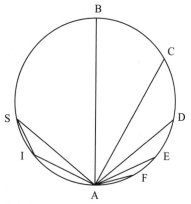

FIG.5   Galileo's Law of Chords

This is close to a proof for isochronism, but not quite. He says to del Monte "But I cannot manage to demonstrate that arcs *SIA* and *IA* are passed in equal times, which is what I am seeking" (Drake 1978, p. 71). He does allude to the pendulum situation and says that two six-foot pendulums keep in synchrony through one thousand swings, one being displaced widely, the other barely displaced from vertical.

In his early work, *On Motion* (1590), Galileo strove for a mathematical proof of isochronic motion; this was his Law of Chords—the time taken to descend any chord in the lower quarter of a circle terminating at the nadir was a constant. He needed a Law of Arcs—the time taken to descend any arc in the lower quarter of a circle terminating at the nadir was a constant. He recognized that he did not have the latter proof. It was his 1638 *Dialogue* that provided what he thought was the mathematical proof of his pendulum laws.

In Theorem VI of the *Discourse* he provides a geometric proof of the Law of Chords. The theorem states:

If from the highest or lowest point in a vertical circle there be drawn any inclined planes meeting the circumference the times of descent along these chords are each equal to the other. (Galileo 1638/1954 p. 188)

This Law of Chords is close to a proof for isochrony of pendulum motion. The law has shown that the time of descent down inclined planes (chords) is the same, provided the planes are inscribed in a circle and originate at the apex or terminate at the nadir. This means that amplitude does not affect the time. This is highly suggestive of a Law of Arcs where amplitude should not affect the time of descent or time of swing. This law is proved later in Theorem XXII of the *Dialogue,* which also demonstrates the counterintuitive proposition that the quickest time of descent in free-fall is not along the shortest path. He says:

If from the lowest point of a vertical circle *C*, a chord *CD* is drawn subtending an arc not greater than a quadrant, and if from the two ends of this chord two other chords be drawn to any point on the arc *B*, the time of descent along the two latter chords *DB*, *BC* will be shorter than along the first, and shorter also, by the same amount, than along the lower of these two latter chords *BC*. (Galileo 1638/1954 p. 237)

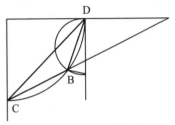

FIG.6   Galileo's Brachistochrone

This is the beginning of Galileo's proof that the arc of a circle is the brachistochrone, or the line of quickest descent in free-fall.

Del Monte was not impressed by these proofs, claiming that Galileo was a better mathematician than a physicist. Reasonably enough, he could not believe that one body would move through an arc of many metres in the same time as another, suspended by the same length of chain, would move only one centimetre. Further, as a mechanic, he conducted experiments on balls rolling within iron hoops and found that Galileo's claims were indeed false: balls released from different positions in the lower quarter of the hoop reached their nadir at different times. But Galileo was not moved by these objections. In his *Dialogue Concerning the Two Chief World Systems* (1633) he says:

Take an arc made of a very smooth and polished concave hoop bending along the curvature of the circumference *ADB*, so that a well-rounded and smooth ball can run freely in it (the rim of a sieve is well suited for this experiment). Now I say that wherever you place the ball, whether near to or far from the ultimate limit *B* . . . and let it go, it will arrive at the point *B* in equal times . . . a truly remarkable phenomenon. (Galileo 1633/1953 p. 451)

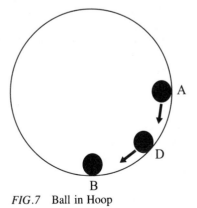

B
FIG.7   Ball in Hoop

In his final great work in mechanics, *Dialogues Concerning Two New Sciences* (1638) Galileo says that:

> It must be remarked that one pendulum passes through its arcs of 180°, 160° etc in the same time as the other swings through its 10°, 8°, degrees. . . . If two people start to count the vibrations, the one the large, the other the small, they will discover that after counting tens and even hundreds they will not differ by a single vibration, not even by a fraction of one (Galileo 1638/1954, p. 254).

Late in his life Galileo proposed using the pendulum as a clock, and his son Vincenzio produced sketches of the proposal.[5]

Empirical Problems with Galileo's Account

These marvellous proofs of Galileo did not receive universal acclaim: on the contrary, learned scholars were quick to point out considerable empirical and philosophical problems with them. The empirical problems were examples where the world did not "correspond punctually" to the events demonstrated mathematically by Galileo. In his more candid moments, Galileo acknowledged that events do not always correspond to his theory; that the material world and his so-called "world on paper," the theoretical world, did not correspond. Immediately after mathematically establishing his famous law of parabolic motion of projectiles, he remarks that:

> I grant that these conclusions proved in the abstract will be different when applied in the concrete and will be fallacious to this extent, that neither will the horizontal motion be uniform nor the natural acceleration be in the ratio assumed, nor the path of the projectile a parabola. (Galileo 1638/1954, p. 251)

One can imagine the reaction of del Monte and other hardworking Aristotelian natural philosophers and mechanicians when presented with such a qualification. It confounded the basic Aristotelian and empiricist objective of science, namely to tell us about the world in which we live. The law of parabolic motion was supposedly true but not of the world we experience: this was indeed as difficult to understand for del Monte as it is for present-day students.

Wolf, the PSSC authors and most science textbook writers who make mention of Galileo's laws of pendulum motion suggest that any old (or young) observers who, at the time, cared to open their eyes would see the isochronic motion that Galileo supposedly saw. Not so. Del Monte, and others, did not see it. As early as 1636 the notable physicist Mersenne reproduced Galileo's experiments and not only agreed with del Monte, but doubted whether Galileo had ever conducted the experiments (Koyré 1968, pp. 113–117). A large and influential part of the scientific community opposed Galileo's claims about isochronism. They were not just being obdurate old heads-in-the-sand, as is so often depicted in texts.

Modern researchers have duplicated the experimental conditions described by Galileo, and have found that they do not give the results that Galileo claimed (Ariotti 1968, Naylor 1974, 1980, 1989). Ronald Naylor for instance found that:

> Using two 76 inch pendulums, one having a brass bob, the other cork, both swinging initially through a total arc of 30°, the brass bob was seen to lead the cork by one quarter of an oscillation after only twenty-five completed swings. (Naylor 1974, p. 33)

Del Monte and others repeatedly pointed out that actual pendulums do not behave as Galileo maintained. Galileo never tired of saying that *ideal* pendulums would obey the mathematically derived rules. Del Monte retorted that physics was to be about this world, not an imaginary mathematical world. Opposition to the mathematizing of physics was a deeply held Aristotelian, and more generally empiricist, conviction.[6] The British empiricist, Hutchinson, would later say of the geometrical constructions of Newton's *Principia* that they were just "cobwebs of circles and lines to catch flies in" (Cantor 1991, p. 219).

It is easy to appreciate the empirical reasons for opposition to Galileo's law. The overriding argument was that if the law were true, pendulums would be perpetual motion machines, which clearly they are not. An isochronic pendulum is one in which the period of the first swing is equal to that of all subsequent swings: This implies perpetual motion. We know that any pendulum, when let swing, will very soon come to a halt; the period of the last swing will be by no means the same as the first. Furthermore it was plain to see that cork and lead pendulums have a slightly different frequency, and that large amplitude swings do take somewhat longer than small-amplitude swings for the same pendulum length. All of this was pointed out to Galileo, and he was reminded of Aristotle's basic methodological claim that the evidence of the senses are to be preferred over other evidence in developing an understanding of the world.

Children have the same difficulty seeing the properties of pendulum motion that the sixteenth-century Aristotelians had. Even with highly refined school laboratory pendulums, they do not see isochrony of large and small amplitude swings, and their cork pendulums soon cease swinging, whilst the brass ones continue much longer. All of this experiential evidence is hard to reconcile with the "laws" of pendulum motion. Children can either think they are stupid and need to take everything on authority, or they can conclude, as one German student did in a recent survey, that "physics is not about the world" (Schecker 1992, p. 75). This is a case of children being in the position of the early pioneers of a science. No amount of looking will reveal isochronic motion; looking is important, but something else is required: a better appreciation of what science is and what it is aiming to do; an epistemology of science. The historian E. J. Dijksterhuis had an appreciation of this when he observed:

> To this day every student of elementary physics has to struggle with the same errors and misconceptions which then [in the seventeenth century] had to be overcome . . . in the teaching of this branch of knowledge in schools, history repeats itself every year. (Dijksterhuis 1986, p. 30)

Dijksterhuis goes on to make the fundamental point that has been labored above: classical mechanics is not only not verified in experience, but its direct verification is fundamentally impossible—"one cannot indeed introduce a material point all by itself into an infinite void and then cause a force that is constant in direction and magnitude to act on it; it is not even possible to attach any rational meaning to this formulation."

Philosophical Problems with Galileo's Account

Apart from the empirical problems with Galileo's claims, del Monte and others had philosophical problems with Galileo's account of pendulum motion. Del Monte had been Galileo's patron, and had secured for Galileo his first teaching position at Pisa largely on the basis of the wonderful mathematics demonstrated in his first work *La Bilancetta* (1586).[7] But del Monte cautioned Galileo that scientists are:

> deceived when they undertake to investigate the balance in a purely mathematical way, its theory being actually mechanical; nor can they reason successfully without the true movement of the balance and without its weights, these being completely physical things, neglecting which they simply cannot arrive at the true cause of events that take place with regard to the balance. (Drake & Drabkin 1969, p. 278)

Vincenzo di Grazia echoed these criticisms when, in 1613, he wrote:

> Before we consider Galileo's demonstrations, it seems necessary to prove how far from the truth are those who wish to prove natural facts by means of mathematical reasoning, among whom, if I am not mistaken, is Galileo. All the sciences and all the arts have their own principles and their own causes by means of which they demonstrate the special properties of their own object. . . . Therefore anyone who thinks he can prove natural properties with mathematical arguments is simply demented, for the two sciences are very different. The natural scientist studies natural bodies that have motion as their natural and proper state, but the mathematician abstracts from all motion. (Shea 1972, p. 34)

Di Grazia here states procedural criticisms of the use of mathematics in physics, and metaphysical criticisms of Galileo's very understanding of motion. What lay behind the procedural criticism was the clear point recognised by Aristotle in his *Physics*. There he held that the speed of an object varies directly as the force applied to it and inversely as the resistance of the medium through which it is being moved, and proposed a form of the formula:

$$V = K \times F/R \quad \text{(speed varies as force over resistance)}$$

Aristotle cautioned that just because ten men pull a boat across a beach at a certain speed, we cannot use the above formula to conclude that one man can pull the boat at one-tenth the speed: in reality, one man may not be able to move the boat at all. That is, our mathematical formula does not allow us to say, independently of experience, what will happen in the world.

To appreciate di Grazia's second criticism, we need to recognize that motion, for Aristotle, was a process that a body undergoes, thus understanding motion depended upon understanding this process. The mathematician abstracts from all motion, in the sense that the mathematician does not consider change as occurring in a body; rather, only the accidents of motion are considered, namely the time and position of a body's displacement. According to Aristotelians these accidents did not get to the "heart of the matter."

Aristotle's understanding of motion is difficult to convey in a brief space, but it is nevertheless central to his natural philosophy.[8] As he says at the beginning of *Physics* Book III:

> Nature has been defined as a "principle of motion and change," and it is the subject of our inquiry. We must therefore see that we understand the meaning of "motion"; for if it were unknown, the meaning of "nature" too would be unknown.

Motion, or change, occurs with respect to substance (fruit decaying), quality (fruit changing color), quantity (fruit getting larger) and location (fruit falling off a tree). The last is called "local motion" and it is what now is regarded as motion—Aristotle's other changes no longer being regarded as motion, but simply as change. He defines motion as:

> The fulfilment of what exists potentially, in so far as it exists potentially, is motion. (*Physics* Book III, 201a, 10)

Thus motion is a *process* undergone by a body, it is the process of having a potential fulfilled; motion is the actualization of an existing potency. Motion is not passed from one body to another, but rather it is the actualization of one thing under the influence of another. Thus, even in local motion, Aristotle's fourfold causation is operative: material (the body undergoing locomotion), formal (actuality), final (the terminal state) and efficient (the agent bringing about change).

Aristotelians argued against Galileo that his mathematical formulations expressed only functional relations, and excluded final causation and teleology from the study of motion: the equations did not tell us what was going on in the process of change, nor why it was occurring. Even the functional relations did not hold between actual measurements, but only between ideal measurements. We can get some sense of their concern when looking at Cartesian responses to Newton's equation for universal gravitation: they said the equation was nice, but it did not tell us what was going on in gravitational attraction, or how the attraction was effective, or what was the mechanism holding the planets in orbit. Aristotelians had similar concerns about Galileo's mathematization of motion.

Another way to appreciate the Aristotelian concern is to compare it with contemporary opponents of quantitative social science: these maintain that statistics, equations, functional relations and so forth do not get to the heart of human behavior because, among other things, they leave out human emotion and intention, which are definitive of human action.[9] Edmund Husserl, in his *The Crisis of European Sciences and Transcendental Phenomenology* (1954/1970), has argued a similar point, saying that mathematics abstracts from the meaning of actions, and thus an entirely mathematical social science is impossible. Husserl also argues that modern physics is limited because of its disregard of the nonmathematical features of experience. Husserl identified the font of this deformation of science as Galileo's idealizations in physics.

Another significant metaphysically based and observationally reinforced argument urged against Galileo's account of pendulum motion, particularly his claims for the pendulum as a measure of the passage of time, was that its motion was discontinuous and thus could not provide a measure of the flow of time which was continuous. This argument goes back to Aristotle's distinction between natural and violent motions, the former being in accord with the nature of a body and "powered" or "motivated" by that nature, and the latter being contrary to the nature of a body. The upward swing of the pendulum was violent motion, the downward swing was natural motion; between the two there had to be a pause. We indeed see a pause at the top of the pendulum swing. The Aristotelians then said that stop-start motion could not be the measure of something which was uniform and continuous. Galileo said that the pendulum only seems to stop, its motion is really continuous. The Aristotelian physicists were left scratching their heads, as are most contemporary schoolchildren when told that something they see stopping actually continues to move, and that a body can reverse direction without pause, and further the body that is apparently at rest at its zenith, is really accelerating vertically downwards.

Herbert Butterfield conveys something of the problem that Galileo and Newton had in forging their new science:

They were discussing not real bodies as we actually observe them in the real world, but geometrical bodies moving in a world without resistance and without gravity—moving in that boundless emptiness of Euclidean space which Aristotle had regarded as unthinkable. In the long run, therefore, we have to recognise that here was a problem of a fundamental nature, and it could not be solved by close observation within the framework of the older system of ideas—it required a transposition in the mind. (Butterfield 1949, p. 5)

An objectivist account of science would stress that the transposition in the mind is really the creation of a new theoretical object or system. Even for Galileo, the pendulum seemed to stop at the top of its swing; it was only in his theory that it continued in motion.

Post-Galileo Developments

It is useful to outline some of the later developments in the science of pendulum motion as they show the interaction of mathematics and experiment in scientific development, and the importance to science of the development of theoretical systems and of conceptual frameworks within which to interpret and interrogate nature. Both of these points are important for the teaching of pendulum motion.

Marin Mersenne and René Descartes corresponded at length about Galileo's pendulum theory; they established that, despite Galileo's claims, a pendulum's period was not independent of its amplitude. Mersenne, in his *Harmonie Universelle* (1636), relates an experiment in which two identical pendulums are set swinging, one with an amplitude of two feet and one with an amplitude of one inch. He claims (Proposition XIX) that the former is retarded by one oscillation after the passage of thirty oscillations. In the following proposition he says that there is a difference in period for a pendulum of eight pounds and one of half a pound. Descartes suspected that pendulum swings were not isochronous. In one of many letters to Mersenne he says that:

I believe that the vibrations will be a little slower toward the end than at the beginning, because the movement, having less force, does not overcome the hindrance of the air so easily. However about this I am not entirely certain. (*Works* vol. I, p. 77)

It was the Dutch mathematician Christiaan Huygens who investigated these empirical claims, and refined Galileo's theoretical object so that the empirical findings were consistent with them. Huygens's magnum opus was the *Horologium Oscillatorium* (1673, trans. R. J. Blackwell 1986). He recognized the problem identified by Descartes—"the simple pendulum does not naturally provide an accurate and equal measure of time since its wider motions are observed to be slower than its narrower motions" (Blackwell 1986, p. 11). Huygens changed two central features of Galileo's theoretical object, namely the claims that period varied with length, and that the circle was the tautochronous curve (the curve on which bodies falling freely under the influence of gravity reach the nadir at the same time regardless of where they were released). In contrast Huygens showed mathematically that period varied with the square root of length, and that the cycloid (the curve traced out by a point on the circumference of a wheel as it rolls) was the tautochronous curve.[10] He then devised a way (cycloid laminates at the fulcrum) of making Galileo's pendulum swing not in a circle, but in an arc of a cycloid. Once this was done the period did become independent of the amplitude and the way was cleared—once he found an effective measure for the length of a cycloid pendulum and its centre of oscillation—for the construction of reliable pendulum clocks.[11] Huygens provides the following account of his discovery of the cycloid as the tautochronous curve:

> We have discovered a line whose curvature is marvelously and quite rationally suited to give the required equality to the pendulum. . . . This line is the path traced out in air by a nail which is fixed to the circumference of a rotating wheel which revolves continuously. The geometers of the present age have called this line a cycloid and have carefully investigated its many other properties. Of interest to us is what we have called the power of this line to measure time, which we found not by expecting this but only by following in the footsteps of geometry. (Blackwell 1986, p. 11)

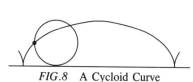

FIG.8 A Cycloid Curve

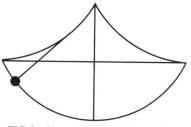

FIG.9 Huygens's Cycloid Pendulum

This development by Huygens of the theory of the pendulum is an example that fits objectivist accounts of scientific development. Despite Galileo's personal brilliance, he nevertheless did not appreciate or work out correctly the implications of the theoretical object that he himself created. The theory had unseen or unintended consequences that needed others to work out or discover. Huygens discovered that the cycloid was the vital tautochronous curve, not the circle, by "following in the footsteps of geometry," a guide that Aristotelian philosophy distrusted in physical affairs. This discovery of the tautochronous curve had very little to do with sensory input. Its justification had even less to do with sense data or other putative empirical foundations for belief so extolled by positivists.

A Comparison: Millikan and Ehrenhaft

The debate between Galileo and del Monte—Galileo convinced that his theoretical object identified a fundamental feature of the world, and del Monte, driven by the facts of the matter, a convinced empiricist—has been often replayed in the history of science. One particularly clear and well documented example is the twenty-year debate that occurred between the young Robert Millikan at the Californian Institute of Technology and the renowned Felix Ehrenhaft of the University of Vienna. This was the debate begun in 1908 over the putative unitary charge of the electron, and concluded in 1927 when Millikan, in victory, received the Nobel Prize for his determination of the charge, *e*.

Millikan set up a model on the assumption that there was a single smallest electric charge, that of the electron. This was the electrical version of atomism, the doctrine that there was in nature a smallest particle from which all bodies are constituted. Millikan was working in a research tradition that went back to G. J. Stoney's postulation of an atomic unit of electricity. J. J. Thomson made a significant contribution to this research tradition when, in 1897, he showed that cathode rays were made of such atomic units, which he called "corpuscles," and then went on to determine the ratio of *e*/*m* for them.

Ehrenhaft on the contrary believed that there was no such minimum charge and that particles existed which had charges that were fractions of that of the electron. He followed Mach in opposing atomism. He saw it as a philosophical doctrine superimposed upon nature, an arbitrary attempt to make nature fit our own limited ideas. Ehrenhaft was the del Monte-like experimentalist whose work on Brownian motion had been widely acclaimed. He took extreme objection to an early comment of Millikan, who said of one of his (Millikan's) aberrant findings:

> I have discarded one uncertain and unduplicated observation, apparently upon a singly charged drop, which gave a value of the charge on the drop some 30 percent lower than the final value of *e*. (Holton 1978b, p. 28)

Ehrenhaft and his associates were busy doing experiments that yielded all sorts of fractional charge readings. He called these subelectronic charges, and maintained that they existed in nature, and were not just an artifact of experimental procedure. Millikan was getting a similar range of results, but instead of believing that this was nature revealing itself, he wrote Galilean-like comments, such as the following, over his result sheet:

very low something wrong; . . . this is almost exactly right; . . . possibly a double drop; . . . something the matter; . . . publish this beautiful result; . . . no something wrong with the thermometer. (Holton 1978b, p. 70)

While Millikan received the Nobel Prize and recognition as one of the foremost physicists in the history of science, Ehrenhaft suffered the fate of del Monte, with his work becoming an obscure footnote to the achievements of a great figure. What can be learnt from this?

Some commentators, having seen Millikan's notebooks, criticize him for failing to be scientific and objective. These critics do not recognise the distinction between the protophysical domain of a science and its empirical domain. In Millikan's case we have another clear example of the theoretical objects governing the empirical object and the interpretation of its measurement. As with Galileo, there is nothing unscientific about this; it may not accord with empiricist orthodoxy, but this orthodoxy champions del Monte and Ehrenhaft, not Galileo and Millikan.

Some Epistemological Lessons

At the outset of this chapter it was said that historical and philosophical study of Galileo's analysis of pendulum motion not only assists with pedagogical matters, but also clarifies central epistemological issues in science; the pendulum is a window onto the nature of the scientific revolution. Before turning to the pedagogical matters, a few of the central epistemological aspects will be amplified, beginning with the key distinction between real bodies and their representation within a theoretical system that works on them. This is at the heart of the differences between empiricist accounts of science and nonempiricist, objectivist, accounts. This distinction also sheds light on practical teaching matters, and on debates about the nature of human learning.

Real versus Theoretical Objects

Galileo's theory of mechanics provides the definitions of key concepts—momentum, acceleration, average speed, instantaneous speed, weight, impetus, force, point mass and so on. These concepts were hard-won, and are utilized in his account of pendulum motion. Acceleration, for instance, was initially defined by Galileo, and by all his predecessors, as rate of increase of speed with respect to distance traversed—a natural enough definition given that accelerating bodies increase speed over both time and distance, and that the passage of distance was both more measurable and more easily experienced by sight and feel. It was only in his middle age that he changed the definition to the modern one of rate of change of speed with respect to time elapsed. Without such a change of definition, the laws of fall would not have been discovered.

These interlocking concepts formed the *conceptual structure* of Galileo's physics, and provided the meaning of key words. This is Galileo's "world on paper," or prototheoretical system. But there is also a real world of material and other objects which exists apart from his, or anyone else's, theorizing about it. But we can see in Galileo's practice, if not in his words, a most important intervening layer emerging between theory and the brute world—the realm of theorized objects. These are natural objects *as conceived and described by* the relevant theoretical concepts.

Planets and falling apples have color, texture, irregular surfaces, heat, solidity and any number of other properties and relations. But when they become the subject matter of mechanics they are merely point masses with specified accelerations; when thus conceptualized and delimited, they are no longer natural objects, but theoretical objects. In a similar way, when apples are considered by economists they become theoretical objects of a different sort—commodities with specific exchange values. When botanists consider apples they create yet other theoretical objects. For Galileo a sphere of lead on the end of a length of rope swinging in air, when it is considered by his mechanical theory, becomes a pendulum conceived as a point mass at the end of a weightless chord suspended from a frictionless fulcrum moving in a void. (John Ziman 1978 chap. 4 is illuminating.)

Historically, grasping the significance of this abstractive or theoretical domain between conceptual schemes and the natural world has not been easy. Pierre Duhem made a similar distinction to that being made here, but did so in terms of concrete and abstract objects. He observed that:

> It is impossible to leave outside the laboratory door the theory that we wish to test, for without theory it is impossible to regulate a single instrument or to interpret a single reading; we have seen that in the mind of the physicist there are constantly two sorts of apparatus; one is the concrete apparatus in glass and metal manipulated by him, the other is the schematic and abstract apparatus which theory substitutes for the concrete and on which the physicist does his reasoning. (Duhem 1906/1954, p. 182)

Experiment

Galileo did not just develop a system of rational mechanics in the same way as the medieval scientists who constructed mathematical models of physical systems and then proceeded no further.[12] In contrast, Galileo's theoretical objects are the means for engaging with and working in the natural world. For him the theoretical object provides a plan for interfering with the material world, and where need be, for making it in the image of the theoretical. When del Monte tells Galileo that he has done an experiment with balls in an iron hoop and the balls do not behave as Galileo asserts, Galileo replies that the hoop must not have been smooth enough, that the balls were not spherical enough and so on. These suggestions for improving the experiment are driven by the theoretical object that Galileo has already constructed. This tells Galileo the things that have to be corrected in the experiment. Without the theoretical object he would not know whether to correct for the color of the ball, the material of the hoop, the diameter of the hoop, the mass of the ball, the time of day or any of a hundred other factors. It is this aspect of Galileo's work which moved Immanuel Kant to say that with Galileo "a light broke upon all students of nature," because he demonstrated that:

> Reason has insight only into that which it produces after a plan of its own . . . It is thus that the study of nature has entered on the secure path of a science, after having for so many centuries been nothing but a process of merely random groping. (*Critique of Pure Reason*, preface to second edition)

Galileo was a technician and an experimentalist. He put great effort into devising, making, and popularizing novel technical instruments. He was responsible for creating the *pulsilogium*, the *bilancetta*, the *compasso di proporzione*, the *thermoscopium*, the telescope, and he drew workable plans for the pendulum clock (Bedini 1986). He also measured and made calculations of pendulum swings. Stillman Drake has unearthed these in the Galilean manuscripts at Florence (Drake 1990, ch. 1). But his measurements and experimentation were directed; they were measurements of behavior in circumstances dictated by his theoretical conceptualizations. Further, as we have seen in his debate with del Monte, the theoretical conceptualization enabled him to identify "accidental" departures from the ideal. Once this was done, allowances could be made, and the experiment refined.

Concept Development

For Aristotle, a person looks at something or at a process and the mind abstracts an essence which typifies or characterizes the phenomenon. The intellectual process is called abstraction. The British empiricists Hume and Locke modify Aristotle's account when they discuss the origin of ideas or concepts: first we have sensations, and then faint images of these are written in the mind. This is more a reflection theory of ideas than an Aristotelian abstraction theory. Galileo's analysis does not fit this scheme at all. As one commentator has said:

> the concept, say, of a "material point with a determinate mass" does not constitute the common essence of apples, planets and projectiles. It is rather a concept of the conceptual scheme of physics which is *produced* together with the other concepts of this system and which is, precisely, *attributed* to such real objects so that their movement may be accounted for by this system as a whole. (Baltas 1988, p. 216)

Looking at the bob of a pendulum could never, as Hume and Locke suggest, produce a faint image of a material point. Nor does watching an accelerating body produce the concept of acceleration as rate of change of velocity with respect to time elasped. This consideration has pedagogical consequences both for the acquisition of concepts and for conceptual change, some of which are discussed in Schecker (1992). This matter is somewhat akin to Popper's recognition that:

> In science it is *observation* rather than perception which plays the decisive part. But observation is a process in which we play an intensely *active* part. . . . An observation is always preceded by a particular interest, a question, or a problem— in short, by something theoretical. (Popper 1972, p. 342)

Inductivism

The pendulum motion episode shows the limitations of inductivism as an account of scientific method. Manifestly, Galileo did not induce his "marvellous properties," or laws, of pendulum motion from looking at various pendulums—balls in hoops, chandeliers, swings, mechanical regulators, cork and iron bobs on strings and so on—and then generalize towards universal statements of what he saw in the particular instances. One enthusiast for inductivism has commented that:

> For him [Galileo], the facts based on them [observations] were treated as facts, and not related to some preconceived idea. . . . The facts of observation might or might not fit into an acknowledged scheme of the universe, but the important thing, in Galileo's opinion, was to accept the facts and build the theory to fit them. (H. D. Anthony in Chalmers 1976, p. 2)

This was, on the contrary, the methodology of the Aristotelians, for whom the facts of experience were the starting points for science and who unsuccessfully urged Galileo to be true to the facts; it was also the methodology of Descartes, who concluded that because the facts were so messy and erratic no science of pendulum motion was possible. What was seen to happen in the world was important, but it did not have the importance that inductivism attributed to it. This is well recognised by I. E. Drabkin, who said of Aristotelian mechanics, that it was "impeded not by insufficient observation and excessive speculation but by too close an adherence to the data of observation . . . an adherence to the phenomena of nature so close as to prevent the abstraction therefrom of the ideal case" (Drabkin 1938, pp. 69, 82).

Falsificationism

Falsificationism, the view that the essence of science is to reject theories that are contradicted by the facts, which is the methodological position associated with Karl Popper, fares not much better than inductivism when dealing with the pendulum example. Inductivism and falsificationism are two sides of the same empiricist coin, so it is to be expected that where the first fails the second will also fail. Galileo acknowledged that there was an inconsistency between his laws and the behavior of pendulums. He certainly did not follow the advice of the writers of the Australian *Web of Life* textbook, who say that scientists must "give up any hypothesis, however much beloved, as soon as facts are shown to be opposed to it." Upholders of this simple version of the Popperian doctrine might better say, as John Henry Cardinal Newman did, when told in 1870 of the proclamation of the doctrine of papal infallibility: "I believe in the dogma but I cannot reconcile it with the facts of history."

In discussing falsificationism one does need to be careful. Karl Popper was not the simple falsificationist that many make him out to be: he said often enough that "criticism of his alleged views was widespread and highly successful, but criticism of his actual views was much rarer." In his first major publication, *The Logic of Scientific Discovery* (1934/1959), he sanctioned the creation of auxiliary hypotheses to rescue theories which were apparently refuted by the evidence, provided these hypotheses were not *ad hoc*. In 1948 he acknowledged that: "Testing proceeds by taking the theory to be tested and combining it with all possible sorts of initial conditions as well as with other theories, and then comparing the resulting predictions with reality" (Popper 1972, p. 360). But after recognizing that falsification is more complicated than many might hope, Popper reasserts the core of his position as one in which: "The proper reaction to falsification is to search for new theories which seem likely to offer us a better grasp of the facts" (Popper 1972, p. 360).

There are at least two questions for this view when applied to Galileo's analysis of pendulum motion. First, what were the facts that were to be so decisive for theory? Second, was it these same facts that a new theory should seek to explain? The relevant facts were not naturally occurring events or episodes: the swinging chandelier would not have been regarded by Galileo as a satisfactory test of his theory; nor would contrived situations such as del Monte's rolling balls in iron hoops. Galileo invents lots of facts—the supposed thousands of oscillations in which large and small amplitude swings (180° versus 5°) are not seen to differ by a "fraction of a vibration"—but these are not what Popper had in mind. However, just about any experimental situation, taken at face value, would falsify Galileo's account, and he plainly does not rectify his theory in the light of such outcomes. Galileo insulates his theory against these recalcitrant facts by detailing *ceteris paribus*, "other things being equal," clauses for the applicability of the theory. So the actual facts were very qualified, they were always suggestive rather than definitive; and ultimately they were not even very suggestive—as the simple fact that most pendulums ceases to swing after a few dozen oscillations is plainly inconsistent with the law of isochronic motion.

Popper also urges that new theories be sought to take account of the supposedly disconfirming facts. This advice was not followed and, if it had been, the research programme started by Galileo and continued by Huygens would have been thwarted in infancy. There is interaction between theoretical development and experiment. Huygens did mathematically alter Galileo's theory partly in the light of recalcitrant observations; but these alterations were refinements of the theory (the cycloid instead of the circle as the tautochronous curve), and the observations were a result of applying the earlier apparently refuted theory. The clearly reformist version of falsificationism proposed by Popper in his 1972 *Objective Knowledge* comes closest to accommodating the history of the analysis of pendulum motion. Imre Lakatos's even more reformist version of falsificationism, his Methodology of Scientific Research Programs, perhaps best fits the example (Lakatos 1970).

Scientific Laws

The regularity account of scientific law has been popular ever since David Hume's 1739 *Treatise on Human Nature*, where he supposedly demolished the necessitarian view of law. For Hume, and those following him, scientific laws state constant relations between observables, they state what is uniformly seen to be the case. The pendulum laws present an overwhelming problem for the Humean account: the regularities do not occur. Under very refined experimental conditions—small oscillations, heavy weights, minimum air and fulcrum resistance—they almost occur, but "almost occurring" is not what regularity accounts of law are about. Moreover, it was a commitment to the truth of the seemingly disproved laws that enabled the approximate conditions for the law's applicability to be devised. That is, the truth of the law is a presupposition for identifying approximations to it, and for identifying when some behavior is to be seen as "almost law-like." But scientific laws are not about the "almost law-like" behavior that we might regularly see in refined conditions, it is about what would happen if a host of conditions, some of them impossible to meet, were actually met. Norwood Hanson has expressed the matter well:

> The great unifications of Newton, Clerk Maxwell, Einstein, Bohr and Schrödinger, were pre-eminently discoveries of terse formulae from which descriptions and explanations of diverse phenomena could be generated. They were not discoveries of undetected regularities. (Hanson 1959, p. 300)

Objectivism

Galileo's analysis of pendulum motion supports nonempiricist views of scientific theory as have been developed by Althusser and Balibar (1970),

Baltas (1988), Chalmers (1976), Lewin (1931), Mittelstrass (1972), Sneed (1979), Ziman (1978) and Suchting (1986). These views are all opposed to empiricist understandings of scientific theory. Firstly, they emphasize the separation of cognitive or theoretical discourse from the real world: the world is neither created by the discourse (as in idealism), nor does it somehow create the discourse (as in various reflection theories), nor does it anchor or provide foundations for the discourse (as in empiricism and positivism). Theoretical discourse and the world are each autonomous. Secondly, the views distinguish within theory between (a) the conceptual foundations of the discourse containing the definitions of theoretical and observational terms (there is no decisive distinction made between these kinds of terms); (b) the conceptual structure of the theory which is the elaboration and manipulation of the basic concepts by techniques (mathematical and logical) that produce the structure of the theory (Galileo's distant theorems and propositions); (c) the theoretical objects of the theory which are the real or imagined objects in the world as they are conceived and described by the theory—the balance treated as a uniform line with parallel weights suspended from it, the pendulum treated as a point mass on a weightless string and so forth.

The concepts and techniques of a theoretical system enable natural events to become scientific events, and as such they can then be considered and analyzed by the scientist in accord with the canons of the appropriate theory. It is as a *scientific* event that they are stripped of their everyday guises and become data or evidence in theoretical debate. The properties ascribed to these theoretical objects are derived from the conceptual foundations of the theory: instantaneous velocity, momentum, acceleration and so on. Likewise, some properties cannot be ascribed because well-developed conceptual foundations exclude them; the particular theoretical discourse does not contain the concepts. Thus Galilean discourse excluded *levitas* as a property of bodies, whereas in Aristotelianism it is one of the fundamental properties of bodies. Eclecticism is a common problem with underdeveloped conceptual foundations, as is the carryover of everyday and ideological concepts into the conceptual foundations of science—the use in science of everyday notions of acceleration, of species, of intentionality or of atoms.

The conceptual foundations of a theoretical discourse or research program, to use Lakatos's terminology, are slowly built up and refined in a process of theoretical production; they generally contain elements, assumptions and aspects of preexisting conceptual schemes, and also elements of commonsense understandings. Despite Galileo's break with so much of the Aristotelian tradition, his conceptual scheme retained Aristotelian notions of natural movement (accelerated movement without an external force) and also circular inertia. It is only very mature theoretical discourses that manage to identify all extraneous elements within them and then either redefine or jettison them. And of course the same concept often has an everyday meaning alongside its theoretical meaning, which can be a cause of confusion. As Baltas points out:

Each concept has, as it were, two faces resembling in that respect a coin. For example "force" is both the cause of "acceleration" and what we éxercise when we try to push some body; and "acceleration" means simultaneously both the "derivative of instantaneous velocity over time" and what we sense when our car speeds up. (Baltas 1988, p. 214)

Educationally, one should not strive to *replace* the commonsense concept with the scientific (a mistake of much constructivist and "conceptual change" teaching), but rather to have children recognize when one concept is appropriate and when the other is appropriate. A child's idea of animal is something that is large and usually having four legs. The scientific idea includes ants and flies. One is not more correct than the other, it is only more, or less, correct in its appropriate domain. To say "there is an animal in the tent," in virtue of there being a fly in the tent, is not to be scientific; it is to be mistaken about when scientific, and when everyday conceptualizations, are required. The French philosopher Gaston Bachelard (Bachelard 1934/1984, 1940/1968) has discussed at length the problems caused by confusing commonsense and scientific concepts that share the same name—it is like, as someone said of British and Americans, "two people divided by a common language." This confusion is one aspect of what Bachelard refers to as "epistemological obstacles" to the development of science. Some of the educational implications of this work have been developed by Jean-Pascal Souque (1988).

The foregoing philosophical remarks on theoretical objects, experiment, concept development, inductivism, falsificationism, law and objectivism are meant to suggest how the Galileo-Huygens analysis of pendulum motion can be used to illustrate key debates about the philosophy of science, and how the pendulum episode better supports certain positions in these debates than other positions. Furthermore, the remarks are made because these philosophical lessons are important for understanding the history of the pendulum motion debate—why people took certain positions, why evidence convinced some and did not convince others and so on. Finally, the remarks are made because both historical and philosophical understanding is important if the episode is to be used in teaching the contemporary science of pendulum motion. Other episodes could have been chosen from fields as diverse as genetics, combustion theory, atomic structure, astronomy, evolutionary theory and so on. In all cases, comparable comments about the interplay of observation, experimental evidence, mathematics and theory could be made.

Some Pedagogical Lessons

We know from Galileo's own hand how central his account of pendulum motion was to the establishment of his new physics, which enabled the Copernican view to eventually triumph over the entrenched Aristotelian worldview supported by common sense and endorsed by culture and the Church. Without this physics there was no effective counter to the mass of sensory evidence in favour of a stationary earth. With the new physics, Copernicus's revolutionary, heliocentric, astronomical system was able to be established. This in turn led to the development of the modern worldview which has transformed human culture and self-understanding.[13] As refined by Huygens, the pendulum became the long-sought-after, accurate and reliable measure of the passage of time. Its use in accurately determining longitude at sea was vital for the great voyages of exploration and for the development of intercontinental commerce and exploitation. A convenient clock also wrought great changes in personal, social and industrial life. The clock became a common metaphor in literature, religion and philosophy; it began to affect people's worldviews.[14] Unlike cloud chambers, electron microscopes, linear accelerators and so on, pendulums are cheap, available and can be studied with a minimum of equipment. On historical, cultural, and practical grounds one would expect the humble pendulum and its marvellous properties to figure prominently in science education programs.

However, when the pendulum appears it is usually a mere shadow of its historical self. The PSSC physics text repeats the story of Galileo looking at the swinging chandelier during a sermon to establish its isochrony. The pendulum then disappears without trace. In the Harvard Project Physics text, the excellent and most contextual of texts, the equation

$$T = 2\pi \sqrt{l/g}$$

is abruptly introduced for the period of the pendulum, and students are told "you may learn in a later physics course how to derive the formula." The influential contemporary curriculum proposal of the US National Science Teachers Association—*Scope, Sequence and Coordination*—highlights the pendulum to illustrate its claims for sequencing and coordination in science: yet nowhere in its discussion of the pendulum are history, philosophy or technology mentioned![15]

The historical experiments can be done very easily. When students are asked to record and interpret what they see, they will see some variant of what del Monte, Mersenne, and Descartes saw: pendulums that come to a halt, pendulums of different weight that lose parity in oscillation, and so on. The process of getting from this data to the above formula can be stimulating and informative. And it can be the occasion for introducing some of the history of Galileo's struggles with del Monte that has been canvassed above. Students can relive the history, and both appreciate and learn from the arguments of the key players. They can see the dependence of science upon mathematics, particularly geometry, and something of its interactions with philosophy.

The example of pendulum motion also focuses and clarifies issues raised for science teachers by the numerous studies of children's learning and thought processes—their alternative frameworks (Hewson 1985), preconceptions (Osborne & Freyberg 1985) and misconceptions (Novak 1983). In the pendulum case did del Monte, Mersenne, Descartes have misconceptions? In one sense they did not (the pendulum behaved roughly as they said it did), but in another sense they clearly did have misconceptions (they did not share the conceptions of Galileo, which became scientific orthodoxy). The important thing for students is that they be introduced to the conceptual discourse of Galileo and contemporary physics. It is with respect to this discourse, or to the theoretical objects of this discourse, that they have misconceptions, it is not with respect to the behavior of the natural world. To confuse matters by saying they do not have misconceptions because the pendulums behave as they (and del Monte) think they do, can lead to problems. It is this commonsense view of the world which science education attempts to change. The task is not easy.

To expect students to learn anything Newtonian by playing around with objects is to underestimate the epistemological revolution inaugurated by Galileo and Newton; and also to underestimate the pedagogical problems in getting children to comprehend the classical scientific worldview. Galileo's conceptual scheme does not emerge by playing around with objects, it emerges by intellectual production using borrowed concepts, and learnt logical and mathematical techniques. There is an important educational role for "messing about," as Hawkings has described it, for being acquainted with the phenomena, as Mach demanded, or for tinkering around, as Feynman has suggested, but this role is not that of producing in itself contemporary scientific concepts and understanding. Teaching does this.

It is notorious how poorly science students and teachers understand pendulum motion. Most teachers and some students can repeat the four laws of pendulum motion, but their conceptualization of the movement is weak. Frederick Reif has conducted revealing studies on this conceptualization. Students and teachers were given Figure 10 for the pendulum's movement and asked to write in the acceleration of the bob at each of the points A, B, C, D, E. Eighty percent of physics students get the answer wrong.[16] The correct answer to the question is given in Figure 11.

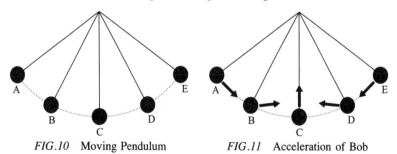

FIG.10 Moving Pendulum   *FIG.11* Acceleration of Bob

One can appreciate the intellectual problems involved in getting the correct answer. At the bob's lowest point, when its tangential speed is greatest, its acceleration is vertically upwards. When the bob is at its top and apparently stationary, it is nevertheless accelerating along the radius of its arc. The first diagram represents the real pendulum, the second diagram represents the theoretical pendulum, or the pendulum as theorized. Being able to represent the second correctly depends upon a very sophisticated grasp of the relevant theoretical system. Such a system is not something generated by looking at, or observing, the first object. This is relevant to di Sessa's remark, on the failure of standard discovery learning, that:

> it seems that very few subjects, if any, had learned much characteristically Newtonian from dealing with the everyday world . . . thought experiments might be more useful than "playing around." (di Sessa 1982, p. 62)

The classroom problems encountered when the theoretical object of science is discordant with everyday experience of material objects is nicely illustrated in the following classroom exchange between a teacher, who has previously introduced the concept of acceleration, and three students who are clearly struggling to apply the concept to the motion of a body thrown upwards, the pendulum situation.

Teacher: Suppose I toss a ball straight up into the air like this (*demonstrates*). What is the ball's acceleration at the top of the trajectory?

Student 1: Zero.

Student 2: Yeah, zero.

T: Why is it zero?

S1: Well, at the top the ball stops moving, so it must be zero.

T: OK. If I place the ball on the table so that it does not move, is it acclerating?

S2: No. It is not moving.

T: What if I roll the ball across the table so that it moves at a constant velocity (*demonstrates*). Is the ball accelerating in this case?

S1 & S2: Yeah.

Student 3: No way! If the ball is rolling at a constant speed it does not have any acceleration because its speed does not change.

T: So it appears that an object can have a zero acceleration if it is standing still or if it is moving at a constant velocity. Let's reconsider the case where the ball is at the top of its trajectory (*demonstrates again*). What is the ball's acceleration when it is at the top?

> *S3:* It would be zero because the ball is standing still at the top. It's not moving—it has to turn around.

> *S2:* I think it might be accelerating because it gets going faster and faster.

> *S1:* Yeah, but that doesn't happen until it gets going again. When it is standing still it is not accelerating. (Mestre 1991, p. 58)

Conclusion

The pendulum case has been introduced in this chapter as an example where the history and philosophy of science can contribute even to routine science education. It provides a wonderful opportunity to learn about science at the same time that one is learning the subject matter of science. With good, HPS-informed teaching the pendulum motion case enables students to appreciate the transition from commonsense and empirical descriptions characteristic of Aristotelian science, to the abstract, idealized and mathematical descriptions characteristic of the scientific revolution. The pendulum provides a manageable, understandable, and straightforward way into scientific thinking and away from everyday and empirical thinking; it shows at the same time how scientific, idealized thinking nevertheless is connected with the world through controlled experiment.

The interplay of experience, mathematics and experiment in Galileo's pendulum analysis is repeated in his account of projectile motion. Giovanni Renieri, a gunner who attempted to apply Galileo's theory to his craft, complained in 1647 to Torricelli that his guns did not behave according to Galileo's predictions. Torricelli replied that his teacher spoke the language of geometry and was not bound by any empirical result (Segre 1991 p. 43). Renieri, as with del Monte, is exposing one of the basic questions about the scientific revolution and modern science: how does science relate to experience and to mathematics? Students can be encouraged to grapple with an answer to this.

Finally, it is clear that "contextual" science, as suggested here, is not a cop-out from serious, or hard science, but the reverse. To understand what happened in the history of science takes effort. Further, it is appealing to students. A frequent refrain from intelligent students who do not go on with study in the sciences is that "science is too boring, we only work out problems." The history of human efforts to understand pendulum motion is far from boring: it is peopled by great minds, their debates are engaging, and the history provides a story line on which to hang the complex theoretical development of science. As well as improved understanding of science, students taught in a contextual way can better understand the nature of science, and have something to remember long after the equation for the period of a pendulum is forgotten.

CHAPTER 7

Constructivism and Science Education

Pope John XXIII spoke of the need for *aggiornamento* (renewal) in the Church: science education has had its share of such calls. Sometimes these calls are for renewal at a tactical or local level, other times they are calls for renewal at a strategic or global level. At various times new teaching methods (group learning, computer-assisted instruction, cooperative learning, inquiry learning), curricula (STS, structure of the discipline, integrated), laboratory procedures and assessment techniques are advanced as the answer to various pedagogical or participation problems in science education. Constructivism is the major plank in the contemporary *aggiornamento* proposals, it is a strategic program that has implications for various tactical-level reforms. In 1991 the president of the US National Association for Research in Science Teaching (NARST) said: "A unification of thinking, research, curriculum development, and teacher education appears to now be occurring under the theme of constructivism . . . there is a lack of polarised debate" (Yeany 1991, p. 1). Peter Fensham, a well-placed observer, has remarked that "The most conspicuous psychological influence on curriculum thinking in science since 1980 has been the constructivist view of learning" (Fensham 1992, p. 801). As the overall claim of this book is that the history and philosophy of science contribute to the theory and practice of science teaching, constructivism will be examined to see how HPS can contribute to debates in the theory side of science education.

Central to constructivism is a view about the nature of human knowledge, and more particularly of scientific knowledge; a view about the origins, transmission mechanisms, and validation procedures of scientific knowledge. Historical and philosophical investigation can shed light upon these constructivist claims. This chapter is critical of constructivism, but the book's thesis is confirmed merely by showing that the history and philosophy of science is *relevant* to the appraisal of constructivist claims. The book's thesis does not require agreement with the critical conclusions here advanced. Many prominent and scholarly constructivists appeal to the history and philosophy of science to establish their epistemological and ontological claims. The crucial point is that the history and philosophy of science are recognized as important by both sides of the constructivist debate.

What Is Constructivism?

There are basically two major traditions of constructivism. The first is psychological constructivism, originating with Jean Piaget's account of children's learning as a process of personal, individual, intellectual construction arising from their activity in the world. This tradition bifurcates into, on the one hand, the more personal, subjective tradition of Piaget that can be seen in von Glasersfeld's work, and on the other hand, into the social constructivism of the Russian Vygotsky and his followers, who stress the importance of language communities for the cognitive constructions of individuals, as can be seen in the work of Duckworth (1987) and Lave (1988).

The second major tradition is sociological constructivism, originating with Emile Durkheim and augmented by sociologists of culture such as Peter Berger and, more recently, by sociologists of science in the Edinburgh School such as Barry Barnes, David Bloor, Harry Collins and Bruno Latour. This sociological tradition maintains that scientific knowledge is socially constructed and vindicated, and it investigates the circumstances and dynamics of science's construction. In contrast to Piaget and Vygotsky, it ignores the individual psychological mechanisms of belief construction, and focuses upon the extraindividual social circumstances which, it claims, determine the beliefs of individuals; the individual becomes a sort of "black box" for the theory. Extreme forms of sociological constructivism claim that science is nothing but a form of human cognitive construction comparable to artistic or literary construction, and having no particular claim to truth. The claims of sociological constructivism, and its contentious and revolutionary implications for science education, are examined in Slezak (1994)

Psychological constructivism inspires reform programs, infuses textbooks, is the topic of major international conferences and of numerous journal articles and papers. One 1992 bibliography lists five hundred constructivist articles, another literature review itemizes twenty-five hundred constructivist-inspired publications (Pfundt & Duit 1991). The doctrine underpins major research programs in science education, such as those conducted at Leeds University, the University of Waikato, Florida State University and the University of British Columbia. Constructivism also influences and is influenced by the prolific misconceptions or alternative framework studies in childrens' science learning. Sixty papers were presented at the first international conference on this topic at Cornell University in 1983 (Helm & Novak 1983), 160 papers were presented at the second conference in 1987 (Novak 1987) and 250 at the third conference in 1993.[1]

Constructivist or interactive teaching methods are being widely advocated and developed.[2] They are contrasted on the one hand with the authoritarian, teacher-dominated, transmission model of science instruction, the model that Paulo Friere called the "banking model" of education; on the other hand, with inquiry methods that were championed as part of the curriculum reforms of the 1960s. Constructivist methods are meant to significantly transform the science classrooom. One important advocate has argued that:

> If the theory of knowing that constructivism builds upon were adopted as a working hypothesis, it could bring about some rather profound changes in the general practice of education. (Glasersfeld 1989, p. 135)

Constructivism is a heterogenous movement. A recent review has identified at least the following varieties: contextual, dialectical, empirical, information-processing, methodological, moderate, Piagetian, postepistemological, pragmatic, radical, realist, social and sociohistorical (Good, Wandersee & St Julien 1993). To this list could be added humanistic constructivism (Cheung & Taylor 1991) and didactic constructivism (Brink 1991). Constructivism, from its origins in developmental psychology, has spread to encompass, often naively, many domains of educational inquiry. The range of constructivist concerns can be seen in the subheadings of a recent science education article: "A constructivist view of learning," "A constructivist view of teaching," "A view of science," "Aims of science education," "A constructivist view of curriculum" and "A constructivist view of curriculum development" (Bell 1991). For many, constructivism has ceased being just a learning theory, or even an educational theory, but rather it constitutes a worldview or *Weltanschuung*, as suggested in remarks such as:

> To become a constructivist is to use constructivism as a referent for thoughts and actions. That is to say when thinking or acting, beliefs associated with constructivism assume a higher value than other beliefs. For a variety of reasons the process is not easy. (Tobin 1991, p. 1)

Epistemological Commitments

Constructivism emphasizes that science is a creative human endeavor which is historically and culturally conditioned, and that its knowledge claims are not absolute. This amounts to a truism shared by most schools of philosophy of science, but nevertheless it is worth restating. Beyond this truism, constructivism is committed to certain epistemological positions that are very contentious and, given the widespread educational influence of the doctrine, deserve close scrutiny. At its core constructivism has a subjectivist, empiricist, and personalist understanding of human knowledge, and consequently of scientific knowledge. As one of the most influential constructivists in science and mathematics education has put it:

> Knowledge is the result of an individual subject's constructive activity, not a commodity that somehow resides outside the knower and can be conveyed or

instilled by diligent perception or linguistic communication. (Glasersfeld 1990, p. 37)

Some extracts from various sources can give a sense of the epistemological and ontological positions adopted by constructivists in science education; they are all variants of a subject-centered, empiricist theory of knowledge:

> The fact that scientific knowledge enables us to cope does not justify the belief that scientific knowledge provides a picture of the world that corresponds to an absolute reality. (Glasersfeld 1989, p. 135)

> Although we may assume the existence of an external world we do not have direct access to it; science as public knowledge is not so much a discovery as a carefully checked construction. (Driver & Oldham 1986, p. 109)

> Put into simple terms, constructivism can be described as essentially a theory about the limits of human knowledge, a belief that all knowledge is necessarily a product of our own cognitive acts. We can have no direct or unmediated knowledge of any external or objective reality. We construct our understanding through our experiences, and the character of our experience is influenced profoundly by our cognitive lens. (Confrey 1990, p. 108)

> Constructivism is, logically, a post-epistemological position. The standard questions of epistemology cannot be answered—or even reasonably asked—from this perspective. Its premises suggest, rather, abandonment of traditional epistemological language. (Noddings 1990, p. 18)

Epistemology, even when supposedly abandoned, is vital to constructivism; indeed it drives constructivist educational theory and practice. Constructivists adopt most of the epistemological theses of postpositivist philosophy of science. These theses have been well laid out in Brown (1979) and Suppe (1977) and summarized in Garrison (1986). They include the following:

1) Observational statements are always dependent upon particular theoretical systems for their expression. There is a difference between "seeing" and "seeing as." The latter, propositional perception, is dependent upon language and theories.[3]
2) The distinction between observational and theoretical terms in a theory can only be made on pragmatic grounds, not on epistemic grounds.[4]
3) Observations themselves are theoretically dependent or determined; what people look for and notice is influenced by what they want to see or what they regard as relevant to an investigation.[5]
4) Theories are always underdetermined by empirical evidence, no matter how much such evidence is accumulated. For any set of data, any number of theories can be constructed to have that data as an implication; for any data points on a graph, any number of curves can be drawn through them.[6]
5) Theories are immune from empirical disproof or falsification because adjust-

ments can always be made to their auxillary assumptions to accommodate the discordant evidence; there can be no crucial experiments in science.[7]

Some constructivists move beyond postpositivism, which after all is still a modern position in that the major postpositivist philosophers believe in the search for truth, to the postmodernism of Lyotard, Rorty, Derrida and Barthes, where the very possibility of truth is abandoned, along with philosophy of science as usually understood (Darusnikova 1992).

Steven Lerman (1989), following Kilpatrick (1987) and earlier, von Glasersfeld, suggests that the core epistemological theses of psychological constructivism are:

1) Knowledge is actively constructed by the cognizing subject, not passively received from the environment.
2) Coming to know is an adaptive process that organizes one's experiential world; it does not discover an independent, preexisting world outside the mind of the knower.

Grayson Wheatley offers a nearly identical summary of the epistemological core of constructivism, saying:

The theory of constructivism rests on two main principles. . . . Principle one states that knowledge is not passively received, but is actively built up by the cognizing subject. . . . Principle two states that the function of cognition is adaptive and serves the organisation of the experiential world, not the discovery of ontological reality. . . . Thus we do not find truth but construct viable explanations of our experiences. (Wheatley 1991, p. 10)

Ontological Commitments

Constructivists often embrace an idealist ontology, or idealist theory about the existential status of scientific and everyday objects. Idealist ontology maintains that the world is created by and dependent upon human thought. Ernst von Glasersfeld's radical constructivism is the best-known idealist variant in educational circles. He says:

The realist believes his constructs to be a replica or reflection of independently existing structures, while the constructivist remains aware of the experiencer's role as originator of all structures . . . for the constructivist there are no structures other than those which the knower constitutes by his very own activity of coordination of experiential particles. (Glasersfeld 1987, p. 104)

And,

Radical constructivism, thus, is *radical* because it breaks with convention and develops a theory of knowledge in which knowledge does not reflect an "objective" ontological reality, but exclusively an ordering and organization of a world constituted by our experience. The radical constructivist has relinquished "metaphysical realism" once and for all. (Glasersfeld 1987, p. 109)

The ontological idealism here embraced by psychological constructivists mirrors and is encouraged by a comparable idealism common among new-style, post-Mertonian sociologists of science, particularly those associated with the Edinburgh school.[8] The influential sociologist Emile Durkheim had long ago written that:

If thought is to be freed, it must become the creator of its own object; and the only way to attain this goal is to accord it a reality that it has to make or construct itself. *Therefore, thought has as its aim not the reproduction of a given reality, but the construction of a future reality.* It follows that the value of ideas can no longer be assessed by reference to objects but must be determined by the degree of their utility, their more or less "advantageous" character. (Durkheim 1972, p. 251)

This idealism has been carried through by the Edinburgh School. Latour and Woolgar at one point say that "'out-there-ness' is the *consequence* of scientific work rather than its *cause*" (Latour & Woolgar 1986, p. 182). They go on to say that reality is the consequence rather than the cause of scientific construction. Other contributors to the Edinburgh program say such things as the planets are "cultural objects" (Lynch, Livingstone, & Garkinkel 1983). Harry Collins says that "the natural world has a small or nonexistent role in the construction of scientific knowledge" (Collins 1981, p. 3). Woolgar embraces idealism, saying that his research program "is consistent with the position of the idealist wing of ethnomethodology that there is no reality independent of the words (texts, signs, documents, and so on) used to apprehend it. In other words, reality is constituted in and through discourse" (Woolgar 1986, p. 312).

One can see here a confusion between ideas of real and theoretical objects, and between physical and intellectual activity. All realists acknowledge that reality does not just imprint itself on the mind of scientists or observers. Science does not deal with real objects *per se* but with real objects as they are depicted by the theoretical apparatus of science—falling colored balls become point masses with specified accelerations, fields of peas become phenotypes of particular descriptions, bubbling solutions become chemical equations and so on. An enormous amount of intellectual effort on the part of the tradition of scientists, and of individual scientists, goes into creating these theoretical objects with their concepts of forces, masses, genes, cells, species, equilibrium conditions and so on. The fact that the theoretical apparatus is humanly constructed, and that natural objects are only considered in theoretical dress, does not imply that the real objects are human creations, or that the real objects have no part in the appraisal of the scientific worth of the conceptual structures brought to bear upon them.

The common constructivist move is from uncontroversial, almost self-evident premises stating that knowledge is a human creation, that it is historically and culturally bound, and that it is not absolute, to the conclusion that knowledge claims are either unfounded or relativist. I shall argue that these premises do not entail the conclusions drawn from them, and further that the best aspects of constructivist teaching practice do not require such conclusions for their justification. But before doing so it is useful to discuss constructivist teaching practice, and to compare this with didacticism on the one hand, and with discovery learning on the other.

Constructivist Teaching Practice

There are many constructivist-inspired teaching methods. Driver and Oldham (1986) describe constructivist teaching as being characterized by a number of stages or steps:

1) *Orientation,* where pupils are given the opportunity to develop a sense of purpose and motivation for learning the topic.
2) *Elicitation,* during which pupils make their current ideas on the topic of the lesson clear. This can be achieved by a variety of activities, such as group discussion, designing posters or writing.
3) *Restructuring of Ideas*; this is the heart of the constructivist lesson sequence. It consists of a number of stages, including:
   Clarification and exchange of ideas during which pupils' meanings and language may be sharpened up by contrast with other, and possibly conflicting, points of view held by other students or contributed by the teacher.
   Construction of new ideas in the light of the above discussions and demonstrations. Students here can see that there are a variety of ways of interpretating phenomena or evidence.
   Evaluation of the new ideas either experimentally or by thinking through their implications. Students should try to figure out the best ways of testing the alternative ideas. Students may at this stage feel dissatisfied with their existing conceptions.
4) *Application of Ideas,* where pupils are given the opportunity to use their developed ideas in a variety of situations, both familiar and novel.
5) *Review* is the final stage in which students are invited to reflect back on how their ideas have changed by drawing comparisons between their thinking at the start of the lesson sequence, and their thinking at the end.

Driver and Oldham liken the final review stage to the learning-about-learning emphasis that Novak and Gowin (1984) claim should be a part of all teaching. That is, as they learn material, students should at the same time be learning something about the process of effective learning. More recently this has been referred to as "metacognition" (White & Gunstone

1989). Constructivist methods emphasize the engagement of the student in the learning process and the importance of prior knowledge or conceptualizations for new learning. Constructivist views of learning have been summarized by Driver and Bell (1986) as:

- Learning outcomes depend not only on the learning environment but also on the knowledge of the learner.
- Learning involves the construction of meanings. Meanings constructed by students from what they see or hear may not be those intended. Construction of a meaning is influenced to a large extent by our existing knowledge.
- The construction of meaning is a continuous and active process.
- Meanings, once constructed, are evaluated and can be accepted or rejected.
- Learners have the final responsibility for their learning.
- There are patterns in the types of meanings students construct due to shared experiences with the physical world and through natural language.

One persistent issue facing constructivist teachers is what happens when, as acknowledged, the child's constructed meaning differs from the one intended by the teacher? It is important to ascertain whether this is the case, and constructivists do well to remind us that not everything taught is caught. But the educational issue is to determine what follows from the recognition of this discrepancy: do we improve our teaching so as to eliminate the discrepancy, or do we accept the child's "misconception," "alternative framework" or just plain error? One prominent constructivist text advises seeking harmony between scientific and children's conceptions only up to that point where continued teaching bears adversely upon a child's self-esteem and their "feeling for what constitutes a sensible explanation" (Osborne & Freyberg 1985, p. 90).

One obvious question is whether or not these constructivist teaching techniques, and understanding of learning, are unique to constructivism. The answer is clearly no. Much of the best constructivist technique—with its emphasis on actively engaging the learner in their own learning and paying attention to the prior beliefs and conceptualizations of students—is at least as old as Socrates' interrogation of the slave boy in the *Meno*. Montaigne, in his delightful 1580 essay on "The Education of Children," observed that:

> Most tutors never stop bawling into our ears, as though they were pouring water into a funnel; and our task is only to repeat what has been told us. I should like the tutor to correct this practice. . . . Socrates and later Arcesilaus first had their disciples speak, and then they spoke to them. *The authority of those who teach is often an obstacle to those who want to learn.* [Cicero] . . . Let him not be asked for an account merely of the words of his lesson, but of its sense and substance, and let him judge the profit he has made not by the testimony of his memory, but by his life. (Montaigne 1580/1943, p. 11)

Driver and Oldham go on to say that constructivist curriculum planners cannot adopt the standard model of a passive student, an active teacher and the curriculum as something the latter transmits to the former. Two changes required are that the curriculum is not seen as a body of knowledge or skills but the program of activities from which such knowledge or skills can possibly be acquired or constructed; and also that there is to be a shift in the status of the curriculum from that which is determined prior to teaching (though negotiable between adults), to something with a problematic status.

These comments illustrate a problem with constructivism: it frequently overreaches itself. It uses claims about learning processes and developmental psychology (the original heart of constructivism) to establish wider educational and social positions. The curriculum, for instance, does not flow from learning theory alone. Learning theory may indicate *how* something should be taught, but *what* and how *much* should be taught to *whom* follow from different or additional considerations. Among these are judgments of social needs, personal needs, the relevant merits of different domains of knowledge and experience and finally, due political decision-making. Constructivists frequently ignore, or implicitly assume, such considerations in extrapolating from learning theory to curriculum matters, and to educational theory more generally.

The Driver and Oldham claims, for instance, do not cast much light upon the difficult matter of curriculum development. Their move from rejecting the curriculum as a body of knowledge or skills, to saying it is a program of activities from which such knowledge and skills might be acquired, does not do away with the need to specify such knowledge or skills. Further, to say that the curriculum has a problematic status is ambiguous. It may be problematic whether particular components are in the curriculum, but this is another truism, as there is always debate about the contents of the curriculum. But it does not follow from this truism that specific contents are problematic. It may be problematic whether geometry is included in high school mathematics, but it does not follow from this that geometry is problematic.

Other constructivists endorse the work of educational theorists such as Michael Apple, Henry Giroux and other critical theorists. But this is frequently done without awareness of the serious debate and opposition that this work has occasioned in the philosophy of education. Jane Gilbert, for instance, says: "There are many parallels between the literature on the development of critical pedagogy [and] the literature on constructivist learning" (Gilbert 1993, p. 35). This is in part because critical theorists "question the value of such concepts as individualism, efficiency, rationality and objectivity, and the forms of curriculum and pedagogy that have developed from these concepts" (Gilbert 1993, p. 20). This endorsement of critical education theory as the partner of constructivist learning theory is not surprising, but it is unfortunate. The philosophy, politics and language of critical theory have been seriously criticised.

Constructivism and Inquiry Learning

Constructivism attempts to steer a path between teacher-dominated instruction, the traditional didactic model of education, and student-led discovery learning, the progressive model of education. The contrast with extreme didacticism is reasonably clear-cut, the contrast with discovery or inquiry learning is less so. A large-scale review of US inquiry teaching has provided a description of the model inquiry classroom:

> Instruction . . . in inquiry classrooms reflects a variety of methodologies—discussions, investigative laboratories, student-initiated inquiries, lectures, debates. Teachers serve as role models in deliberating issues, in examining values, in admitting error, and in confronting areas of their own ignorance. The classroom atmosphere is conducive to inquiry. It is easy for students to ask questions. Risk-taking is encouraged and student responses are listened to, clarified, and deliberated upon with high frequency of student-student transactions. Classroom climate stimulates a thorough, thoughtful exploration of objects and events, rather than a need to finish the text. Inquiry transactions are concerned with students' developing meaning. Thus, in an inquiry classroom there is a time for doing . . . a time for reflection . . . a time for feeling . . . and a time for assessment. (Welch 1981, p. 35)

This classroom would pass equally as a model constructivist class.[9]

The failures of inquiry learning can be attributed to a number of factors, some of which are external, having to do with teacher education, provision of resources, school and society expectations, assessment demands, methods of implementation and so on.[10] But the central causes of failure are internal ones, having to do with a series of errors in the intellectual foundations of inquiry learning. It is worth detailing some of these errors, as the passage of time has by no means laid them to rest and, further, constructivists are in danger of reviving them. These core philosophical problems of inquiry learning can be illustrated from many sources. Consider, for instance, the following:

> Inquiry Training . . . gives the child a plan of operation that will help him to discover causal factors of physical change through his own initiative and control and not to depend on the explanations and interpretations of teachers or other knowledgeable adults. He learns to formulate hypotheses, to test them through a verbal form of controlled experimentation, and to interpret the results. In a nutshell, the program is aimed at making pupils more independent, systematic, empirical, and inductive in their approach to problems of science. (Suchman 1960, quoted in Sund & Trowbridge 1967, p. 37)

We see here a number of propositions, all of which are central to discovery learning, and all of which are either false or highly contentious.

1) That a child in isolation can discover and vindicate scientific truths.
2) That the language and concepts required for hypothesis development can be acquired independently of teachers or, more generally, independently of social interaction and participation in language communities.
3) That the testing of a hypothesis, and the interpretation of the test, is straightforward, and indeed simple enough even for elementary schoolchildren.
4) That scientific concepts are formed by abstraction from particulars.
5) That the scientific method is inductive.

The earlier chapter on Galileo's discovery of the laws of pendulum motion have illustrated the deficiency of all the foregoing claims. In general, such claims are more characteristic of Aristotelianism than they are of modern science. The earlier arguments for rejecting these positions will not be rehearsed here; suffice it to say that the claims made fail to recognize that:

1) Concepts do not emerge from sensory experience in the way assumed. This is the mistaken legacy not only of Aristotle, but of Locke, Hume and the British empiricists. Much has been written on this matter in the light of the "theory dependence of observation" thesis.
2) Scientific hypotheses are formulated using the conceptual foundations of scientific discourses, and these conceptual foundations have to be acquired by instruction and participation. As Paulo Freire, repeating Hegel, has said: "The 'we think' determines the 'I think' and not the reverse."
3) There is a qualitative difference between discovery in the sense of formulating and even supporting a hypothesis about some matter, and discovery in the sense of vindicating such a hypothesis. This traditionally has been called the difference between the context of discovery and the context of justification. The latter essentially requires public discourse and agreed canons of justification; it is not a Robinson Crusoe matter.
4) Discovery in any educationally serious sense implies knowledge claims, which in turn imply students having good reasons for their beliefs or hypotheses, and this in turn implies some account of what constitutes good reasons, which finally requires an epistemological position that cannot be purely individually generated. Such epistemology, or protoepistemology, arises from more or less sophisticated social interaction. A good reason for a putative knowledge claim might initially be, "I believe it," subsequently it might be "My mother told me," then it might be "The book says so," then it might be "This very well-received book says so" and so on with increasing epistemological sophistication.

The wholehearted adoption of inductivism by the science education community in the 1960s was as unfortunate as it was unnecessary. By the mid-1960s there was enough written in the history and philosophy of science to cast doubt upon the inductivist views so characteristic of inquiry learning.[11] The clear and detrimental effects of this separation of science education from the history and philosophy of science in the 1960s is a powerful argument for doing everything possible to prevent the separation recurring.[12] As James Rutherford remarked in 1964, teachers need some familiarity with the history and philosophy of their subject in order to teach it well, but also they need it in order to appraise the various edicts, policies and curricula that they are asked to implement. This reminder is especially timely given the influence of constructivism, with its frequent commitment to contentious, if not plain false, theses in philosophy of science.

Radical Constructivist Theory

Ernst von Glasersfeld[13] has had great influence on the development of constructivist theory in mathematics and science education in the past decade. He has published well over one hundred papers, book chapters and books in fields such as mathematics and science education, cybernetics, semantics and epistemology. His major papers are gathered together in his *The Construction of Knowledge* (1987). Von Glasersfeld is an advocate of "Radical Constructivism," a position based on "the practice of psycholinguistics, cognitive psychology, and . . . the works of Jean Piaget" (Glasersfeld 1990, p. 1). He gives perhaps the most systematic account of the epistemological and ontological underpinnings of psychological constructivism that can be found in the educational literature—see, in particular, his 1989 and 1992 papers. It is for this reason that his work will be examined here in some detail. The examination intends to illustrate some philosophical problems with constructivist theory, and more generally illustrate how the history and philosophy of science can bear upon important disputes in educational theory.

Von Glasersfeld sees himself in a constructivist tradition begun in the "18th century by Giambattista Vico, the first true constructivist" and continued by "Silvio Ceccato and Jean Piaget in the more recent past" (Glasersfeld 1987, p. 193). This tradition tends to undermine a large "part of the traditional view of the world," above all "the relation of knowledge and reality" (Glasersfeld 1987, p. 193). Von Glasersfeld concludes his discussion of Vico with the claim that, for constructivists:

> The word "knowledge" refers to a commodity that is radically different from the objective representation of an observer-independent world which the mainstream of the Western philosophical tradition has been looking for. Instead "knowledge" refers to conceptual structures that epistemic agents, given the range of present experience within their tradition of thought and language, consider *viable*. (Glasersfeld 1989, p. 124)

This can be referred to as von Glasersfeld's principle, or perhaps von Glasersfeld's philosophy (VGP), as it subsumes a number of epistemological and ontological theses, among which are the following:

1) Knowledge is not about an observer-independent world.
2) Knowledge does not represent such a world; correspondence theories of knowledge are mistaken.
3) Knowledge is created by individuals in a historical and cultural context.
4) Knowledge refers to individual experience rather than to the world.
5) Knowledge is constituted by individual conceptual structures.
6) Conceptual structures constitute knowledge when individuals regard them as viable in relationship to their experience; constructivism is a form of pragmatism.

There are some ambiguities and obscurities in this formulation, but there are other statements of VGP which illuminate some of these constitutive theses. In one place von Glasersfeld says:

> Our knowledge is useful, relevant, viable, or however we want to call the positive end of the scale of evaluation, if it stands up to experience and enables us to make predictions and to bring about or avoid, as the case may be, certain phenomena (i.e., appearances, events, experiences). . . . Logically, that gives us no clue as to how the "objective" world might be; it merely means that we know one viable way to a goal that we have chosen under specific circumstances in our experiential world. It tells us nothing . . . about how many other ways there might be. (Glasersfeld 1987, p. 199)

This supports the foregoing delineation and suggests a further thesis implicit in the former statement:

7) There is no preferred epistemic conceptual structure; constructivism is a relativist doctrine.

And finally, in a move that many idealists before him have made, von Glasersfeld proceeds from an epistemological position to an ontological one:

> Radical constructivism, thus, is *radical* because it breaks with convention and develops a theory of knowledge in which knowledge does not reflect an "objective" ontological reality, but exclusively an ordering and organization of a world constituted by our experience. The radical constructivist has relinquished "metaphysical realism" once and for all. (Glasersfeld 1987, p. 199)

This claim suggests two further constitutive theses of VGP:

8) Knowledge is the appropriate ordering of an experiential reality.
9) There is no rationally accessible, extraexperiential reality.

In his 1989 paper, von Glasersfeld approvingly quotes Ludwik Fleck[14] and Richard Rorty. From Fleck, he repeats: "The content of our knowledge must be considered the free creation of our culture. It resembles a traditional myth" (p. 122). From Rorty, he repeats that the pragmatist "drops the notion of truth as correspondence with reality altogether, and says that modern science does not enable us to cope because it corresponds, it just enables us to cope" (p. 124). These endorsements strengthen the nine-part delineation of VGP proposed above. It is easy to see the influence of VGP in the list of constructivist-inspired epistemological claims listed at the beginning of this chapter. Some problems with VGP as delineated will be considered under five headings: its empiricism, its confusion of real and theoretical objects of science, its individualism, its account of concept acquisition and its idealism.

VGP's Empiricist Problematic

The basic problem with VGP is that it is a variant of the empiricist conception of knowledge which the scientific revolution discredited. All the root commitments of empiricism are preserved and endorsed in VGP: knowledge is something that individuals create and adjudicate; experience is the raw material of knowledge claims; thus there is no immediate, epistemic access to the external world; once individual cognitive activity is recognized, it is assumed that cognitive claims are compromised, and knowledge of an external reality becomes impossible. VGP (1–9) both embraces and elaborates the consequences of empiricist epistemology.

Any epistemology which formulates the problem of knowledge in terms of a subject looking at an object and asking how well his or her experience or sensations reflects the nature or essence of the object, is quintessentially Aristotelian, or more generally empiricist—even if the conclusion is that sensory experience does not reflect properties of objects at all. Aristotelians were direct realists about perception; that is, the objects of perception were material bodies. Later empiricists were largely indirect realists; that is the objects of perception were sense impressions generated, it was supposed, by material objects. Locke, an avowed opponent of Aristotle, puts the matter this way in his *Essay*: "The mind, in all its thoughts and reasonings, hath no other immediate object but its own ideas, which it alone does or can contemplate." Variations of this recur in modern constructivist formulations. Experience, rather than a means to knowledge, becomes the object of knowledge. This substitution is fatal. As is well known, Locke's formulation of the problem of knowledge was used by Berkeley to support idealism and relativism. Berkeley's argument in his *Treatise* was simple but devastating: "As for our senses, by them we have the knowledge *only of our sensations*, ideas, or those things that are immediately perceived by sense, call them what you will: but they do not inform us that things exist without the mind, or unperceived." It is not coincidental that modern constructivists, once having formulated the epistemological problem in Aristotelian-Lockean terms (VGP 4, 8), then endorse versions of Berkeley's savage critique of it and end up with relativism (VGP 7) and, for the more consistent, idealism (VGP 9).

Within this Aristotelian-empiricist tradition the possibility of knowledge was weakened once it was pointed out that the mind is active in cognition. The possibility of knowledge evaporated once it was claimed that the immediate objects of the intellectual faculty were sense impressions rather than nature itself. Nature, or in Kant's terms, the thing-in-itself, became unknowable, because we only ever see it through a distorting lens, and there is no privileged position from which to check the correspondence of thought to reality.

Following Kant, Piaget, and the host of postpositivist philosophers such as Toulmin, Kuhn, Feyerabend, Rorty and others, modern constructivism asserts that, because individuals are active in knowledge acquisition, knowledge of an external reality is impossible. The argument sets up the epistemological situation as an observer facing reality, and then argues that, in as much as the observer contributes to the resulting knowledge, it cannot be undiluted knowledge of reality.

Constructivism's acceptance of the fundamentals of the Aristotelian-empiricist epistemological problematic is indicated when von Glasersfeld speaks of "looking through distorting lens and [agreeing] on what they see"; when Confrey speaks of "cognitive lens"; when Desautels and Larochelle write of "making sense of observations which are themselves theory-laden"; and when numerous others have recourse to this looking/seeing/observing vocabulary for stating the problem of knowledge. The empiricist assumptions of constructivism are also revealed by the frequent use of the Kuhn/Hanson ambiguous or hidden figures examples to establish facts about the theory dependence of observation; or when gestalt-switch terminology is used to describe scientific revolutions. Whether subjects are seeing through the lens clearly or darkly, it is the metaphor of seeing through a lens which signals commitment to an empiricist theory of knowledge.

The one-step argument from the psychological premise (1) "the mind is active in knowledge acquisition," to the epistemological conclusion (2) "we cannot know reality," is endemic in constructivist writing. Lerman speaks for many when he says, of these two theses, that "the connections between hypothesis (1) and (2) seem to be quite strong" (1989, p. 212).

However, this conclusion only follows on the assumption that the empiricist tradition has correctly delineated the problem of knowledge. If one rejects the assumption that the problem of knowledge arises when a subject looks at an object and wonders whether his or her mental representation corresponds to the object, then none of the sceptical conclusions of radical constructivism follow. Nonempiricist theories of knowledge are not subject to this sceptical argument.

Confusion of Theoretical and Real Objects of Science

Another fundamental, but related, problem is that VGP systematically confuses the scientific categories elaborated in Chapter 5: the conceptual foundations of science, the conceptual scheme of science, the theoretical objects of science and the material or natural objects of science. Constructivism is correct in stressing the culturally and temporally dependent aspects of creating the *theoretical* apparatus and hence theoretical objects of science—but none of this bears, of itself, upon truth. Wheatley provides a pristine example of this confusion when he says:

> From a constructivist perspective, knowledge originates in the learner's activity performed on *objects*. But objects do not lie around ready made in the world but are mental constructs. (Wheatley 1991, p. 10)

Wheatley is partially correct when he says that the objects of science do not just lie around. Where he and most constructivists, in company with Aristotle and the empiricists, go wrong is in failing to distinguish the theoretical objects of science, which do not lie around, from the real objects of science, which do lie around and fall on people's heads. The real falling apple is represented in physics as a colorless point mass and as a variable in an equation, and it is on this object, the equation, that physics works, not on the falling apple. But this does not mean that there is no falling apple, and that ultimately the worth of the equation (and the theoretical apparatus that generates it) is tested by seeing whether the apple reaches the ground at the appointed time and place.

Importantly, the theoretical object, once produced, has a reality, although it is not exactly lying around. This is the point that Popper saw in his account of "objective knowledge," or knowledge without a knowing subject (Popper 1972, chs. 3, 4). It is also a point stressed by Althusser (Althusser & Balibar 1970) and other objectivists, including the German "protophysics" school (Butts & Brown 1989). Newton's mechanics, Darwin's evolutionary theory and Mendel's genetics all exist and can affect and be apprehended by subsequent thinkers. But they are not to be confused with falling apples, Galapagos turtles, or fields of peas; nor are they to be confused with the thought processes inside the heads of Newton, Darwin and Mendel. Newton's head was full of all sorts of thoughts that came and went—some clear, others less clear. It was not these thoughts that are true or false, it was the contents of the thoughts as expressed in propositions or statements that are true or false. In turn the propositions depend for their expression upon the system of definitions and principles that constitute the theoretical objects of Newton's mechanical system.

It has been stressed earlier that science has a creative and constructive dimension: this is the production of the theoretical discourse of science, the positing or adopting of a conceptual foundation and the elaboration of a conceptual scheme. VGP 3 is correct, but trivially so. What science develops are systems of theoretical or scientific objects with specified properties, and natural objects are conceived in terms of the theory—fields of colored pea plants become in theory, but crucially not in reality, a genetics equation, and a rusting iron bar becomes a chemical equation. Again, VGP is partially correct in stressing that science is not the direct sensory knowledge of the world of natural or material objects; what VGP fails to see is that scientific knowledge is mediated by a science's theoretical objects.

VGP's Individualism

Von Glasersfeld is thoroughly individualist in his analysis of the problem of knowledge. A person's mental states (or structures) are the repository of knowledge (VGP 4, 5), and it is the individual who adjudicates knowledge claims (VGP 6). This individualism might be understandable in discussing "everyday knowledge," where people think about what to have for dinner, and whether the kettle is boiling, but it is completely inadequate for analyzing the adequacy or otherwise of scientific knowledge. Is acceleration invariant in inertial systems and why? What is produced in photosynthesis and why? What is the order of crystallization of minerals in a cooling acidic magma and why? In these cases individual cognition depends upon public cognition. Feral children have absolutely no prospect of thinking anything about inertial systems or rates of crystallization because they have no language, or at least none that encapsulates any scientific content. They have lots of Lockean experience and stimulation, but none of this gives rise to concepts of gravity, acidity or inertia.

When suitably interested and educated, individuals may think about the order of crystallization of minerals from a magma. But they think in terms of the concepts developed in a geological discourse—crystals, minerals, acidic magma. Moreover their thoughts are not knowledge because they make sense and are personally viable, but rather because they embody the appropriate and publicly vindicated parts of the extraindividual geological discourse (in this case the theory of Bowen's Reaction Series and its various experimental tests).

Once this point is recognized, then the essential epistemological tasks of evaluating different modes of knowledge production—in terms of fecundity, accuracy, simplicity, utility, problem-solving—can be tackled. Individualism and its concomitant relativism short-circuit these tasks.

VGP and Language and Concept Acquisition

VGP recognizes that individual knowledge claims have to be formulated in a language, that concepts presuppose words, that words entail meanings, and meanings presuppose communities of language users. VGP's private, individualist, subjective account of language and concept acquisition is prevalent in the Piagetian tradition within which von Glasersfeld works. Piaget, of course, recognized the importance of other subjects for the development of a child's intellectual capacities and beliefs, but overall there is a tendency in Piaget and the tradition to treat other people as just one more item in the child's environment. Von Glasersfeld says that:

> From the constructivist point of view . . . language users must individually *construct* the meaning of words, phrases, sentences, and texts. Needless to say, this semantic construction does not always have to start from scratch. Once a certain amount of vocabulary and combinatorial rules ("syntax") have been built up in interaction with speakers of the particular language, these patterns can be used to lead a learner to form novel combinations and, thus, novel conceptual compounds. But the basic elements out of which an individual's conceptual structures are composed and the relations by means of which they are held together cannot be transferred from one language user to another . . . they must be abstracted from individual experience. (Glasersfeld 1989, p. 132)

Von Glasersfeld here asserts:

1) Semantic construction can *sometimes* start from scratch—presumably meaning that an isolated individual, a feral child, can, before social contact, build up some stock of concepts and their associated meanings and references.[15]
2) Social interaction accelerates the above process, but it remains primarily an individual one.
3) The elements of language—ideas, concepts, words, meanings—cannot be transferred from one user to another.
4) Even with social interaction, the concepts, ideas, meanings, must be abstracted from individual experience.

There are good grounds for believing that all of these assertions are false. The fundamental error is the endorsement of an individual, abstractive theory of language acquisition. To put the matter starkly, individuals do not *construct* the meaning of words, they *learn*, or *mislearn*, the meaning of words. This is the point on which Vygotsky's social constructivism diverges from the more individual constructivism of Piaget. It is, of course, individuals who come to learn a language, and in this trivial sense one might say they construct a language, but this terminology is most misleading. Learning does require attention and intellectual activity on the part of the learner; in this sense there is intellectual construction occurring. But this undisputed sense of construction does not imply any full-bodied construction of meaning by individuals. For the most part individuals learn, not construct, meanings.

The first assertion, that semantic construction can start from scratch, was the target of Wittgenstein's arguments against the possibility of a private language. Language requires words and the precontact individual is not going to have these. Further language requires stability of reference for words; this can be known only in a community of language users. These considerations, and the work of language theorists such as Vygotsky (1962, 1978), have inclined some constructivists to abandon this individualist account of language acquisition and become social constructivists (Duckworth 1987, Lave 1988, Newman et al. 1989). Vasili Davydov, a Russian linguist and follower of Vygotsky, has stated the social, as against the private, view of the origin of language and concept formation:

> The child does not create his own speech, his own verbal meanings, and does not determine the range of their object attributions—he masters the speech of adults and receives a number of visible objects from them, which are designated by these words. (Davydov 1990, p. 179)

The inherently social and conceptual dimension of experience asserted by Vygotsky and Davydov was a major plank in Marx's theory of knowledge, first stated in his 1844 *Paris Manuscripts*, and starkly asserted in his 1845 *Theses on Feuerbach*.[16]

The issue is of some moment for science and mathematics education. Most constructivists do recognize that there is a public, symbolic, created world of science and mathematics that children have to be introduced to, and whose concepts they have to internalize. They recognize further that children are not going to discover this world, its concepts and their relationships, merely by private inquiry. One leading constructivist has said that "learning science is essentially a process of enculturation into the ideas and models of conventional science" (Driver 1989, p. 103). This recognition is a major departure from individualist constructivism where students create their own meanings and adjudicate their own knowledge claims. This enculturation involves decisions about curriculum objectives and content and about teaching methods. These decisions are not simple; they involve considerations of social need, cultural worth, human purposes, learning styles and capacities, educational theory and economic necessities. Introducing children to the symbolic and practical world of science in a way that alienates them from this world, that confuses them, that makes the scientific world completely unintelligible, makes no sense on any account of teaching and education: constructivists and nonconstructivists are agreed upon this point. The problem for constructivists is how, given their principles, to get children to believe, understand and make meaningful scientific ideas that not only transcend their experience, but are often in outright contradiction with their experience. Some have likened learning science to learning a foreign language: there is an awful lot that just has to be learnt before the totality begins to make sense, and before one can be a critical user of the language.

The third assertion, that meaning cannot be transferred, is in one sense true, but trivially true: ideas and concepts are mental (however this is construed) entities and thus cannot literally be transferred; transportation having a material connotation in the sense that bread can be put in the hand and transferred, whilst ideas cannot be. But if transfer is interpreted as "can teach" or "can learn from" or "can assist the development of," then there would have to be powerful arguments produced in order to establish the truth of 3) against all the good sense and everyday experience that refutes it—parents have been telling children lots of things for a long time; teachers have long been instructing children in complex matters of history, mathematics and science. No such arguments are given for this assertion which so undermines the profession of teaching.[17]

Von Glasersfeld often defends teaching against attempts to reduce it to training. He reconciles this defense with his nontransferability thesis by saying "language is not a means of transporting conceptual structures from teacher to student, but rather a means of interacting that allows the teacher here and there to constrain and thus to guide the cognitive structure of the student" (Glasersfeld 1990, p. 36). It is then a moot point as to how constraint and guidance can occur unless some meaning is conveyed or transferred to students. Transferability does not imply transfer without loss; not everthing taught is caught, but some meaning needs to be transfered if facilitation or guidance is to occur.

The final assertion, that meaning must be abstracted from individual experience, embodies the core weakness of VGP's account of language acquisition. In order for (4) to be distinctive, experience needs to be interpreted in a nonsocial, or at least nonconceptual manner; experience has to become pure experience, or sense data, as the positivists used to say. In its pure form, (4) is the assertion of a Robinson Crusoe theory of language and concept development. This only needs to be stated in order for its inadequacy to be apparent. Wallis Suchting, in a long and detailed criticism of von Glasersfeld's constructivism, has observed that:

> Abstraction theories in general are essentially circular because the alleged process of abstraction already *presupposes* the concept which is supposed to be formed as a *result* of that process. For example, if I am supposed to learn the meaning of "red" by "abstracting" the common property "redness" from various items that are red, this assumes that I can already form a class of "red" things from which the abstraction can be made. . . . The situation is not changed in principle [with] the process of so-called "ostensive definition" . . . here too, since everything always instantiates different concepts at the same time, I must already have at least a rudimentary command of the concept intended if I am to realise what is meant. (Suchting 1992, p. 239)

These considerations apply to the acquisition of everyday concepts; *mutatis mutandis* they apply to the acquisition of scientific concepts. Theoretical concepts neither arise from immediate experience, nor do they even refer directly to such experience. This is the point labored in Chapter 5 about the momentous transition from Aristotelian to Galilean philosophy. The concept of instantaneous velocity, for example, is of crucial importance for modern mechanics, yet is not given in experience: it is difficult to conceive of, let alone perceive, the displacement of position divided by a near-zero moment of time. This was part of the problem that Galileo confronted in saying that pendulums keep moving at their apex even though they were seen to come to momentary halt. With mathematical notation, including graphs, most children can be taught the meaning of instantaneous velocity: ds/dt as t approaches zero. The concept is derived by language acquisition and a thoroughly conceptualized set of learning experiences: the experiences come complete with concepts, and the richness of the experiences depends upon the richness of the enveloping concepts.

Learning experiences do not come first and then get labels afterwards. This was the mistake of discovery learning. It is the reason that di Sessa observed that "very few subjects, if any, had learned much characteristically Newtonian from dealing with the everyday world" (di Sessa 1982, p. 62). An implication of VGP is that students should or can learn Newtonian categories by dealing with the everyday world. The fact that they do not and cannot either refutes VGP, or causes such massive rewriting and qualifications of it as to dissolve the distinction between VGP and more social accounts of concept acquisition. On this matter von Glasersfeld does say that he, along with Piaget, maintains that theoretical concepts, including number, causality and so on, arise from "reflective abstraction" and that this presupposes social interaction. Thus there is a blurring of the lines between radical and social constructivism.

VGP's Idealism

Von Glasersfeld highlights an important issue for constructivism, namely what to make of the claims of scientific realism. VGP 9 is thoroughly idealist in that, Berkeley-like, it claims there is no extraexperiential reality, or, if atheism about the world is eschewed, then agnosticism at least takes its place. Von Glasersfeld is admittedly ambiguous on this ontological point. However, there is no ambiguity in his claim that the scientific world picture tells us nothing about the constitution of the world, and thus, why should we believe there is a world? This might loosely be called epistemological antirealism. It is expressed throughout von Glasersfeld's writings. One statement of this antirealism is:

> The organism's representation of his environment, his knowledge of the world, is under all circumstances the result of his own cognitive activity. The raw material of his construction is "sense data," but by this the constructivist intends "particles of experience"; that is to say, items which do not entail any specific "interaction" or causation on the part of an already structured "reality" that lies beyond the organism's experiential interface. . . . Though externalization is a

necessary condition for what we call "reality," this reality is wholly our construct and can in no sense be considered to reflect or represent what philosophers would call "objective" reality; for no organism can have cognitive access to structures that are not of his own making. (Glasersfeld 1987, p. 113)

In his 1992 interview, when asked about constructivism and reality, he replied:

The main difficulty of the question arises from the word "exist." In our human usage, it means to have some location in space, or time, or both. But since space and time are our experiential constructs, "to exist" has no meaning outside the field of our experience, and whatever an independent ontological reality may do, it is not something we can visualize or understand. (Glasersfeld 1992, p. 174).

These claims about realism are important both for philosophy and for science education. Whether or not the scientific world view purports to tell us about reality affects curriculum decisions and how we teach. It affects the rationale we give ourselves, parents, society and students for initiating children into the activities and conceptual schemes of science; and affects the motivation students have for learning science. The issue, which will be addressed in the next chapter, is of great consequence for other problems, such as teaching science in non-Western and multicultural situations.

Constructivism and Relativism

Constructivist epistemology is fraught with grave educational and cultural implications that are seldom thought through. Constructivism leads directly to relativisms of all kinds, and not just in science. Clearly lots of different things can make sense to people, and people can disagree about whether a particular proposition makes sense to them or does not make sense. The ways in which a proposition can make sense are independent of the reference of the proposition; matters about the truth of a proposition are not so liberal, they depend upon how the world is. Consequently "making sense" is a very unstable plank with which to prop up curriculum proposals and adjudicate debates about curriculum content.

Furthermore, most scientific advances have entailed commitment to propositions that literally defied sense—Copernicus's rotating earth, Galileo's point masses and colorless bodies, Newton's inertial systems that in principle cannot be experienced and also his ideas of action at a distance, Darwin's gradualist evolutionary assumptions so at odds with the fossil record, Einstein's mass-energy equivalence and so forth. Indeed, the topic of pendulum motion, as we have seen, exhibits the problems with using "sense" as a goal and arbiter in science education. In the theoretical object of classical mechanics, the bob at its highest point is both at rest and accelerating with the acceleration of gravity, at its lowest point it is moving with maximum speed in a tangential direction, yet its acceleration is vertically upwards. Neither of these propositions makes immediate sense, yet they are consequences of the physical theory that allows construction of the pendulum clock and successful predictions to be made about the behavior of the real, material objects that constitute pendulums. Within the theory of circular motion the propositions "make sense." But the theory does not emerge from sensations; and not only is it not traceable to experience, it contradicts immediate experience, and is only roughly in accord with refined, experimental experience. This is why Wolpert among others comments that "if something fits in with common sense it almost certainly isn't science . . . the way in which the universe works is not the way in which common sense works" (Wolpert 1992, p. 11).

If the conceptual schemes of science purport to be about the real world, and if they are intended to make true statements about the world, it is more likely that the effort necessary to change students' scientific misconceptions will be made and financed. If science is not about the real world, or is not thought to be true in any serious sense, then it becomes difficult to justify attempts to change students' understandings and beliefs when such change is at the cost of their self-confidence, is in opposition to the feelings of their parents, or is in conflict with important cultural values. The Scopes Trial, and the contemporary debate over creationism in schools, highlight these issues.[18]

Flowing directly from constructivism's individualistic empiricism is the neglect of the inherently social aspect of scientific development. It is not just that individuals are dependent upon others for their language and conceptual furniture, but as far as science is concerned, the growth of scientific understanding goes hand in hand with initiation into a scientific tradition, a tradition within which point masses and instantaneous accelerations make sense. A valuable tradition is passed on, not reinvented by each generation. There are serious educational questions posed by the business of selecting those aspects of a tradition worthy of transmission, and the processes whereby they are passed on. But these questions only arise and can be addressed if this apprenticeship dimension of education is recognized. Subjective, or psychological, constructivism only dimly recognizes this. Social constructivism sees it more clearly, but then needs to address the epistemological or normative elements in the social construction of knowledge.

Children's thoughts are private, but their concepts are public. Whether or not particular thoughts are going to constitute knowledge is not a matter for the individual to determine; or rather, if they do so determine, then it is against a public standard. Teachers mediate between students and this public standard. Without such public criteria, the word "knowledge" is reducible to "belief." What constitutes knowledge and what makes something knowledge are issues of great epistemological and political importance. On the facile, personal, constructivist view of knowledge, these questions evaporate. For social constructivism they also evaporate, but just more slowly: What will be the social group whose agreement will constitute some proposition as knowledge?

Still further, these constructivist ideas have very mixed consequences for culture. All cultures build up traditions and understandings, some of which are worthy of being passed on. Tradition is the hallmark of a healthy culture. Each new generation should not have to start completely anew the task of making meaning. Extreme constructivism makes tradition nugatory. The history of science plays a minor, if any, part in constructivist curriclar proposals.

On the other hand, it is notorious that people have for centuries thought that the grossest injustices and the greatest evils have all made sense. The subjection of women to men has, and still does, make perfectly good sense to millions of people and to scores of societies; explaining illness in terms of possession by evil spirits makes perfectly good sense to countless millions; the intellectual inferiority of particular races is perfectly sensible to millions of people, including some of the most advanced thinkers; to very sophisticated Germans it made sense to regard Jewish people as subhumans and to institute extermination programs for them; apartheid made sense to South Africans, just as racial discrimination did to US citizens until very recently. The list of atrocities and stupidities that have made perfect sense at some time or other, or in some place or other, is endless. It seems clear that the appeal to sense is not going to be sufficient to refute such views. But the appeal to truth, or right, which is independent of human desires or power, may be able to overturn such opinions and practices. Certainly the interests of the less powerful and marginalized are not advanced by championing the view that power is truth; minority rights have always been better advanced by holding on to the view that truth is power.

The relativism and subjectivism of constructivism are particularly ill-suited to deal with the complex, transsocial problems facing the contemporary world. There is a need for the sustained application of reason and the rejection of self-interest in the attempt to deal with pressing environmental, political and social questions—think of the political situation in Africa or the Balkans. Karl Popper recognised this socially corrosive aspect of constructivism, when he said:

> The belief of a liberal—the belief in the possibility of a rule of law, of equal justice, of fundamental rights, and a free society—can easily survive the recognition that judges are not omniscient and may make mistakes about facts. . . . But the belief in the possibility of a rule of law, of justice, and of freedom, can hardly survive the acceptance of an epistemology which teaches that there are no objective facts; not merely in this particular case, but in any other case. (Popper 1963, p. 5)

Conclusion

This chapter has given an indication of the enormous impact of psychological constructivism on the theory and practice of contemporary science education. It has drawn attention to the explicit epistemological and ontological claims made by advocates of constructivism, and in particular by Ernst von Glasersfeld. The general conclusion reached has been that, inasmuch as there are arguments advanced for the epistemological and ontological positions, they are weak arguments. Constructivism amounts to a restatement of standard empiricist theory of science, and suffers all the well-known faults of that theory. As mentioned at the beginning of this chapter, some constructivists adopt a version of social constructivism so as to avoid some of the problems associated with subjective or psychological constructivism. But this move just delays the day of epistemological reckoning. Whose group will be judged correct in its knowledge?

However, the interactive, antidogmatic teaching practices supported by constructivism need not be abandoned. Von Glasersfeld acknowledges that: "Good teachers . . . have practiced much of what is suggested here, without the benefit of an explicit theory of knowledge . . . their approach was intuitive and successful" (Glasersfeld 1989, p. 138). Other epistemologies and other educational theories can equally suggest and demand humane, engaged, interactive, antidogmatic and intellectual teaching aimed at the development of critical capacities and well-formed understandings. Since Socrates this has characterized the best teaching, but as with Socrates, realists and nonskeptics have been prepared to challenge students' firmly held beliefs, which may well be reinforced by an overwhelming amount of commonsense experience and deeply held cultural values. It is less clear that either personal or social constructivist pedagogy will do this, or at least it is not clear on what grounds it would do so, given that truth is not available as a ground for criticism.

Perhaps the most basic issue at stake in the evaluation of constructivism is this: To what extent is scientific thinking natural? In most of its guises, constructivism assumes that scientific thought is natural—witness the use of "facilitation," "children's science," etc. Two fundamental problems for the "naturalness of science" position is that science developed so late in human history, some 10,000 years after the development of agriculture, and 2,000 years after the intellectual achievements of the Greeks; and that it developed in only one culture despite numerous cultures having advanced thought, literature, art, education and commerce. The argument of this book is that Western science is not natural, it does not automatically unfold as children either confront the world, or participate in their culture. Scientific understanding and modes of thought require initiation into a scientific tradition, an initiation provided by school science teachers.

CHAPTER 8

What is Science?
Realism and Empiricism

Discussion of constructivism leads naturally into discussion of a debate that has echoed through the history of science, and that bears significantly upon the nature of science: namely that between realists and empiricists. This debate will be elaborated not just because it clarifies the argument about constructivism, but because it is so central to science that only a truncated science education can ignore it. The debate can be appreciated, if not joined, by teachers and students alike, with benefit to both. What is at issue are the goals of scientific investigation and the reality or otherwise of theoretical entities and mechanisms postulated in scientific theories to explain observable events and phenomena.

In the ancient world some philosophers disputed the reality of the Aristotelian crystalline spheres that were proposed as the mechanism that kept the planets moving regularly and at fixed distances from each other; others disputed the reality of Ptolemaic epicycles that were to explain the complex observed motion of planets. It was not just that the philosophers doubted the existence of the spheres or epicycles; rather, some regarded the theories of crystalline spheres and epicycles as mere mathematical devices, or useful images for calculating the positions of the planets; they were not meant to make ontological claims about the world. This view became known as empiricism or instrumentalism, or much later, positivism. On the other hand, there were those in the ancient world who thought that the epicycles and the crystalline spheres proposed by astronomers were real, and it was their reality that bestowed legitimacy on the explanations of planetary motion proposed. Some may have thought that particular explanatory theories were mistaken—that, for instance, there were no crystalline spheres, or no planetary intelligences—but nevertheless the business of science, or philosophy as it then was, was to seek such real entities or mechanisms to explain observable phenomena. These people were realists concerning the claims of science.

Empiricism is the doctrine that knowledge is confined to the world of experience or phenomena, and that the aim of science is to produce theories that predict phenomena and connect economically—usually mathematically—items of experience. In contrast, epistemological realism is the view that the aim of science is to reveal the causal mechanisms that generate the realm of experience; science aims to produce knowledge of an extrasensory world. From the ancient debate about crystalline spheres, through to the instrumentalist position urged upon Galileo by Cardinal Bellarmine, to the bitter debates between Newtonians and Cartesians over the reality of gravitational attraction, to the equally heated debates over the reality of atoms that engaged Ernst Mach and others in the nineteenth century, to the controversy between the realist Einstein and the instrumentalist Bohr over the Copenhagen interpretation of quantum mechanics—the issue of realist versus empiricist interpretation of scientific theory has always been close to the centre of philosophical debate about science.

There are many ways of posing the realist/empiricist distinction. The fundamental distinction is that empiricists wish to confine the claims of science to what we can experience, saying that any claims that go beyond experience have to be treated only as aids, tools, models or heuristic devices for coordinating sensory or observable phenomena. For empiricists, the theoretical, as distinct from observational, terms of a theory do not refer, and are not meant to refer, to existing entities (the reference even of observational terms is controversial, as will be seen). In medieval terms, an empiricist maintains that the aim of science is to "save the phenomena"— that is, to be consistent with and predict phenomena, not to speculate about unobservable features of reality. Medieval nominalists, and most contemporary constructivists, are empiricists in this sense.

Realists, on the contrary, believe that the point of science is to postulate theoretical entities and to test the accuracy of these postulates. Realists are usually not so naive as to believe that all of what science postulates at any time is accurate, but they do believe that science strives to uncover the hidden nature of reality. Galileo expressed the realist view of science when he said that:

> Nature did not make human brains first, and then construct things according to their capacity of understanding, but she first made things in her own fashion and then so constructed the human understanding that it, though at the price of great exertion, might ferret out a few of her secrets. (In Burtt 1932, p. 68)

There are, of course, varieties of empiricism, and varieties of realism; not everyone in each camp is committed to a single set of propositions about science and reality. The history of the debate illustrates these varieties. Clarification is important in reading the literature of science education because different authors use the terms in different ways, with "empiricist" and "realist" often being interchangeable terms, referring to whatever is opposed to constructivist theory. Often "instrumentalism" is used as a synonym for "empiricism," "positivism" is frequently used to describe "realist" positions, and so on.

Platonic Empiricism and Aristotelian Realism

Plato was a realist about Forms, which were the object of true and proper knowledge claims, but he provided an early statement of the empiricist or instrumentalist view of scientific devices or theories. Simplicius says of Plato that he:

> lays down the principle that the heavenly bodies' motion is circular, uniform, and constantly regular. Thereupon he sets the mathematicians the following problem: What circular motions, uniform and perfectly regular, are to be admitted as hypotheses so that it might be possible to save the appearances presented by the planets? (Duhem 1908/1969, p. 5)

Ancient mathematicians were asked by Plato for a model of the movement of heavenly bodies that would conform to, and enable predictions about, astronomical phenomena—times of rising and setting of the planets, changes of season, planetary regression, periods of the planets, time of the equinoxes, and other matters. The model was not meant to conform to reality, it needed only to be consistent with and predict astronomical events.

In opposition to this there was a realist tradition in ancient astronomy that sought mechanisms for planetary motion. For instance, Eudoxus and Aristotle held that planets rotate on crystalline spheres. This mechanism accounted both for their motion, their spacing, and their regularity, but unfortunately, over time, the theory had less and less success in saving the astronomical appearances. Ptolemy provided the first full-blooded empiricist astronomical account when he cut himself loose from the constraints of realism and proposed a system of cyclic and epicyclic motions for the planets that violated most of Aristotle's physical principles. Ptolemy's epicycles, for instance, passed through the crystalline spheres, and his eccentric orbits had planets rotating in circles whose centers were empty. But to a remarkable extent, Ptolemy's complicated, earth-centered theory was able to save the appearances; it worked very well as a calculating device.[1] Koestler describes the situation as follows:

> Astronomy after Aristotle becomes an abstract sky-geometry, divorced from physical reality, ... It serves a practical purpose as a method for computing tables of the motions of the sun, moon, and planets; but as to the real nature of the universe, it has nothing to say. (Koestler 1964, p. 77)

Copernican and Galilean Realism and Osiander's Empiricism

Copernicus, in his *Six Books Concerning the Revolutions of the Heavenly Spheres* (1543), resurrected the Aristotelian realist program in astronomy. Copernicus believed that both astronomy and physics should propose hypotheses that not only saved the phenomena, but were in accord with the Platonic conception of the world. To this end he revived the ancient but overlooked heliocentric, moving earth, model of Aristarchus of Samos. Copernicus, in his Dedication, says of the Ptolemaic tradition that:

These, on the other hand who have devised systems of eccentric circles, although they seem in great part to have solved the apparent movements by calculations which by these eccentrics are made to fit, have nevertheless introduced many things which seem to contradict the first principles of the uniformity of motion. (Matthews 1989, p. 42)

As Copernicus lay dying, Osiander, the Lutheran scholar charged with arranging publication of the *Revolutions*, inserted a Preface which is the embodiment of empiricist and instrumentalist understanding of scientific theory. It says in part:

For the astronomer's job consists of the following: To gather together the history of the celestial movements by means of painstakingly and skilfully made observations, and then—since he cannot by any line of reasoning reach the true causes of these movements—to think up or construct whatever hypotheses he pleases such that, on their assumption, the self-same movements, past and future both, can be calculated by means of the principles of geometry. . . . It is not necessary that these hypotheses be true. They need not even be likely. This one thing suffices, that the calculation to which they lead agree with the result of observation. (Duhem 1908/1969, p. 66)

This instrumentalist preface is remarkably like the statement of Ernst von Glasersfeld quoted in the last chapter: "our knowledge is useful, relevant, viable . . . if it stands up to experience and enables us to make predictions . . . [it] gives us no clue as to how the 'objective' world might be." This similarity is not surprising: constructivism leads directly to instrumentalism. George Bodner, an American constructivist, provides a pleasingly frank endorsement of instrumentalism:

The constructivist model is an instrumentalist view of knowledge. Knowledge is good if and when it works, if and when it allows us to achieve our goals. (Bodner 1986, p. 874)

and goes on to champion Osiander's interpretation of Copernicus's theory. Constructivists need to carefully explain this support to their students, who might have expected science teachers to come down on the side of Copernicus and Galileo in this confrontation.

Galileo adopted the Copernican hypothesis some time around 1600. The hypothesis was, of course, scientifically and theologically controversial.[2] In 1615 the illustrious Cardinal Bellarmine proposed to Galileo the sort of empiricism and instrumentalism that Osiander had deviously thrust upon Copernicus. The Cardinal said:

It seems to me that [you] are proceeding prudently by limiting yourselves to speaking suppositionally and not absolutely, as I have always believed Copernicus spoke. For there is no danger in saying that, by assuming the earth moves and the sun stands still, one saves all the appearances better than by postulating eccentrics and epicycles; and that it is sufficient for the mathematician. However it is different to want to affirm that in reality the sun is in the center of the world . . . this is a very dangerous thing. (Finocchiaro 1989, p. 67)

However, Galileo did not embrace the instrumentalist olive branch offered by Bellarmine: he maintained a resolute realism about the Copernican hypothesis. In his *Two Chief World Systems* (1633) he repeats Copernicus's claim against Ptolemy that:

> However well the astronomer might be satisfied merely as a calculator, there was no satisfaction and peace for the astronomer as a scientist . . . although the celestial appearances might be saved by means of assumptions essentially false in nature, it would be very much better if he could derive them from true suppositions. (Galileo 1633/1953, p. 341)

Newton's Realism and Berkeley's Empiricism

Newton was a realist in the tradition of Aristotle and Galileo. He proposed a mechanism (gravitational attraction) that gave rise to the celestial laws of planetary motion uncovered by Kepler, and the terrestrial laws discovered by Galileo. His realism underlies his insistence on the reality of absolute space and time in contradiction to those who maintain that only relative space and time exist, the space and time of our experience. In his Scholium on "Space and Time," Newton says:

> But because the parts of space cannot be seen, or distinguished from one another by our senses, therefore in their stead we use sensible measures of them. . . . And so, instead of absolute places and motions, we use relative ones; and that without any inconvenience in common affairs; but in philosophical disquisitions, we ought to abstract from our senses, and consider things themselves, distinct from what are only sensible measures of them. (Newton 1729/1934, p. 8)

Absolute space and time were thus theoretical constructs in Newton's system, in contrast to actual measures of space and time—ruler measurements and clock readings—which were observational terms. It goes without saying that the fact that Newton regarded absolute space and time as real existents does not prove their existence: his, and other arguments, need to be evaluated on their merits.

Newton was also a realist about forces: when a body accelerates there was a *real* force acting upon it, something is making the body accelerate. Forces were not just mathematical conveniences or conventions useful in linking together successive locations of a moving body. Force was responsible for the body moving; it had the same ontological status as the body moved. Although, in free-fall and planetary motion for instance, only the accelerating body could be seen, Newton believed that a real, unseen, force is responsible for the acceleration. Force is a theoretical construct to explain observational occurrences. It is not, to use a methodological concept common in psychology, an intervening variable that merely links variables in a mathematical manner (MacCorquodale & Meehl 1948); nor is it, as Mach would later claim, a mere convenience for the economy of thought.

It is worth noting that although Newton believed that gravity was a real attractive force, he was less certain of the means of its operation. The concluding remarks of the General Scholium that he appended to his *Principia* are well known:

> Hitherto we have explained the phenomena of the heavens and of our sea by the power of gravity, but have not yet assigned the cause of this power. This is certain that it must proceed from a cause that penetrates to the very centres of the sun and planets, without suffering the least diminution of its force. . . . But hitherto I have not been able to discover the cause of those properties of gravity from phenomena, and I frame no hypotheses . . . to us it is enough that gravity does really exist, and act according to the laws which we have explained, and abundantly serves to account for all the motions of the celestial bodies, and of our sea. (Newton 1729/1934, p. 547)

Newton resisted the interpretation of his followers that gravity was action at a distance. This struck him, as well as Leibniz and the Continental Cartesian philosophers, as occult. His physics dictated that there had to be a real force of gravitational attraction, his mathematics had ascertained the inverse-square law expressing its action, but he hesitated to pronounce on the mechanism of its action. His letter of 1693 to his supporter Bentley illustrates this hesitancy:

> That gravity should be innate, inherent, and essential to matter, so that one body may act upon another at a distance in a vacuum without the mediation of anything else by and through which their action and force may be conveyed from one to another, is to me so great an absurdity that I believe no man, who has in philosophical matters a competent faculty of thinking, can ever fall into it. (McMullin 1978, p. 58)

In the period between the first and second editions of his *Principia*, Newton expended effort in trying to give realist flesh to "gravity." An aether, light, an active "most subtle spirit," God—all were investigated as possible causes of the attraction we call gravity. The issue became so problematic that Newton inserted a special Scholium on the topic in the 1713 second edition of the *Principia*:

> I here use the word *attraction* in general for any endeavour whatever, made by bodies to approach to each other, whether that endeavour arise from the action of the bodies themselves, as tending to each other or agitating each other by spirits emitted; or whether it arises from the action of the ether or of the air, or

of any medium whatever, whether corporeal or incorporeal, in any manner impelling bodies placed therein towards each other. (Newton 1729/1934, p. 192)

He stressed that he was providing a *mathematical* treatment of the effects of gravitational forces, rather than a *physical* account of the means of their operation. In the opening definitions of the *Principia* he says that:

I here design only to give a mathematical notion of those forces, without considering their physical causes and seats. . . . [I] use the words attraction, impulse, or propensity of any sort towards a centre, promiscuously, and indifferently, one for another; considering those forces not physically, but mathematically. (Newton 1729/1934, p. 5)

But Newton was more and more embarrassed by being unable to specify the mode of action of the linchpin of his physics: How does one body have causal effects on another at a distance across empty space? Without such specification, gravitational attraction was in danger of becoming, as Galileo said of the Aristotelian categories, a name without content. Newtonian gravitation was looking as if it could save the phenomena, and be very useful in mathematical calculations, but have no reality. Leibniz in 1716 wrote to Dr Clarke, a supporter of Newton's science:

But what does he mean, when he will have the sun to attract the globe of the earth through an empty space? Is it God himself who performs it? But this would be a miracle if ever there was any. . . . Or, are perhaps some immaterial substances, or some spiritual rays, or some accident without a substance, or some kind of *species intentionalis*, or some other I know not what, the means by which this is pretended to be performed? Of which sort of things, the author seems to have a still good stock in his head, without explaining himself sufficiently . . . it must be a perpetual miracle: and if it is not miraculous, it is false. (Alexander 1956, p. 94)

Bishop George Berkeley, in his 1721 *De Motu* (*On Motion*), continued this empiricist attack on the reality of gravitational attraction, but in addition he argued against the reality of forces more generally. Berkeley said:

Force, gravity, attraction and similar terms are convenient for purposes of reasoning and for computations of motion and of moving bodies, but not for the understanding of the nature of motion itself. (Berkeley 1721/1901, p. 506)

This is an extension of his earlier, 1710, *Principles of Human Knowledge*, idealist argument for the nonreality of extrasensory existence. There he had said:

All the choir of heaven and furniture of the earth, in a word all those bodies which compose the mighty frame of the world, have not any subsistence without a mind—that their *being* is *to be perceived* or known . . . let anyone consider those arguments which are thought manifestly to prove that colours and tastes exist *only* in the mind, and he shall find they may with equal force be brought to prove the same thing of extension, figure, and motion. (Berkeley 1710/1962, pp. 67–71)

David Hume expanded Berkeley's empiricist attack to cover not just the notion of force, but the notion of causation more generally. Reality is what we see: cause is nothing over and above the constant conjunction of events, and we simply designate the earlier event the cause; it has no powers, nor is there any necessary connection between it and the effect. According to Hume "we know nothing farther of causation of any kind than merely the *constant conjunction* of objects, and the consequent *inference* of the mind from one to another" (Hume 1777/1902, p. 92). Causal powers, and necessary connections, are just as occult for Hume as gravitational attraction was for Leibniz and Berkeley.

Planck's Realism and Mach's Empiricism

A century after Hume's treatise, the antirealist view of science was forcibly restated by the physicist-philosopher Ernst Mach. He said gravitational attraction, for instance, was not just unknowable, but there was no such thing: it was merely a human construct useful for the economy of thought and for the mathematization of particular experimental relationships. Mach recognised Berkeley and Hume as like-minded philosophers (although his ideas were developed in advance of reading them). For Mach,

What we represent to ourselves behind the appearances exists *only* in our understanding, and has for us only the value of a *memoria technica* or formula, whose form, because it is arbitrary and irrelevant, varies very easily with the standpoint of our culture. (Mach 1872/1911, p. 49)

Mach carried the empiricist standard in the great intellectual war of turn-of-the-century science: the reality or nonreality of atoms, the meaningfulness or meaninglessness of the atomic hypothesis. This hypothesis had its origin in the materialism of Democritus, where it was said that the basic constituent of all matter was atoms, and nothing apart from atoms and the void existed. Boyle transformed the philosophical concept into a scientific concept with his 1674 *The Excellency and Grounds of the Corpuscular or Mechanical Philosophy*. He said:

The chymical ingredient itself, whether sulphur, or any other must owe its nature and other qualities to the union of insensible particles, in a convenient size, shape, motion, or rest, and texture. (Matthews 1989, p. 118)

Boyle's atoms, with their particular masses and shapes, were theoretical terms that were postulated to explain the known chemical regularities and reactions. Newton enshrined atomism in his "Rules of Reasoning in Philosophy." Subsequently the hypothesis had a chequered career in both science and philosophy.[3] The nineteenth-century empiricist philosopher, Alexander Bain, remarked on the realist interpretation of the atomic hypothesis that:

> Some hypotheses consist of assumptions as to the minute structure and operation of bodies. From the nature of the case these assumptions can never be proved by direct means. Their merit is their suitability to express phenomena. They are Representative Fictions. (Hacking 1984, p. 169)

Mach's first public refutation of atomism was in his 1872 *History and Root of the Principle of the Conservation of Energy*. There he held the hypothesis to be useless, saying that it contributed nothing to what phenomenal knowledge already told us. His argument is almost exactly the same as the one Carl Hempel would use against realism a century later in his famous paper "The Theoretician's Dilemma" (Hempel 1958).[4] Mach argued:

> But let us suppose for a moment that all physical events can be reduced to spatial motions of material particles (molecules). What can we do with that supposition? Thereby we suppose that things which can never be seen or touched and only exist in our imagination and understanding can have the properties and relations only of things which can be touched. We impose on the creations of thought the limitations of the visible and tangible. . . . In a complete theory, to all details of the phenomenon details of the hypothesis must correspond, and all rules for these hypothetical things must also be directly transferable to the phenomenon. But then molecules are merely a valueless image. (Mach 1872/1911, p. 49)

Beyond being useless, Mach said of realist hypotheses that:

> If the hypotheses are so chosen that their subject can never appeal to the senses and therefore also can never be tested, as is the case with the mechanical molecular theory, the investigator has done more than science, whose aim is facts, requires of him—and this work of superogation is an evil. (Mach 1896, p. 57)

Mach's greatest adversary was Max Planck, who for a time, as with nearly all physicists of his generation, shared Mach's empiricist viewpoint (Heilbron 1986, pp. 44–46). During his Machian phase he had opposed Boltzmann's atomic interpretation of the Second Law of Thermodynamics. After his own 1900 work on black-body radiation, he converted to the realist and atomist camp. As with many converts, he became more of a realist than most realists—he maintained that atoms were as real as planets, and probably looked the same except scaled down (Toulmin 1970, p. 24).

The kinetic theory of gases was one area in which the realist/empiricist war was waged. The empirical gas laws of Boyle and Gay-Lussac had long been known. Boltzmann, Maxwell and others were successful in deriving the laws from the assumption of molecules that behaved in specified ways—elastic collisions and so on. Mach, and the research chemist Ostwald denied that this warranted belief in such entities. Eventually Planck disagreed with this, and said that the kinetic theory was so confirmed as to warrant belief in the reality of molecules.

The interpretation of Brownian motion was another area in which the argument was fought out. The botanist Robert Brown, was a vitalist who, in searching for confirmation of his view that the small male parts of flowers were active self-movers, had in 1827 described the phenomenon of extremely small pollen particles moving randomly in a liquid. Long after vitalism had been banished in biology, upholders of the kinetic-atomic theory said that Brownian motion was visible proof of the existence of mobile, but not self-moving, unseen molecules. In 1905, the same year as his Special Relativity Theory was published, Einstein, assuming the atomic hypothesis, developed the mathematical theory for the movement of Brownian particles. He calculated that the displacement distance of a single particle which was being moved randomly was given by the formula:

$$X^2 = 2RTt \,/NA$$

Where X is the displacement, R is the gas constant, T is absolute temperature, N is Avogadro's number, A is a resistance factor, and t is time elapsed. In 1909 Perrin experimentally confirmed this formula and, indirectly, the kinetic-atomic theory on which it was based. One century after Brown identified the motion, Perrin was given a Nobel prize for showing that it established precisely the opposite microscopic world-picture to the one Brown set out to confirm. This is an instance of the interplay between science and philosophy—a scientific development is held to disprove one philosophical position and confirm another.

Planck's first public rejection of Mach's ideas occurred in his 1908 lecture "The Unity of the Physical World-Picture" that he gave in Leyden at the invitation of Lorentz (reproduced in Toulmin 1970). Planck says, against Mach's fundamental claim that science has to be anchored in our psychological elements or experiences, that:

> The whole development of theoretical physics until now has been marked by a unification achieved by emancipating the system from its anthropomorphous elements, in particular from specific sense impressions. (Toulmin 1970, p. 6)

He says of Mach's system that:

It deserves full credit for having rediscovered, in the face of a menacing skepticism, the one legitimate point of departure for all natural science in the sense impressions. But when it degrades the whole physical world-picture along with the mechanical one, it overshoots the target . . . the outstanding characteristic of all scientific research—the demand for a *constant* world-picture, independent of changing times and peoples—is alien to it . . . this constant element, independent of every human (and indeed of every intellectual) individuality, is what we call "the Real." (Toulmin 1970, p. 25)

And he criticized the thesis of Mach's acclaimed history of physics, *The Science of Mechanics*, saying:

When the great masters of the exact sciences introduced their ideas into science: when Nicolaus Copernicus removed the earth from the center of the universe, . . . when Isaac Newton discovered the laws of gravitation, . . . when Michael Faraday created the foundations of electrodynamics . . . "economical" points of view were certainly the last to fortify these men in their battle against traditional attitudes and overriding authorities. No: it was their unshaken faith, whether based on artistic or religious foundations, in the reality of their world-picture. (Toulmin 1970, p. 26)

Planck believed that the history of science progressively reveals the secrets of nature; he had as little time for relativist notions in epistemology as he had for instrumental or economic ones:

A constant, unified world-picture is, as I have tried to show, the fixed goal which true natural science, in all its forms, is perpetually approaching; and in physics we may justly claim that our present world-picture, although it shimmers with the most varied colors imparted by the individuality of the researcher, nevertheless contains certain features which can never be effaced by any revolution, either in nature or in the human mind. (Toulmin 1970, p. 25)

Planck finished his lecture with the claim that Machian empiricism was antithetical to the progress of science:

if the Machian principle of economy were ever to become central to the theory of knowledge, the thought processes of such leading intellects would be disturbed, the flights of their imagination would be paralyzed, and the progress of science might thus be fatally impeded. (Toulmin 1970, p. 26)

These of course were provocative words, and notwithstanding his seventy-two years, Mach responded. His reply, titled "The Guiding Principles of My Scientific Theory of Knowledge," was published in 1910 (reproduced in Toulmin 1970). Mach, in polemical style, says of Planck and his supporters that they:

are on the way to founding a church. . . . To this I answer simply: If belief in the reality of atoms is so important to you, I cut myself off from the physicists' mode of thinking, I do not wish to be a true physicist, I renounce all scientific respect—in short: I decline with thanks the communion of the faithful. I prefer freedom of thought. (Toulmin 1970, p. 37)

Some Philosophical Considerations

This sketch of the history of debate between realist and empiricist accounts of the development of mechanics shows that some distinctions are important in order to discuss the issue; approaching the subject with too limited, black-and-white contrasts will not allow the nuances of the history to be appreciated. The sketch also illustrates one of the central themes of this book: the close relationship between science and philosophy, and the importance of understanding *both* fields in order to understand the history of either. It consequently raises the question of how the history of science relates to the philosophy of science.

Much has been written, for instance, on Mach's empiricist opposition to atomism and his debates with Einstein, Planck and Boltzmann.[5] One should be cautious in drawing philosophical lessons from the debate: the issues and personalities are as complex as they are interesting and important. Concerning the accepted histories of this period in physics, Feyerabend wisely counsels that "the received versions most of the time are not only incorrect, but much simpler . . . than the events they describe" (Feyerabend 1987, p. 217). Keeping this caution in mind, some useful things can be said. Mach and the empiricist tradition wanted to keep science close to its experiential and specifically observational base, and expressed scepticism about constructions that passed beyond this firm base. Planck, Einstein and the realist tradition sought to understand an extrasensory reality, and believed that science was gradually revealing the features of that reality.

One obvious problem is that Planck and other realists too readily accepted a transitory scientific theory as a final one—eighteenth- and nineteenth-century atomistic hopes of giving a mechanical interpretation of all physical phenomena including electromagnetism, for instance, proved illusory. Mach's scepticism was more prescient, although, given that he was sceptical about *all* scientific theories, his skepticism in this particular instance perhaps ought not be labeled "prescient"—the economic doomsayer *eventually* has to be right, this does not make him or her prescient. Late nineteenth- and early twentieth-century realism too often identified old-fashioned mechanism with the realist and scientific worldview, and consequently fought for the truth of specific mechanistic pictures as the truth about reality. A realist need not be committed to any particular account of what constitutes the ultimate "stuff" of the world. Materialism is one version of realism, dualism is another. Even versions of ontological idealism can be realist provided they maintain that their nonmaterial reality exists independently of individuals, and that science is an attempt to know the properties of this nonmaterial substance.

It is one thing to show how different historical figures held various philosophical positions, but this alone, of course, does not prove the truth or otherwise of the actual positions. Specifically we need to know whether realism or empiricism is entailed by different scientific theories, and whether there can be independent arguments for the truth of one as against the other.

The three most powerful arguments that empiricists urge against realists are: first, the fact that the history of science is littered with discarded theoretical entities which earlier were firmly ensconced in the best science of their time; second, the fact that theoretical terms are always underdetermined by the evidence available, and consequently the same evidence will also support other extant or potential, theoretical entities; third, the fact that scientific conceptions are determined by the theory in which they occur as well as by the reality they purportedly describe. Versions of these empiricist and constructivist challenges to realism have been made recently by distinguished philosophers such as Fine (1984), Hesse (1980), Kuhn (1970) and Laudan (1977, 1984).[6] Arguably Bas van Fraassen (1980) has provided the most wide-ranging critique of realism, and the most sophisticated restatement of empiricism as a viable philosophy of science. Van Fraassen says that:

> To be an empiricist is to withhold belief in anything that goes beyond the actual, observable phenomena, and to recognize no objective modality in nature . . . [it] involves throughout a resolute rejection of the demand for an explanation of the regularities in the observable course of nature, by means of truths concerning a reality beyond what is actual and observable. (Fraassen 1980, p. 202)

The first empiricist argument against realism has traditionally been most convincing: the fact of change in science, not just of incremental change or accretion of knowledge, but of upheaval or paradigm change, has, repeating Kant's reaction to Hume, jolted realists out of their dogmatic slumber. Planck tells a nice story which illustrates the depth of this slumber. In 1924 he gave an address at the University of Munich, where fifty years earlier he had begun his scientific career. In the address he recalled how he had been advised against a career in physics because the discipline was just about to be finalized and there would be no research to complete:

> When I began to study physics, I went for advice about the conditions and prospects of my studies to my esteemed teacher Philip von Jolly. He portrayed physics to me as a highly developed almost wholly mature science, which in a sense had been crowned by the discovery of the principle of the conservation of energy and therefore should soon assume its final stable form. Of course, here and there in a corner there could perhaps still be a speck of dust or a bubble that remained to be explored and assigned its proper place. The system as a

whole, however, was rather firmly established, and theoretical physics clearly approached the same degree of perfection which geometry had possessed for several centuries already. (Melsen 1961, p. 208)

Planck was recalling a view of science which was widespread in the 1870s, and was comparable to the view of many medieval Aristotelians that Aristotle had essentially finished the task of finding out about the world, and that henceforth one only had to look up his books. Yet within just a few decades, this idea of the stability of physics would be challenged by Planck's own achievements, and those of Einstein and others.

A number of realists have offered defenses against the empiricist arguments outlined above, and have proposed augmented and chastened versions of realism.[7] Ian Hacking (1983) has said that, if science is conceived as simply a representation of the world, then the empiricist arguments are so strong that realism has no satisfactory reply; realism has to look to new forms of justification, which Hacking finds in the success of scientific intervention and experimentation: "You cannot spray electrons around unless they are really there."

It is useful to delineate some of the forms that realism can take in order to clarify what is being defended in the name of realism, and what is not being defended. Leplin (1984, p. 1) provides a comprehensive list of theses that span the range of realist philosophical positions. He points out that realists can be said to be affirming one of a number of slightly different theses, these being:

1) The best current scientific theories are at least approximately true.
2) The central terms of the best current theories are genuinely referential.
3) The approximate truth of a scientific theory is sufficient explanation of its predictive success.
4) The approximate truth of a scientific theory is the only possible explanation of its predictive success.
5) A scientific theory may be approximately true even if referentially unsuccessful.
6) The history of at least the mature sciences shows progressive approximation to a true account of the physical world.
7) The theoretical claims of scientific theories are to be read literally, and so read are definitively true or false.
8) Scientific theories make genuine, existential claims.
9) The predictive success of a theory is evidence for the referential success of its central terms.
10) Science aims at a literally true account of the physical world, and its success is to be reckoned by its progress toward achieving this aim.

A strong form of realism might, for instance, hold the combination of theses (1), (2), (4), (7) and (10). A modest form of realism might, for instance, hold the combination of theses (6), (8) and (9). Modest realism is in effect saying that science aims to provide a true account of a world which is beyond and independent of our own mental state; but it is not committed to the current view being correct. It says that over time well-proven and accepted scientific theories are well proven because they are making existential claims about how the world works, and that these claims are approximately true. Philosophers have raised problems with the idea of approximate truth, or "verisimilitude" as Popper called it, but these can and have been answered (Devitt 1991, Oddie 1986). Modest realism is enough to go on with, and it is incompatible with empiricism, with constructivism and particularly with idealist forms of radical constructivism. Modest realism contains the standardly accepted realist theses:

- Theoretical terms in a science *attempt* to refer to some reality.
- Scientific theories are confirmable.
- Scientific progress, in at least mature sciences, is due to their being increasingly true.
- The reality that science describes is largely independent of our thoughts and minds.

Conclusion

The debate between realists and empiricists over the status of scientific theory—whether theoretical statements about nonobservables are meant to refer to real existing entities, and to what degree do they so refer—has been canvassed for a number of reasons. Firstly, it has so dominated the history of philosophical reflection on the nature of science that it ought to feature in school discussions about the nature of science. Secondly, school textbooks frequently endorse one or other of the views, but with very little understanding of the historical or philosophical issues involved. One study of seventeen widely used school science textbooks in Britain and South Africa concluded that the majority endorsed an "inductive-empiricist" view of science (Jacoby & Spargo 1989). Familiarity with the debate allows teachers to be more critical of the texts and widen students' appreciation of this core matter. Aspects of this question of truth and science teaching have been discussed by Derek Hodson (1982) and Stephen Norris (1984). Thirdly, constructivism, at least the radical variant, is decidedly empiricist in its view of science and the goals of scientific inquiry; indeed in many cases where it is asserted that people can only know about their experiences, it is positivist. These empiricist commitments flow over to classroom practice and curriculum deliberations, where statements such as "science involves people exploring and investigating their biological, physical, and technological worlds, and making sense of them in logical and creative ways" (Bell 1990) are commonly found. A realist might respond that there are countless logical and creative ways in which people can make sense of the world around them. Science is concerned with finding those ways which provide truth about the world. Because of the educational influence of constructivism, its empiricist underpinnings need to be scrutinized.

This chapter has outlined the history of empiricism as a doctrine about the aims of science. In this sense of empiricism, science should seek to tell us about the world of observables and eschew reference to unobservables except in so far as they are considered, as with Mach, mere shorthand ways of talking about relations between observables. Thus science should seek the laws of falling bodies and planetary motion—accounts of observable relations—and even make use of the notion of gravitational attraction as a convenient way of summarising the empirical laws, but science should not pretend that there is in fact gravitational attraction. Likewise science should seek relations between an individual's performance on a variety of tests, and it may even refer to "intelligence" as a short-hand way of summarising such relations, but it should not assert the existence of intelligence—having high intelligence simply means performing well on a variety of designated tests, having low intelligence simply means performing poorly on those tests. Behaviorism in psychology is perhaps the quintessential scientific expression of empiricist doctrine—B.F. Skinner learnt this philosophy by reading Ernst Mach. Most empiricists are ontological realists about the observables of science, believing that the planets, falling apples, individuals, and test booklets actually exist and enter into causal relations. Some empiricists, beginning with Bishop Berkeley and ending with the positivists and radical constructivists, maintain that science tells us only about our experiences and not about external objects at all.

If discarded theoretical entities and mechanisms—crystalline spheres, phlogiston, humours etc.—are a problem for realists, then the long litany of such entities that have been effectively revealed and scrutinised is a bigger problem for empiricists. One-time theoretical entities—molecules, electrons, genes, chromosomes, molten cores, the planet Neptune—have a habit of turning into respectable observable entities. The empiricist doctrine is predicated upon a distinction between observation terms and theoretical terms that the advance of science and technology renders untenable. The doctrine has to retreat merely to skepticism about putative entities that are in-principle unobservable.

But empiricism is also an epistemological doctrine about the grounds of knowledge, namely that knowledge claims must be validated by experience, or for positivists, sense data. There are different sets of problems for this version of empiricism—universal statements outrun experience, mathematics is not obviously reducible to experiential claims, scientific idealisations are counterfactual, and so on.

CHAPTER 9

Multicultural Science Education

The history and philosophy of science can contribute to debates occurring in and about science education: constructivism, discovery learning, values in science, children's naive conceptions and feminist critiques of science have already been mentioned. These debates hinge upon conceptions of the nature of science—its aims, methodology, limitations and achievements. This chapter will examine one such debate that is increasingly important for science education, namely multicultural science education. In the last decade many people have claimed that orthodox science is culturally biased and that our schools need to allow for more diverse understandings of nature to be expressed and studied. It is also widely claimed that science education in non-Western cultures needs to be different from that in the West; it needs to be more multicultural, if not completely ethno-scientific. The instructional part of this debate is philosophically uncontroversial, it is a concern about the overdue recognition of non-Western understandings and technologies, and about the effective, and sensitive, teaching of science to cultures that do not share the traditions and philosophy of the West. The philosophically controversial part of the debate begins when claims are made that there are a number of equally valid, and equally good sciences, and that both Western and ethnic sciences should be accorded the same status in schools, or that in certain circumstances, local ethnic science ought replace Western science in schools.[1]

Criticism of Science Education

The debate about multicultural science education is just one part of a larger argument about schooling and culture in the West. Criticism of schooling in the 1960s centered on issues of inequality, access, and the ideological and political function of schools. More recently critiques have focused upon curriculum matters, and the school's role in the creation of public knowledge. Some maintain that the supposedly public knowledge transmitted in the curriculum is really partisan knowledge; it is knowledge created by, and furthering the interests of, particular groups. This can be seen in the arguments about "political correctness" that have engulfed many universities.[2]

Beginning in the 1960s, it was recognised that in all societies there are a multitude of ways in which school structures, regulations, pedagogical methods and curricula favor the dominant cultural group, and disadvantage and silence minority cultures. Sexual, class and racial biases in education have been exhaustively documented, as has been the political function of educational systems. Among the thousands of such studies, some landmark ones are Thorstein Veblen (1969) on the class biases in higher education, Brian Simon (1971) on the class and racial bias of intelligence testing and school streaming, Michael Young (1971) on the curriculum as socially organized knowledge, Paulo Freire (1972) on the domination of native cultures by colonial education, Christopher Jencks (1972) on inequality in education, Samuel Bowles and Herbert Gintis (1976) on the economic determinants of school success, and Michael Apple (1979) on the ideological function of the school curriculum.[3]

In this radical tradition, some writers focused on the specific ways in which school science contributes to the patterns of domination and subjection. David Layton (1973) wrote on the deskilling and alienating effects of theoretical and impractical science curricula. Michael Young (1976) wrote on the culture of positivism in school science and its contribution to the functioning of science as a gatekeeper, restricting access to scientific knowledge and leaving the majority of the population scientifically ignorant and dependent upon a usually middle-class, white, male, professional elite. Numerous studies were conducted on the appallingly low participation rates of women and minorities in science—the low numbers who finished school science, and the dramatically lower numbers who enrolled in, let alone finished, university science and engineering programs.[4]

The criticisms of the 1960s and seventies have been well summarized by Jacques Desautels:

> By perpetuating overloaded curricula for years, often poorly suited to the intellectual development of the majority of students, the system has guaranteed that only a minority will eventually have access to scientific careers. By arranging curriculum content strictly according to logic and discipline, with no reference whatever to the history of science, apart from parenthetical anecdotes, it ensures that students do not absorb a *critical view of knowledge*. By divorcing curriculum content from everyday or cultural reality, the knowledge acquired is rendered useless for the individual in his or her daily actions. By disassociating science and technology, the framework is already prepared for the division of labour. By carefully avoiding the integration of the social problems related to scientific and technological development, generations of young people are prepared for a passive, naive acceptance of what passes for progress. (In Aikenhead 1985, p. 135)

These criticisms of science education were written on the assumption that science itself is epistemologically unproblematic: the problems were pragmatic ones of how best to teach science, and how to create pedagogies and structures that did not exclude, or discourage women, minorities or the poor. The contemporary debate about multicultural science education is occuring in a different, postmodernist, intellectual environment, where the truth status of Western science is challenged, and its monopoly on scientific understanding is questioned, if not denied. As one advocate has put the matter:

> The postmodern perspective reveals the world as composed of an indefinite number of meaning-generating agencies, all relatively self-sustained and autonomous, all subject to their own respective logics and armed with their own facilities of truth validation. (Bauman 1988, p. 799)

The issue facing science educators is to ascertain whether and, if so to what extent, the cultural and postmodern critiques that are applied to literature and social science apply to Western natural science. Is Western science just one among a number of equally valid and truthful sciences, each of which has its own logic and its own facilities for truth validation? To the extent that postmodernist epistemological appraisals of science are correct, to that extent the epistemological arguments for multicultural science education will be advanced. Conversely, if such arguments are mistaken, then the epistemological arguments for multicultural science education will be weakened. Matters of great moment concerning human well-being and educational quality depend upon a satisfactory answer to these questions. The Minister of Education in one South Pacific state is currently proposing, on multicultural grounds, to replace Western science in its schools with traditional science. The curriculum recommendations in the Portland *African-American Baseline Essays* have been adopted in many major US education districts, including Atlanta, Baltimore, Detroit and Indianapolis.[5]

The Universalist Tradition

Universalism is the epistemological position associated with Western, mainstream science. Such a view was expressed in 1921 by Norman Campbell, who said that "Science is the study of those judgements concerning which universal agreement can be obtained" (Campbell 1921/1952, p. 27). In the following year, George Sarton, the founding editor of *Isis*, the first history of science journal, said:

> The development of knowledge knows no political or racial boundaries. It is the only development which is truly international. If we wish to bring the peoples of the earth together should we not draw their attention to the treasures which are their common heirlooms, to the things which unite them? The history of the quest for truth is the history of no single nation; it is the history of mankind. (In Pyenson 1992, p. 96).

Universalists regard science as an intellectual activity whose truth-finding goal is not, in principle, affected by national, class, racial or other differences: science transcends human differences. It is a hard-won vehicle for common engagement across cultures, religions and races. This universalist view recognizes that while aspects of culture do influence science, nevertheless cultural considerations do not determine the truth claims of science.

Max Planck was one of many who shared this universalist creed. He regarded his formula for the distribution of energy in a heated cavity as something "which will necessarily retain its importance for all times and cultures, even for nonterrestrial and nonhuman ones" (Heilbron 1986, p. 6). This is a statement of the widest possible independence of scientific truth from all human and nonhuman interests. Albert Einstein, while a great humanitarian, and acutely aware of the cultural roots and impact of science, nevertheless endorsed Planck's view that the basic aim of science is "the complete liberation of the physical world picture from the individuality of separate intellects" (Holton 1975, p. 107). Their attitude was shared by the French physicist-philosopher Pierre Duhem, who was concerned to trace the influence upon science of different national characteristics. However, having done this in various works, including one on German science written during World War One, he went on to say:

> Considered under its perfect form, science ought to be absolutely impersonal. Since no discovery in it would bear the signature of its author, neither would anything allow one to say in what land the discovery saw the light of day . . . there is no trace of the English mind in Newton, nothing of the German in the work of Gauss or Helmholtz. In such works one no longer divines the genius of this or that nation, but only the genius of humanity. (Duhem 1916/1991, p. 80)

The core universalist idea is that the material world ultimately judges the adequacy of our accounts of it. Scientists propose, but ultimately, after debate, negotiation and all the rest, it is the world that disposes. The character of the natural world is unrelated to human interest, culture, religion, race or sex. Ultimately the concept is judged by the object, not the other way around. Just as volcanic eruptions are indifferent to the race or sex of those in the vicinity, and lava kills whites, blacks, men, women, believers, nonbelievers equally, so also the science of lava flows will be the same for all. For the universalist, our science of volcanoes is assuredly a human construction with negotiated rules of evidence and justification, but it is the behavior of volcanoes that finally judges the adequacy of our vulcanology, not the reverse.

Universalism and Imperialism

Undoubtedly universalism has been used for political and ideological ends. It provided a justification and rationale for the teaching of Western science as the West expanded among, and subjugated, native cultures in the Americas, Asia, Africa and the Pacific. To bring scientific understanding to alien cultures was often explicitly stated as one part of the "civilizing mission" of the West; the teaching of science was second only to the teaching of religion as part of the "white man's burden."

Lewis Pyenson, in a series of detailed publications on colonial science (Pyenson 1985, 1989, 1992), has drawn attention to this putative civilizing mission of science. Just a few of numerous adulatory accounts of science that he has marshalled suffice to give the flavor of the civilizing hope held for science. Juan Bautista Menen, the nineteenth-century Ecuadorian professor of astronomy, stated that "science in general may be called a divine gift; and it may reasonably be said that through science man in particular and society in general progress and develop" (Pyenson 1992, p. 87). Claude Bernard, a French physicist in Hanoi in the 1920s, argued for the inclusion of history of science in the university curriculum because scientists propose "ideas of beauty and harmony that raise mankind well above immediate, practical interests and contribute to moral progress" (Pyenson 1992, p. 88). Jacob Clay, the Dutch physicist-philosopher in Java in the 1920s, argued that Indonesian students ought to learn about the Greek miracle (Archimedes) and its utilization by Galileo because the latter's achievements were the "greatest wonder known to the history of mankind," and that studying the Western scientific classics was "an especially excellent way" for Indonesians "to be raised up to higher civilization" (Pyenson 1992, p. 90). Science was highly valued.

Pyenson's observations are echoed by most who have studied the history of colonial science education. Dart and Pradham, for instance, record that:

> Beginning with the earliest missionary schools and continuing through the period of colonial schools, the attitude and often the intent of western education has been that a primitive or decadent civilization is to be replaced with a more modern and "better" one. The attitude tends to continue even though colonialism is no longer a force behind it, and it tends to be particularly strong in science teaching; science teaching is taken to be the one really unique and powerful offering of the western world. (Dart & Pradham, 1976, p. 655)

The technological horrors unleashed in two world wars and numerous lesser ones—all the way up to Operation Desert Storm with its electronically guided, nose-camera equipped missiles bringing death, mutilation and destruction to living rooms throughout the world—have dampened the enthusiasm of those who naively thought that the advancement of science would eliminate human suffering. So also has, for instance, the clear-felling of rain forests, radar-guided pursuit and killing of whales, and drift-net fishing of oceans; the Chernobyl catastrophe; the spending (wasting?) of thirty billion dollars on the Strategic Defense Initiative (Star Wars) and realization that the bulk of government-funded science research in the US goes on war-related projects. The civilizing function of the West, and the virtues of its science and technology, are no longer as obvious and uncontested as was earlier thought. Not that this affects the cognitive claims.

Some proponents of radical science education reform and proponents of multicultural science education assert that the constellation of science-related catastrophes arise from the intellectual sources of Western science, and not just from its accidental associations with particular Western interests. They maintain that Western, or mainstream, science is intrinsically connected with materialism and reductionism, and that it is dominated and tainted by instrumental and technological reason. At the intellectual heart of the multicultural science education debate is the issue of whether orthodox science is inextricably connected to Western culture, and whether the truth claims of Western science are relative to its philosophical framework, and more broadly, to its interests.

Epistemology and Multicultural Science Education

There are a spectrum of alternatives that have been adopted by science teachers when teaching science in multicultural or bicultural situations:

Imperialist, where traditional understandings of nature and phenomena are ignored and Western science is taught as it is in the metropolitian centres: PSSC Physics in Polynesia, Nuffield in Newfoundland, CBA Chemistry in Colombia and so on. Traditional beliefs and systems are only attended to in order to prepare the ground for new knowledge which will supplant the old.

Integrationist, where alternative understandings and ways of thinking about nature are recognized, respected and made use of, but in the last resort only as a more effective means of having students learn about Western science. Ethnoscience is dealt with in an anthropological way: what other cultures believe and the reasons for their beliefs are pointed out. Efforts are made to interpret traditional beliefs and practices in terms of Western scientific understanding, in order to facilitate the understanding of Western science.

Robust or *noninterventionist*, where ethnic or traditional science is recognised as an intellectually legitimate alternative to Western science and cultivated in its own terms along with varying degrees of Western science and technique. In some places both traditions are fully taught and a "best of both worlds" approach is taken; in other places, just traditional sciences are taught.

The robust view is partly supported by ethical and political considerations that say that existing belief systems and cultures need to be respected, and that only internally instigated changes ought be sanctioned. As one African educator has said:

The purpose of education in Africa is not to destroy its own civilization or its own culture, in order to replace it with something that is conceived to be "better."

To proceed in that direction or with that implicit attitude is to create unnecessary difficulties in science education in Africa. (Urevbu 1988, p. 8)

It is not intended here to appraise these complex cultural, ethical and political arguments for robust multiculturalism; instead only the epistemological arguments proffered for the position will be examined.[6]

The core epistemological argument for nonintervention is the rejection of universalism (or objectivism, as it is frequently referred to in educational literature) as a theory of knowledge. Universalism is rejected in favor of some form of relativism which says that different knowledge systems are equally valid, and so there is no good cognitive reason to introduce Western science to traditional cultures. One can find many statements of this in the literature on multicultural science education. The following are a sample:

> Science is a way of knowing and generating reliable knowledge about natural phenomena. Other cultures have generated reliable knowledge about natural phenomena, therefore reason invites exploration of the possibility that other cultures may have different sciences. But science teachers wanting to celebrate this diversity have been so indoctrinated in the Western cultural tradition of science that they lack a methodology enabling examination of the science of other cultures with little more than tokenism. (Pomeroy 1992, p. 257)

> The American approach to multicultural science education is problematic. It seems to me that the movement encourages "universal science for all Americans" without ever considering the possibility of multi-sciences. (Ogawa 1989)

> There is a need to struggle to assert the equal validity of Maori knowledge and frameworks and conversely to critically engage ideologies which reify Western knowledge (science) as being superior, more scientific, and therefore more legitimate. (Smith 1992, p. 7)

> In developing new science curriculum materials, the African world view of nature must form the foundation. Concepts should be structured in such a way that harmonious co-existence between the Western scientific and the traditional view points are guaranteed. (Jegede 1989, p. 192)

Philosophical versus Psychological Coexistence

The possibility of coexistence between the Western scientific and traditional worldviews is a problem posed by multicultural science education: can Western scientific and traditional viewpoints harmoniously coexist? And if they are brought into harmony, is the intellectual and educational price too high? Unfortunately there is systematic ambiguity about the meaning of "harmonious." There is no doubt that subjectively, within an individual, all sorts of mutually inconsistent worldviews can coexist. Individuals are frequently unaware of the contradictions. Even when contradictions between intellectual commitments are apparent, individuals can live with enormous amounts of cognitive dissonance.

Many examples can be cited of this private accommodation of apparent contradictions. For instance, astromony and astrology happily coexist for numerous US science graduates. Fundamentalist Christianity thrives in centers of high-technology and space research (the witnesses for creationism at the 1981 Arkansas trial were all scientists, whilst the witnesses against creationism were mostly theologians and philosophers!). Many well-trained, fundamentalist scientists maintain that dinosaur and human foot-prints occur alongside each other in rock strata, whilst others spend time excavating for Noah's Ark in the Turkish mountains. Animist beliefs pose no apparent obstacle to biological research in much of Asia. Christianity and Marxism have coexisted for countless intellectuals.

Eminent scientists have included idealists and deeply religious Christians, Jews, Muslims and Hindus; others have been materialists and militantly anti-religious. Isaac Newton was an unconventional Christian whose library con-tained 138 books on alchemy, and who wrote 650,000 words on the subject; Michael Faraday was a devout member of the obscure Victorian Sandemanian sect; Darwin was an atheist whilst Lyell, his acknowledged inspirer, was a theist; the physicist Pierre Duhem was a devout Roman Catholic while his contemporary, the equally eminent physicist and philosopher, Ernst Mach, was an atheist, a socialist and a positivist; the physics Nobel laureates Philipp Lenard and Johannes Stark were Nazis and anti-Semites, while their contem-porary laureate, Albert Einstein, was a Jewish anti-Nazi; the mathematician Ramanujan said daily prayers to the Goddess Namagiri, the consort of the Hindu lion-god Narasimba; Erwin Schrödinger was a non-Christian idealist who regarded mind and matter as equivalent and who chose to end one of his books (1956) with the equation: "ATHMAN = BRAHMAN (the personal self equals the omnipresent, all-comprehending eternal self)."

This kaleidoscopic canvas of beliefs that have coexisted with the most sophisticated scientific practice suggests some caution in pronouncing what worldviews are and are not compatible with education in mainstream sci-ence. There may be limits, but the limits seem wider than might initially be thought. There is an important question about how science education should relate to worldviews or metaphysics. When we read that, for many, belief in astrology is unaffected by completion of a US science degree, we feel that their science education has been inadequate—what kind of a science education allows students to graduate believing in astrology?—but if maintenance of astrological belief is to count against the adequacy or effectiveness of a science program, then what of New Age ideas, fundamen-talist religion, orthodox religion, superstitions and so on? Once we say that science should connect with worldviews, then we need to say how it connects, and with what worldviews.[7]

Some Traditional Non-Western Metaphysics

The issue to be focused upon here is not the psychological possibility of conflicting worldviews being accommodated by individuals, but the possibility of their objective coexistence. That is, are there formal contradictions between the ontological and epistemological assumptions of mainstream science and those of other worldviews? Olugbemiro Jegede is representative of African science educators who hold a robust form of multiculturalism. He states that there is:

> the need to design science education curricula that satisfactorily meet the needs of the traditional person within Africa in such a way that the African view of nature, socio-cultural factors, and the logical dialectical reasoning embedded in African metaphysics are catered for. (Jegede 1989, p. 192)

Whether such views can be catered for in modern science is the question. Jegede elaborates what these worldviews are that "all African communities" have in common, and that science education must be "rooted in." These are:

1) The belief in a separate being whose spiritual powers radiate through gods (of thunder, fire, iron) and ancestors.
2) Reincarnation and the continuation of life after death.
3) The human as the centre of the universe in traditional African thought.
4) The theory of causality. (Jegede 1989, p. 193)

Jegede cites the work of thirteen anthropologists and educators who "now confirm the position that the African [view of nature] is anthropomorphic as opposed to the mechanistic view of nature of Western science."

Deborah Pomeroy, who works with Alaskan Indians, is another representative of robust multicultural science education. She invites teachers "to develop meaningful comparisons between the sciences of different cultures," so that students can engage in inquiries "which explore and validate some of the different ways of developing knowledge about natural phenomena" (Pomeroy 1992, p. 258). This is suggested not only because of the need to respect other cultures and traditions, but also because she detects "a general sense among people today that traditional [Western] ways of solving problems may not be adequate for some of the extraordinarily complex problems facing the world today" (p. 257).

Pomeroy characterizes the epistemology of the Indians as one where "Native cultures present us with traditions which accept the knowledge of observation, the dream, the sense, and the mystical as most valuable" (p. 260). The Alaskan culture is antiexperimentalist because it does not "believe in exerting control over nature," consequently "the process of gathering knowledge is longer and more complicated, but the knowledge gained is rich and encompasses all the variables interacting in their natural complexity" (p. 262). Traditional Alaskan Indians lived in and with nature, taking great care and time to observe the behaviors of the spirit-imbued animals, and "the power of this experience sometimes manifests itself as voices. In this case the test of the knowledge appears to be an external consistency with observations and the communion with the spirit world, often in the form of animal people" (p. 262).

The ontology of native Alaskans is one wherein "there are spirits in everything, including rocks, animals, and plants. Because of these spirits, animals possess knowledge which humans do not have, and to gain access to this knowledge, humans must be receptive to the animal spirits" (p. 261). The culture's understanding of nature is embodied and transmitted, but in ways that are different from the Western tradition: "indigenous people have built significant sites of learning, such as . . . the petroglifs of the Alaskan coast. These sites would be comparable to Western universities or libraries, but they are built in such a way that knowledge was manifest to the visible eye" (p. 263).

This is not the place to canvass the myriad non-Western worldviews that activate contemporary cultures and inform their sciences—Selin (1992) is a useful introduction to the literature. Nor is it the place to canvass the detailed and rich empirical knowledge of animal life, astronomy, horticulture and technology that traditional societies possess. I wish to concentrate upon the worldview, or "theoretical" aspects, of traditional belief systems. The observations of Jegede and Pomeroy are sufficient to illustrate the threads of the argument that I wish to advance, namely that some core epistemological and ontological assumptions of Western science are in objective conflict with core assumptions of some traditional belief systems. If this is so, then thoughtful educational responses are required.

The matters of ontological contention are the following:

1) Is the world constituted in such a way as to serve human interests?
2) Are processes in the world teleological? That is, do events and behaviors occur in order to bring about some fitting end state?
3) Are inanimate and nonhuman animate processes activated and controlled by spiritual influences?

The Western scientific tradition, after centuries of investigation and tumultuous debate, answers "no" to each of the above questions, while traditional belief systems affirm some or all of the propositions. One can recognise among the pre-Socratic philosophers the slow, awkward attempts to distance their thought about the world from the surrounding mythical worldviews that were characterized by the above anthropomorphic, animistic and teleological dimensions. Western science has slowly continued this process of jettisoning these features, and thus becoming less egocentric.[8]

The basic matters of epistemological contention are the following:

1) Does knowledge come from the observation of things as they are in their natural states?
2) Are knowledge claims validated by successful predictions?

3) Do particular classes or authority figures define knowledge or become the custodians of knowledge?
4) Is knowledge a fixed and unchanging system?

The Western scientific tradition, again after centuries of debate, answers "no" to each of these questions, whilst many traditional societies affirm some or all of them. Of course, there is some debate about these questions of natural states, prediction, the institutionalization of knowledge, and accretion versus revolutions in knowledge. I believe that even with more nuanced elaboration the conflict between scientific ontology and epistemology and numerous traditional ontologies and epistemologies is still apparent. This was the view of Robin Horton, in his classic 1971 study of African and Western science. After outlining many points of similarity between African and Western science, he concluded by drawing attention to deep differences. For Horton:

> The key difference is a very simple one. It is that in traditional cultures there is no developed awareness of alternatives to the established body of theoretical tenets; whereas in scientifically orientated cultures, such an awareness is highly developed. It is this difference we refer to when we say that traditional cultures are "closed" and scientifically oriented cultures are "open." (Horton 1971, p. 153)

One of the reasons for concern about teaching Western science in traditional societies is that this conflict very quickly spills over into other domains. Almost all commentators make the observation that traditional science is much more integrated with other important cultural systems than is usually apparent in the West. Traditional science is connected with religion, with health, with politics, with social customs and so on. The fear is that Western science will not only subvert traditional science, but that it will as a consequence subvert a range of other significant social institutions and beliefs. A minor example of this is provided by Howard Woodhouse and Theresa Ndognko, who conducted a study of the depressingly few women in Cameroon who persist with science courses to university level. One of the few woman graduates relates how:

> I have found it quite impractical to follow the traditional belief that women should not have sexual intercourse with their husbands while breastfeeding a child. As a result, I no longer follow this practice. (Woodhouse & Ndognko 1993, p. 144)

This fear of Western science's possible disruption of culture and traditional institutions is often misplaced, and indeed, often indicates a paternalist attitude; an assumption that other cultures are so feeble that they cannot make intelligent and sensible decisions about what accommodations to make and not to make in the light of modern science. Presumably the above Cameroonian woman is no less a member of her culture for making her accommodation to Western scientific knowledge.

What Is Good Science?

Deborah Pomeroy advances a view of knowledge—reliable belief constitutes knowledge—which is widely adopted among advocates of robust multiculturalism. As quoted above, she says: "Science is a way of knowing and generating reliable knowledge about natural phenomena. Other cultures have generated reliable knowledge about natural phenomena, therefore reason invites exploration of the possibility that other cultures may have different sciences" (Pomeroy 1992, p. 257).

There are two problems with this widespread multiculturalist position: First, is predictive success a guarantor of knowledge? Second, even if predictive success constitutes knowledge, can we move from the existence of different knowledge systems to the proposition that different knowledge systems are equally valid? The multiculturalist position seems in error on both counts.

The magnitude of the first problem depends upon the detail or depth at which the predictability thesis is spelt out. Given the onset of night, most people can soon predict that in about twelve hours daylight will occur; and that the colder the season the longer it will be before daylight. But such predictive success is hardly grounds for proclaiming knowledge of planetary motion. Likewise given the observation of lightning, the prediction of thunder to follow is easily and reliably made, but this does not constitute knowledge of atmospheric electrical conditions. As Plato so long ago realized, to lay claim to knowledge requires not just successful predictions but good reasons why the predictions are successful. Without adequate reasons, mere reliable inference hardly constitutes knowledge in any serious sense. A part of this first problem is the failure to distinguish empirical from theoretical knowledge. The account given by Pomeroy is at best an account of empirical knowledge, knowledge of regularities among events. But this "surface level" knowledge is of a different order from theoretical knowledge, where some account of causal mechanisms is postulated for the regularities seen.

Consider, for instance, the discovery of aspirin. In the Western world it is usually traced to the English clergyman, the Rev. Edward Stone, who, in 1758, while suffering from a bout of fever, chewed a twig of white willow, *salix alba*. He noticed an immediate improvement in his condition. Subsequently he dried and pulverized the bark of the willow, and tried to interest chemists in ascertaining its vital ingredients. A century later, the German chemist, Hoffman, made a usable form of the medicine by tacking on an acetyl group to the active salicylic acid. The Bayer firm in 1897 then made the first commercial aspirin. In Latin America, Hispanic people had known for centuries that tea made from the Daisy Fleabane plant was a cure for many illnesses. It was widely prescribed by healers or *curanderos*. It turns out that this also has salicylic acid as its active ingredient. In one sense then, the discovery of aspirin could be accredited to Hispanic people in the remote past, or to the Rev. Stone in the less remote past, but neither made the scientific discovery of aspirin. Their achievements were obviously important, but they were not scientific achievements; or rather they were, at best, low-level scientific achievements. They were the typical achievements of a great deal of traditional science and technology.

Comparison of Knowledge Systems

One should remember the important function of mathematics, experimentation, theory, open communication and public testing in mainstream science. This is not to assert that only Western science has these characteristics, but it is to assert that other sciences should not be lumped together with Western science unless they have these characteristics. It is clearly not the case that all ethnic sciences are "just like Western science except they believe different things," as is often maintained. Some ethnic sciences are more Western-like than others, but all sciences, Western and non-Western, can be compared with respect to their ability to provide control over events, to successfully predict the unknown and to grasp the truth of the matter.

Advocates of robust multicultural science education maintain that Western and traditional sciences cannot be compared. This is the second problem in Pomeroy's formulation of the difference between Western and traditional science. Supposing that a traditional account of agricultural practice or of medical practice is well formed, it does not follow from this that it is the best available knowledge. It may be well formed, predictively reliable and yet completely wrong—as was Ptolemaic astronomy for over one thousand years. Or it might be well formed, accurate and just inadequate when compared to other accounts of the same phenomena.

In general, the educational imperative is to teach the best of what is known, not the second best, or the discredited. This imperative is of course to be related to student understanding and levels of attainment, but it is an odd sort of education which sets out knowingly to teach falsehood or inadequate understanding. Thus there is a requirement upon educators, at least those who share broadly liberal ideals for education, to compare and evaluate putative systems of understanding or theories about phenomena prior to teaching them. Phlogiston theory can usefully be included in a science program in order to illustrate certain things about the history of science, or to illustrate certain things about the alternative oxygen theory of combustion, or to facilitate the learning of oxygen theory, but it can hardly be included as *the* scientific theory of combustion, notwithstanding the fact that phlogiston theory was very reliable, had good predictive properties, and highly intelligent people believed in it to the end of their days. Thus the common move from the existence of different sciences

192 • *Science Teaching*

to the necessity or desirability of teaching different sciences ignores the educational imperative to ascertain and teach the best of current understanding in ways that are engaging and comprehensible to students. It is the departures from this ideal that need to be justified. The foregoing has suggested that there are no epistemological reasons to justify such departures. And thus political, ethical or cultural reasons will need to be advanced, but these should not be dressed up as epistemology.

History of Science and Multiculturalism

The history of science is useful in appraising the epistemological arguments for robust multiculturalism. Furthermore, there has been a long tradition of conflict and accommodation between science and culture in the West from which lessons perhaps can be learned for the teaching of science in non-Western cultures.

The history of science shows how dependent European science has been upon the achievements of non-European cultures. Some of this is fairly obvious. Without the rediscovered Archimedes—of whom Galileo said, "his name should not be mentioned except in awe"—there would not have been a Galilean physics or a scientific revolution. Archimedes' geometry had its origins in Euclid, and this, in turn, in north African traditions. The base ten, the decimal place system of numbers, the number zero—all of which were crucial to Western scientific advance—were not of European invention. Science as a way of thinking has its origins in non-Hebrew, non-Christian, classical Greek thought.

As well as European dependence upon non-European scientific and mathematical achievements, good history of science shows the numerous autonomous scientific and technical achievements of non-Western cultures. Ubitrain D'Ambrosio has directed a research project in São Paulo, Brazil, on ethno-science and ethno-mathematics, and the latter is now a research field in history of mathematics congresses.[9] Eva Krugly-Smolska (1992) is a useful source of writings on Indian, Chinese and Islamic science. Helen Selin has published a guide to over eight hundred books on non-Western science (Selin 1993), and is now editing an encyclopedia on non-Western science and technology.

There is a wide literature that can be made available to students that conveys the wealth of technical, medicinal, astronomic, horticultural and scientific understanding of traditional societies. Such information can contribute to the expansion of student understanding of other cultures and also, by contrast, the better understanding of their own culture's achievements and presuppositions. But the fact of impressive traditional scientific and technological achievement does not in itself mean that these achievements cannot be compared to modern achievements, or that they should be taught in place of mainstream science. The latter two claims require, first, an argument about incommensurability that is generally lacking and, second, an argument that science education does not need to convey the best available understanding of nature. Of course where local science is adequate for local needs, then the argument is diminished, but no ethnic science is going to adequately explain how radios work, why the moon stays in orbit, why hundreds of thousands of Africans are dying of AIDS and so on. Mainstream science may not give us complete answers, but my claim is that it gives better answers than others.

Science and Social Influence

The history and sociology of science shows the influence of personal, social, sexual and cultural interests on the development of science. The recognition of such influences is an important component of good science education. Often it is only from the perspective of history, or of another culture, that these assumptions become apparent. Few have expressed this idea better than Ernst Mach, who, in his 1883 history of mechanics, said that:

> The historical investigation of the development of a science is most needful, lest the principles treasured up in it become a system of half-understood precepts, or worse, a system of *prejudices*. Historical investigation not only promotes the understanding of that which now is, but also brings new possibilities before us. (Mach 1883/1960, p. 316)

This recognition of the personal, social and cultural influences upon science has been long-standing. Francis Bacon, in his 1620 *Novum Organum,* wrote about the Idols of the Mind and the need to recognize and correct for psychological, linguistic, economic and cultural influences which might distort understanding.

Many who reject objectivity as a norm or goal in science seem to suggest that all biases compromise science, and that, further, such biases cannot be corrected. One feminist historian of science writes:

> The dominant categories of cultural experience—race, gender, religion, and class—will be reflected in the institution of science itself: in its structure, theories, concepts, values, ideologies and practices . . . scientists are not magically capable of suspending belief and judgement in their approach to the problem. (Bleier 1984)

In contrast to such positions, one may, with Mach, Duhem and Bacon, recognize the operation of deep-seated cultural and other assumptions, yet say that a task of science is to identify and test the adequacy of such assumptions. Some such assumptions might be deleterious to scientific advancement, other such assumptions might be advantageous to science. An argument is frequently advanced that, because Western science in general, or particular Western research traditions, or particular scientists, are influenced by some factor—sex, gender, race, class, religion—then the resulting science is necessarily compromised.

This argument from influence to epistemological deficiency is simply invalid. That Ethiopian marathon runners are influenced by their high-altitude climate, and presumably by their genetic endowment, does not make them any the less capable as marathon runners. That Japanese students are influenced by their family and culture to perform well at school, does not cast doubt upon their scholastic achievement. Some argue that Protestantism was the chief intellectual influence that brought about the scientific revolution (Hooykaas 1972, p. 161). This is very debatable, but if it were true, it would not affect the cognitive achievements of Newton, Boyle and others. The "influence therefore deficit argument" is peculiar in education, as so much effort goes into identifying and improving influences that will enhance learning and achievement.

A more challenging form of the "influence means deficit" argument is that which maintains that external factors determine the epistemology of science; they determine the criteria whereby claims are judged to be true or false. In the above example this would be the case if Ethiopians had the power to decree that only marathons will be run in the Olympic Games. This argument is advanced by a number of feminist critics of science, for instance Jane Roland Martin (1989).

A general problem with the influence argument is that it is by no means clear what assumptions are internal to science and thus "legitimate" and what are external to science and consequently "illegitimate." Positivists thought that all philosophical positions were external to science and so ought be treated as cultural assumptions to be eradicated. This is by no means clear. Many see Galileo's religion as external to his science, but this is by no means clear. He thought that the Church did have a legitimate teaching role in and authority on diverse matters, and that the Book of Nature could be read by mathematical philosophers because it was written by God. The attempt to delineate internal from external factors in science is complex; thus the project of separating valid from invalid science in terms of its biases *per se* is fraught with difficulty.[10]

The fact that scientists carry cultural baggage does not imply subjectivity in their discoveries, or that their work is intellectually compromised. Over the centuries, scientists from diverse cultural, racial and religious milieu have built upon the work of scientists from other cultures and earlier centuries. Today, "Western" science is contributed to by scientists from all corners of the globe; indeed, some non-Western cultures are putting more effort into, and having more success with, Western science education than Britain and the US. This fact accords with structuralist or objectivist theories of science; theories that maintain that science has an independence from any particular scientist's experience and that, in general, it is the state of science that determines the experience of scientists, rather than the experience of scientists determining the state of science (Chalmers 1990). Important personal scientific achievements occur within objective contexts.

Conflict Between Science and Culture

The fact that science deals with important questions, mostly in ways that are counterintuitive and in opposition to common sense, makes conflict with traditional belief systems inevitable. The dramatic moments in the history of conflict between religion and science in the West deal with many of these same conflicts; the West has had its share of conflict between science and culture. The effect of Copernican astronomy and the New Physics on medieval society, the effect of Darwinian naturalism and evolutionary theory on nineteenth-century religion, are Western examples of scientific conflict with fundamental cultural values, causing pain in many circles, and readjustments of fundamental belief systems.[11] Yet few would argue that the pain was without gain.

Galileo championed the new science, but he did so in the tradition of Augustine and Aquinas, who were very cautious about tying culture and religion to any particular scientific understanding.[12] Augustine had said: "One does not read in the Gospel that the Lord said: I will send you the Paraclete who will teach you about the course of the sun and moon. For He willed to make them Christians, not mathematicians" (Langford 1966, p. 65). And Aquinas restated the point as follows: "since Holy Scipture can be explained in a multiplicity of senses, one should adhere to a particular explanation only in such measure as to be ready to abandon it if it be proved with certainty to be false; lest Holy Scripture be exposed to the ridicule of unbelievers and obstacles placed to their believing" (Langford 1966, p. 66). This Augustinian tradition recognized the primacy of science in understanding the world; culture and theology were to adjust to what science established as the indisputable facts of the matter—much hinged, of course, on what was to be regarded as indisputable, but that is another issue.

Western society has undergone enormous change since Galileo's time, much of it related to changing scientific beliefs. In the last century or two, this rate of change has been astonishingly rapid, not just in the West, but in most nations. Yet where Western science has been wholeheartedly embraced, there has been no loss of confidence or of sense of distinctive cultural achievement. Changing beliefs do not need to undermine a culture. If other social, economic and cultural matters are in order, societies are very resilient. Science and culture are in a complex interaction. Giving priority to one or the other alone is usually not a sensible alternative.

The Multiscience Thesis

Central to the epistemological arguments for robust multicultural science education is the multiscience thesis, which rejects epistemological universalism and objectivity as an attainable or desirable goal for intellectual activity. This thesis is not peculiar to the multicultural science debate: a form of it, the two-science doctrine, had a long history in the Marxist tradition. The weaknesses of the Marxist two-science doctrine are now reasonably apparent, and they are apposite in considering the multiscience doctrine. Its seeds were sown in Marx's *German Ideology*, where he says:

> The phantoms formed in the human brain are also, necessarily, sublimates of their life-process. . . . Morality, religion, metaphysics, all the rest of ideology and their corresponding forms of consciousness, thus no longer retain the semblance of independence. . . . Life is not determined by consciousness, but consciousness by life.

On this formulation of historical materialism, economic life determines the form of morality, religion, and philosophy developed in a society and, arguably, the form of science developed.[13]

The two-science thesis had its culmination with Stalin's efforts to promote proletarian mathematics, chemistry, biology and so on. Not just mathematics, chemistry, biology to serve proletarian needs and interests, but full-fledged alternative sciences to bourgeois science. The most documented part of this programme was the battle fought between 1927 and 1964 in the Soviet Union between Mendelian genetics and the Lysenko's theories of environmental influence on heredity.[14] Lysenko's theory was culturally supportive (at least of official ideology) and politically very correct (he was a farmer and directed his research to the transformation of agriculture). His doctrine was advocated with passion, and opponents were swept aside, many to their graves.

Unfortunately, although culturally sensitive and politically very correct, Lysenko's doctrine was false. The world, in particular the mechanism of heredity, was not the way he described it, not the way he wished it to be. The painful lesson for the Soviet Union, after purges of politically incorrect scientists and massive crop failures, was that ideology and science had to adjust to the way the world is.[15] There are lessons here for advocates of the social construction of scientific facts: Lysenkoists certainly constructed, or enforced, widespread scientific agreement. Unfortunately for the USSR, their crops did not confirm such agreements.

The Nazis also were opponents of universalism and advocates of the multiscience doctrine.[16] In 1936, at an anniversary of the University of Heidelberg, Dr. Bernhard Rust, the Nazi Minister of Science and Education, stated that:

> The old idea of science based on the sovereign right of abstract intellectual endeavour has gone forever. The new science is quite the opposite of uncontrolled search for truth which has been the ideal heretofore. The true freedom of science

is to support the State and share its destiny and make the search for truth subservient to this aim. (Taylor 1941, p. 39)

The previous year, Professor Philipp Lenard, a Nobel laureate, remarked that:

We must recognise that it is unworthy of a German—and indeed only harmful to him—to be the intellectual follower of a Jew. Natural science properly so-called is of completely Aryan origin and Germans must today also find their own way out into the unknown. Heil Hitler! (Taylor 1941, p. 39)

Before climbing into the multiscience bed, or jumping on the multiscience bandwagon, educators and others ought to be cautious and look carefully at who else is in the bed or aboard the wagon. Some bedfellows or fellow-travellers are unsavory. This is not the unworthy accusation of guilt by association. The caution has its force because the unpalatable fellows are sanctioned by the core of the multiscience doctrine. The doctrine rejects universalism and objectivity as ideals for science; it elevates interest to the rank of epistemological arbiter, and consequently elevated are race, class, sex, religion, politics, sexual preference, age and whatever else demarcates interest. In this situation, the determination of truth reduces to whose interest is most powerful or most politically correct. And so, on this postmodern view, Stalinists and Nazis can legitimately point to the class or race of scientists or research programs as an element, if not the main element, in their evaluation of the scientist or program.

The counterargument, leaving aside Stalinists and Nazis, is that mainstream science is in fact partisan but does not recognize itself to be; that universalism is an ideology to mask special interest. Postmodernists need to substantiate this argument, keeping in mind that it is intellectual or cognitive partisanship and interests that need to be established, not just material interests. The latter claim is uncontroversial.

Conclusion

A nation or society can, of course, decide upon the type of education it prefers. Education is, however, very expensive, both in individual and social effort. So the type of education is an important decision. Social class and gender have often been used as a basis for deciding what is appropriate education for different groups within a society. The liberal tradition has generally opposed this, and has tended towards the idea that the best should be available to everyone. Another basis for deciding what is an appropriate education may be ethnicity. A group may decide that their own cultural orientation is of overriding importance, and that they wish to give preeminence in education to their own cultural tradition. Few would argue with a people's right to make such a decision, but as with all decision-making, it needs to be informed, and decisions need to be made with regard for the consequences. To make decisions on the basis that ethno-sciences are cognitively equivalent to Western science is a mistake. There may be other bases for the decision, but this equivalence contention merely clouds the pressing educational and instructional issues. Paradoxically, a modern education and technological competence may be necessary for the survival of some traditional cultures and people. A society can usually adjust to changing beliefs; impoverishment, dispossession, powerlessness and marginalization are less easy to cope with.

We know enough about learning to know that cultural beliefs affect understanding of what is taught, and we know that teachers need to appreciate the ideas that children bring to their classes. This suggests that traditional sciences ought to be acknowledged in multicultural situations. But it is an altogether different matter to suggest that traditional sciences ought to be cultivated as science. The African educator Ogunniyi has said that:

> the aim of education should not be to supplant or denigrate a traditional culture but to help the people meet modern challenges. (Ogunniyi 1988, p. 8)

Modern challenges, as distinct from traditional life-style challenges, are best met by modern science. How to teach this science effectively in multicultural settings is the challenge: this challenge is not met by diversions into multiscience doctrines, or adoption of questionable relativisms.[17]

CHAPTER 10

Teacher Education

Everyone agrees that intelligent, knowledgeable and engaging teachers, who are interested in children, and know how to manage classrooms and teach creatively, are crucial for good education. Furthermore, teachers increasingly have to do more than just teach: they need either to develop local curricula, or to interpret national or provincial curricula for local use, they take part in school governance, and in policy-making that bears upon subjects taught in their school, and the levels to which subjects are taught to what students and so on. Good, well-prepared teachers are necessary for these complex and important tasks. There has, however, been less agreement on how best to prepare such teachers (Yager & Penick 1990). This question has been long debated, with contributions from entrenched professional and academic interests, and with political and economic expediency looming over most policy decisions. There is, of course, a prior question about how to recruit science teachers. Economics, cultural values, industrial matters and other extraeducational factors affect people's desire to become a teacher. Recruitment is a pressing problem, as indicated in the American Physical Society's warning that: "The young person, fresh out of college or graduate school, who wants to teach physics in high school or middle school may soon be extinct" (APS 1986, p. 1033).[1]

In the US 1986 saw the publication of two reports on teacher education that galvanized debate on the subject—the Carnegie Foundation's *A Nation Prepared*, and the Holmes Group's *Tomorrow's Teachers*.[2] There is a range of views about the best organization of teacher training programs. Some advocate no training at all: just take interested science graduates and put them in front of classes, or into apprenticeship roles in schools. In the UK the government has moved to partly bypass university teacher training in favour of a nineteenth-century in-school apprenticeship mode of training. In New Zealand, training requirements have been dropped, and employing bodies can employ whomever they wish, regardless of teacher training. The more usual arrangement is to require formalized teacher training. Where education studies are required for prospective teachers, their content has been contentious. Such studies usually consist of both theoretical or foundation studies (typically philosophy, sociology and psychology of education)[3] and applied or pedagogic studies (typically curriculum, teaching methods, and practice teaching). Notoriously, foundation studies are regarded by trainee teachers as the least relevant part of their program.

This chapter will suggest ways in which HPS-inspired philosophy and psychology programs can substitute for, or enrich, the usual foundation offerings, and greatly diminish the "irrelevance" factor. Further, HPS can enrich the standard methods or curriculum and instruction courses.

History and Philosophy of Science in Teacher Education

Many have argued that HPS should be part of the education of science teachers—the British *Thompson Report* in 1918 said "some knowledge of the history and philosophy of science should form part of the intellectual equipment of every science teacher in a secondary school" (Thompson 1918, p. 3). The Science Council of Canada, after advocating increased attention to HPS matters in the science curriculum, said: "Although Council does not expect children or adolescents to be trained in the philosophy of science, it does expect science educators to be trained in this area" (SCC 1984, p. 37). A 1981 review of the place of philosophy of science in British science-teacher education said:

> This more philosophical background which is being advocated for teachers would, it is believed, enable them to handle their science teaching in a more informed and versatile manner and to be in a more effective position to help their pupils build up the coherent picture of science—appropriate to age and ability—which is so often lacking. (Manuel 1981, p. 771)

Michael Polanyi suggested that HPS should be as much a part of science teacher education as literary and musical criticism is part of literary and musical education. So also it should be odd to think of a science teacher who has no knowledge of the terms of the discipline—"cause," "law," "explanation," "model," "theory," "fact"; no knowledge of the often conflicting objectives of his or her own discipline—to describe, to control, to understand; or no knowledge of the cultural and historical dimensions of his or her own discipline—the momentous issues involved in Galileo's trial, the cultural impact of Darwin's theory, the transformation in the quality of life brought about by Pasteur's and Jenner's discoveries, the challenges of genetic engineering and so on. Others have also indicated the advantages of including HPS in science teacher education programs (Eger 1987, Robinson 1969, Summers 1982).

Many examples have been given where HPS can contribute to better, more coherent, stimulating and critical teaching of specific curriculum topics, where HPS can increase participation rates and so on. These examples from the educational "bottom line" are compelling, but they are not the only ones that can be advanced. Teachers, as professionals, should have historical and philosophical knowledge of their subject matter quite independently of whether this knowledge is directly used in classrooms: teachers ought to know more about their subject than what they are required to teach. Teachers have a professional responsibility to see beyond the school fence. They are dealing with the formation of children's minds, and introducing children into what John Dewey called the intellectual conversation of mankind. Science teachers, in particular, are introducing children to a tradition that is complex, rich, influential and of great cultural significance. In contrast to drill sergeants or political commissars, teachers should have some perspective on their tradition. They have a responsibility to society, to their profession, and to their students both to understand science and to see science in its broad historical, philosophical and cultural contexts.

The opening pages of a 1929 text for science teachers make salutory reading. There a successful science teacher is described as one who:

> knows his own subject . . . is widely read in other branches of science . . . knows how to teach . . . is able to express himself lucidly . . . is skilful in manipulation . . . is resourceful both at the demonstration table and in the laboratory . . . is a logician to his finger-tips . . . is something of a philosopher . . . is so far an historian that he can sit down with a crowd of [students] and talk to them about the personal equations, the lives, and the work of such geniuses as Galileo, Newton, Faraday and Darwin. More than this he is an enthusiast, full of faith in his own particular work. (Westaway 1929, p. 3)

This ideal of a successful science teacher—putting aside the masculine language, for which Westaway himself apologizes (p. 4)—is timely. As has been mentioned, the new curricula being developed and implemented in Britain, the US, Denmark and other places will require such qualities in a teacher if the curricula are to be successfully taught—episodes in the history of science, and questions about the nature (philosophy) of science are part of these curricula.

The Stanford-based, Carnegie-funded, National Teacher Assessment Project, directed by Lee Shulman, is the foremost teacher assessment program in the US. Shulman rejects the behaviorist, managerial measures of teacher competence so long enshrined in evaluation practice. He asks about the "missing paradigm," the command of subject matter, and the ability to make it intelligible to students. For Shulman,

> Teachers must not only be capable of defining for students the accepted truths in a domain. They must also be able to explain why a particular proposition is deemed warranted, why it is worth knowing, and how it relates to other propositions, both within the discipline and without, both in theory and in practice. (Shulman 1986, p. 9)

To explain why a particular proposition is deemed warranted—for instance a proposition about genetic inheritance, or the conservation of energy, or the valency of sodium—assumes an epistemology of science. Teachers who have thought through some basic epistemological questions will be much better able to explain why a proposition is deemed warranted than those who have not had philosophical training. In classrooms this need to be able to explain belief in propositions is crucial when children's experimental results and observations are usually so at variance with what they are asked to believe.

Shulman's ideas are reflected in the National Board for Professional Teaching Standards—*What Teachers Should Know and Be Able To Do* (1989). An evaluation package for biology teachers that has been developed as part of the Carnegie project, this tries to assess teachers' grasp of the nature of science, its processes and determinants. In their words, "Do teachers hold a rich conception of the scientific enterprise as an interaction of the facts, laws and theories of a domain, mastering the skills to construct such knowledge, and recognizing that this knowledge is influenced by and has influence on human society?" (Collins 1989, p. 64).

What Type of Course?

Recent literature contains accounts of a number of HPS courses for trainee and practicing science teachers.[4] There is general agreement that in initial teacher training such courses should be applied or practical courses. Sending education students to a philosophy department to do "HPS I," is not the best way to proceed. HPS courses for teachers should begin with problems, literature or material that teachers can see as pertinent to their own professional development, or to the development of HPS-informed classroom materials and programs of study. Some of these courses have been aimed at bringing history and science teachers together to develop pedagogical material. The outcomes have been positive.[5]

Gerald Bakker and Len Clark have written a text (1988) and designed a course (1989) around the concept of explanation. Students can immediately appreciate that science is about explaining things, and that teaching is also about explaining things. This idea provides a pedagogically relevant path along which historical, philosophical and psychological matters can be traversed. Bakker and Clark deal with the distinction between science and pseudoscience, explanation and description, the covering law model of explanation, other models of scientific explanation and religious explanation. Science students are generally willing to read and think about these matters because they see their relevance to science. They can be led to investigate the current state of philosophical discussion about scientific explanation, which is well presented by, for instance, Philip Kitcher and Wesley C. Salmon (1989) Trainee teachers can also see the purpose of thinking about what it is to explain something to someone, and what it is for a pupil to understand something. The notions of understanding, explanation and reasons were central in the work of the philosopher of education Richard Peters, whose *Ethics and Education* (1966) argued for such notions as the hallmark of liberal education in contrast to mere training or indoctrination. There is a considerable philosophy of education literature on this topic to which students can be introduced.[6]

Ronald Good and James Wandersee (1992) have developed a graduate course on HPS for trainee science teachers. Central to their course are the ideas that: (1) the history of science should serve as an introduction to the philosophy of science; (2) the philosophy of science should be introduced in a nontechnical way; (3) both history and philosophy should be linked directly to science teaching. The focal question for the course is, What constitutes scientific progress? The course begins with Darwin's *Voyage of the Beagle*, in which Good and Wandersee identify twenty philosophical and methodological issues that students can identify or be presented with. Students then study Larry Laudan's *Science and Relativism* (1990), a Galileo-like dialogue between a pragmatist, a relativist, a positivist and a realist. Students were able to develop a richer understanding of science, and produced HPS-inspired units of work for classes.

Arthur Stinner and Harvey Williams have developed a science education course that examines "the major achievements of science as well as the practices of scientists throughout history." Their students design science stories, one for each of the major historical epochs, that are then used in classrooms (Stinner & Williams 1993).

My own course (Matthews 1990b), which has run with some success for a number of years, deals with two episodes in the history of science: the seventeenth-century revolution in astronomy and physics, and the nineteenth-century revolution in biology. The course is based upon selections of the writings of Galileo, Boyle, Newton, Huygens, Darwin and others.[7] These are "heroes" in science yet they have seldom been read by teachers who teach about them.[8] I have found, not suprisingly, that teachers appreciate the opportunity to read something of their work. As one teacher stated, "teachers are hungry for this knowledge." The philosophical issues—realism, instrumentalism, authority, reductionism, causality, explanation, idealization—are dealt with as they arise out of the text. The text also provides the opportunity for contextualizing the science; for discussing its intellectual, economic, religious, ideological contexts; and for considering the interaction between science and these broader contexts.[9] There is ample opportunity to take up issues of internal/external history of science, and of the sociology of science. The idea is not to produce historians and philosophers of science, but to stimulate teachers' interest in the subject and give them enough training to identify HPS issues as they arise in the classroom, texts and curriculum.

These HPS-for-science-teaching courses could replace more orthodox philosophy-of-education courses in science teacher education programs. Unfortunately, the orthodox philosophy courses often do not engage would-be science teachers, who often do not see their relevance to classroom practice. HPS courses wear their relevance on their sleeve, or at least on their course descriptions, and so this first hurdle to satisfactory progress is easily overcome. Israel Scheffler (1970), the philosopher of science and of education, made such a recommendation in a largely overlooked paper.[10]

Teachers' Epistemology

It is not just the subject matter of science that raises philosophical questions for teachers and students, it is also the context and conduct of classes and the development of curricula that raise these questions. The teacher needs to have an idea of what science is, needs to have a sense of the "essence" of science, an image of science that is going to be conveyed to classes and which is going to inform decision-making about texts, curriculum, lesson preparation, assessment and other pedagogic matters. Joseph Novak remarked that "any attempt to teach the content of science that does not consider its complex 'conceptual web,' and its evolving nature, is destined to failure, provided that our objective is *meaningful*, rather than verbatim, rote learning" (In Good & Wandersee 1992). This image of science is an important part of the background knowledge that teachers bring to their work; it structures the "pedagogical content knowledge" that Shulman has identified as so important for teaching. Beyond the specific concepts, the meaning of which is better grasped by philosophical elucidation, are broader questions of: What is this thing called Science? What typifies scientific method? Has the "nature" of science remained the same over the centuries? Does its epistemology change? What are its characteristic tests for truth claims? How do these differ from other intellectual pursuits? What is the relevant role of observation and reason in the conduct of science? Do and should ethics and politics enter into science? What is the role of authority in science? Are there any typically scientific attitudes that characterize good scientists and that might be encouraged in pupils? A teacher's epistemology or theory of science influences the understanding of science that students retain after they have forgotten the details of what has been learnt in their science classes.

Answers to these foregoing and other questions constitute a teacher's view of the "nature of science" which is conveyed to students in class. After four or more years in a science classroom, students come away with some teacher-influenced image of science: this ought to be as sophisticated and realistic as is possible in the circumstances. A teacher's theory about the nature of science, his or her epistemology, can be conveyed explicitly or implicitly. This epistemology affects the classroom behavior of teachers: How it is formed and what effects it has on teacher practice have been the subject of many recent studies.[11]

One thing that is known is that a teacher's epistemology is picked up indirectly. In 1989 only four of fifty-five institutions providing science teacher training in Australia offered a course in HPS. In 1990, of the fifteen leading centres of science teacher training in the US, only half required a course in philosophy of science; the proportion in the remaining hundreds of centres is likely to be far lower (Loving 1991). The situation in the UK is no more encouraging. In this situation a teacher's epistemology is thus largely picked up during his or her own science education; it is seldom consciously examined or refined. This is less than desirable for the formation of something so influential in teaching practice, and so important for professional development. There is a clear opportunity for fruitful collaboration between education and philosophy departments.

Analogy, Metaphor and Scientific Thinking

Analogy and metaphor is used constantly in textbooks and by teachers to explain science in terms that students can comprehend: the apt metaphor is often the key to pedagogical success. A good deal of science method courses are devoted to practice in the use of metaphor and models in the science classroom. Lee Shulman, in his elaboration of pedagogical content knowledge, wrote:

> Within the category of pedagogical content knowledge I include, for the most regularly taught topics in one's subject area, the most useful forms of representation of those ideas, the most powerful analogies, illustrations, examples, explanations, and demonstrations—in a word, the ways of representing and formulating the subject that make it comprehensible to others. (Shulman 1986, p. 9)

The use of metaphor and analogy in science teaching is increasingly researched (Duit 1991, Lawson 1993). What is often overlooked in this research is the degree to which metaphor is present in the content of scientific theory. It is not the case that there is nonmetaphorical science content that then has to be made intelligible by metaphor: analogy and metaphor are present within science. The use of metaphor in both science and education gives rise to interesting epistemological questions that can be encouraged in teacher training. This is another way in which philosophy can contribute to reflective and informed science teacher education. Some examples will indicate the issues.

Newton's *Principia* exemplifies the problem of metaphor in science. He goes to great length in the introductory definitions to point out that his treatment of motion will be a mathematical treatment:

> The words "attraction," "impulse" or any "propensity" to a centre, however, I employ indifferently and interchangeably, considering these forces not physically but merely mathematically. The reader should hence beware lest he think that by words of this sort I anywhere define a species or mode of action, or a physical cause or reason.

Having derived the mathematical relation between bodies, he gave it a commonplace name—"attraction"—because that was the only way to make the relation intelligible, but stressed that this was to be understood metaphorically. It is well known how his followers, and the originators of the corpuscularian worldview, lost sight of the metaphorical quality of Newton's descriptions. Newton's correspondence with Richard Bentley, the first Boyle lecturer, is in part concerned with pulling Bentley back'from his literalist, nonmathematical interpretation of the *Principia*'s definitions. Newton urges caution:

> You sometimes speak of gravity as essential and inherent to matter. Pray do not ascribe that notion to me, for the cause of gravity is what I do not pretend to know and therefore would take more time to consider it. (Thayer 1953, p. 53)

John Locke (1632–1704), the philosopher-champion of Newton and self-styled "underlaborer" in Newton's garden, struggled over the same matters as Bentley. In the first three editions of his famous *Essay Concerning Human Understanding* (1690, 1694, 1695) Locke enunciated the basic tenets of the mechanical worldview, saying that "bodies operate one upon another . . . by impulse, and nothing else." Increasingly he came to appreciate the contradiction between these tenets and the foundations of the *Principia*, which had been published in 1687. In a letter to Stillingfleet he admits that:

> It is true, I say, "that bodies operate by impulse, and nothing else." And so I thought when I writ it, and can yet conceive no other way of their operation. But I am since convinced by the judicious Mr. Newton's incomparable book, that it is too bold a presumption to limit God's power, in this point, by my narrow conceptions. The gravitation of matter towards matter, by ways inconceivable to me, is not only a demonstration that God can, if he pleases, put into bodies powers and ways of operation, above what can be derived from our idea of body, or can be explained by what we know of matter, but also an unquestionable and every where visible instance, that he has done so. And therefore in the next edition I shall take care to have that passage rectified. (Stein 1990, p. 32)

Book 2 of the fourth edition of the *Essay* (1700) contained these changes, which were the first changes within philosophical atomism, or the mechanistic worldview, prompted by modern science. This is an example of the interaction of physics and metaphysics that this book has discussed.[12] The problem with which Newton was grappling in the seventeenth century was felt more acutely after the scientific advances of the nineteenth and early twentieth centuries. Arthur Eddington said, in 1928, that:

> It is difficult to school ourselves to treat the physical world as purely symbolic. We are always relapsing and mixing with the symbols incongruous conceptions taken from the world of consciousness. Taught by long experience we stretch a hand to grasp the shadow, instead of accepting its shadowy nature. Indeed, unless we confine ourselves altogether to mathematical symbolism it is hard to

avoid dressing our symbols in deceitful clothing. When I think of an electron there rises to my mind a hard, red, tiny ball. (Eddington 1928/1978, p. xvii)

This comment was made in the context of Eddington's idealist worldview, but the problem of clothing the unknown in comfortable and familiar garb—the problem of speaking metaphorically—is just as pressing for realists. One aid to untangling the conceptual issues is to distinguish the realms of the natural world and the theorized world with which science deals. Eddington confuses the mathematical nature of the latter with the supposed mathematical nature of the former. Eddington's comment also invites the criticism that the Aristotelians made against Galileo's mathematization of science: the mathematics abstracts from the very physical processes that physics is meant to understand.

Darwinian theory, with its "struggle for existence," "war of nature," "tree of life," and "survival of the fittest," is full of metaphorical expression that can aid and also deflect understanding. Darwin's reconciliation of his gradualist assumptions with the abrupt breaks found in the fossil record, by use of the analogy of the damaged book with chapters, pages, paragraphs, sentences and words missing, is an outstanding instance of analogy in science.

How much science could proceed without metaphor is a moot point. Mach saw metaphor as indispensible for the growth and communication of science, but regarded it as only an aid to understanding that could be jettisoned:

What a simplification it involves if we can say, the fact *A* now considered comports itself, not in one, but in many or in *all* its features, like an old and well-known fact *B* . . . light like a wave motion or an electric vibration; a magnet, as it were laden with gravitating fluids. (Mach 1893/1986, p. 240)

As with theories more generally, Mach denied any truth value to metaphorical description; such description had only heuristic value. Max Black has taken a similar view: "Perhaps every science must start with metaphor and end with algebra; and perhaps without the metaphor there would never have been any algebra" (Black 1962, p. 242). An alternate view might be to accept that there is a continuum between description, representation and depiction, and, consequently, a continuum between description, model, metaphor, analogy, theory and so on. They are all ways of representing something about the world, and thus are all to some degree making truth claims about the world. This view is consistent with, as Wartofsky (1979) says, a modest realism.

Science thus makes powerful use of metaphor and analogy, both of which draw upon everyday or prescientific conceptions.[13] A constant problem for teachers and students is to keep apart the technical or scientific meaning of concepts and the commonplace images so often used to make the technical images comprehensible. An HPS component in teacher training allows consideration of the myriad number of rich epistemological, ontological and psychological issues occasioned by the constant metaphorical and analogical conversation of classrooms and textbooks. HPS can also contribute to the more standard instructional concerns with finding metaphors that work.

History of Science and the Psychology of Learning

Thus far, the argument for HPS in teacher education has been made in terms of HPS's contribution to the teaching of specific subject matter, its integrative function in bringing science and other disciplines—history, mathematics, technology, literature—together, and its importance for a professional's understanding of his or her occupation. But increasingly, HPS is being shown to be also relevant to problems in the learning of the sciences.

A significant part of the recent HPS and science teaching literature has been concerned with the conjunction of HPS and the psychology of learning. Concerning history, the question asked is: In which ways do the histories of individual cognitive development and the process of historical conceptual development shed light upon each other? This issue has had a long history, and has received new impetus from cognitive theories of science in which the concepts and methods of cognitive science have been used to study science and its processes (Giere 1987, Jung 1993).

The view was given its most influential exposition in the writings of Jean Piaget; indeed, it underlies his account of cognitive development. Thomas Kuhn popularized the "cognitive ontogeny recapitulates scientific phylogeny" thesis among historians and philosophers of science. He said:

> Part of what I know about how to ask questions of dead scientists has been learned by examining Piaget's interrogations of living children. (Kuhn 1977, p. 21)

Conversely, the historian of science, Alexander Koyré, observed that it was Aristotle's physics that taught him to understand Piaget's children. The philosopher Philip Kitcher has recently (1988) affirmed that developmental psychologists can gain insights into the linguistic advances of young children by studying the shifts that have occurred in the history of science; and that historians and philosophers of science can learn from the experimental results and analyses of the child psychologists.

Joseph Nussbaum (1983) provided an early review of the relevant science education literature dealing with individual learning and the history of science. Subsequent contributors to this area of research have included Gauld (1991), Nersessian (1989), Niedderer (1992) and Wandersee (1985). A model paper in this research tradition is that of Melvin Steinberg and others (1990), on how the study of Newton's slow conceptual development out of impetus theory towards the inertial mechanics of his 1687 *Principia* can illuminate the conceptual journey that modern students have to make from their naive noninertial misconceptions to an understanding of the mechanics of the mature Newton. Gruber (1974) has provided a Piagetian study of Darwin's conceptual development.

More generally, important studies of individual conceptual change in science, that is, science learning, have made use of historical and philosophical theses. Peter Hewson's (1981) initial formulation of the conceptual change model of science learning quotes Kuhn and Lakatos on the conditions for theory change and, following the latter, reports that "some of the most important conceptions influencing conceptual change in an individual were found to be . . . the metaphysical [and epistemological] commitments which he or she held" (Hewson 1981, p. 391). The influential Posner et al. (1982) study, to which Hewson contributed, on "Accommodation of a Scientific Conception: Toward a Theory of Conceptual Change" also draws upon the accounts of scientific theory change given by Kuhn, Toulmin and Lakatos. They propose that, for individual conceptual change or learning to take place, four conditions must be met:

1) There must be dissatisfaction with current conceptions.
2) The proposed replacement conception must be intelligible.
3) The new conception must be initially plausible.
4) The new conception must offer solutions to old problems and to novel ones; it must suggest the possibility of a fruitful research program.

Strike and Posner, in retrospect, describe their original conceptual change theory as "largely an epistemological theory, not a psychological theory . . . it is rooted in a conception of the kinds of things that count as *good* reasons" (Strike & Posner 1992, p. 150). Their original theory is concerned with the "formation of rational belief" (p. 152); it does not "describe the typical workings of student minds or any laws of learning" (p. 155). Their theory of individual learning is dependent upon the historical and philosophical analyses of scientific change provided by Thomas Kuhn and Stephen Toulmin.[14] Consequently science education students should have some knowledge of these analyses in order to competently appraise and understand the Strike and Posner thesis.

Susan Carey, a psychologist, has suggested that success in comprehending the complexity of conceptual change in science students will "require the collaboration of cognitive scientists and science educators, who together must be aware of the understanding of science provided by both historians and philosophers of science" (Carey 1986, p. 1125). Richard Duschl, Richard Hamiliton and Richard Grandy—a science educator, a cognitive psychologist and a philosopher of science—have taken up Carey's suggestion and have provided an extensive review of the ways in which the process of theory development by scientists can be compared to an individual's acquisition of knowledge of the world (Duschl et al. 1992). They rely upon cognitive studies of science to make their connections between epistemology and learning theory.[15]

Not everyone has been as convinced of the utility of this interaction between cognitive psychology and the history of science. Richard Kitchener, in a review of philosophical responses to Piaget's program of research, commented that "Unfortunately, Piaget's program of a genetic epistemology has not been widely discussed by philosophers, nor critically evaluated in a comprehensive and scholarly way" (1985, p. 4).[16] Kitchener has provided a normative interpretation of Piaget that is squarely based upon the Galilean method of idealization, which seeks to clearly separate the epistemological from the psychological issues involved in the appraisal of Piaget's theory and in its application to science education (Kitchener 1992, 1993).

Piaget's work leads to one obvious area of investigation: Do the intuitive, immediate conceptions of children mirror the early stages in the development of scientific understanding in different domains? At one level of simplification the answer is "yes." Children do seem to have preinstruction understanding, or naive beliefs, that parallel early scientific, or prescientific notions.[17] This has been demonstrated for the field of mechanics, where children and adults routinely believe versions of Aristotelian mechanics and of impetus theory.[18] Bartov has shown that intuitive conceptions of biological processes are highly teleological (Bartov 1978). Others point to children's Lamarckian-like account of inheritance (Lucas 1971, Brumby 1979). Mas, Perez and Harris (1987) conducted a study on adolescent beliefs in chemistry among students who had studied up to five years of chemistry at school. A significant proportion continued to hold the Aristotelian-like belief that gases had no mass despite repeated teaching of the atomic hypothesis of gases.

The persistence of intuitive or naive beliefs in the face of science instruction has generated productive exchanges between teachers, psychologists, philosophers and historians, of the type asked for by Carey. McCloskey (1983a, b) found that eighty percent of college physics students continued to believe in impetus despite instruction to the contrary. Studies by Finegold and Gorsky (1988), Gauld (1989), Linn (1983) and Osborne (1983) are just some of many that document this resistance of intuitive ideas to instruction. The embarrassing film, "A Private Universe," taken at a Harvard commencement ceremony in which the brightest in America confidently talk nonsense about the cause of the seasons is startling confirmation of the strength of intuitive beliefs and/or the weakness of instruction (Schneps 1987). Martin Eger, in a series of articles, has shown the usefullness of hermeneutical analysis for understanding these problems with meaning acquisition, and more generally, understanding the interpretative role of science learning (Eger 1992, 1993a, b).

It has been indicated that the major research programs in science learning are based on assumptions about, and replete with references to, the history and philosophy of science. Therefore preservice or in-service courses for science teachers in the psychology of learning ought to include or be augmented with studies of the history and philosophy of science. Without such courses, students and teachers must take on faith the views attributed to philosophers such as Kuhn, Toulmin and Lakatos. This is less than satisfactory preparation for a profession committed to rational inquiry.

Idealizations in Science and the Learning of Science

Idealization in science has been recognized as one of the major stumbling blocks to meaningful learning of science. This is in part because intuitive beliefs are so strongly influenced by everyday, concrete experience. Lewis Wolpert, in a recent book on *The Unnatural Nature of Science* (1992), has correctly remarked that:

> Scientific ideas are, with rare exceptions, counter-intuitive: they cannot be acquired by simple inspection of phenomena and are often outside everyday experience . . . doing science requires a conscious awareness of the pitfalls of "natural" thinking. (Wolpert 1992, p. xi)

He is essentially repeating what Pierre Duhem said at the turn of the century, when he warned against grounding science instruction in common sense.[19] Not just the content, but the method of science is alien.

HPS can contribute a good deal to trainee teachers' understanding of this fundamental issue. Schecker (1992) has addressed some of these questions in an interesting way. He asked 254 high school students to comment upon the following statement:

> In physics lessons there are often assumptions or experiments of thought, which obviously cannot be realized in actual experiments, like completely excluding air resistance and other frictional effects or assuming an infinitely lasting linear motion.

The students were asked to comment on whether the method was useful or not useful. Eleven percent said it was useless, "Why should I consider something that does not exist?" A large group, up to fifty percent said it was useful, but only for physics because physics did not deal with reality: "I don't need to refer everything to reality. I am simply interested in physics." Only about twenty-five percent had any comprehension of the method of idealization in science. Champagne and others expressed the matter in the following terms: "the arduousness of learning mechanics is expressed in the effort required as students shift their thinking from one paradigm to another. Paradigm shifts are not accomplished easily, neither in the scientific enterprise nor in the minds of students" (Champagne et al. 1980, p. 1077).

Floden and others (1987), and Brandon (1989), have discussed many pedagogical problems occasioned by the rupture of science education from everyday experience. Garrison and Bentley (1990) develop the theme in a discussion of the influential Posner et al. theory of conceptual change. Ginev provides a very sophisticated account of science curricula built upon the recognition that: "The very process of idealisation is considered as the epistemological *differentia specifica* of science" (1990, p. 65).

History and philosophy can make the idealizations of science more understandable, and can explain them as scientific tools of trade, or instruments, whereby the complex concrete world can be investigated. Just as material tools—spanners, beaters, microscopes—can be more or less useful, or more or less elegant, so also can the particular idealizations in science. To represent a planet as a point mass, and its orbit as an ellipse, was the precondition for Newton's masterful mathematical analysis of planetary motion. In the light of refined measurements and observations, the initial assumptions can be altered and the picture of planetary motion made more realistic or concrete. Eventually, the idealizations allow a person to step out of a rocket and walk on the moon's surface. Some understanding of this is important for students being introduced to the "world of science." A failure to appreciate what idealization is and is not has been at the basis of a lot of antiscience criticism. It was, of course, Newtonian idealization that the Romantic reaction was directed against. For them (Keats, Goethe and so on) the rich world of lived experience was not captured by the colorless point masses of Newton.[20] In the twentieth century, Marcuse, Husserl, Tillich and others have repeated versions of this charge. At the end of World War Two, Aldous Huxley commented on the matter, saying:

> The scientific picture of the world is ´inadequate, for the simple reason that science does not even profess to deal with experience as a whole, but only with certain aspects of it in certain contexts. All of this is quite clearly understood by the more philosophically minded men of science. . . . [Unfortunately] our times contains a large element of what may be called "nothing but" thinking. (Huxley 1947, p. 28)

The prominent German science educator, Martin Wagenschein, has written on this dichotomy at the heart of an education in science:

> My deepest motive force is the cleavage between an original feeling-at-home within nature and a strong fasination by physics and mathematics, and the ensuing irritation by the growing alienation between man and nature effected by science, starting early at school. My pedagogical aim is to overcome—still better to avoid—the cleavage by an educationally centered humanistic physics teaching. (Wagenschein 1962, p. 9, W. Jung trans.)

A historically and philosophically literate science teacher can assist students to grasp just how science captures, and does not capture, the real, subjective, lived world. An HPS-illiterate teacher leaves students with the unhappy choice between disowning their own world as a fantasy, or rejecting the world of science as a fantasy.[21] Sutton (1992) is illuminating.

Conclusion

There are many reasons why study of the history and philosophy of science should be part of preservice and in-service science teacher education programs. Increasingly school science courses address historical, philosophical, ethical and cultural issues occasioned by science. Teachers of such curricula obviously need knowledge of HPS. Without such knowledge they either present truncated versions of the curricula, or repeat uncritical gossip about the topics mentioned. Either way their students are done a disservice. But even where curricula do not include such "nature of science" sections, HPS can contribute to more interesting and critical teaching of science.

Beyond these "practical" arguments for HPS in teacher education, there are compelling "professional" arguments. A teacher ought to know more than just what he or she teaches. As educators, teachers need to know something about the body of knowledge they are teaching, something about how this knowledge has come about, how its claims are justified and what its limitations are. Teachers should have a feel for, or appreciation of, the tradition of inquiry into which they are initiating students. HPS fosters this.

Enough has been said in this book to suggest that many of the issues in the history and philosophy of science are complex and contentious. The jury is still out on important matters. The art of the teacher is to judge the sophistication of his or her students, and present a picture of science that is intelligible to them without being overwhelming. Students need to get their feet, to become familiar with a tradition, before they are confronted with the "cutting-edge" questions. The teacher may have strong opinions on various HPS issues, but the point of education is to develop the students' minds, which means giving students the knowledge and wherewithal to develop informed opinions. If HPS in science teaching becomes a catechism, then it defeats one of its major purposes. HPS in teacher training programs can do something towards broadening the vision of teachers, and having their students not only arrive at destinations (scientific competence), but arrive with broader horizons, having travelled with a different view. In the long run this contributes to the health of science, and of society.

Education systems have a responsibility to identify and transmit the best of our cultural heritage. Science is one of the most important parts of this heritage. The history and philosophy of science allows science teachers to better understand their own social and professional responsibilities as part of a great tradition of achievement and intellectual orientation.

Notes

Preface

1. The proceedings of the 1989 Tallahassee conference are available in Herget (1989, 1990); those of the 1992 Kingston conference are in Hills (1992).
2. The journal special issues include the following: *Educational Philosophy and Theory* 20(2), (1988); *Synthese* 80(1), (1989); *Interchange* 20(2), (1989); *Studies in Philosophy and Education* 10(1), (1990); *Science Education* 75(1), (1991); *Journal of Research in Science Teaching* 29(4), (1992); *International Journal of Science Education* 12(3), (1990); and *Interchange* 23(2,3), (1993)
3. The journal is published by Kluwer Academic Publishers, P.O. Box 17, 3300 AA Dordrecht, The Netherlands. It is available at reduced rates through the International HPS&ST Group (inquiries to the author).

1. The Rapprochement Between History, Philosophy and Science Education

1. There is a large literature on the theory and practice of liberal education. Peters (1966, chs. 1, 2) and Bantock (1981, ch. 4) are useful introductions. The contributions to Obler & Estrin (1962) focus on the contribution of science to a liberal education, as do the arguments in Holton (1973) and Schwab (1945).
2. In the seventeenth century Giambattista Vico turned his back on the new science of Galileo and the new mathematics of Descartes. Subsequently, many other critics, including the literary Romantics, some religious traditions and various countercultural movements, have repeated Vico's stand. A good account of "Science and Its Critics" can be found in Passmore (1978) and Holton (1993c). Phenomenological philosophers such as Husserl (Husserl 1954/1970) also criticize the mathematization of science inaugurated by Galileo on account of its failure to grasp the experiential realities of the life world.
3. Jon D. Miller has conducted a series of large-scale studies on scientific literacy in the US. On the basis of ability to say something intelligible about concepts such as "molecule," "atom," "byte," in 1985 he judged only three percent of high school graduates, twelve percent of college graduates, and eighteen percent of college doctoral graduates to be scientifically literate. See Miller (1983, 1987, 1992).
4. The British National Curriculum is documented in NCC (1988). It is discussed in Akeroyd (1989), Ray (1991), and Solomon (1991). The Danish curriculum in the History of Science and Technology is discussed in Nielsen & Nielsen (1988), and Nielsen & Thomsen (1990). In The Netherlands there has been

a Physics in Society course since 1981 (Eijkelhof & Swager 1983), and since 1972 various materials generated by the PLON project have incorporated an HPS dimension (Project Curriculum Development in Physics, PO Box 80.008, 3508 TA Utrecht, The Netherlands). The Project 2061 proposals are contained in AAAS (1989) and republished in Rutherford & Ahlgren (1990); they are discussed in Stein (1989). A discussion of STS programs and a guide to the literature can be found in McFadden (1989) and Yager (1993).

5. Inquiries about the international group can be made to the author. The third international conference will be held in Minneapolis in October 1995. Inquiries to Professor Fred Finley, Department of Curriculum and Instruction, University of Minnesota, Minneapolis, MN 55455–0208.

6. These were held in Pavia (1983), Munich (1986), Paris (1988), Cambridge (1990) and Madrid (1992). For *Proceedings* of the conferences see Bevilacqua & Kennedy (1983), Thomsen (1986), Blondel & Brouzeng (1988), and Moreno (1992). Inquiries about the European History of Physics and Physics Teaching group can be made to Professor Fabio Bevilacqua, Physics Department, Pavia University, Pavia, Italy.

7. The US group meet during the US History of Science Society conferences. They can be contacted through Dr David Rhees, The Bakken Museum, 3537 Zenith Ave. S., Minneapolis, MN 55416, USA. The British group held a conference on History of Science and Science Teaching at Oxford University in 1987 (Shortland & Warwick 1989), and at the University of Sheffield in 1992. They can be contacted through Mr Peter Ellis, 12 Belvedere St, Isle of Wight, PO33 2JW, England.

8. Fifteen percent of US high school physics students were following this program at its peak, and it was widely used outside the US. The philosophy behind this program can be read in Gerald Holton (1978a), and in the symposium published in *The Physics Teacher* (1967, vol. 5 no. 2). Other evaluations of Harvard Project Physics can be found in Aikenhead (1974), Brush (1978, 1989), Russell (1981), and Welch & Walberg (1972).

9. This was first published in 1963 and went through four editions up to 1980.

2. Historical Debates About the Science Curriculum

1. Rodger Bybee has reminded science education reformers of the need to seek information from the history of past reforms (Bybee 1982). Others to stress the same point are Leo Klopfer and Audrey Champagne (1990), and Senta Raizen (1991).

2. DeBoer (1991) provides a comprehensive history of leading ideas in science education. Other accounts of the history of science education are Bybee (1993), Glass (1970), Hodson (1987) and Waring (1979). A good source of materials for charting the history of US science education are the occasional yearbooks published by the National Society for the Study of Education. These include the 3rd, *Nature Study* (1904), the 31st, *A Program for Teaching Science* (1932), the 46th, *Science Education in American Schools* (1947) and the 59th, *Rethinking Science Education* (1960).

3. Two standard histories of nineteenth-century schooling are, for the US, Butts & Cremin (1953), and for the UK, Curtis & Boultwood (1964).

4. Some of this seminal debate can be read in Armstrong (1903), Dewey (1910), Huxley (1885/1964), Mach (1895/1986) and Nunn (1907). In England there was a celebrated exchange between Thomas Huxley and Matthew Arnold, occasioned by the former's 1880 essay "Science and Culture" in Bibby (1971). Arnold's reply "Literature and Science" is in Brown (1947).

5. The "new movement" should really have been called the "old movement," but this, one surmises, was not thought a progressive enough name. Accounts of this turn-of-the-century debate can be read in Hodson (1910), Mann (1912) and Woodhull (1910).

6. The titles of other commonly used texts were: *Applied Biology*, Bigelow & Bigelow, 1911; *A Civic Biology*, Hunter (1914); *Practical Biology*, Smallwood, Reveley, & Bailey (1916); *Civic Biology*, Hodge & Dawson (1918); *Biology and Human Welfare*, Peabody & Hunt (1924).

7. The history of this 1950s crisis, and its attendant educational reforms, can be found in numerous sources. Some useful ones are: Bybee (1993), Crane (1976), DeBoer (1991), Dede & Hardin (1973), Jackson (1983), Klopfer & Champagne (1990), Raizen (1991) and Welch (1979).

8. Jerome Bruner says of Zacharias that "it was Zack more than anybody else who converted *Sputnik* shock into the curriculum reform movement that it became rather than taking some other form" (Bruner 1983, p. 180).

9. A discussion of the educational theory behind PSSC can be found in Easley (1959), Finlay (1962) and less directly in Bruner (1960).

10. During the boom period, millions of students studied the NSF-supported curricula: PSSC (one million in 1956–1960), CHEMS (one million in 1959–1963), BSCS (ten million in 1959 –1990), IPS (one million in 1963–1972), ESS (one million in 1961–1971), SAPA (one million in 1963–1974). These constituted the major league of curricula. In 1976–1977 it was estimated that nineteen million students were using the new curriculum materials; this number represented forty-three percent of the school population (Welch 1979, Klopfer & Champagne 1990).

11. Another review of these case studies can be found in Klopfer (1969).

12. Other reviews of inquiry learning and the NSF reforms can be found in Shymansky et al. (1983) and Shymansky et al. (1990).

13. It was not until the Education Act of 1870 that state-funded primary education appeared, and not until the Acts of 1902 and 1903 that state secondary schools appeared.

14. A history of the nineteenth-century development of science education in England and the competing demands upon it can be found in Layton (1973).

15. In the 1868 lecture he said:

> If I am justified in my conception of the ideal of a liberal education; and if what I have said about the existing educational institutions of the country is also true, it is clear that the two have no sort of relation to one another; that the best of our schools and the most complete of our university trainings give but a narrow, one-sided, and essentially illiberal education—while the worst give what is really next to no education at all. (In Bibby 1971, p. 96)

16. Accounts of the life and achievements of Armstrong can be found in Richmond & Quraishi (1964), and Brock (1973). A collection of twenty-four of his own

articles and addresses were published as *The Teaching of Scientific Method and other Papers on Education* (1903). A selection of these articles can be found in Praagh (1973).

17. This didactic teaching style was praised in a review of a 1892 *Practical Physics* textbook which commended the book because it contained "a very complete list of experiments and practical exercises with full directions as to how to do them, why they are done and what to observe" (Richmond & Quraishi 1964, p. 512). The style was made notorious by Dickens's Mr. Gradgrind in *Hard Times,* with his insistence on "facts, facts, facts, and nothing but the facts" in the classroom.

18. His views are presented in numerous *The School Science Review* articles over a span of forty years. His first journal article was in 1933. He elaborated his approach to molecular chemistry in a series of articles in 1957, vol. 39, 1958, vol. 39, 1959, vol. 40, 1961, vol. 42. His famous "The Copper Problem," where he defends Armstrong's heurism against Nuffield science is elaborated in eight articles in *The School Science Review*: 1963, vol. 44, 1964, vol. 45, 1964, vol. 46, 1965, vol. 47, 1966, vol. 47, 1967, vol. 48, 1967, vol. 49, 1968, vol. 49. G. van Praagh's *Chemistry by Discovery* (London 1949) is another example of Armstrong's heurism.

19. He wrote an important book on Mach's philosophy of science (Bradley 1971).

20. As in the US there were personnel problems. A survey by Smithers and Robinson at Manchester University indicated that thirty percent of senior physics classes and twenty percent of chemistry classes were taught by teachers who did not have majors in these subjects. Primary science was in an even more precarious state. A 1978 Her Majesty's Inspectorate (HMI) Report said that most primary teachers spent no more than forty-five minutes per week teaching science, and that many lacked the skills to effectively use inquiry and problem solving strategies. They lacked the confidence to teach science.

21. Bruner wrote a chairperson's report on the Woods Hole conference which was published as *The Process of Education* (1960). This immediately became an international best-seller, being translated into nineteen languages, and was described in the *New York Herald Tribune* as a "classic, comparable in its philosophical centrality and humane concreteness to Dewey's essays on education." A more personal account of the conference can be found in his autobiography *In Search of Mind* (Bruner 1983, pp. 181–188).

22. He was in large part responsible for initiating this turn with his 1956 *The Study of Thinking*. At the time psychology had been colonized by behaviorism, and his own Harvard Department was "locked in a standoff between Skinner's operant conditioning and Steven's psychophysics" (Bruner 1983, p. 122). Whatever the advances of the cognitive turn were in psychology departments, they were much slower in departments of education, where some such departments in the 1960s made successful pigeon training a precondition for the award of the doctorate. My own psychology professor in the early 1970s said, only half jokingly, that he would like to study human beings, but he doubted whether they could tell us anything about rats! Novak (1977) outlines the lingering grip of behaviorism on educational psychology.

23. Among the more substantial contributions were Bruner (1961), Romey (1968), Rutherford (1964), Schwab (1962), and Shulman & Keislar (1966).

3. Contemporary Curricular Developments

1. This publication received wide media coverage. Articles appeared with headings such as "Can American Schools Produce Scientifically Literate High School Graduates?" and "Can Democracy Survive Scientific Illiteracy?" (Bauer 1992, p. 1). American business establishments expressed their concern, with the Committee for Economic Development reporting that "far too many American children continue to grow up without the fundamental skills and knowledge necessary to be productive in the workplace . . . unless we act swiftly and decisively . . . we are jeopardizing America's survival as a free and prosperous society and condemning much of a new generation to lives of poverty and despair" (Committee for Economic Development 1991, p. 12).

2. The NAEP reports are titled *The Science Report Card*. They can be obtained from the Educational Testing Service, Princeton, NJ.

3. For example, the twenty-five percent of Canadian eighteen-year-olds taking chemistry knew more than the very select one percent of their US peers taking chemistry. The twenty-eight percent of Canadian eighteen-year-olds taking biology knew more than the six percent of US students who took the subject. Whereas only one percent of US eighteen-year-olds took a physics class, twenty-four percent of their Norwegian peers took physics. The situation in elementary school was no more encouraging. One study showed that at the time, the best students in twenty fifth-grade mathematics classrooms in Minneapolis were bettered by every single classroom in Sendai, Japan and by students in nineteen of twenty classrooms studied in Taipeh, Taiwan (Stevenson, Lee & Stigler, 1986). Stevenson's study has ranged over twelve years, looking at 204 classrooms in Beijing, Taipei, Sendai and Chicago (Stevenson 1992). Some government and educational representatives maintained that at least the very best US students held their own against other countries. Not so, maintained Lawrence Feinberg from the National Assessment Governing Board: "Actually, when compared with the same top slice of students in the 15 countries that tested representative samples of their population, the top 10% of US students rank near the bottom for 13-year-olds in both math and science. That's where the average scores for the US rank too" (Fisher 1992a, p. 59).

4. Information on the National Science Standards can be obtained from The Standards Group, National Research Council, 2101 Constitution Ave, Washington, DC 20418.

5. John Penick has recently published an annotated bibliography of 250 articles on the subject of science literacy (Penick 1993). This publication exposes the full range of opinions on the topic.

6. US high school seniors spend as much time watching television (twenty-four hours per week) as they do on learning-related tasks at school. A staggering twenty-five percent of fourth-graders watch television for more than six hours per day; while forty percent of twelfth-graders watch it for more than three hours per day. The number of rapes, shootings, car smashes, situational idiocies, political evasions, crass advertisements, and so on, seen on television per hundred hours viewed, is best not tabulated. It is little wonder that fourteen percent of American seventeen-year-olds are functionally illiterate, and that

few American children read more than eleven pages a day either at home or at school (Fisher 1992b, p. 51).

7. Both the AAAS's Project 2061, and the NSTA's Scope, Sequence, and Coordination programs speak of the need to limit curriculum content so that understanding may be developed. The NSTA program admirably does away with the century old "layer cake" curriculum structure—astronomy in the first year of high school, biology in the second, chemistry in the third and physics in the fourth—in favor of an integrated approach. Sadly it is largely bereft of historical, philosophical or cultural dimensions. This neglect is illustrative of the ground that needs to be made up in bringing HPS and science education together.

8. The director of the project is Dr James F. Rutherford, who in the 1960s was an assistant director of the Harvard Project Physics course. The AAAS distributes a Newsletter outlining the ongoing implementation and evaluation of Project 2061. It is available from their headquarters at 1333 H Street NW, Washington DC 20005.

9. This can be seen in representative documents such as the 1966 *Education and the Spirit of Science*, published by the Education Policies Commission. There it is stated that in science "generalizations are induced from discrete bits of information gathered through observation conducted as accurately as the circumstances permit," and that science seeks for "verification" of its claims (Education Policies Commission 1966, p. 18).

10. The Biological Sciences Study Committee have recently published a collection of background papers on HPS for teachers that can assist this engagement; the paper of Peter Machamer (1992) on "Philosophy of Science: An Overview for Educators" is particularly useful.

11. Some useful discussions of the interconnection between history of science and philosophy of science can be found in Hacking (1992), Lakatos (1971), McMullin (1970, 1975), Shapere (1984b) and Wartofsky (1976).

12. Too often philosophy of science courses neglect the history of science. Commonly students read of the debates over scientific methodology engaged in by Carnap, Nagel, Popper, Kuhn, Lakatos, Feyerabend, Laudan, van Fraassen, and others, but have to take the contenders' historical examples and interpretations on faith. What should be a course that enhances critical thinking can, in the absence of history, become a catechism lesson.

13. The unpleasant politics of the revision are described by Duncan Graham, the first chairperson of the NCC (Graham 1993). There are serious questions about the degree to which the clear HPS attainments of the 1988 report can be met within the guidelines of the second report. The political origins and educational implications of the 1988 Act are discussed in Flude & Hammer (1990).

14. Eight papers surveying principles and issues in contemporary US science education curriculum reform are in Shymansky & Kyle (1992). See also Bybee (1993). Raizen identifies the central tension in the contemporary US reforms as the fact that "science, by its very nature, is elitist, whereas education has become more and more populist" (Raizen 1991, p. 1).

4. History of Science in the Curriculum

1. Informed and cogent arguments for a historical dimension in the teaching of science have been provided by, among others, Stephen Brush (1969), Bernard

Cohen (1950), James Conant (1947), Gerald Holton (1978a), Leo Klopfer (1969, 1992), Helge Kragh (1992), Thomas Russell (1981) and Walter Jung (1983).

2. For the writings and arguments of Fleck, see the collection of essays in Cohen & Schnelle (1986).

3. Piaget's position is stated most fully in Piaget & Garcia (1989). Franco & Colinvaux-de-Dominguez (1992) and Kitchener (1986, chs. 6, 7) discuss the matter. Strauss (1988) contains articles on the theme.

4. Nahum Kipnis, at the Bakken Musuem in Minneapolis, has produced an exemplary book of lesson suggestions and activities on optics for teachers that is based upon the history of optics (Kipnis 1992).

5. For the life, times and influence of Galileo, see, for example, the essays in McMullin (1967); for Newton, see the essays in Fauvel (1988); for Darwin, see the essays in Appleman (1970).

6. Reviews of its chequered career can be found in Brush (1989) and Klopfer (1969, 1992). Kauffman (1989) examines specifically the use of history in teaching chemistry.

7. See the articles of Sammis (1932), Oppe (1936) and Jaffe (1938); and the texts of Jaffe (1942) and Hogg (1938).

8. For good or bad, Kuhn's personal transformation caused a massive transformation of professional history and philosophy of science, and indeed of many other academic fields: for three decades the ambiguous and oft-misunderstood idea of "paradigm" and its relativist epistemology has been a loose cannon on the intellectual deck. Critical accounts of Kuhn's epistemology are in Gutting (1980), Shapere (1984a) and Shimony (1976). A comprehensive account of pre- and post-Kuhnian philosophy of science is in Suppe (1977).

9. Holton was subsequently instrumental in developing in the early 1960s—with Stephen Brush, Fletcher Watson, James Rutherford, and others—the Harvard Project Physics course for secondary schools. Holton produced a number of substantial defenses of the liberal view of science education (Holton 1973, 1975, 1978a), and wrote a college physics text embodying historical and philosophical themes (Holton 1952). At the end of the 1980s James Rutherford was appointed director of the Project 2061 program of the AAAS.

10. This was a 1950 address to the American Association of Physics Teachers—"A Sense of History in Science" (Cohen 1950). After obtaining his PhD in the history of science, the second such degree awarded in the US, Cohen taught in the General Science course, and wrote his own best seller, *The Birth of a New Physics* (Cohen 1961), for the PSSC school physics committee.

11. Klopfer later said that scientific literacy encompasses five components

  • Knowledge of significant science facts, concepts, principles and theories.
  • The ability to apply relevant science knowledge in situations of everyday life.
  • An understanding of general ideas about the organization of the scientific enterprise, the important interactions of science, technology and society, and the characteristics of scientists.
  • The ability to utilize the processes of scientific inquiry, and an understanding of the nature of scientific inquiry.
  • The possession of informed attitudes and interests related to science. (Klopfer 1990, p. 3)

12. The first edition contained eight cases: three in biology—The Sexuality of Plants, Frogs and Batteries, Cells of Life; two in chemistry—Discovery of Bromine, Chemistry of Fixed Air; and three in physics—Fraunhofer Lines, Speed of Light, Air Pressure.

13. The instrument used for measuring students' understanding of science was the Test of Understanding of Science (TOUS), published by the Educational Testing Service. This is described in the *Journal of Research in Science Teaching*, vol. 1, pp. 73–80. A critical review of the assumptions of the TOUS test can be found in Lucas (1975).

14. Joseph Schwab was long associated with the University of Chicago and was imbued with its "great books" tradition. He had, independently of Kuhn and contemporaneously with him, enunciated a distinction between "fluid" and "stable" periods of scientific inquiry which parallels Kuhn's better-known distinction between "revolutionary" and "normal" science. A list of Schwab's publications occurs in Matthews & Winchester (1989). Selections of his articles are contained in Ford & Pugno (1964), and Westbury & Wilkof (1978).

15. The philosopher and historian, William Whewell, was one of the first to advocate the contributions of the history of science to educational development (Whewell 1855). This tradition has been well documented by Bill Brock (1989), Edgar Jenkins (1979, 1990), and W. J. Sherratt (1982, 1983).

16. Brief accounts can be found for West Germany (Teichmann 1986a), for Italy (Galdabini 1986), for France (Blondel 1986), for Denmark (Thomsen 1986), and for Sweden (Vedin 1986).

17. An excellent and beautifully illustrated text has been produced for the course (Nielsen, Nielsen, and Jensen 1990, currently available only in Danish). The book is reviewed by Svante Lindqvist in *Science & Education* 2(2), 1993.

18. For a discussion of Galileo's erroneous theory of the tides see Brown (1976).

19. A nice sequence of such lessons can be seen in Ekstig (1990). A second-year university science student, training to be a secondary teacher, wrote the following about the Ekstig article:

> I am a student who did not do physics for the Higher School Certificate and only did half a year of university physics before dropping out after failing the mid-year exam. I have heard myself say many times that I dislike immensely and cannot do physics. After reading this article I wonder at my negative attitude. Basically I have never given the subject much of a chance, but on the other hand I have never heard it or read it presented in such an interesting and relevant way . . . The thing that amazed me was that I actually understood . . . Because my exposure to physics generally left me confused and I was convinced that it was beyond me.

> This is a pleasing testimony for the pedagogical worth of history in professional science courses.

20. The contemporary Aristotelian, Mortimer J. Adler, recognised this when he observed in his *Introduction to Aristotle* that:

> In an effort to understand nature, society, and man, Aristotle began where everyone should begin—with what he already knew in the light of his ordinary, commonplace experience. Beginning there, his thinking used notions that all of us possess, not

because we are taught them in school, but because they are the common stock of human thought about anything and everything. (Adler 1978, p. xi)

21. For a discussion of the sixteenth-century controversy about a void see Schmitt (1967).

22. The history of the science of air pressure is complex, and experts disagree on various aspects of it. A useful history is Middleton (1964). Shapin & Schaffer (1985) have provided an extensive case study of the interactions of science and philosophy in the debate between Hobbes and Boyle over the latter's famous air-pump experiments.

23. The director of the project is John A. Moore, who was director of the Yellow Version of the 1961 BSCS *High School Biology* text. *Science as a Way of Knowing* has been published in the *American Zoologist*, 1984 and following, as well as in separate monographs.

24. Neugebauer, in his *The Exact Sciences in Antiquity* (1969), says:

I do not consider it as the goal of historical writing to condense the complexity of historical processes into some kind of "digest" or "synthesis." On the contrary, I see the main purpose of historical studies in the unfolding of the stupendous wealth of phenomena which are connected with any phase of human history and thus to counteract the natural tendency toward oversimplification and philosophical constructions which are the faithful companions of ignorance (p. 208).

25. See Kragh (1992) for an account of these.

26. From the time of Vivani, Galileo's first biographer, most commentators have remade Galileo in their own methodological image. Viviani presented the first "empiricist" account of the work of Galileo (Segre 1991); this interpretation was adopted by Whewell, for whom Galileo had a "preponderating inclination towards facts" (Whewell 1840/1947, vol. 2, p. 220); Mach of course developed it at great length, saying that Galileo "investigated and established, wholly without preformed opinions, the actual facts of falling" (Mach 1883/1960, p. 167); Stillman Drake has written extensively on Galileo from this perspective (Drake 1978, 1990). The 1914 Crew and de Salvio translation of Galileo's *Dialogues* is corrupted in a few instances by these empiricist presuppositions. An alternative "rationalist" reading of Galileo was first provided by Alexandre Koyré (1939/1978), who doubted whether Galileo performed many of the experiments he wrote about and who, anyway, insisted that mathematics and Platonic metaphysics were more important for the development of Galileo's physics than experiment. This tradition has been continued by a number of others, including William Shea (1972). Paul Feyerabend, in his influential *Against Method* (1975), sees Galileo as the harbinger of Feyerabend's own style of methodological anarchism, thus "whenever possible he replaced old facts by a new type of experience which he simply invented for the purpose of supporting Copernicus" (p. 160). Much has been written on the effects of philosophical presuppositions upon the historical interpretations of Galileo (Crombie 1981).

27. Stephen Brush has been a very important figure over the past few decades in encouraging good history in science teaching and in the historical training of science teachers. He was a convenor of the 1970 International Commission on Physics Education conference, an editor of the conference proceedings,

an instigator of the History of Physics section within the American Physical Society, the founding chairperson of the Education Committee of the US History of Science Society; the editor of a book of scholarly reprints especially designed for teachers (Brush 1988a), the author of a substantial guide to the Second Scientific Revolution (Brush 1988b), and the author of three important articles on the place of history in science teaching (Brush 1969, 1974, 1989).

28. See Chapter 10 of Kragh (1987) for a review of such influences.

5. Philosophy in the Curriculum

1. The philosopher who contributed most to exploring the usefulness of philosophy to science education was Michael Martin, who published a series of articles (1971, 1974, 1979, 1986, 1994), and wrote a popular book, *Concepts of Science Education* (1972) on the subject. The book's five chapters, dealing with Inquiry, Explanation, Definition, Observation and Goals, provide ample evidence of the usefulness of philosophical training for the improvement of instruction, texts and statements of aims and objectives in science courses. Other philosophers of science, not otherwise mentioned in this chapter, who have written on science education include Gerd Buchdahl (1993), Robert Cohen (1964), Rom Harré (1983), Gerald Holton (1973, 1975), Noretta Koertge (1970), Ernst Nagel (1969) and Wallis Suchting (1992, 1994).

2. Among a score of articles on philosophy of science and science education, the following, from those not otherwise mentioned in this book, could be consulted: Abimbola (1983), Albury (1983), Cawthron & Rowell (1978), Cleminson (1990), Connelly (1969), Elkana (1970), Hodson (1988), Norris (1984), Robinson (1968), Burbules & Linn (1991), Forge (1979), Terhart (1988), Herron (1972) and Rogers (1982). Also Herget (1989, 1990) and Hills (1992).

3. The interconnections between science and metaphysics are discussed in Amsterdamski (1975), Buchdahl (1969), Burtt (1932), Gjertsen (1989) and Wartofsky (1968).

4. Finocchiaro (1980, p. 149) has provided a table of fourteen philosophical topics to be found in Galileo's *Dialogue on the Two Chief World Systems* (1633).

5. There has been a regretable tendency for histories of science to be written as if science was not influenced by philosophy, and on the other hand there has been a tendency for histories of philosophy to be written as if science had no impact on philosophical ideas. Students in philosophy courses standardly deal with Bacon, Locke, Descartes, Leibniz, Berkeley, Hobbes, Hume, Kant, Hegel, Dewey, Husserl, Popper and other philosophers with little attention to the scientific developments to which the philosophers were reacting. On this theme see Matthews (1989).

6. Susan Stebbing in her *Philosophy and the Physicists* (1937) wrote critically of the philosophical mistakes of Eddington and Jeans. Comparable criticisms can be made of much contemporary literature.

7. The papers in Woolnough (1987) provide one introduction to this issue of how to treat faith and science in science education.

8. In the United Kingdom the best known STS course is *SISCON: Science in a Social Context* (Solomon 1983, 1985). Another set of materials to supple-

ment a chemistry course is *SaTiS: Science and Technology in Society*, Association for Science Education, 1986.

9. See the PLON senior physics course as described in Eijkelhof & Kortland (1988).

10. Most Canadian provinces have STS courses. The Atlantic Science Curriculum Project based in New Brunswick is one (McFadden 1989), and Alberta has a large programme (Alberta Education 1990). Early Canadian STS initiatives are described in Aikenhead (1980).

11. See the two NSTA Yearbooks *Redesigning Science and Technology Education* (Bybee et al. 1984) and *Science, Technology, Society* (Bybee 1985), and their volume *The Science, Technology, Society Movement* (Yager 1993).

12. Pierre Duhem's *To Save the Phenomena: An Essay on the Idea of Physical Theory from Plato to Galileo* (1908/1969) is an excellent source book on this tradition.

13. A good collection of papers on the Duhem-Quine thesis is Harding (1976)

14. For some of the debates about critical thinking—what it is, how to promote it, and how generalizable it is—see Baron & Sternberg (1987), Levine & Linn (1977), McPeck (1981, 1990), Resnick (1987) and Siegel (1988, 1989a). See also the special issue of *Educational Philosophy and Theory* (23(1), 1991) edited by Paul Hagar. An excellent book dealing with the theory of good reasoning in science, and containing a multitude of realistic student exercises, is Giere (1984). A comparable book addressing just the life sciences is Steen (1993).

15. For a sample of cogent defenses of rationalism and the truth-seeking function of science see Brown (1994), Shimony (1976), Shapere (1964, 1984), Scheffler (1982) and Siegel (1987).

16. The antecedents of the strong program include Karl Mannheim (1936/1960) and Robert Merton (1957). The harbinger of the revival was David Bloor's *Knowledge and Social Imagery* (Routledge & Kegan Paul, London, 1976), then followed Barry Barnes's *Interests and the Growth of Knowledge* (Routledge & Kegan Paul, London 1977), and Bruno Latour and Stephen Woolgar's *Laboratory Life: The Social Construction of Scientific Facts* (Sage, London, 1979). Two reviews of the first wave of sociological literature, each citing hundreds of articles, are Mulkay (1982) and Shapin (1982). For critiques of the strong program see, for instance, Brown (1984), Bunge (1991, 1992), Nola (1991) and Slezak (1994). The last treats educational issues.

17. Some commentators maintain that Foucault considers his "power is knowledge" thesis applies only to the social sciences and humanities; it was not meant to cover the natural sciences (Gutting 1989, p. 4).

18. An account of the development of intelligence testing and theory can be found in Matthews (1980), ch.6.

19. John Bradley, the English chemist and educator, organized his chemistry instruction on Machian principles (Bradley 1963–68), and wrote a useful book on Mach's philosophy of science (Bradley 1971). Mach has had much more influence in European science education. The writings of Th. Litt and Martin Wagenschein are noteworthy here. Litt advocated "paradigmatic" teaching of physics, where a little is taught, but taught in such a way as to develop understanding. "All I propose is to teach the child to really understand, even to understand understanding." (Litt 1959, Walter Jung trans.). Wa-

genschein has written a voluminous amount in defense of teaching physics as it historically developed. This tradition is discussed in writings of Walter Jung, to whom I am indebted (Jung 1983, 1989, 1993). Accounts of Mach's educational ideas and activities can be found in Blackmore (1972, ch. 10), Blüh (1970), Matthews (1990a) and Pyenson (1983, ch. 4).

20. Accounts of Mach's life and achievements can be found in the entries in *The Encyclopedia of Philosophy*, and in *The Dictionary of Scientific Biography*. Additionally, see Blackmore (1972), Bradley (1971), Cohen & Seeger (1970) and Hintikka (1968).

21. Besso in a 1947 letter to Einstein says of this influence that "As far as the history of science is concerned, it appears to me that Mach stands at the center of the development of the last 50 or 70 years" (Holton 1970, p. 169).

22. In his 1906 *Aim and Structure of Physical Theory* Duhem comments that:

> The legitimate, sure, and fruitful method of preparing a student to receive a physical hypothesis is the historical method . . . that is the best way, surely even the only way, to give those studying physics a correct and clear view of the very complex and living organisation of this science. (Duhem 1906/1954, p. 268)

23. The classic treatments of thought experiments in the history of science are Koyré (1960), Kuhn (1964) and Mach (1896/1976). More recently their historical and philosophical function has been discussed by Brown (1986), Sorensen (1992) and in the edited collection of Horowitz & Massey (1991).

24. It is important to distinguish the then "received view" from that of Aristotle, with which it is often confused. The common view is perhaps an Aristotelian one, but as Lane points out, there is little textual evidence to attribute it to Aristotle himself. Galileo, on p. 68 of the *New Sciences*, attributes to Aristotle the claim that a "hundred-pound iron ball falling from the height of a hundred braccia hits the ground before one of just one pound has descended a single braccio." No one has been able to find this text in Aristotle. Lane calls it "a sheer invention" by Galileo. The episode is discussed in Brackenridge (1989).

25. Two particularly useful articles are Helm et al. (1985) and Winchester (1990).

26. These are "Mapping and Sequencing the Human Genome: Science, Ethics and Public Policy" (BSCS 1992), "Genethics—Ball State Model" (Ball State University, Muncie IN) and "Teacher Education in Biology" (San Francisco State University, San Francisco CA). The programs are discussed in Blake (1994).

27. The recent exchange between Eger, Hesse, Shimony, and others (*Zygon* 23(3), 1988) on "rationality in science and ethics" (reproduced in Matthews 1991) shows the benefits of striving for some modicum of philosophical sophistication in these matters. Eger (1989a) has also addressed the question of the "interests" of science, taking up issues that the work of Habermas and the Frankfurt School pose for understanding the social role of science and the fundamental structures of the discipline. Cordero (1992) and Martin (1986) provide insightful and disciplined discussion of the interplay of science, ethics and education. A guide to some of the considerable literature on ethics in science education can be found in the contributions to Musschenga & Gosling (1985). Many of the issues are well canvassed in Cross & Price (1992).

6. History and Philosophy in the Classroom: The Case of Pendulum Motion

1. There is no adequate history of the medieval pendulum. Lynn White (1962, pp. 117, 172–173) and (1966, p. 108) discusses some aspects of the topic.
2. Drake (1976) and Fredette (1972) discuss the work. Some have described it as "thoroughly medieval" in its approach (Dijksterhius 1961/1986, p. 334).
3. This vital idealizing feature of Galileo's physics is discussed in Koertge (1977) and McMullin (1985).
4. See the Drake translation of del Monte's *Mechanics* in Drake & Drabkin (1969), where he is described as the greatest mechanician of the sixteenth century.
5. Discussion and references can be found in White (1966, p. 109).
6. This claim needs to be nuanced as there was, beginning with Aristotle himself, a lively tradition of the "mixed sciences" in the Aristotelian tradition. Astronomy and optics made extensive use of mathematics, but they did not substitute mathematics for science, and did not replace the phenomena with an equation. On this issue see Lennox (1986).
7. This is translated in Fermi & Bernardini (1961).
8. For an exposition of Aristotle's concept of motion see Buckley (1971), Hanson (1965), McWilliams (1943), Melsen (1959) and Weiher (1967).
9. The classic, yet neglected, treatment of Galilean and Aristotelian approaches to social science is by Kurt Lewin (1931)
10. The cycloid curve had been studied by Galileo and his pupil Torricelli. Huygens recognized that, for large amplitudes, the effective length of the pendulum had to be shortened with respect to the amplitude; a cycloid enabled this to happen.
11. Some of this development can be seen in Kline 1959, ch.18.
12. One historian of technology has summed up medieval science by saying: "The truth is that medieval science generally was a very bookish business, conducted by means of abstract thought rather than by experiment . . . [it was] an autonomous speculative activity" (White 1966, p. 101).
13. Much has been written on Copernicus and the origins of the modern worldview. Some of the more substantial works are Blumenberg (1987), Boas (1962) and Kuhn (1957).
14. For discussion of the clock as a metaphor in culture and philosophy see Laudan (1981).
15. See Aldridge (1992) for the rationale of the curriculum proposal, and discussion of the pendulum. The absence of historical and philosophical considerations reflects the unfortunate gap in the US between science educators and the community of historians and philosophers of science.
16. The author has done the test a number of times at gatherings of physics teachers, each time with worse results than Reiff's.

7. Constructivism and Science Education

1. This research deals with ways that children and adults misconceive scientific notions; and how misconceptions and alternative belief systems often persist

despite instruction in science. Reviews of this literature can be found in Driver & Easley (1978), Gilbert & Watts (1983) and Duit (1995). Cumulative indexes of this literature are contained in Pfundt & Duit (1985, 1991).

2. For accounts of constructivist teaching practice, see the papers in Helm & Novak (1983), Novak (1987), Osborne & Freyberg (1985) and Tobin (1993). Additionally see Driver & Bell (1986) and Duckworth (1987).

3. The distinction between "seeing" and "seeing as" is made in Wittgenstein's *Philosophical Investigations* (1969). Norwood Russell Hanson's *Patterns of Discovery* (1958) gave the distinction prominence in philosophy of science. Popper's distinction between "perception" and "observation" mentioned in the previous chapter is another version.

4. This claim attacks the chief plank of empiricist and positivist theories of science which depend upon unsullied sensations or sense data to ground genuine scientific claims. Carnap's "protocol sentences" are a clear expression of the positivist claim (Carnap 1936). It is such sentences that Popper criticized in 1934/1959, maintaining that scientific universals—"All *A*s are *B*"—always outrun experience, and thus can never be established by experience.

5. Francis Bacon, in his *New Organon* (1620), was well aware of this feature of observation, and spelled out some of its determinations in his discussion of the Idols of the Mind. Karl Popper's *The Logic of Scientific Discovery* (1934/1959) restates the matter: we never just look, we always look for something.

6. This is the logical point recognised by Aristotle and the medievals when they spoke of the fallacy of affirming the consequent, and why Aquinas and others said that empirically derived scientific claims could never rise above the status of probable knowledge.

7. This is the Duhem-Quine thesis. Quine expressed the matter this way:

    Science is like a field of force whose boundary conditions are experience. A conflict with experience at the periphery occasions readjustments in the interior of the field . . . but there is much latitude of choice as to what statements to reevaluate in the light of any single contrary experience. (Quine 1953, p. 42)

8. The idealism of these sociologists has been well surveyed by Bunge (1992), on whom the discussion in this section is dependent.

9. Among the vast literature on the inquiry approach of the 1960s the following are useful: Bruner (1961), Romey (1968), Rutherford (1964), Schwab (1962) and Shulman & Keislar (1966).

10. The Welch review went on to comment on the vital role of teacher preparation for the success of inquiry teaching, a concern shared by contemporary constructivists:

     Many teachers are ill-prepared, in their own eyes and in the eyes of others, to guide students in inquiry learning, and over one-third feel they receive inadequate support for such teaching. Most teachers had not had adequate training for responding instinctively to the fruitful observations or the penetrating questions of a thoughtful student. (Welch 1981, p. 37)

     This, when coupled with a number of other factors (for instance, only half the American states had as much as one person working three-fourths-time as a science supervisor), accounts for the fact that at the end of the 1960s only thirty percent of elementary schools, and sixty percent of secondary schools were using any of the new inquiry-based curriculum materials; and that in those schools inquiry activities went on for only about ten percent of the time allocated to science.

For discussion of some of the difficulties and mistakes of inquiry learning see: Atkinson & Delamont (1977), Dearden (1967), Harris & Taylor (1983), Herron (1971), Wellington (1981), Shulman & Keislar (1966) and Strike (1975).

11. On the Continent, Duhem (1906), Bachelard (1934, 1940), Fleck (1935), Popper (1934), Piaget (1950); in the UK, Collingwood (1945), Toulmin (1953), Polanyi (1958), Popper (1934/1959); and in the US, Einstein (1944), Hanson (1958), Kuhn (1962), and Feyerabend (1962)—had all written persuasively against the inductivist model of science that inquiry teaching was enthusiastically adopting.

12. Richard Duschl (1985) provides a good overview of the degree of separation between HPS and science education in the US.

13. I am indebted to Professor von Glasersfeld for reading the penultimate draft of this chapter, for correcting a number of factual and stylistic errors, and for pointing out places where my account of his position needs qualification. He largely concurs with my nine-point characterization of his epistemological and ontological positions. The final, ninth point on ontology is the most contentious. He does not, of course, concur with my criticism of these positions. He emphasizes, against my characterization, that his radical constructivism "proposes to *substitute* the notion of viability for the notion of Truth," that he and Piaget regard scientific concepts as arising from reflective abstraction, not just Lockean sense impressions that supposedly create faint conceptual images in a passive mind, and finally he stresses that the constructivist assertion of noncommunicability of meaning does not have the deleterious consequences for teaching that I claim it does.

14. Ludwik Fleck, the interwar Polish physician and bacteriologist, whom Kuhn acknowledges as a precusor, was an early sociological constructivist. His central work was *Genesis and Development of a Scientific Fact* (1935/1979) in which he studied the history of the identification and treatment of syphilis. He holds that "syphilis as such does not exist" and that "objective reality can be resolved into historical sequences of ideas belonging to the collective" (p. 41). Some of Fleck's less well-known papers and discussion of his views can be found in Cohen & Schnelle (1986).

15. In the above private communication, von Glasersfeld points out that his view does not allow conceptual learning by feral children, as children's experiences need to be associated with words in order for learning to occur; in which case the quotation should have read "semantic construction cannot start from scratch."

16. For an elaboration of some of these themes in Marx's epistemology see Matthews (1980, ch. 6), and Suchting (1986, ch. 1).

17. Von Glasersfeld has constantly maintained this thesis on the nontransferability

of ideas, or more correctly, the propositional content of ideas. Subsequent to the above 1989 statement he wrote:

> once we have come to see this essential and inescapable subjectivity of linguistic meaning, we can no longer maintain the preconceived notion that words convey ideas or knowledge and that the listener who apparently "understands" what we say must necessarily have conceptual structures identical to ours. (Glasersfeld 1990, p. 36)

18. The pedagogical issues are not clear-cut, as many antirealists in epistemology—Ernst Mach being preeminent—have certainly championed rigorous science education. These antirealists need to produce additional arguments that do not depend upon science giving us knowledge of the world.

8. What is Science? Realism and Empiricism

1. Ptolemy's system predicted astronomical events, and served practical purposes so well, that it was undisputed from around AD 150 to the time of Copernicus in the early sixteenth century. For accounts of the life, times and achievements of Ptolemy see Taub (1993), and for accounts of ancient astronomy more generally, see, among others, Crowe (1990) and O'Neil (1986).
2. For accounts of the astronomy of Copernicus, Brahe, Galileo and Kepler, see Cohen (1961), Crowe (1990), Goodman & Russell (1991), Koyré (1957) and Kuhn (1957).
3. Discussion of the history of atomism in science and in philosophy can be found in Harman (1982), McMullin (1963) and Melsen (1952).
4. Hempel regarded all scientific terms as belonging to either of two realms: the observable or the theoretical. The function of the latter was to explain or enjoin the former, so that given one set of observations, a second set could be predicted. After quoting the behaviorists Hull and Skinner on the subject, he then poses the theoretician's dilemma as follows:

> If the terms and principles of a theory serve their purpose they are unnecessary . . . if they do not serve their purpose they are surely unnecessary. But given any theory, its terms and principles either serve their purpose or they do not. Hence the terms and principles of any theory are unnecessary. (Hempel 1958/1965, p. 186)

5. See for instance Blackmore (1985, 1989), Bradley (1971), Brush (1968), Feyerabend (1980, 1981, 1987), Holton (1970, 1993b) and Laudan (1981).
6. Two anthologies in which both sides of the argument can be found are Churchland & Hooker (1985) and Leplin (1984).
7. See for instance Boyd (1984), Bhaskar (1975), Brown (1994), Glymour (1985), Harré (1970), Hooker (1985), McMullin (1984) and Schlagel (1986).

9. Multicultural Science Education

1. Terminology can be a problem in this discussion. Western science is used in the debate, but it should perhaps be called orthodox or mainstream science. Although Western science had its modern origins in Western Europe, it has long been contributed to by Africans, Asians, East Europeans and just about all other geographical communities.

2. For some of the arguments and issues, see Berman (1992).
3. These radical critiques of schooling are discussed in Matthews (1980).
4. In the US the American Council on Education publishes annual reports on *Minorities in Higher Education*. These document science, mathematics and engineering participation rates. The reports are available from ACE, 1 Dupont Circle, Washington DC 20036, US.
5. The Portland Baseline Essays are a series of essays and curricula dealing with different subject matters and aimed at developing "an appreciation, respect, and tolerance for people of different ethnic and cultural backgrounds" (O'Neil 1991, p. 24). The science essay was written by Hunter Adams. One sympathetic reviewer of this essay and curriculum has said that it is "severely compromised throughout by its presentation of pseudoscientific concepts as legitimate science" (Martel 1991, p. 22). Others regard the Essays as intellectual drivel. This simply highlights the need for teachers to have some basis for judging epistemological claims made by curricular writers.
6. In this matter, as in so many educational and political controversies, there is a certain degree of self-serving that is operative, and intellectual analysis is somewhat beside the point. Cultures and social institutions can be respected, and even supported, without endorsing their cognitive claims. Supporters of ethnoscience might rely just on ethical arguments.
7. William Cobern has researched the interactive effects of worldviews on science education (Cobern 1993).
8. That we know what metaphysics is incompatible with Western science is not to say that there is agreement on *a* metaphysical system for Western science. Tom Settle (1990), for instance, disputes the claims of physicalism to be *the* metaphysics of modern science, and discusses the implications for science teachers of these metaphysical issues. See also the previously cited literature on metaphysics and science.
9. D'Ambrosio can be contacted at: The Centre for the Improvement of Science Education, UNICAMP, Caixa Postal 6063, 13081 Campinas, SP, Brazil.
10. Ernan McMullin (1984) provides a good discussion of the problems in separating internal from external factors in science.
11. Moore (1979) is an excellent discussion of religious reactions to Darwin. The "Galileo affair" is documented in Finocchiaro (1989). It is discussed in Langford (1966), Poupard (1987) and Redondi (1988). Brooke (1991), Funkenstein (1986), Hooykaas (1972) and Mascall (1956) are four, among legion, general discussions of the interactions between Western science and religion.
12. The central document is Galileo's 1615 *Letter to the Grand Duchess Christina* in Drake (1957).
13. Some maintain that Marx ends up affirming this position, although the matter is contentious. See Dianne Paul (1979) for a guide to the literature on the topic.
14. As with the Galileo and Darwin episodes, the Lysenko episode is more complex than meets the eye. Joravsky (1970), Lecourt (1977) and Lewontin & Levins (1976) discuss some of the scientific, philosophical and political issues involved.
15. Louis Althusser has remarked on the twilight of this two-science tradition.

In the Introduction of his 1969 *For Marx* he says:

> In our philosophical memory it [1950s] remains the period of intellectuals in arms, hunting out error from all its hiding-places . . . we were making politics out of all writing, and slicing the world up with a single blade, arts, literatures, philosophies, sciences with the pitiless demarcation of class—the period summed up in caricature by a single phrase, a banner flapping in the void: "bourgeois science, proletarian science."

16. On Nazi science see Beyerchen (1977). For an engaging account of the struggle of one great scientist to maintain universalist commitments in the middle of the Third Reich see Heilbron's biography of Max Planck (Heilbron 1986).
17. None of which is to say that modern science should be taught uncritically. The whole thrust of this book is to argue for the critical, contextual teaching of science. History allows us to see the successes as well as the failures of Western science, the achievements and the distortions. Hopefully we can learn from this.

10. Teacher Education

1. The dimension of this problem in the US can be gauged by the fact that in 1993 there are approximately twelve physics graduates training to be teachers in the entire state of New York, and less than five in the state of Louisiana. The problem is not confined to the US. In Australia, teacher education programs are among the least desired of all university courses.
2. The Holmes Group is comprised of the deans of most of the major US University Education Schools. Their reports, *Tomorrow's Teachers* (1986) and *Tomorrow's Schools* (1990), can be obtained from The Secretary, Holmes Group, 501 Erickson Hall, East Lansing, MI 48824–1034, US (cost $10). Both the Carnegie and Holmes reports are discussed in Fraser (1992).
3. Arguments for the place of foundation studies in teacher education can be found in the contributions to Tozer et al. (1990).
4. Such courses are described in Bakker & Clark (1989), Brickhouse (1990), Bybee (1990), Eger (1987), Matthews (1990b) and Ruse (1990).
5. The US National Endowment for the Humanities has sponsored such programs. A book of one hundred lesson plans produced in one such two-year program can be obtained from the program director, Professor Robert A. Hatch, History Department, University of Florida, Gainesville, Florida, US.
6. See Green (1971), Halstead (1975), Martin (1970) and Waks (1968).
7. Most of the scientific revolution texts used have been published in Matthews (1989), the Darwinian texts are in Appleman (1970), and secondary papers on HPS and science teaching are in Matthews (1991).
8. In twenty years of teaching hundreds of biology graduates I have found about ten who have read any of Darwin's work; among physics graduates I have yet to find one who has read any of Galileo's work.
9. An excellent and well-illustrated text which deals with the development of modern science in its social context is Goodman & Russell (1991).
10. Reprinted in *Science & Education* 1(4), 1992.
11. See, for instance, the research of Abell (1989), Akindehin (1988), Billeh &

Hasan (1975), Gallagher (1991), Jacoby & Spargo (1989), Koulaidis & Ogborn (1989), Lederman & Zeidler (1987), Mackay (1971), Proper et al.(1988), Robinson (1969) and Rowell & Cawthron (1982).

12. For something of the history of the interaction of science and philosophy in the development and decline of atomism, see Einstein & Infeld (1938/1966), Harman (1982) and Melsen (1952).

13. For a discussion of metaphor, models and analogy in science, see Black (1962), Hesse (1966), Leatherdale (1974) and Wartofsky (1979).

14. Although Strike and Posner's theory has been very influential in science education, they nevertheless say that: "We have always regarded attempts to turn our four components of conceptual change into four steps of instruction as misinterpretations of our intent" (Strike & Posner 1992, p. 172). They acknowledge that the move from normative theory to classroom practice is not direct.

15. The precise nature of the useful connections between epistemology and psychology have of course been much debated. The orthodox philosophical view has been that there is no epistemologically useful connection. C. I. Lewis expressed this view as follows: "Epistemology is not psychological description of mental states, but is the critique of their cognitive claim; the assessment of their veracity and validity, and the eliciting of those criteria by which such claim may be attested" (In Siegel 1979, p. 63). Karl Popper has endorsed this view, as has Israel Scheffler, in his *Science and Subjectivity* (1982).

At one level it is unexceptional and correct: psychology as the study of learning does not, of itself, have the competence to pronounce upon the truth or otherwise of what is learnt: presumably the same mechanisms are involved in learning truth as are involved in learning error. This is a matter of confusion in much constructivist writing. But aspects of the orthodox position have been challenged by Quine (1969) and others who are proposing a naturalized epistemology. On this project see the contributions to Kornblith (1985). For critiques of naturalized epistemology, and discussion of its implications for rationality and science education, see Siegel (1993).

16. A bibliography of philosophical writings on Piaget is provided in Kitchener (1985) which is a contribution to a special issue of *Synthese* journal devoted to the topic.

17. Of course it was a noteworthy contribution of Piaget to have shown that children did indeed have preinstruction beliefs about scientific subject matter. So often they had been assumed to be "empty buckets," or *tabulae rasas* to be filled by the science teacher. As demonstrated by Ausubel, and popularised by Novak, these naive conceptions affected how the new scientific conceptions were internalized. If teachers ignored them, or were ignorant of them, then often they were in a position of saying one thing to students, while an altogether different thing was being heard by the students.

18. Clement (1983), Champagne et al. (1980), di Sessa (1982), Driver & Easley (1978), McCloskey (1983a,b), McDermott (1984), Robin & Ohlsson (1989) and Whitaker (1983) are just a few to suggest that naive conceptions of force and motion mirror the fundamentals of Aristotelian dynamics. Piaget & Garcia (1989) provide an analysis of the history of mechanics to Newton and its connection to the development of children's cognition.

19. Duhem remarked that:

> Now is it clear merely in the light of common sense that a body in the absence of any force acting on it moves perpetually in a straight line with constant speed? Or that a body subject to a constant weight constantly accelerates the velocity of its fall? On the contrary such opinions are remarkably far from common-sense knowledge; in order to give birth to them, it has taken the accumulated efforts of all the geniuses who for two thousand years have dealt with dynamics. (Duhem 1906/1954, p. 263)

> An extensive treatment of the logic of idealization in science is given by Leszek Nowak (1980). He draws out the problems that scientific idealization provides for simple inductivist, empiricist and falsificationist theories of science. This was a topic widely studied by the Polish Poznań group, some of whose work can be found in Krajewski (1982). Ronald Laymon (1985) has also written on the subject.

20. For discussion of the interaction of science and poetry in the West, see Bush (1967) and Heath-Stubbs & Salman (1984).
21. Some of these matters are discussed in Eger (1972), Holton (1993c), Jung (1989) and Passmore (1978).

References

Abell, S. K.: 1989, "The Nature of Science as Portrayed to Preservice Elementary Teachers via Methods Textbooks." In D. E. Herget (ed.), *The History and Philosophy of Science in Science Teaching*, Florida State University, Tallahassee, FL, pp. 1–11.

Abimbola, I. O.: 1983, "The Relevance of the 'New' Philosophy of Science for the Science Curriclum," *School Science and Mathematics* 83(3), 181–193.

Achilles, M.: 1986, "History of Physics and the Historical Experiment." In P. V. Thomsen (ed.), *Science Education and the History of Physics*, University of Aarhus, Denmark, pp. 222–234.

Adler, M. J.: 1978, *Aristotle for Everybody*, Macmillan, New York.

Aikenhead, G. S.: 1974, "Course evaluation II: interpretation of student performance on evaluation tests," *Journal of Research in Science Teaching* 11, 23–30.

————: 1985, "Science Curricula and Preparation for Social Responsibility." In R. Bybee (ed.), *Science, Technology, Society: 1985 Yearbook of the National Science Teachers Association*, NSTA, Washington, DC, pp. 129–143.

————: 1980, *Science in Social Issues: Implications for Teaching*, Science Council of Canada, Ottawa.

Akeroyd, F. M.: 1989, "Philosophy of Science in a National Curriculum." In D. E. Herget (ed.), *The History and Philosophy of Science in Science Teaching*, Florida State University, Tallahassee, FL, pp. 15–22.

Akindehin, F.: 1988, "Effect of an Instructional Package on Preservice Science Teachers' Understanding of the Nature of Science and the Acquisition of Science-Related Attitudes," *Science Education* 72(1), 73–82.

Alberta Education: 1990, *Unifying the Goals of Science Education*, Curriculum Support Branch, Alberta, Canada.

Albury, R.: 1983, "Science Teaching or Science Preaching? Critical Reflections on School Science," In R. W. Home (ed.), *Science Under Scrutiny*, Reidel, Dordrecht, The Netherlands.

Aldridge, B. G.: 1992, "Project on *Scope, Sequence, and Coordination*: A New Synthesis for Improving Science Education," *Journal of Science Education and Technology* 1(1), 13–21.

Alexander, H. G. (ed.): 1956, *The Leibniz-Clarke Correspondence*, Manchester University Press, Manchester, UK.

Althusser, L. & Balibar, E.: 1970, *Reading Capital*, New Left Books, London.

————: 1969, *For Marx*, Penguin, Harmondsworth, UK.

American Association for the Advancement of Science (AAAS): 1989, *Project 2061: Science for All Americans*, AAAS, Washington, DC.

————: 1990, *The Liberal Art of Science: Agenda for Action*, AAAS, Washington, DC.

————: 1993, *Benchmarks for Science Literacy: Draft*, AAAS, Washington DC.

American Physical Society (APS): 1986, "Report of the Committee on Education—1985," *Bulletin of the American Physical Society* 31(6), 1033–1034.

Amsterdamski, S.: 1975, *Between Experience and Metaphysics*, Reidel, Dordrecht, The Netherlands.

Apple, M. W.: 1979, *Ideology and Curriculum*, Routledge & Kegan Paul, London.

Appleman, P. (ed.): 1970, *Darwin*, Norton, New York.

Ariotti, P.: 1968, "Galileo on the Isochrony of the Pendulum," *Isis* 59, 414–426.

Armstrong, H. E.: 1903, *The Teaching of Scientific Method*, Macmillan, London.

Arons, A. B.: 1965, *Development of Concepts of Physics*, Addison-Wesley, Reading, MA.

————: 1977, *The Various Language: An Inquiry Approach to the Physical Sciences*, Oxford University Press, New York.

————: 1983, "Achieving Wider Scientific Literacy," *Daedalus* 112(2), 91–122.

————: 1988, "Historical and Philosophical Perspectives Attainable in Introductory Physics Courses," *Educational Philosophy and Theory* 20(2), 13–23.

————: 1989, "What Science Should We Teach?" In *Curriculum Development in the Year 2000*, BSCS, Colorado Springs, CO.

————: 1974, "Education Through Science," *Journal of College Science Teaching* 13, 210–220.

Association for Science Education (ASE): 1963, *Training of Graduate Science Teachers*, ASE, Hatfield, Herts, UK.

————: 1979, *Alternatives for Science Education*, ASE, Hatfield, Herts, UK.

————: 1981, *Education Through Science*, ASE, Hatfield, Herts, UK.

————: 1986, *SaTiS: Science and Technology in Society*, ASE, Hatfield, Herts, UK.

Atkinson, P. & Delamont, S.: 1977, "Mock-ups & Cock-ups." In M. Hammersley & P. Woods (eds.), *The Process of Schooling*, Routledge, London, pp. 87–108.

Bachelard, G.: 1934/1984, *The New Scientific Spirit*, Beacon Books, Boston.

————: 1940/1968, *The Philosophy of No*, The Orion Press, New York.

Bakker, G. R. & Clark, L.: 1988, *Explanation: An Introduction to the Philosophy of Science*, Mayfield Publishing Company, Mountain View, CA.

————: 1989, "The Concept of Explanation: Teaching the Philosophy of Science to Science Majors." In D. E. Herget (ed.), *The History and Philosophy of Science in Science Teaching*, Florida State University, Tallahassee, FL, pp. 23–29.

Baltas, A.: 1988, "On the Structure of Physics as a Science." In D. Batens & J. P. van Bendegens (eds.), *Theory and Experiment*, Reidel, Dordrecht, The Netherlands, pp. 207–225.

Bantock, G. H.: 1981, *The Parochialism of the Present*, Routledge & Kegan Paul, London.

Baron, J. & Sternberg, R. (eds.): 1987, *Teaching Thinking Skills: Theory and Practice*, Freeman, New York.

Barrow, R. & Woods, R.: 1988, *An Introduction to Philosophy of Education*, Routledge, London, 3rd ed.

Bartov, H.: 1978, "Can Students be Taught to Distinguish Between Teleological and Causal Explanations?" *Journal of Research in Science Teaching* 15, 567–572.

Bauer, H. H.: 1992, *Scientific Literacy and the Myth of the Scientific Method*, University of Illinois Press, Urbana, IL.

Bauman, Z.: 1988, "Sociology and Postmodernity," *Sociological Review* 36, 790–823.

Beardsley, T.: 1992, "Teaching Real Science," *Scientific American* October, 78–86.

Bedini, S. A.: 1986, "Galileo and Scientific Instrumentation." In W. A. Wallace (ed.), *Reinterpreting Galileo*, Catholic University of America Press, Washington, DC, pp.127–154.

Bell, B.: 1988, "Girls and Science." In S. Middleton (ed.), *Women and Education in Aotearoa*, Allen & Unwin, Auckland, pp.153–160.

———: 1990, *Draft Forms 1–5 Science Syllabus for Schools*, Ministry of Education, Wellington, New Zealand.

———: 1991, "A Constructivist View of Learning and the Draft Forms 1–5 Science Syllabus," *SAME Papers 1991*, pp. 154–180.

Bent, H. A.: 1977, "Uses of History in Teaching Chemistry," *Journal of Chemical Education* 54, 462–466.

Berg, K. C. de: 1990, "The Historical Development of the Pressure-Volume Law for Gases," *The Australian Science Teachers Journal* 36(1), 14–20.

Bergmann, P.: 1949, *Basic Theories of Physics*, Prentice-Hall, New York.

Berkeley, G.: 1710/1962, *The Principles of Human Knowledge*, G. J. Warnock (ed.), Collins, London.

———: 1721/1901, *De Motu*. In A. Fraser (ed.), *The Works of George Berkeley*, Oxford University Press, Oxford.

Berman, P. (ed.): 1992, *Debating P.C.: The Controversy Over Political Correctness on College Campuses*, Bantam Doubleday, New York.

Bernal, J. D.: 1939, *The Social Function of Science*, Routledge & Kegan Paul, London.

———: 1946, "Science Teaching in General Education," *School Science Review* 27, 150–158. Reproduced in his *The Freedom of Necessity*, Routledge & Kegan Paul, London.

Bevilacqua, F. & Kennedy, P. J. (eds.): 1983, *Proceedings of the International Conference on Using History of Physics in Innovatory Physics Education*, University of Pavia, Pavia, Italy.

Beyerchen, A. D.: 1977, *Scientists Under Hitler: Politics and the Physics Community in the Third Reich*, Yale University Press, New Haven.

Bhaskar, R.: 1975, *A Realist Theory of Science*, Leeds Books, Leeds, UK.

Bibby, C. (ed.): 1971, *T. H. Huxley on Education*, Cambridge University Press, Cambridge, UK.

Billeh, V. Y. & Hasan, O. E.: 1975, "Factors Affecting Teachers' Gain in Understanding the Nature of Science," *Journal of Research in Science Teaching* 12(3), 209–219.

Biological Science Curriculum Committee (BSCS): 1992, *Mapping and Sequencing the Human Genome: Science, Ethics and Public Policy*, BSCS, Colorado Springs, CO.

Black, M.: 1962, *Models and Metaphors*, Cornell University Press, Ithaca, NY.

Black, P. J. & Lucas, A. M. (eds.): 1993, *Children's Informal Ideas in Science*, Routledge, London.

Blackmore, J. T.: 1972, *Ernst Mach: His Work, Life and Influence*, University of California Press, Berkeley, CA.

————: 1985, "An Historical Note on Ernst Mach," *British Journal for the Philosophy of Science* 36, 299–329.

————: 1989, "Ernst Mach Leaves 'The Church of Physics'," *British Journal for Philosophy of Science* 40, 519–540.

Blackwell, R. J. (ed.): 1986, *Christiaan Huygens "The Pendulum Clock or Geometrical Demonstrations Concerning the Motion of Pendula as Applied to Clocks,"* Iowa State University Press, Ames, IA.

Blake, D. D.: 1994, "Revolution, Revision or Reversal: Genetics-Ethics Curricula," *Science & Education* 3(4).

Bleier, R.: 1984, *Science and Gender*, Pergamon Press, New York.

Blondel, C.: 1986, "History of Physics and Physics Education in France." In P. V. Thomsen (ed.), *Science Education and the History of Physics*, University of Aarhus, Denmark, pp. 264–271.

———— & Brouzeng, P. (eds.): 1988, *Science Education and the History of Physics*, Université Paris-Sud, Paris.

Blüh, O.: 1970, "Ernst Mach: His Life as a Teacher and Thinker." In R. S. Cohen & R. J. Seeger (eds.), *Ernst Mach: Physicist and Philosopher*, Reidel, Dordrecht, The Netherlands, pp. 1–22.

Blumenberg, H.: 1987, *The Genesis of the Copernican World*, MIT Press, Cambridge, MA.

Boas, M.: 1962, *The Scientific Renaissance 1450—1630*, Harper & Row, New York.

Bodner, G. M.: 1986, "Constructivism: A Theory of Knowledge," *Journal of Chemical Education* 63(10), 873–878.

Bohning, J. J.: 1984, "Integration of Chemical History into the Chemical Literature Course," *Journal of Chemical Information and Computer Science* 24, 101–107.

Bowles, S. & Gintis, H.: 1976, *Schooling in Capitalist America*, Routledge & Kegan Paul, London.

Bown, W.: 1993, "Classroom Science goes into Freefall," *New Scientist* December, 12–13.

Boyd, R. N.: 1984, "The Current Status of Scientific Realism." In J. Leplin (ed.), *Scientific Realism*, University of California Press, Berkeley, CA, pp. 41–82.

Boyer, E. L.: 1983, *High School: A Report on Secondary Education in America*, Harper & Row, New York.

Brackenridge, J. B.: 1989, "Education in Science, History of Science and the 'Textbook,'" *Interchange* 20(2), 71–80.

Bradley, J.: 1963–68, "A Scheme for the Teaching of Chemistry by the Historical Method," *School Science Review* 44, 549–553; 45, 364–368; 46, 126–133; 47, 65–71, 702–710; 48, 467–474; 49, 142–150, 454–460.

————: 1971, *Mach's Philosophy of Science*, London.

Brandon, E. P.: 1989, "Subverting Common Sense: Textbooks and Scientific Theory." In D. E. Herget (ed.), *The History and Philosophy of Science in Science Teaching*, Florida State University, Tallahassee, FL, pp. 30–40.

Brickhouse, N. W.: 1990, "The Teaching of the Philosophy of Science in Secondary Classrooms: Case Studies of Teachers' Personal Theories," *International Journal of Science Education* 11(4), 437–450.

Brink, J. van den: 1991, "Didactic Constructivism." In E. von Glasersfeld (ed.), *Radical Constructivism in Mathematics Education*, Kluwer, Dordrecht, The Netherlands, pp.195–227.

Brock, W. H.: 1973, *H. E. Armstrong and the Teaching of Science 1880–1930*, Cambridge University Press, Cambridge, UK.

————: 1989, "History of Science in British Schools: Past, Present & Future." In M. Shortland & A. Warwick (eds.), *Teaching the History of Science*, Basil Blackwell, Oxford, pp. 30–41.

Brooke, J. H.: 1991, *Science and Religion: Some Historical Perspectives*, Cambridge University Press, Cambridge, UK.

Brouwer, W. & Singh, A.: 1983, "Historical Approaches to Science Teaching," *Science Education* 21(4), 230–235.

Brown, E. K. (ed.): 1947, *Matthew Arnold: Four Essays on Life and Letters*, New York.

Brown, H. I.: 1976, "Galileo, the Elements, and the Tides," *Studies in History and Philosophy of Science* 7(4), 337–351.

————: 1979, *Perception, Theory and Commitment: The New Philosophy of Science*, University of Chicago Press, Chicago.

Brown, J. R. (ed.): 1984, *Scientific Rationality: The Sociological Turn*, Reidel, Dordrecht.

————: 1986, "Thought Experiments Since the Scientific Revolution," *International Studies in the Philosophy of Science* 1(1), 1–15.

————: 1991, *The Laboratory of the Mind: Thought Experiments in the Natural Sciences*, Routledge, New York.

————: 1994, *Smoke and Mirrors: How Science Reflects Reality*, Routledge, New York.

Brumby, M.: 1979, "Problems in Learning the Concept of Natural Selection," *Journal of Biological Education* 13, 119–122.

Bruner, J. S., Goodnow, J. J., & Austin, G. A.: 1956: *A Study in Thinking*, John Wiley, New York.

————: 1960, *The Process of Education*, Random House, New York.

————: 1961, "The Act of Discovery," *Harvard Educational Review* 31, 21–32. Reprinted in R. C. Anderson & D. P. Ausubel (eds.), *Readings in the Psychology of Cognition*, Holt, Rhinehart & Winston, New York.

————: 1974, "Some Elements of Discovery." In his *Relevance of Education*, Penguin, Harmondsworth, pp. 84–97. Originally published in L. Shulman & E. Keislar (eds.), *Learning by Discovery*, Rand McNally, Chicago, 1966.

————: 1983, *In Search of Mind: Essays in Autobiography*, Harper & Row, New York.

Brunkhorst, H. K. & Yager, R. E.: 1986, "A New Rationale for Science Education," *School Science and Mathematics* 86(5), 364–374.

Brush, S. G.: 1968, "Mach and Atomism," *Synthese* 18, 192–215.

————: 1969, "The Role of History in the Teaching of Physics," *The Physics Teacher* 7(5), 271–280.

————: 1974, "Should the History of Science be Rated X?" *Science* 18, 1164–1172.

————: 1978, "Why Chemistry Needs History and How It Can Get Some," *Journal of College Science Teaching* 7, 288–291.

————: 1979, "Comments on 'On the Distortion of the History of Science in Science Education'," *Science Education* 63, 277–278.

———— (ed.): 1988a, *History of Physics: Selected Reprints*, American Association of Physics Teachers, College Park, MD.

————: 1988b, *The History of Modern Science: A Guide to the Second Scientific Revolution, 1800–1950*, Iowa State University Press, Ames, IA.

————: 1989, "History of Science & Science Education," *Interchange* 20(2), 60–70.

———— & King, A. L. Y. (eds.): 1972, *History in the Teaching of Physics*, University Press of New England, Hanover, NH.

Buchdahl, G.: 1969, *Metaphysics and the Philosophy of Science*, Basil Blackwell, Oxford.

Buchdahl, G.: 1993, "Styles of Scientific Thinking," *Science & Education* 2(2), 149–168.

Buckley, M. J.: 1971, *Motion and Motion's God*, Princeton University Press, Princeton, NJ.

Bunge, M.: 1991, "A Critical Examination of the New Sociology of Science: Part 1," *Philosophy of the Social Sciences* 21(4), 524–560.

————: 1992, "A Critical Examination of the New Sociology of Science: Part 2," *Philosophy of the Social Sciences* 22(1), 46–76.

Burbules, N. C.: 1992, "Two Perspectives on Reason as an Educational Aim: The Virtues of Reasonableness," *Philosophy of Education 1991*, 215–224.

———— & Linn, M.C.: 1991, "Science Education and Philosophy of Science: Congruence or Contradiction?" *International Journal of Science Education* 13(3), 227–241.

Burtt, E. A.: 1932, *The Metaphysical Foundations of Modern Physical Science* (2nd ed.), Routledge & Kegan Paul, London.

Bush, D.: 1967, *Science in English Poetry: A Historical Sketch 1590–1950*, Oxford University Press, London (first published 1950).

Butterfield, H.: 1949, *The Origins of Modern Science*, G. Bell and Sons, London.

Butts, R. E. & Brown, J. (eds.): 1989, *Construction and Science. Essays in Recent German Philosophy*, Kluwer Academic Publishers, Dordrecht, The Netherlands.

Butts, R. F. & Cremin, L.: 1953, *A History of Education in American Culture*, Holt, Rhinehart & Winston, New York.

Bybee, R. W.: 1982, "Historical Research in Science Education," *Journal of Research in Science Teaching* 19, 1–13.

———— (ed.): 1985, *Science, Technology, Society, Yearbook of the National Science Teachers Association*, NSTA, Washington, DC.

————, Carlson, J. & McCormack, A. J. (eds.): 1984, *Redesigning Science & Technology Education*, National Science Teachers Association, Washington, DC.

———— et al.: 1990, "Teaching History and the Nature of Science in Science Courses: A Rationale," *Science Education* 75(1), 143–156.

———— et al. (eds.): 1992, *Teaching About the History and Nature of Science and Technology: Background Papers*, BSCS/SSEC, Colorado Springs, CO.

———— et al.: 1992, *Teaching About the History and Nature of Science and Technology: A Curriculum Framework*, BSCS/SSEC, Colorado Springs, CO.

Bybee, R. W.: 1993, *Reforming Science Education: Social Perspectives and Personal Reflections,* Teachers College Press, New York.

Callahan, R. E.: 1962, *Education and the Cult of Efficiency*, University of Chicago Press, Chicago.

Campbell, N. R: 1921/1952, *What Is Science?* Dover, New York.

Cantor, G.: 1991, *Michael Faraday: Sandemanian and Scientist*, St. Martin's Press, New York.

Capra, F.: 1975, *The Tao of Physics*, Shambhala Press, Berkeley, CA.

Carey, S.: 1985, *Conceptual Change in Childhood*, MIT Press, Cambridge, MA.

———: 1986, "Cognitive Psychology and Science Education," *American Psychologist* 41, 1123–1130.

———: 1987, "Theory Change in Childhood." In B. Inhelder, D. Caprona & A. Cornu-Wells (eds.), *Piaget Today*, Lawrence Erlbaum, London.

———: 1988, "Reorganization of Knowledge in the Course of Acquisition." In S. Strauss (ed.), *Ontogeny, Philogeny and Historical Development*, Ablex, Norwood.

Carnap, R.: 1936/1937, "Testability and Meaning," *Philosophy of Science* 3, 4. Reprinted in H. Feigl & M. Brodbeck (eds.), *Readings in the Philosophy of Science*, Appleton-Century-Crofts, New York, 1953.

Carr, E. H.: 1964, *What Is History?* Penguin, Harmondsworth, UK.

Cawthorn, E. R. & Rowell, J. A.: 1978, "Epistemology and Science Education," *Studies in Science Education* 5, 31–59.

Chalmers, A. F.: 1976, *What Is This Thing Called Science?* University of Queensland Press, St Lucia, Queensland, Australia.

Champagne, A. B, Klopfer, L. E. & Anderson, J.: 1980, "Factors Influencing Learning of Classical Mechanics," *American Journal of Physics* 48, 1074–1079.

Cheung, K. C. & Taylor, R.: 1991, "Towards a Humanistic Constructivist Model of Science Learning: Changing Perspectives and Research Implications," *Journal of Curriculum Studies* 23(1), 21–40.

Churchland, P. M. & Hooker, C. A. (eds.): 1985, *Images of Science*, University of Chicago Press, Chicago.

Clagett, M.: 1959, *The Science of Mechanics in the Middle Ages*, University of Wisconsin Press, Madison, WI.

Clement, J.: 1983, "A Conceptual Model Discussed by Galileo and Intuitively Used by Physics Students." In D. Genter & A. L. Stevens, (eds.), *Mental Models*, Erlbaum, Hillsdale, NJ, pp. 325–339.

———: 1987, "Overcoming Students' Misconceptions in Physics: The Role of Anchoring Intuitions and Analogical Validity." In J. D. Novak (ed.), *Proceedings of the Second International Seminar on Misconceptions & Educational Strategies in Science & Mathematics*, Education Department, Cornell University, Ithaca, NY, pp. 84–97.

Cleminson, A.: 1990, "Establishing an Epistemological Base for Science Teaching in the Light of Contemporary Notions of the Nature of Science and of how Children Learn Science," *Journal of Research in Science Teaching* 27(5), 429–445.

Cobern, W. W.: 1991, "Introducing Teachers to the Philosophy of Science," *Journal of Science Teacher Education* 2(3), 45–47.

———: 1993, "Contextural Constructivism: The Impact of Culture on the Learning and Teaching of Science," In K. Tobin (ed.) *Constructivist Perspectives on Science and Mathematics Education*, American Association for the Advancement of Science, Washington DC.

Cochaud, G.: 1989, "The Process Skills of Science," unpublished paper, Australian Science Teachers Association Annual Conference.

Cohen, I. B.: 1950, "A Sense of History in Science," *American Journal of Physics* 18, 343–359. Reprinted in *Science & Education* 2(3), 1993.

———: 1961, *The Birth of a New Physics*, Heineman, London.

Cohen, R. S.: 1964, "Individuality and Common Purpose: The Philosophy of Science," *The Science Teacher* 31(4). Reprinted in *Science & Education* 3(4), 1994.

——— & Schnelle, T. (ed.): 1986, *Cognition and Fact: Materials on Ludwick Fleck*, Reidel, Dordrecht, The Netherlands.

——— & Seeger, R. J. (eds.): 1970, *Ernst Mach: Physicist and Philosopher*, Reidel, Dordrecht, The Netherlands.

Collingwood, R. G.: 1945, *The Idea of Nature*, Clarendon Press, Oxford.

Collins, A.: 1989, "Assessing Biology Teachers: Understanding the Nature of Science and Its Influence on the Practice of Teaching." In D. E. Herget (ed.), *The History and Philosophy of Science in Science Teaching*, Florida State University, Tallahassee, FL, pp. 61–70.

Collins, H. M.: 1981, "Stages in the Empirical Programmes of Relativism," *Social Studies of Science* 11, 3–10.

Committee for Economic Development: 1991, *The Unfinished Agenda: A New Vision for Child Development and Education*, CED, New York.

Conant, J.B.: 1945, *General Education in a Free Society: Report of the Harvard Committee*, Harvard University Press, Cambridge, MA.

———: 1947, *On Understanding Science*, Yale University Press, New Haven.

———: 1951, *Science and Common Sense*, Yale University Press, New Haven, CT.

——— (ed.): 1957, *Harvard Case Histories in Experimental Science*, 2 vols., Harvard University Press, Cambridge, MA.

Confrey, J.: 1990, "What Constructivism Implies for Teaching." In R. Davis, C. Maher & N. Noddings (eds.), *Constructivist Views on the Teaching and Learning of Mathematics*, National Council of Teachers of Mathematics, Reston, VA, pp. 107–124.

Connelly, F. M.: 1969, "Philosophy of Science and the Science Curriculum," *Journal of Research in Science Teaching* 6, 108–113.

Cooper, L.: 1935, *Aristotle, Galileo, and the Tower of Pisa*, Cornell University Press, Ithaca, NY.

Cordero, A.: 1992, "Science, Objectivity and Moral Values," *Science & Education* 1(1), 49–70.

Crane, L. T.: 1976, *The National Science Foundation & Pre-College Science Education: 1950–1975*, US Government Printing Office, Washington, DC.

Crombie, A. C.: 1952, *Augustine to Galileo*, Heinemann, London.

———: 1981, "Philosophical Presuppositions and the Shifting Interpretations of Galileo." In J. Hintikka et al. (eds.), *Theory Change, Ancient Axiomatics, and Galileo's Methodology*, Reidel, Boston, pp. 271–286.

Cromer, A.: 1993, *Uncommon Sense: The Heretical Nature of Science*, Oxford University Press, New York.

Cross, R. T. & Price, R. F.: 1992, *Teaching Science for Social Responsibility*, St Louis Press, Sydney, Australia.

Crow, L. W. (ed.): 1989, *Enhancing Critical Thinking in the Sciences*, NSTA, Washington, DC.

Crowe, M. J.: 1990, *Theories of the World from Antiquity to the Copernican Revolution*, Dover Publications, New York.

Curtis, S. J. & Boultwood, M. E. A.: 1964, *An Introductory History of English Education since 1800*, University Tutorial Press, London, 3rd ed.

Dart, F. E. & Pradham, P. L.: 1976, "Cross Cultural Teaching in Science," *Science* 155, 649–656.

Darusnikova, Z.: 1992, "Is a Postmodern Philosophy of Science Possible?" *Studies in History and Philosophy of Science* 23(1), 21–37.

Davies, P.: 1983, *God and the New Physics*, Simon & Schuster, New York.

Davis, R. B.: 1990, "Discovery Learning and Constructivism." In R. B. Davis, C. A. Maher, & N. Noddings (eds.), *Constructivist Views on the Teaching and Learning of Mathematics*, National Council of Teachers of Mathematics, Reston, VA, pp. 93–106.

Davson-Galle, P.: 1990, "Philosophy of Science Done in the 'Philosophy for Children' Manner in Lower-Secondary Schools." In D. E. Herget (ed.), *More The History and Philosophy of Science in Science Teaching*, Florida State University, Tallahassee, FL, pp. 223–230.

Davydov, V. V.: 1990, *Soviet Studies in Mathematics Education: Volume 2. Types of Generalization in Instruction*, National Council of Teachers of Mathematics, Reston, VA.

Dearden, R. F.: 1967, "Instruction and Learning by Discovery." In R. S. Peters (ed.), *The Concept of Education*, Routledge & Kegan Paul, London, pp. 135–155.

DeBoer, G. E.: 1991, *A History of Ideas in Science Education*, Teachers College Press, New York.

Dede, C. & Hardin, J.: 1973, "Reforms, Revisions, Re-examinations: Secondary Science Education since World War II," *Science Education* 57(4), 485–491.

Department of Education (NZ): 1989, *Draft Syllabus for Schools: Forms 1–5 Science*, Curriculum Development Division, Wellington, New Zealand.

Derkse, W.: 1981, "Popper's Epistemology as a Pedagogic and Didactic Principle," *Journal of Chemical Education* 58(7), 565–567.

Devitt, M.: 1991, *Realism & Truth*, 2nd ed., Basil Blackwell, Oxford.

Dewey, J.: 1910, "Science as Subject-Matter and as Method," *Science* 31, 121–127.

Di Sessa, A. A.: 1982, "Unlearning Aristotelian Physics : A Study of Knowledge-Based Learning," *Cognitive Science* 6, 37–75.

Dick, B. G.: 1983, "An Interdisciplinary Science Humanities Course," *American Journal of Physics* 51, 702–708.

Dijksterhuis, E. J.: 1961, "The Origins of Classical Mechanics from Aristotle to Newton." In M. Claggett (ed.), *Critical Problems in the History of Science*, University of Wisconsin Press, Madison, WI, pp. 163–189.

———: 1961/1986, *The Mechanization of the World Picture*, Princeton University Press, Princeton, NJ.

Drabkin, I. E.: 1938, "Notes on the Laws of Motion in Aristotle," *American Journal of Philology* 59, 60–84.

Drake, S.: 1957, *Discoveries and Opinions of Galileo*, Doubleday, New York.

———: 1976, "The Evolution of De Motu," *Physis* 14, 321–348.

———: 1978, *Galileo At Work*, University of Chicago Press, Chicago.

————: 1990, *Galileo: Pioneer Scientist*, University of Toronto Press, Toronto.

———— & Drabkin, I. E. (eds.): 1969, *Mechanics in Sixteenth-Century Italy*, University of Wisconsin Press, Madison, WI.

Driver, R.: 1983, *The Pupil as Scientist?* Open University, Milton Keynes, UK.

————: 1989, "The Construction of Scientific Knowledge in School Classrooms." In R. Millar (ed.), *Doing Science: Images of Science in Science Education*, Falmer Press, Lewes, East Sussex, pp. 83–106.

———— & Bell, B.: 1986, "Students' Thinking and the Learning of Science: A Constructivist View," *School Science Review* 67, 443–456.

———— & Easley, J.: 1978, "Pupils & Paradigms: A Review of Literature Related to Concept Development in Adolescent Science Students," *Studies in Science Education* 5, 61–84.

————, Guesne, E. & Tiberghien, A. (eds.): 1985, *Children's Ideas in Science*, Open University Press, Milton Keynes, UK.

———— & Oldham, V.: 1986, "A Constructivist Approach to Curriculum Development in Science," *Studies in Science Education* 13, 105–122.

Duckworth, E.: 1987, *The Having of Wonderful Ideas*, Teachers College Press, New York.

Duhem, P.: 1906/1954, *The Aim and Structure of Physical Theory*, trans. P. P. Wiener, Princeton University Press, Princeton, NJ.

————: 1908/1969, *To Save the Phenomena: An Essay on the Idea of Physical Theory from Plato to Galileo*, University of Chicago Press, Chicago.

————: 1916/1991, *German Science*, trans. J. Lyon & S. L. Jaki, Open Court Publishers, La Salle, IL.

Duit, R.: 1991, "The Role of Analogy and Metaphor in Learning Science," *Science Education* 75, 649–672.

————: 1995, "Research on Students' Conceptions: Developments and Trends," *Science & Education* 4(4).

Durkheim, E.: 1972, *Selected Writings*, A. Giddens ed., Cambridge University Press, Cambridge, UK.

Duschl, R. A.: 1985, "Science Education and Philosophy of Science: Twenty-Five Years of Mutually Exclusive Development," *School Science and Mathematics* 87(7), 541–555.

————: 1990, *Scientific Theories, Theory Development, and Science Education*, Teachers College Press, New York.

———— & Hamilton, R. J. (eds.): 1992, *Philosophy of Science, Cognitive Psychology, and Educational Theory and Practice*, State University of New York Press, Albany, NY.

————, Hamilton, R. J., & Grandy, R. E.: 1992, "Psychology and Epistemology: Match or Mismatch When Applied to Science Education?." In R. A. Duschl & R. J. Hamilton (eds.), *Cognitive Psychology, and Educational Theory and Practice*, State University of New York Press, Albany, NY.

Easley, J.: 1959, "The Physical Science Study Committee and Educational Theory," *Harvard Educational Review* 29, 4–11.

Eddington, A.: 1928, *The Nature of the Physical World*, University of Michigan Press, Ann Arbor, MI.

Education Policies Commission: 1966, *Education and the Spirit of Science*, National Education Association, Washington, DC.

Egan, K.: 1986, *Teaching As Story Telling*, University of Chicago Press, Chicago.

Eger, M.: 1972, "Physics and Philosophy: A Problem for Education Today," *American Journal of Physics* 40, 404–415.

———: 1987, "Philosophy of Science in Teacher Education," In J. D. Novak (ed.), *Misconceptions and Educational Strategies*, Cornell University, Ithaca, NY, vol I, pp. 163–176.

———: 1988, "A Tale of Two Controversies: Dissonance in the Theory and Practice of Rationality," *Zygon* 23(3), 291–326. Reprinted in M. R. Matthews (ed.), *History, Philosophy, and Science Teaching: Select Readings*, OISE Press, Toronto, 1991.

———: 1989a, "The 'Interests' of Science and the Problems of Education," *Synthese* 80(1), 81–106.

———: 1989b, "Rationality and Objectivity in a Historical Approach: A Response to Harvey Siegel." In D. E. Herget (ed.), *The History and Philosophy of Science in Science Teaching*, Florida State University, Tallahassee, FL, pp. 143–153.

———: 1992, "Hermeneutics and Science Education: An Introduction," *Science & Education* 1(4), 337–348.

———: 1993a, "Hermeneutics as an Approach to Science: Part 1," *Science & Education* 2(1), 1–30.

———: 1993b, "Hermeneutics as an Approach to Science: Part II," *Science & Education* 2(4), 303–328.

Eijkelhof, H. M. C. & Swager, J.: 1983, *Physics in Society: New Trends in Physics Teaching IV*, UNESCO, Paris.

——— & Kortland, K.: 1988, "Broadening the Aims of Physics Education." In P. Fensham (ed.) *Development and Dilemmas in Science Education*, Falmer Press, London, pp. 282–305.

Einstein, A.: 1944, "Remarks on Bertrand Russell's Theory of Knowledge." In P. A. Schilpp (ed.), *The Philosophy of Bertrand Russell*, Northwestern University Press, Evanston IL.

——— & Infeld, L.: 1938, *The Evolution of Physics*, Simon & Schuster, New York.

Eisner, E.: 1979, *The Educational Imagination: On the Design and Evaluation of the School Program*, Macmillan, New York.

Ekstig, B.: 1990, "Teaching Guided by the History of Science: The Discovery of Atmospheric Pressure." In M. R. Matthews (ed.), *History, Philosophy, and Science Teaching: Selected Readings*, OISE Press, Toronto, pp. 213–217.

Elbers, G. W. & Duncan, P. (eds.): 1959, *The Scientific Revolution: Challenge and Promise*, Public Affairs Press, Washington, DC.

Elkana, Y.: 1970, "Science, Philosophy of Science, and Science Teaching," *Educational Philosophy & Theory* 2, 15–35. (Reprinted in *Science & Education* 4(4))

Engelhardt, H. T. & Caplan, A. L. (eds.): 1987, *Scientific Controversies: Case Studies in the Resolution and Closure of Disputes in Science and Technology*, Cambridge University Press, Cambridge, UK.

Ennis, R. H.: 1979, "Research in Philosophy of Science Bearing on Science Education." In P. D. Asquith & H. E. Kyburg (eds.), *Current Research in Philosophy of Science*, Philosophy of Science Association, East Lansing, MI, pp. 138–170.

Epstein, L. C.: 1979, *Thinking Physics*, Insight Press, San Francisco, 2nd ed.

Fauvel, J. et al. (eds.): 1988, *Let Newton Be!* Oxford University Press, Oxford.

Fensham, P. (ed.): 1988, *Development and Dilemmas in Science Education*, Falmer Press, London.

Fensham, P. J.: 1992, "Science and Technology." In P. W. Jackson (ed.), *Handbook of Research on Curriculum*, Macmillan, New York, pp. 789–829.

Fermi, L. & Bernardini, G.: 1961, *Galileo and the Scientific Revolution*, New York.

Feyerabend, P. K.: 1962, "Explanation, Reduction and Empiricism," *Minnesota Studies in the Philosophy of Science* 3, 28–97.

————: 1975, *Against Method*, New Left Books, London.

————: 1980, "Zahar on Mach, Einstein and Modern Science," *British Journal for the Philosophy of Science* 31, 273–282.

————: 1981, "Mach, Einstein and the Popperians." In his *Problems of Empiricism: Philosophical Papers Volume Two*, Cambridge University Press, Cambridge, UK, pp. 89–98.

————: 1987, "Mach's Theory of Research and its Relation to Einstein." In his *Farewell to Reason*, Verso, London, pp. 192–218.

Fine, A.: 1984, "The Natural Ontological Attitude." In J. Leplin (ed.), *Scientific Realism*, University of California Press, Berkeley, CA, pp. 83–107.

Finegold, M. & Gorsky, P.: 1988, "Learning About Force: Simulating the Outcomes of Pupils' Misconceptions," *Instructional Science* 17, 251–261.

Finlay, G. C.: 1962, "The Physical Science Study Committee," *The School Review* Spring, 63–81.

Finocchiaro, M. A.: 1980, *Galileo and the Art of Reasoning*, Reidel, Dordrecht, The Netherlands.

————: 1989, *The Galileo Affair*, University of California Press, Berkeley, CA.

Fisher, A.: 1992a, "Science + Math = F," *Popular Science* 241(2), 58–63.

————: 1992b, "Why Johnny Can't Do Science and Math," *Popular Science* 241(3), 50–55.

Fitzpatrick, F. (ed.): 1960, *Policies for Science Education*, Teachers College, Columbia University, New York.

Fleck, L.: 1935/1979, *Genesis and Development of a Scientific Fact*, T. J. Trenn & R. K. Merton (eds.), University of Chicago Press, Chicago.

Floden, R. E., Buchmann, M., & Schwille, J. R.: 1987, "Breaking with Everyday Experience," *Teachers College Record* 88(4), 485–506.

Flude, M. & Hammer, M.: 1990, *The Education Reform Act 1988*, Falmer Press, Basingstoke, Hants, UK.

Ford, G. W. & Pugno, L. (eds.): 1964, *The Structure of Knowledge and the Curriculum*, Rand McNally, Chicago.

Forge, J.C.: 1979, "A Role for the Philosophy of Science in the Teaching of Science," *Journal of Philosophy of Education* 13, 109–118.

Fraassen, B. C. van: 1980, *The Scientific Image*, Clarendon Press, Oxford.

Franco, C. & Colinvaux-de-Dominguez, D.: 1992, "Genetic Epistemology, History of Science, and Science Education," *Science & Education* 1(3), 255–272.

Fraser, J. W.: 1992, "Preparing Teachers for Democratic Schools: The Holmes and Carnegie Reports Five Years Later—A Critical Reflection," *Teachers College Record* 94(1), 7–40.

Fredette, R.: 1972, "Galileo's *De Motu Antiquiora*," *Physis* 14, 321–348.

Freire, P.: 1972, *Pedagogy of the Oppressed*, Penguin, Harmondsworth.

Funkenstein, A.: 1986, *Theology and the Scientific Imagination: From the Middle Ages to the Seventeenth Century*, Princeton University Press, Princeton, NJ.

Galdabini, S.: 1986 "Information About the Italian Group." In P. V. Thomsen (ed.) *Science Education and the History of Physics*, University of Aarhus, Denmark, pp. 272–277.

Galileo, G.: 1590/1960, *De Motu*. In I. E. Drabkin & S. Drake (eds.), *Galileo Galilei On Motion and On Mechanics*, University of Wisconsin Press, Madison, WI.

———: 1633/1953, *Dialogue Concerning the Two Chief World Systems*, S. Drake (trans.), University of California Press, Berkeley, CA.

———: 1638/1954, *Dialogues Concerning the New Science*, H. Crew & A. de Salvio (trans.), Dover Publications, New York (orig. 1914).

Gallagher, J.: 1991, "Prospective and Practicing Secondary School Science Teachers' Knowledge and Beliefs About the Philosophy of Science," *Science Education* 75(1), 121–134.

Garnett, J. P. & Tobin, K. G.: 1984, "Reasoning Patterns of Preservice Elementary and Middle School Science Teachers," *Science Education* 68, 621–631.

Garrison, J. W.: 1986, "Some Principles of Postpositivist Philosophy of Science," *Educational Researcher* 15(9), 12–18.

——— & Bentley, M.: 1990, "Science Education, Conceptual Change, and Breaking with Everyday Experience," *Studies in Philosophy and Education* 10(1), 19–36.

Gauld, C. F.: 1988, "The 'Pupil-as-Scientist' Metaphor in Science Education," *Research in Science Education* 18, 35–41.

———: 1989, "A Study of Pupils' Responses to Empirical Evidence." In R. Millar (ed.), *Doing Science: Images of Science in Science Education*, Falmer, London, pp. 62–82.

———: 1991, "History of Science, Individual Development and Science Teaching," *Research in Science Education* 21, 133–140.

———: 1992, "Wilberforce, Huxley and the Use of History in Teaching About Evolution," *The American Biology Teacher* 54(7), 406–410.

Giere, R. N.: 1984, *Understanding Scientific Reasoning*, Holt, Rinehart & Winston, New York.

———: 1987, "The Cognitive Study of Science." In N. J. Nersessian (ed.), *The Process of Science*, Martinus Nijhoff, Dordrecht, The Netherlands, pp. 139–160.

Gilbert, J.: 1993, "Constructivism and Critical Theory." In B. Bell (ed.), *I Know About LISP But How Do I Put It into Practice?: Final Report of the Learning in Science Project (Teacher Development)*, Centre for Science and Mathematics Education Research, University of Waikato, Hamilton, New Zealand.

Gilbert, J. K. & Watts, D. M.: 1983, "Concepts, Misconceptions and Alternative Conceptions: Changing Perspectives in Science Education," *Studies in Science Education* 10, 61–98.

Ginev, D.: 1990, "Toward a New Image of Science," *Studies in Philosophy and Education* 10(1), 63–72.

Gjertsen, D.: 1989, *Science and Philosophy*, Penguin, Harmondsworth, UK.

Glasersfeld, E. von: 1987, *Construction of Knowledge*, Intersystems Publications, Salinas, CA.

————: 1989, "Cognition, Construction of Knowledge, and Teaching," *Synthese* 80(1), 121–140.

————: 1990, "Environment and Communication." In L. P. Steffe & T. Wood (ed.), *Transforming Children's Mathematics Education: International Perspectives*, Lawrence Erlbaum, Hillsdale, NJ, pp. 30–38.

————: 1992, "Questions and Answers About Radical Constructivism." In M. K. Pearsall (ed.), *Scope, Sequence, and Coordination of Secondary School Science, Vol.11, Relevant Research*, NSTA, Washington, DC, pp. 169–182.

Glass, B.: 1958, "Liberal Education in a Scientific Age." In P. C. Obler & H. A. Estrin (ed.) *The New Scientist: Essays on the Methods and Values of Modern Science*, Doubleday & Co., New York, pp. 215–236.

————: 1970, *The Timely and the Timeless: The Interrelations of Science Education and Society*, London.

Glymour, C.: 1985, "Explanation and Realism." In P. M. Churchland & C. A. Hooker (eds.), *Images of Science*, University of Chicago Press, Chicago, pp. 99–117.

Good, R. G. & Wandersee, J. H.: 1992, "A Voyage of Discovery: Designing a Graduate Course on HPST." In S. Hills (ed.), *History and Philosophy of Science in Science Education*, Vol.1, Queen's University, Kingston, Ontario, pp. 423–434.

Good, R., Wandersee, J. & St. Julien, J.: 1993, "Cautionary Notes on the Appeal of Constructivism in Science Education." In K. Tobin (ed.), *Constructivism in Science and Mathematics Education*, AAAS, Washington, DC, pp. 71–90.

Goodman, D. & Russell, C. A.: 1991, *The Rise of Scientific Europe*, Hodder & Stoughton, London.

Gosling, D. & Musschenga, B. (eds.): 1985, *Science Education and Ethical Values*, Georgetown University Press, Washington, DC.

Gotschl, J.: 1990, "Philosophical and Scientific Conceptions of Nature and the Place of Responsibility," *International Journal of Science Education* 12(3), 288–296 .

Graham, D.: 1993, *A Lesson for Us All*, Routledge, London.

Graham, L. R.: 1972, *Science and Philosophy in the Soviet Union*, Alfred A. Knopf, New York.

Green, T. F.: 1971, *The Activities of Teaching*, McGraw-Hill, New York.

Gruber, H.: 1974, "Courage and Cognitive Growth in Children and Scientists." In M. Schwebel & J. Ralph (eds.), *Piaget in the Classroom*, Routledge and Kegan Paul, London, pp. 73–105.

Gutting, G. (ed.): 1980, *Paradigms and Revolutions*, University of Notre Dame Press, Notre Dame, IN.

————: 1989, *Michel Foucault's Archaeology of Scientific Reason*, Cambridge University Press, Cambridge, UK.

Hacking, I.: 1983, *Representing and Intervening*, Cambridge University Press, Cambridge, UK.

————: 1984, "Experimentation and Scientific Realism." In J. Leplin (ed.), *Scientific Realism*, University of California Press, Berkeley, CA, pp. 154–172.

————: 1992, "'Style' for Historians and Philosophers," *Studies in History and Philosophy of Science* 23(1), 1–20.

Hall, A. R.: 1962, *The Scientific Revolution: 1500—1800*, 2nd ed., Beacon Press, Boston. (Third updated edition 1983.)

Halstead, R. F.: 1975, "Teaching for Understanding," *Philosophy of Education*, 52–62.

Hamburg, D. A.: 1992, *Today's Children: Creating a Future for a Generation in Crisis*, Random House, New York.

Hanson, N. R.: 1958, *Patterns of Discovery*, Cambridge University Press, Cambridge, UK.

————.: 1959, "Broad and the Laws of Dynamics." In P. A. Schilpp (ed.), *The Philosophy of C. D. Broad*, Tudor Publishing Company, New York, pp. 281–312.

————: 1965, "Aristotle (and others) on Motion Through Air," *Review of Metaphysics* 19, 133–147.

Harding, S. G (ed.): 1976, *Can Theories Be Refuted? Essays on the Duhem-Quine Thesis*, Reidel, Dordrecht, The Netherlands.

————: 1986, *The Science Question in Feminism*, Cornell University Press, Ithaca, NY.

Harman, P. M.: 1982, *Energy, Force and Matter: The Conceptual Development of Nineteenth-Century Physics*, Cambridge University Press, Cambridge, UK.

Harms, N. C. & Yager, R. E. (eds.): 1981, *What Research Says to the Science Teacher*, vol.3, NSTA, Washington, DC.

Harré, R.: 1970, *The Principles of Scientific Thinking*, University of Chicago Press, Chicago.

————: 1983, "History and Philosophy of Science in the Pedagogical Process," In R. W. Home (ed.), *Science Under Scrutiny*, Reidel, Dordrecht, The Netherlands, pp.139–157.

Harris, D. & Taylor, M.: 1983, "Discovery Learning in School Science: The Myth & the Reality," *Journal of Curriculum Studies* 15, 277–289.

Hawking, S. W.: 1988, *A Brief History of Time*, Bantam Books, London.

Heath-Stubbs, J. & Salman, P.: 1984, *Poems of Science*, Penguin, Harmondsworth, UK.

Heilbron, J. L.: 1983, "The Virtual Oscillator as a Guide to Physics Students Lost in Plato's Cave." In F. Bevilacqua & P. J. Kennedy (eds.), *Using History of Physics in Innovatory Physics Education*, Pavia, Italy, pp. 162–182. Republished in *Science & Education* 3(2), 1994.

————: 1986, *The Dilemmas of an Upright Man: Max Planck as Spokesman for German Science*, University of California Press, Berkeley, CA.

————: 1987, "Applied History of Science," *Isis* 78, 552–563.

Helgeson, S. L., Blosser, P. E. & Howe, R. W.: 1977, *The Status of Pre-College Science, Mathematics, and Social Science Education: 1955–1975*, US Government Printing Office, Washington, DC.

Helm, H. & Gilbert, J.: 1985, "Thought Experiments and Physics Education—Part I," *Physics Education* 20, 124–131.

————, Gilbert, J. & Watts, D. M.: 1985, "Thought Experiments and Physics Education—Part II," *Physics Education* 20, 211–217.

———— & Novak, J. D. (eds.): 1983, *Proceedings of the International Seminar on Misconceptions in Science & Mathematics*, Education Department, Cornell University, Ithaca, NY.

Hempel, C. G.: 1958/1965, "The Theoretician's Dilemma," *Minnesota Studies in the Philosophy of Science* 2, 37–98. Reprinted in his *Aspects of Scientific Explanation*, Macmillan, New York, 1965, pp. 173–226.

Herget, D. E. (ed.): 1989, *The History and Philosophy of Science in Science Teaching*, Florida State University, Tallahassee, FL.

—— (ed.): 1990, *More History and Philosophy of Science in Science Teaching*, Florida State University, Tallahassee, FL.

Herron, M. D.: 1971, "The Nature of Scientific Inquiry," *School Review* 79, 170–212.

Hesse, M. B.: 1963, *Models and Analogies in Science*, London.

——: 1980, *Revolutions and Reconstructions in the Philosophy of Science*, Harvester Press, Brighton, UK.

Hessen, B. M.: 1931, "The Social and Economic Roots of Newton's *Principia*." In *Science at the Crossroads*, Kniga, London.

Hewson, P. W.: 1981, "A Conceptual Change Approach to Learning Science," *European Journal of Science Education* 3(4), 383–396.

——: 1985, "Epistemological Commitments in the Learning of Science: Examples from Dynamics," *European Journal of Science Education* 7(2), 163–172.

Hiebert, E. N.: 1976, "Introduction." In E. Mach *Knowledge and Error*, Reidel, Dordrecht, The Netherlands, (orig. 1905).

Hills, S. (ed.): 1992, *The History and Philosophy of Science in Science Education*, two volumes, Queen's University, Kingston, Ontario.

Hintikka, J. (ed.): 1968, "A Symposium on Ernst Mach," *Synthese* 18, 132–301.

Hodson, D.: 1982, "Science—the Pursuit of Truth? Parts I, II," *School Science Review* 63(225), 643–652; 63(226), 23–30.

——: 1987, "Social Control as a Factor in Science Curriculum Change," *International Journal of Science Education* 9, 529–540.

——: 1988a, "Experiments in Science and Science Teaching," *Educational Philosophy and Theory* 20(2), 53–66.

——: 1988b, "Toward a Philosophically More Valid Science Curriculum," *Science Education* 72, 19–40.

Hodson, F.: 1910, *Broad Lines in Science Teaching*, Macmillan, London.

Höfler, A.: 1916, "Ernst Mach: Obituary," *Zeitschrift für den Physikalischen und Chemischen Unterricht* 29(2).

Hogg, J. C.: 1938, *Introduction to Chemistry*, Oxford University Press, New York.

Holton, G.: 1952, *Introduction to Concepts and Theories in Physical Science*, Addison-Wesley, New York.

——: 1970, "Mach, Einstein, and the Search for Reality." In R. S. Cohen & R. J. Seeger (eds.), *Ernst Mach Physicist and Philosopher*, Reidel, Dordrecht, The Netherlands, pp. 165–199.

——: 1973, "Physics and Culture: Criteria for Curriculum Design" and "Modern Science and the Intellectual Tradition." In his *Thematic Origins of Scientific Thought*, Harvard University Press, Cambridge.

——: 1975, "Science, Science Teaching, and Rationality," In S. Hook et al. (eds.), *The Philosophy of the Curriculum*, Promethus Books, Buffalo, NY.

——: 1978a, "On the Educational Philosophy of the Project Physics Course." In his *The Scientific Imagination: Case Studies*, Cambridge University Press, Cambridge, UK, pp. 284–298.

——: 1978b, "Subelectrons, Presuppositions, and the Millikan-Ehrenhaft Dis-

References • 251

pute." In his *The Scientific Imagination: Case Studies*, Cambridge University Press, Cambridge, UK.
———: 1993a, "Ernst Mach and the Fortunes of Positivism." In his *Science and Anti-Science*, Harvard University Press, Cambridge, MA, pp. 1–55.
———: 1993b, "More on Mach and Einstein." In his *Science and Anti-Science*, Harvard University Press, Cambridge, MA, pp. 56–73.
———: 1993c, "The Anti-Science Phenomenon." In his *Science and Anti-Science*, Harvard University Press, Cambridge, MA, pp. 145–190.
Hooker, C. A.: 1985, "Surface Dazzle, Ghostly Depths: An Exposition and Critical Evaluation of van Fraassen's Vindication of Empiricism against Realism." In P. M. Churchland & C. A. Hooker (eds.), *Images of Science*, University of Chicago Press, Chicago, pp. 153–196
Hooykaas, R.: 1972, *Religion and the Rise of Modern Science*, Scottish Academic Press, Edinburgh, UK.
Horowitz, T. & Massey, G. J. (eds.): 1991, *Thought Experiments in Science and Philosophy*, Rowman & Littlefield, Savage, MD.
Horton, R.: 1971, "African Traditional Thought and Western Science." In M. F. D. Young (ed.), *Knowledge and Control*, Collier-Macmillan, London, pp. 208–266.
Hume, D.: 1777/1902, *Enquiries Concerning the Human Understanding and Concerning the Principles of Morals*, Clarendon Press, Oxford.
Hurd, P. D.: 1958, "Science Literacy: Its Meaning for American Schools," *Educational Leadership* 16, 13–16.
———: 1961, *Biological Education in American Secondary Schools 1890–1960*, American Institute of Biological Science, Washington, DC.
———: 1985, "A Rationale for a Science, Technology, and Society Theme in Science Education." In Bybee, R. W. (ed.), *Science, Technology, Society*, Yearbook of the National Science Teachers Association, NSTA, Washington, DC, 94–101.
———: 1987, "A Nation Reflects: The Modernisation of Science Education," *Bulletin of Science, Technology, & Society* 7, 9–13.
Husserl, E.: 1954/1970, *The Crisis of European Sciences and Transcendental Phenomenology*, Northwestern University Press, Evanston, IL.
Huxley, A.: 1947, *Science, Liberty and Peace*, Chatto & Windus, London.
Huxley, T. H.: 1868, "A Liberal Education; and Where to Find It." In C. Bibby (ed.), *T. H. Huxley on Education*, Cambridge University Press, Cambridge, UK, pp. 74–98.
———: 1885/1964, *Science and Education*, Citadel Press, New York.
Ihde, A. J.: 1971, "Let's Teach History of Chemistry to Chemists," *Journal of Chemical Education* 48, 686–687.
Jackson, P. W.: 1983, "The Reform of Science Education: A Cautionary Tale," *Daedalus* 112(2), 143–166.
Jacoby, B. A. & Spargo, P. E.: 1989, "Ptolemy Revived?" *Interchange* 20(2), 33–53.
Jaffe, B.: 1938, "The History of Chemistry and Its Place in the Teaching of Chemistry," *Journal of Chemical Education* 15, 383–389.
———: 1942, *New World of Chemistry*, Silver Burdett, New York. Revised editions 1947, 1952, 1955, 1959 and 1964.
Jeans, J.: 1943/1981, *Physics and Philosophy*, Dover Publications, New York.

Jegede, O.: 1989, "Toward a Philosophical Basis for Science Education of the 1990s: An African View-Point." In D.E. Herget (ed.), *The History and Philosophy of Science in Science Teaching*, Florida State University, Tallahassee, FL, pp. 185–198.

Jencks, C.: 1972, *Inequality*, Penguin, Harmondsworth.

Jenkins, E. W.: 1979, *From Armstrong to Nuffield*, John Murray, London.

———: 1990, "History of Science in Schools: Retrospect and Prospect in the U.K.," *International Journal of Science Education* 12(3), 274–281. Reprinted in M. R. Matthews (ed.), *History, Philosophy and Science Teaching: Selected Readings*, OISE Press, Toronto, 1991, pp. 33–42.

Johnson, S. & Stewart, J.: 1991, "Using Philosophy of Science in Curriculum Development: An Example from High School Genetics." In M. R. Matthews (ed.), *History, Philosophy, and Science Teaching: Selected Readings*, OISE Press, Toronto, pp. 201–212.

Jones, G. S.: 1972, "History: The Poverty of Historicism." In R. Blackburn (ed.), *Ideology in Social Science*, Collins, London.

Joravsky, D.: 1970, *The Lysenko Affair*, University of Chicago Press, Chicago.

Jung, W.: 1983, "Toward Preparing Students for Change: A Critical Discussion of the Contribution of the History of Physics to Physics Teaching." In F. Bevilacqua & P. J. Kennedy (eds.), *Using History of Physics in Innovatory Physics Education*, Pavia University, Italy, pp. 6–57. Reprinted in *Science & Education* 3(2), 1994.

———: 1989, "Philosophy of Science and Education," unpublished manuscript.

———: 1993, "Uses of Cognitive Science to Science Education," *Science & Education* 2(1), 31–56.

Jungwirth, E.: 1987, "Avoidance of Logical Fallacies: A Neglected Aspect of Science Education and Science-teacher Education," *Research in Science and Technological Education* 5(1), 43–58.

Kant, I.: 1783/1970, *Metaphysical Foundations of Natural Science*, J. Ellington trans., Bobbs-Merrill, Indianapolis, IN.

Kauffman, G. B.: 1989, "History in the Chemistry Curriculum," *Interchange* 20(2), 81–94. Reprinted in M. R. Matthews (ed.), *History, Philosophy and Science Teaching: Selected Readings*, OISE Press, Toronto, 1991, pp. 185–200.

Keller, E. F.: 1985, *Reflections on Gender and Science*, Yale University Press, New Haven.

Kelly, A.: 1985, "The Construction of Masculine Science," *British Journal of Sociology of Education* 6, 133–154.

Kenealy, P.: 1989, "Telling a Coherent 'Story': A Role for the History and Philosophy of Science in a Physical Science Course." In D. E. Herget (ed.), *The History and Philosophy of Science in Science Teaching*, Florida State University, Tallahassee, FL, pp. 209–220.

Kilpatrick, J.:1987, "What Constructivism Might Be in Mathematics Education." In J. C. Bergeron, N. Herscovics, & C. Keiran (eds.), *Psychology of Mathematics Education*, Proceedings of the Eleventh International Conference, Montreal, pp. 3–27.

Kipnis, N.: 1992, *Rediscovering Optics*, BENA Press, Minneapolis, MN.

Kitchener, R. F.: 1985, "A Bibliography of Philosophical Work on Piaget," *Synthese* 65(1), 139–151.

————: 1986, *Piaget's Theory of Knowledge: Genetic Epistemology and Scientific Reason*, Yale University Press, New Haven.

————: 1992, "Piaget's Genetic Epistemology: Epistemological Implications for Science Teaching." In R. A. Duschl & R. J. Hamilton (eds.), *Philosophy of Science, Cognitive Psychology, and Educational Theory and Practice*, State University of New York Press, Albany, NY, pp. 116–146.

————: 1993, "Piaget's Epistemic Subject and Science Education: Epistemological Versus Psychological Issues," *Science & Education* 2(2), 137–148.

Kitcher, P.: 1988, "The Child as Parent of the Scientist," *Mind and Language* 3(3), 217–228.

———— & Salmon, W. C. (eds.): 1989, *Scientific Explanation*, University of Minnesota Press, Minneapolis, MN.

Klein, M. J.: 1972, "Use and Abuse of Historical Teaching in Physics," In S. G. Brush & A. L. King (eds.), *History in the Teaching of Physics*, University Press of New England, Hanover, NH.

Kline, M.: 1959, *Mathematics and the Physical World*, Dover Publications, New York.

Klopfer, L. E.: 1969a, *Case Histories and Science Education*, Wadsworth Publishing Company, San Francisco.

————: 1969b, "The Teaching of Science and the History of Science," *Journal of Research in Science Teaching* 6, 87–95.

————: 1990, "Scientific Literacy." In *The International Encyclopedia of Curriculum*, Pergamon Press, Oxford.

————: 1992, "An Historical Perspective on the History and Nature of Science in School Science Programs." In R. W. Bybee et al. (eds.), *Teaching About the History and Nature of Science and Technology: Background Papers*, BSCS/SSEC, Colorado Springs, CO.

———— & Champagne, A. B.: 1990, "Ghosts of Crisis Past," *Science Education* 74(2), 133–154.

———— & Cooley, W. W.: 1961, *The Use of Case Histories in the Development of Student Understanding of Science and Scientists*, Graduate School of Education, Harvard University, Cambridge, MA.

———— & Cooley, W. W.: 1963, "The History of Science Cases for High Schools in the Development of Student Understanding of Science and Scientists: A Report on the HOSC Instruction Project," *Journal of Research in Science Teaching* 1, 33–47.

———— & Watson, F. G.: 1957, Historical Materials and High School Science Teaching, *The Science Teacher* 24, 264–265, 292–293.

Koertge, N.: 1970, "Towards an Integration of Content and Method in the Science Curriculum," *Curriculum Theory Network* 4, 26–43.

————: 1977, "Galileo and the Problem of Accidents," *Journal of the History of Ideas* 38, 389–408.

————: 1981, "Methodology, Ideology and Feminist Critiques of Science." In P. D. Asquith & R. N. Giere (eds.), *Proceedings of the Philosophy of Science Association 1980*, Edwards Bros, Ann Arbor, pp. 346–359.

Koestler, A.: 1964, *The Sleepwalkers*, Penguin Books, Harmondsworth, UK.

Kornblith, H. (ed.): 1985, *Naturalizing Epistemology*, MIT Press, Cambridge, MA.

Koulaidis, V. & Ogborn, J.: 1989, "Philosophy of Science: An Empirical Study of Teachers' Views," *International Journal of Science Education* 11(2), 173–184.

Koyré, A.: 1939/1978, *Galileo Studies*, J. Mepham trans., Harvester Press, Hassocks, Sussex, UK.

———: 1957, *From the Closed World to the Infinite Universe*, The Johns Hopkins University Press, Baltimore, MD.

———: 1960, "Galileo's Treatise 'De Motu Gravium': The Use and Abuse of Imaginary Experiments," *Revue d"Historire des Sciences* 13. Reprinted in his *Metaphysics and Measurement*, Harvard University Press, Cambridge, MA, 1968, pp. 44–88.

———: 1968, *Metaphysics and Measurement*, Harvard University Press, Cambridge, MA.

Kozol, J.: 1991, *Savage Inequalities*, Harper, New York.

Kragh, H.: 1986, "Physics and History: Noble Lies or Immoral Truths?" In P. V. Thomsen (ed.), *Science Education and the History of Physics*, University of Aarhus, Denmark, pp. 70–76.

———: 1987, *An Introduction to the Historiography of Science*, Cambridge University Press, Cambridge, UK.

———: 1992, "A Sense of History: History of Science and the Teaching of Introductory Quantum Theory," *Science & Education* 1(4), 349–364.

Krajewski, W. (ed.): 1982, *Polish Essays in the Philosophy of the Natural Sciences*, Reidel, Dordrecht.

Krugly-Smolska, E.: 1992, "A Cross-Cultural Comparison of Conceptions of Science." In S. Hills (ed.), *History and Philosophy of Science in Science Education* vol.1, Queen's University, Kingston, Ontario, pp. 583–593.

Kuhn, D., Amsel., E. & O'Loughlin, M.: 1988, *The Development of Scientific Reasoning Skills*, Academic Press, New York.

Kuhn, T. S.: 1957, *The Copernican Revolution*, Random House, New York.

———: 1959, "The Essential Tension: Tradition and Innovation in Scientific Research," *The Third University of Utah Research Conference on the Identification of Scientific Talent*, University of Utah Press, Salt Lake City. Reprinted in his *The Essential Tension*, University of Chicago Press, Chicago, 1977, pp. 225–239.

———: 1962, *The Structure of Scientific Revolutions*, University of Chicago Press, Chicago.

———: 1964, "A Function for Thought Experiments." In his *The Essential Tension*, University of Chicago Press, Chicago, 1977, pp. 240–265.

———: 1970, *The Structure of Scientific Revolutions*, (2nd ed.), University of Chicago Press, Chicago.

———: 1977, "Concepts of Cause in the Development of Physics." In his *The Essential Tension*, University of Chicago Press, Chicago, 1977, pp. 21–30.

Kumar, D. D. & Berlin, D. F.: 1993, "Science-Technology-Society Policy Implementation in the USA: A Literature Review," *The Review of Education* 15, 73–83.

Lakatos, I.: 1970, "Falsification and the Methodology of Scientific Research Programmes." In I. Lakatos & A. Musgrave (eds.), *Criticism and the Growth of Knowledge*, Cambridge University Press, Cambridge, UK, pp. 91–196.

———: 1971, "History of Science and Its Rational Reconstructions." In R. C.

Buck & R. S. Cohen (eds.), *Boston Studies in the Philosophy of Science 8*, pp. 91 –135. Reproduced in J. Worrall and G. Currie (eds.), *The Methodology of Scientific Research Programmes*, Cambridge University Press, Cambridge, UK, 1978, pp. 102–138.

———— & Musgrave, A. (eds.): 1970, *Criticism and the Growth of Knowledge*, Cambridge University Press, Cambridge, UK.

Langford, J. J.: 1966, *Galileo, Science and the Church*, University of Michigan Press, Ann Arbor, MI.

Latour, B. & Woolgar, S.: 1986, *Laboratory Life: The Social Construction of Scientific Facts*, Sage Publications, London, revised ed. (1st ed. 1979.)

Laudan, L.: 1977, *Progress and Its Problems*, University of California Press, Berkeley, CA.

————: 1981, "The Clock Metaphor and Hypotheses: The Impact of Descartes on English Methodological Thought." In his *Science and Hypothesis*, Reidel, Dordrecht, The Netherlands, pp. 27–58.

————: 1984, "A Confutation of Convergent Realism." In J. Leplin (ed.), *Scientific Realism*, University of California Press, Berkeley, CA, pp. 218–249.

————: 1990, *Science and Relativism*, University of Chicago Press, Chicago.

Lave, J.: 1988, *Cognition in Practice: Mind, Mathematics and Culture in Everyday Life*, Cambridge University Press, New York.

Lawson, A. (ed.): 1993, "The Role of Analogy in Science and Science Teaching." A special issue of *Journal of Research in Science Teaching* 30(10).

Laymon, R.: 1985, "Idealizations and the Testing of Theories by Experimentation." In P. Achinstein & O. Hannaway (eds.) *Observation, Experiment, and Hypothesis in Modern Physical Science*, MIT Press, Cambridge, MA, pp. 147–173.

Layton, A. D. & Powers, S. R.: 1949, *New Directions in Science Teaching*, McGraw-Hill, New York.

Layton, D.: 1973, *Science for the People*, George Allen & Unwin, London.

Leacock, R. A. & Sharlin, H. I.: 1977, "The Nature of Physics and History : a Cross Disciplinary Inquiry," *American Journal of Physics* 45(2), 146–153.

Leatherdale, W. H.: 1974, *The Role of Analogy, Model and Metaphor in Science*, Oxford University Press, Oxford.

Lecourt, D.: 1977, *Proletarian Science? The Case of Lysenko*, Manchester University Press, Manchester, UK.

Lederman, N. G. & Zeidler, D. L.: 1987, "Science Teachers Conceptions of the Nature of Science: Do They Really Influence Teaching Behaviour?" *Science Education* 71(5), 721–734.

Leibniz, G. W.: 1686/1969, "A Brief Demonstration of a Notable Error of Descartes and Others Concerning a Natural Law." In L. E. Loemker (ed.), *Gottfried Wilhelm Leibniz: Philosophical Papers and Letters*, Reidel, Dordrecht, The Netherlands, pp. 296–302.

Lennox, J. G.: 1986, "Aristotle, Galileo, and the 'Mixed Sciences'." In W. A. Wallace (ed.), *Reinterpreting Galileo*, Catholic University of America Press, Washington, DC, pp. 29–51.

Leplin, J. (ed.): 1984, *Scientific Realism*, University of California Press, Berkeley, CA.

Lerman, S.: 1989, "Constructivism, Mathematics, and Mathematics Education," *Educational Studies in Mathematics* 20, 211–223.

Lerner, L. S. & Gosselin, E. A.: 1975, "Physics and History as a Bridge Across the 'Two Cultures' Gap," *American Journal of Physics* 43, 13–19.

Levine, D. I. & Linn, M. C.: 1977, "Scientific Reasoning Ability in Adolescence: Theoretical Viewpoints and Educational Implications," *Journal of Research in Science Teaching* 14, 371–384.

Lewin, K.: 1931, "The Conflict Between Aristotelian and Galilean Modes of Thought in Contemporary Psychology," *Journal of General Psychology* 5, 141–177. Reprinted in his *A Dynamic Theory of Personality*, McGraw Hill, New York, 1935.

Lewontin, R. & Levins, R.: 1976, "The Problem of Lysenkoism." In H. Rose & S. Rose (ed.), *The Radicalisation of Science*, Macmillan, London, pp. 32–64.

Linn, M. C.: 1983, "Content, Context and Process in Adolescent Reasoning," *Journal of Early Adolescence* 3(1), 63–82.

Lipman, M. & Sharp, A. M. (eds.): 1978, *Growing Up with Philosophy*, Temple University Press, Philadelphia, PA.

Litt, Th.: 1959, *Naturwissenschaft und Menschenbildung*, Quelle & Meyer, Heidelberg.

Lochhead, J. & Dufresne, R.: 1989, "Helping Students Understand Difficult Science Concepts Through the Use of Dialogues with History." In D. E. Herget (ed.), *The History and Philosophy of Science in Science Teaching*, Florida State University, Tallahassee, pp. 221–229.

Longino, H. E.: 1989, "Can There Be a Feminist Science?" In N. Tuana (ed.), *Feminism & Science*, Indiana University Press, Bloomington, IN, pp. 45–57.

Loving, C. C.: 1991, "The Scientific Theory Profile: A Philosophy of Science Model for Science Teachers," *Journal of Research in Science Teaching*, 28(9), 823–838.

Lucas, A. M.: 1971, "Creativity, Discovery, and Inquiry in Science Education," *Australian Journal of Education* 15(2), 185–196.

————: 1975, "Hidden Assumptions in Measures of Knowledge About Science and Scientists," *Science Education* 59, 481–485.

Lynch, M., Livingstone, E. & Garkinkel, H.: 1983, "Temporal Order in Laboratory Work." K. D. Knorr-Cetina & M. Mulkay (eds.), *Science Observed*, Sage Publications, London.

MacCorquodale, K. & Meehl, P.: 1948, "On a Distinction Between Hypothetical Constructs and Intervening Variables," *Psychological Review* 55, 95–107.

Mach, E.: 1872/1911, *The History and Root of the Principle of the Conservation of Energy*, trans. P. E. B. Jourdain, Open Court Publishing Company, La Salle, IL.

————: 1883/1960, *The Science of Mechanics*, Open Court Publishing Company, LaSalle, IL.

————: 1886/1986, "On Instruction in the Classics and the Sciences." In his *Popular Scientific Lectures*, Open Court Publishing Company, La Salle, IL.

————: 1895/1986, *Popular Scientific Lectures*, Open Court Publishing Company, La Salle, IL.

————: 1896/1976, "On Thought Experiments." In his *Knowledge and Error*, Reidel, Dordrecht, The Netherlands, pp. 134–147.

————: 1910/1970, "The Guiding Principles of My Scientific Theory of Knowledge and Its Reception by My Contemporaries." In S. Toulmin (ed.), *Physical Reality: Philosophical Essays on Twentieth-Century Physics*, Harper & Row, New York, pp. 28–43.

Machamer, P.: 1992, "Philosophy of Science: An Overview for Educators." In R. W. Bybee et al. (eds.), *Teaching About the History and Nature of Science and Technology: Background Papers*, BSCS/SSEC, Colorado Springs, CO, pp. 9–18.

Mackay, L. D.: 1971, "Development of Understanding About the Nature of Science," *Journal of Research in Science Teaching* 8, 57–66.

MacLachlan, J.: 1976, "Galileo's Experiments with Pendulums: Real and Imaginary," *Annals of Science* 33, 173–185.

Mann, C. R.: 1912, *The Teaching of Physics for Purposes of General Education*, Macmillan, New York.

Mannheim, K.: 1936/1960, *Ideology and Utopia*, Routledge & Kegan Paul, London.

Mansell, A. E.: 1976, "Science for All," *School Science Review* 57, 579–585.

Manuel, D. E.: 1981 "Reflections on the Role of History and Philosophy of Science in School Science Education," *School Science Review* 62(221), 769–771.

Martel, E.: 1991, "How Valid are the Portland Baseline Essays?" *Educational Leadership* Dec./Jan., 20–23.

Martin, B., Kass, H. & Brouwer, W.: 1990, "Authentic Science: A Diversity of Meanings," *Science Education* 74(5), 541–554.

Martin, J. R.: 1970, *Explaining, Understanding & Teaching*, McGraw-Hill, New York.

————: 1989, "Ideological Critiques and the Philosophy of Science," *Philosophy of Science* 56, 1–22.

Martin, M.: 1971, "The Use of Pseudo-Science in Science Education," *Science Education* 55, 53–56.

————: 1972, *Concepts of Science Education*, Scott, Foresman & Co., New York. (Reprinted, University Press of America, 1985.)

————: 1974, "The Relevance of Philosophy of Science for Science Education," *Boston Studies in Philosophy of Science* 32, 293–300.

————: 1979, "Connections Between, Philosophy of Science & Science Education," *Studies in Philosophy and Education* 9.

————: 1986, "Science Education and Moral Education," *Journal of Moral Education* 15(2), 99–108. Reprinted in M. R. Matthews (ed.), *History, Philosophy, and Science Teaching: Selected Readings*, OISE Press, Toronto, 1991, pp. 102–114.

————: 1994, "Pseudoscience, the Paranormal, and Science Education," *Science & Education* 3(4).

Mas, C. J., Perez, J. H., & Harris, H. H.: 1987, "Parallels between Adolescents' Conception of Gases and the History of Chemistry," *Journal of Chemical Education* 64(7), 616–618.

Mascall, E.L.: 1956, *Christian Theology and Natural Science*, Longmans, Green & Co., London.

Matthews, M. R.: 1980, *A Marxist Theory of Schooling: A Study in Epistemology and Education*, Harvester Press, Brighton, UK.

———— (ed.): 1989, *The Scientific Background to Modern Philosophy*, Hackett Publishing Company, Indianapolis, IN.

————: 1990a, "Ernst Mach and Contemporary Science Education Reforms," *International Journal of Science Education* 12(3), 317–325.

————: 1990b, "History, Philosophy and Science Teaching: What Can Be Done in an Undergraduate Course?" *Studies in Philosophy and Education* 10(1), 93–98.

———— (ed.): 1991, *History, Philosophy, and Science Teaching: Selected Readings*, OISE Press, Toronto and Teachers College Press, New York.

———— & Winchester, I. (eds.): 1989, "History, Science, and Science Teaching: A Special Issue," *Interchange* 20(2).

Mayer, J.: 1987, "Consequences of a Weak Science Education," *Boston Globe*, September.

Mayr, E.: 1982, *The Growth of Biological Thought*, Harvard University Press, Cambridge, MA.

McCloskey, M.: 1983a, "Intuitive Physics," *Scientific American* 248, 114–122.

————: 1983b, "Naive Theories of Motion." In D. Gentner & A. L. Stevens (eds.), *Mental Models*, Lawrence Erlbaum, Hillsdale, NJ, pp. 299–324.

McDermott, L. C.: 1984, "Research on Conceptual Understanding in Mechanics," *Physics Today* 37, 24–32.

McFadden, C. P.: 1989, "Redefining the School Curriculum." In D. E. Herget (ed.), *The History and Philosophy of Science in Science Teaching*, Florida State University, Tallahassee, FL, pp. 259–270.

McGrath, E. (ed.): 1948, *Science in General Education*, W. C. Brown & Co., Dubuque, IA.

McMullin, E. (ed.): 1963, *The Concept of Matter in Modern Philosophy*, University of Notre Dame Press, Notre Dame, IN.

———— (ed.): 1967, *Galileo Man of Science*, Basic Books, New York.

————: 1970, "The History and Philosophy of Science: A Taxonomy," *Minnesota Studies in the Philosophy of Science* 5, 12–67.

————: 1975, "History and Philosophy of Science: a Marriage of Convenience?" *Boston Studies in the Philosophy of Science* 32, 515–531.

————: 1978, *Newton on Matter and Activity*, University of Notre Dame Press, Notre Dame, IN.

————: 1984, "A Case for Scientific Realism." In J. Leplin (ed.), *Scientific Realism*, University of California Press, Berkeley, CA, pp. 8–40.

————: 1985, "Galilean Idealization," *Studies in History and Philosophy of Science* 16, 347–373.

McPeck, J.: 1981, *Critical Thinking and Education*, St. Martin's, New York.

————: 1990, *Teaching Critical Thinking, Dialogue and Dialectic*, Routledge, New York.

McWilliams, J. A.: 1943, "Aristotelian and Cartesian Motion," *New Scholasticism* 17, 307–321.

Melsen, A. G. van: 1952, *From Atomos to Atom*, Duquesne University Press, Pittsburgh, PA.

————: 1959, *The Philosophy of Nature*, Duquesne University Press, Pittsburgh, PA.

————: 1961, *Science and Technology*, Duquesne University Press, Pittsburgh, PA.

Merton, R. K.: 1957, "The Sociology of Knowledge." In his *Social Theory and Social Structure*, Free Press, New York.

Mestre, J. P.: 1991, "Learning and Instruction in Pre-College Physical Science," *Physics Today*, September, 56–62.

Middleton, W. E. K.: 1964, *A History of the Barometer*, Baltimore, MD.

Miller, J. D.: 1983, "Scientific Literacy: A Conceptual and Empirical Review," *Daedalus* 112(2), 29–47.

———: 1987, "Scientific Literacy in the United States." In E. David & M. O'Connor (eds.), *Communicating Science to the Public*, John Wiley, London.

———: 1992, *The Public Understanding of Science and Technology in the United States, 1990*, National Science Foundation, Washington, DC.

Millikan, R. A.: 1950, *Autobiography*, Prentice-Hall, New York.

Mittelstrass, J.: 1972, "The Galilean Revolution: The Historical Fate of a Methodological Insight," *Studies in the History and Philosophy of Science* 2, 297–328.

Montaigne, M. de: 1580/1943, *Selected Essays*, Van Nostrand Co., New York.

Moody, E. A.: 1951, "Galileo and Avempace: The Dynamics of the Leaning Tower Experiment," *Journal of the History of Ideas* 12, 163–193, 375–422.

Moore, J. R.: 1979, *The Post-Darwinian Controversies*, Cambridge University Press, Cambridge, UK.

Moreno, A. G. (ed.): 1992, *History of the Physical-Mathematical Sciences and the Teaching of Sciences*, European Physical Society, Madrid.

Mulkay, M.: 1982, "Sociology of Science in the West," *Current Sociology* 28(3), 1–116.

Musschenga, B. & Gosling, D. (eds.): 1985, *Science Education and Ethical Values: Introducing Ethics and Religion into the Science Classroom and Laboratory*, Georgetown University Press, Washington, DC.

Nagel, E.: 1969, "Philosopohy of Science and Educational Theory," *Studies in Philosophy and Education* 7(1), 16–27. Reprinted in J. Park (ed.), *Selected Readings in Philosophy of Education*, Macmillan, New York, 1974.

National Commission on Excellence in Education: 1983, *A Nation At Risk: The Imperative for Education Reform*, US Department of Education, Washington, DC.

National Curriculum Council (NCC): 1988, *Science in the National Curriculum*, NCC, York, UK.

———: 1989, *Science: Non-Statutory Guidance*, NCC, York, UK.

———: 1991, *Science for Ages 5 to 16*, DES, London.

National Science Board: 1991, *Science & Engineering Indicators—1991*, US Government Printing Office, Washington, DC.

National Science Foundation (NSF): 1980, *What are the Needs in Precollege Science, Mathematics, and Social Science Education? Views from the Field*, NSF, Washington, DC.

National Science Teachers Association (NSTA): 1971, *School Science Education for the 1970s*, NSTA, Washington, DC.

———: 1982, *Science-Technology-Society: Science Education for the 1980s*, NSTA, Washington, DC.

———: 1992, *Scope, Sequence and Coordination*, NSTA, Washington, DC.

National Society for the Study of Education (NSSE): 1960, *Rethinking Science Education. 59th Yearbook*, University of Chicago Press, Chicago.

Naylor, R. H.: 1974, "Galileo's Simple Pendulum," *Physis* 16, 23–46.

————: 1980, "The Role of Experiment in Galileo's Early Work on the Law of Fall," *Annals of Science* 37, 363–378.

————: 1989, "Galileo's Experimental Discourse." In D. Gooding et al. (eds.), *The Uses of Experiment*, Cambridge University Press, Cambridge, UK.

Nersessian, N. J.: 1989, "Conceptual Change in Science and in Science Education," *Synthese* 80(1), 163–184. Reprinted in M. R. Matthews (ed.), *History, Philosophy, and Science Teaching: Selected Readings*, OISE Press, Toronto, 1989, pp. 133–148.

Neugebauer, O.: 1969, *The Exact Sciences in Antiquity*, 2nd ed., Dover, New York.

Newman, D., Griffin, P., & Cole, M.: 1989, *The Construction Zone: Working for Cognitive Change in School*, Cambridge University Press, New York.

Newton, I.: 1729/1934, *Mathematical Principles of Mathematical Philosophy*, (trans. A. Motte, revised F. Cajori), University of California Press, Berkeley, CA.

Niedderer, H.: 1992, "Science Philosophy, Science History, and the Teaching of Physics." In S. Hills (ed.), *History and Philosophy of Science in Science Education* Vol.II, Queen's University, Kingston, Ontario, 201–214.

Nielsen, H. & Nielsen, K.: 1988, "History of Technology in Education—Why and How." In C. Blondel & P. Brouzeng (eds.), *Science Education and the History of Physics*, pp. 51–68.

Nielsen, K., Nielsen, H. & Jensen, H. S.: 1990, *Skruen uden Ende*, Teknisk Forlag, Köbenhavn, Denmark.

Nielsen H. & Thomsen, P.: 1990, "History and Philosophy of Science in the Danish Curriculum," *International Journal of Science Education* 12(4), 308–316.

Noddings, N.: 1990, "Constructivism in Mathematics Education." In R. Davis, C. Maher & N. Noddings (eds.), *Constructivist Views on the Teaching and Learning of Mathematics*, National Council of Teachers of Mathematics, Reston, VA, pp. 7–18.

Nola, R.: 1991, "Ordinary Human Inference as Refutation of the Strong Programme," *Social Studies of Science* 21, 107–129.

Norris, S. P.: 1984, "Cynicism, Dogmatism, Relativism, and Scepticism: Can All These Be Avoided?" *School Science and Mathematics* 84(6), 484–495.

Novak, J. D.: 1977, *A Theory of Education*, Cornell University Press, Ithaca.

————: 1983, "Overview." In H. Helm & J. D. Novak (eds.), *Proceedings of the International Seminar on Misconceptions in Science and Mathematics*, Cornell University, Ithaca, NY, pp. 1–4.

———— (ed.): 1987, *Misconceptions and Educational Strategies in Science and Mathematics*, 3 vols., Cornell University, Ithaca, NY.

———— & Gowin, D. R.: 1984, *Learning How to Learn*, Cambridge University Press, New York.

Nowak, L.: 1980, *The Structure of Idealization*, Reidel, Dordrecht.

Nunn, T. P.: 1907, *The Aims and Achievements of the Scientific Method*, Macmillan, London.

————: 1919, "Science." In J. Adams (ed.), *The New Teaching*, Hodder and Stoughton, London.

Nussbaum, J.: 1983, "Classroom Conceptual Change: The Lesson to be Learned from the History of Science." In H. Helm & J. D. Novak (eds.), *Misconceptions in Science & Mathematics*, Department of Education, Cornell University, pp. 272–281.

Nye, M. J.: 1975, "The Moral Freedom of Man and the Determinism of Nature: The Catholic Synthesis of Science and History in the *Revue des Questions Scientifiques*," *British Journal for the History of Science* 8, 274–292.

Obler, P. C., Estrin, H. A. (eds.): 1962, *The New Scientist: Essays on the Methods and Values of Modern Science*, Doubleday, New York.

Oddie, G.: 1986, *Likeness to Truth*, Reidel, Dordrecht, The Netherlands.

Ogawa, M.: 1989, "Beyond the Tacit Framework of 'Science' and 'Science Education' among Science Educators," *International Journal of Science Education* 11(3), 247–250.

Ogunniyi, M. B.:1988, "Adapting Western Science to Traditional African Culture," *International Journal of Science Education* 10(1), 1–9.

Oliver, J. S. & Nichols, B. K.: 1993, "An Intellectual Tradition of Science as a Way of Knowing in the Stated Goals of Science Education: 1900–1950." Paper presented at the annual meeting of the National Association for Research in Science Teaching, Atlanta, GA.

O'Neil, J.: 1991, "On the Portland Plan: A Conversation with Matthew Prophet," *Educational Leadership* Dec./Jan., 24–27.

O'Neil, W. M.: 1986, *Early Astronomy from Babylonia to Copernicus*, University of Sydney Press, Sydney, Australia.

Oppe, G: 1936, "The Use of Chemical History in the High School," *Journal of Chemical Education* 13, 412–414.

Osborne, R. J.: 1983, "Towards Modifying Children's Ideas about Electric Current," *Research in Science and Technological Education* 1, 73–82.

——— & Freyberg, P.: 1985, *Learning in Science: The Implications of Children's Science*, Heinemann, London.

Pais, A.: 1982, *Subtle is the Lord: The Science and Life of Albert Einstein*, Oxford University Press, New York.

Passmore, J.: 1978, *Science and Its Critics*, Rutgers University Press, Rutgers NJ.

Patterson, E. C.: 1980, "History as an Introduction to Science," *Journal of College Science Teaching* 10(1), 15–18.

Paul, D. B.: 1979, "Marxism, Darwinism and the Theory of Two Sciences," *Marxist Perspectives* 5, 116–143.

Paul, H.: 1979, *The Edge of Contingency: French Catholic Reaction to Scientific Change from Darwin to Duhem*, University of Florida Press, Gainesville, FL.

———: 1985, *From Knowledge to Power: The Rise of the Science Empire in France 1860–1939*, Cambridge University Press, Cambridge, UK.

Pearce, G. & Maynard, P. (eds.): 1973, *Conceptual Change*, Reidel, Dordrecht, The Netherlands.

Penick, J. E.: 1993, *Scientific Literacy: An Annotated Bibliography*, UNESCO, Paris.

Peters, R. S.: 1966, *Ethics and Education*, George Allen and Unwin, London.

Pfundt, H. & Duit, R.: 1985, *Bibliography of Students' Alternative Frameworks and Science Education*, 2nd ed. Institute for Science Education, University of Kiel, Germany.

———: 1991, *Bibliography of Students' Alternative Frameworks and Science*

Education, 3rd ed., Institute for Science Education, University of Kiel, Germany.

Physical Science Study Committee (PSSC): 1960, *Physics*, Heath & Co., Boston.

Piaget, J.: 1950, *Introduction a l'Epistemologie Genetique*, 3 vols., Presses Universitaires de France, Paris.

———: 1970, *Genetic Epistemology*, Columbia University Press, New York.

———: 1972, *Psychology and Epistemology: Towards a Theory of Knowledge*, Penguin, Harmondsworth, UK.

——— & Garcia, R.: 1989, *Psychogenesis and the History of Science*, Columbia University Press, New York.

Piel, E. J.: 1981, "Interaction of Science, Technology, and Society in Secondary Schools." In N. C. Harms & R. E. Yager (eds.), *What Research Says to the Science Teacher*, vol.3, NSTA, Washington, DC, pp. 94–112.

Pitt, J. C. (ed.): 1985, *Change and Progress in Modern Science*, Reidel, Dordrecht, The Netherlands.

———: 1992, *Galileo, Human Knowledge, and the Book of Nature: Method Replaces Metaphysics*, Kluwer Academic Publishers, Dordrecht, The Netherlands.

Polanyi, M.: 1958, *Personal Knowledge*, Routledge and Kegan Paul, London.

Pomeroy, D.: 1992, "Science Across Cultures: Building Bridges Between Traditional Western and Alaskan Native Cultures." In S. Hills (ed.), *History and Philosophy of Science in Science Education* vol.2, Queen's University, Kingston Ontario, pp. 257–268.

Popper, K. R.: 1934/1959, *The Logic of Scientific Discovery*, Hutchinson, London.

———: 1963, *Conjectures and Refutations*, Routledge Kegan Paul, London.

———: 1972, *Objective Knowledge*, Clarendon Press, Oxford.

Posner, G. et al.: 1982, "Accommodation of a Scientific Conception : Toward a Theory of Conceptual Change," Science Education 66(2), 211–227.

Postman, N.: 1985, *Amusing Ourselves to Death*, Methuen, New York.

Poupard, P. (ed.): 1987, *Galileo Galilei: Toward a Resolution of 350 Years of Debate—1633–1983*, Duquesne University Press, Pittsburgh, PA.

Praagh, G. van (ed.): 1973, *H.E. Armstrong and Science Education: Selections from "The Teaching of Scientific Method" and Other Papers on Education*, John Murray, London.

Proper, H., Wideen, M. F. & Ivany, G.: 1988, "World View Projected by Science Teachers," Science Education 72(5), 542–560.

Pumfrey, S.: 1991, "History of Science in the British National Science Curriculum: A Critical Review of Resources and Their Aims," *British Journal for the History of Science* 24, 61–78.

Pyenson, L.: 1983, *Neohumanism and the Persistence of Pure Mathematics in Wilhelmian Germany*, American Philosophical Society, Philadelphia, PA.

———: 1985, *Cultural Imperialism and the Exact Sciences: German Expansion Overseas, 1900–1930*, Verlag Peter Lang, New York and Berne.

———: 1989, *Empire of Reason: Exact Sciences in Indonesia, 1840–1940*, E. J. Brill, Leiden.

———: 1992, "The Ideology of Western Rationality: History of Science and the European Civilizing Mission." In A. G. Moreno (ed.), *History of the Physical-*

Mathematical Sciences and the Teaching of Sciences, European Physical Society, Madrid, pp. 86–102. Reprinted in *Science & Education* 2(4) 329–344.

Quine, W. V. O.: 1953, *From a Logical Point of View*, Harper & Row, New York.

———: 1960, *Word and Object*, MIT Press, Cambridge, MA .

———: 1969, "Epistemology Naturalised." In his *Ontological Relativity and Other Essays*, Columbia University Press, New York.

Raizen, S. A.: 1991, "The Reform of Science Education in the U.S.A. Déjà Vu or De Nova," *Studies in Science Education* 19, 1–41.

Ramage, H. P.: 1983, "The Treatment of the Philosophy of Science in the *Science in Society* Project," *School Science Review* 64(229), 786–787.

Ray, C.: 1991, "Science Education, Philosophy of Science, and Scientific Prejudice," *Science Education* 75(1), 87–94.

Redondi, P.: 1988, *Galileo Heretic*, Allen Lane, London.

Reichenbach, H.: 1938, *Experience and Prediction*, University of Chicago Press, Chicago.

Resnick, L. B.: 1987, *Education and Learning to Think*, National Academy Press, Washington, DC.

Richmond, P. E. & Quraishi, A. R.: 1964, "Armstrong's Heuristic Method in 1964," *School Science Review* 45, 511–520.

Roberts, D. A.: 1982, "Developing the Concept of 'Curriculum Emphases' in Science Education," *Science Education* 66, 243–260.

Robin, N. & Ohlsson, S.: 1989, "Impetus Then and Now: A Detailed Comparison between Jean Buridan and a Single Contemporary Subject." In D. E. Herget (ed.), *The History and Philosophy of Science in Science Teaching*, Florida State University, Tallahassee, FL, pp. 292–305.

Robinson, J. T.: 1968, *The Nature of Science and Science Teaching*, Wadsworth, Belmont CA.

———: 1969, "Philosophy of Science: Implications for Teacher Education," *Journal of Research in Science Teaching* 6, 99–104.

Rogers, P. J.: 1982, "Epistemology and History in the Teaching of School Science," *European Journal of Science Education* 4(1), 1–10.

Romey, W. D. (ed.): 1968, *Inquiry Techniques for Teaching Science*, Prentice-Hall, Englewood Cliffs, NJ.

Rosenthal, D. B.: 1984, "Social Issues in High School Biology Textbooks: 1963–1983," *Journal of Research in Science Teaching* 21(8), 819–831.

———: 1985, "Biology Education in a Social and Moral Context." In R. W. Bybee (ed.), *Science, Technology, Society*, Yearbook of the National Science Teachers Association, NSTA, Washington, DC, pp. 102–116.

Rowell, J. A. & Cawthron, E. R.: 1982, "Images of Science: An Empirical Study," *European Journal of Science Education* 4(1), 79–94.

Rubba, P. et al.: 1991, "The Effects of Infusing STS Vignettes into the Genetics Unit of Biology on Learner Outcomes in STS and Genetics: A Report of Two Investigations," *Journal of Research in Science Teaching* 28(6), 537–552.

Ruse, M.: 1990, "Making Use of Creationism: A Case-study for the Philosophy of Science Classroom," *Studies in Philosophy and Education* 10(1), 81–92.

Russell, T. L.: 1981, "What History of Science, How Much and Why?" *Science Education* 65, 51–64.

Rutherford, F. J.: 1964, "The Role of Inquiry in Science Teaching," *Journal of Research in Science Teaching* 2, 80–84. Reprinted in W. D. Romey (ed.), *Inquiry Techniques for Teaching Science*, Prentice Hall, Englewood Cliffs, NJ, 1968, pp. 264–270.

——— & Ahlgren, A.: 1990, *Science for All Americans*, Oxford University Press, New York.

Sammis, J. H.: 1932, "A Plan for Introducing Biographical Material into Science Courses," *Journal of Chemical Education* 9, 900–902.

Schecker, H.: 1992, "The Paradigmatic Change in Mechanics: Implications of Historical Processes on Physics Education," *Science & Education* 1(1), 71–76.

Scheffler, I.: 1970, "Philosophy and the Curriculum." In his *Reason and Teaching*, London, Routledge, 1973, pp. 31–44. Reprinted in *Science & Education* 1(4), 285–294.

———: 1982, *Science and Subjectivity*, 2nd ed., Hackett, Indianapolis, IN. (1st ed. 1966)

Schilpp, P. A. (ed.): 1951, *Albert Einstein*, 2nd ed., Tudor, New York.

Schlagel, R.: 1986, *Contextual Realism: A Meta-physical Framework for Modern Science*, Paragon House, New York.

Schmitt, C. B.: 1967, "Experimental Evidence For and Against a Void: The Sixteenth-Century Arguments," *Isis* 58, 352–366.

Schneps, M. H.: 1987, *A Private Universe* [film], Harvard University, Cambridge, MA.

Schrödinger, E.: 1956, *What is Life? and Other Scientific Essays*, Cambridge University Press, Cambridge, UK.

Schwab, J. J.: 1945, "The Nature of Scientific Knowledge as Related to Liberal Education," *Journal of General Education* 3, 245–266. Reproduced in I. Westbury & N. J. Wilkof (eds.), *Joseph J. Schwab: Science, Curriculum, and Liberal Education*, University of Chicago Press, Chicago, 1978.

———: 1950, "The Natural Sciences: The Three Year Programme." In University of Chicago Faculty, *The Idea and Practice of General Education*, University of Chicago Press, Chicago.

———: 1962, "The Concept of the Structure of a Discipline," *Educational Record* 43, 197–205.

———: 1963, *Biology Teacher's Handbook*, Wiley, New York.

Science Council of Canada (SCC): 1984, *Science for Every Student: Educating Canadians for Tomorrow's World*, Report 36, SCC, Ottawa.

Segre, M.: 1991, *In the Wake of Galileo*, Rutgers University Press, New Brunswick, NJ.

Selin, H.: 1992, "Science Across Cultures: Introducing the Science, Technology and Medicine of Non-Western Cultures into the Classroom." In S. Hills (ed.), *The History and Philosophy of Science in Science Education*, vol.2, Queen's University, Kingston, Ontario, pp. 407–417.

———: 1993, *Science Across Cultures: A Bibliography of Books on Non-Western Science and Medicine*, Garland Press, New York.

Settle, T.: 1990, "How to Avoid Implying that Physicalism is True: A Problem for Teachers of Science," *International Journal of Science Education* 12(3), 258–264. Reproduced in M. R. Matthews (ed.), *History, Philosophy, and*

Science Teaching: Selected Readings, OISE Press, Toronto, 1991, pp. 225–234.

Shapere, D.: 1984a, "The Structure of Scientific Revolution," In his *Reason and the Search for Knowledge*, Reidel, Dordrecht, The Netherlands, pp. 37–48.

———: 1984b, "What can the Theory of Knowledge Learn from the History of Knowledge?" In his *Reason and the Search for Knowledge*, Reidel, Dordrecht, The Netherlands, 182–202.

Shapin, S.: 1982, "History of Science and Its Sociological Reconstructions," *History of Science* 22, 157–211.

——— & Schaffer, S.: 1985, *Leviathan and the Air-Pump: Hobbes, Boyle, and the Experimental Life*, Princeton University Press, Princeton, NJ.

Shea, W. R.: 1972, *Galileo's Intellectual Revolution*, Macmillan, London.

Sheehan, H.: 1985, *Marxism and the Philosophy of Science*, Humanities Press, Atlantic Highlands, NJ.

Sherratt, W. J.: 1982, "History of Science in the Science Curriculum: An Historical Perspective Part I" *School Science Review* 64, 225–236.

———: 1983, "History of Science in the Science Curriculum: An Historical Perspective Part II," *School Science Review* 64, 418–424.

Shimony, A.: 1976, "Comments on Two Epistemological Theses of Thomas Kuhn." In R. S. Cohen et al. (eds.), *Essays in Memory of Imre Lakatos*, Reidel, Dordrecht, The Netherlands, pp. 569–588.

Shortland, M. & Warwick, A. (eds.): 1989, *Teaching the History of Science*, Basil Blackwell, Oxford.

Shulman, L. S.: 1986, "Those Who Understand: Knowledge Growth in Teaching," *Educational Researcher* 15(2), 4–14.

——— & Keislar, E. R. (eds.): 1966, *Learning by Discovery: A Critical Appraisal*, Rand McNally, Chicago, IL.

Shymansky, J. A. et al.: 1983, "The Effects of New Science Curricula on Student Performance," *Journal of Research in Science Teaching* 20, 387–404.

——— et al.: 1990, "A Reassessment of the Effects of Inquiry-Based Science Curricula of the 1960s on Student Performance," *Journal of Research in Science Teaching* 27, 127–144.

——— & Kyle, W. C. (eds.): 1992, "Special Issue: Science Curriculum Reform," *Journal of Research in Science Teaching* 29(8).

Sibum, H. O.: 1988, "The Beginning of Electricity: Social and Scientific Origins and Experimental Setups." In C. Blondel & P. Brouzeng (eds.), *Science Education and the History of Physics*, Université Paris-Sud, Paris, pp. 139–146.

Siegel, H.: 1979a, "Can Psychology be Relevant to Epistemology?" *Philosophy of Education*, 55–64.

———: 1979b, "On the Distortion of the History of Science in Science Education," *Science Education* 63, 111–118.

———: 1987, *Relativism Refuted*, Reidel, Dordrecht, The Netherlands.

———: 1988, *Educating Reason: Rationality, Critical Thinking, and Education*, Routledge, London.

———: 1989a, "Epistemology, Critical Thinking, and Critical Thinking Pedagogy," *Argumentation* 3, 32–42.

———: 1989b, "The Rationality of Science, Critical Thinking, and Science Education," *Synthese* 80(1), 9–42. Reprinted in M. R. Matthews (ed.), *History, Philosophy, and Science Teaching: Selected Readings*, OISE Press, Toronto and Teachers College Press, New York 1991, pp. 45–62.

———: 1992, "Two Perspectives on Reason as an Educational Aim: The Rationality of Reasonableness," *Philosophy of Education 1991*, 225–233.

———: 1993, "Naturalized Philosophy of Science and Natural Science Education," *Science & Education* 2(1), 57–68.

Silverman, M. P.: 1992, "Raising Questions: Philosophical Significance of Controversy in Science," *Science & Education* 1(2), 163–180.

Simon, B.: 1971, *Intelligence, Psychology and Education: A Marxist Critique*, Lawrence & Wishart, London.

Slezak, P.: 1994, "Sociology of Scientific Knowledge and Science Education," *Science & Education* 3(3).

Smith, C., Carey, S. & Wiser, M.: 1985, "On Differentiation: A Case Study of the Development of Concepts of Size, Weight and Density," *Cognition* 21, 177–237.

Smith, G. H.: 1992, "Kura Kaupapa Maori Schooling: Implications for the Teaching of Science in New Zealand," unpublished paper, Education Department, University of Auckland.

Sneed, J. D.: 1979, *The Logical Structure of Mathematical Physics*, 2nd ed., Reidel, Dordrecht, The Netherlands.

Snow, C. P.: 1963, *The Two Cultures: A Second Look*, Cambridge University Press, Cambridge, UK. (Originally 1957.)

Solomon, J. (ed.): 1983, *Science in a Social Context*, Basil Blackwell, Oxford.

———: 1985, "Science in a Social Context: Details of a British High School Course." In R. W. Bybee (ed.), *Science, Technology, Society*, Yearbook of the National Science Teachers Association, NSTA, Washington, DC, pp. 144–157.

———: 1989a, *The Big Squeeze*, Association for Science Education, Hatfield Herts., UK.

———: 1989b, "Teaching the History of Science: Is Nothing Sacred?." In M. Shortland & A. Warwick (eds.), *Teaching the History of Science*, Basil Blackwell, Oxford, pp. 42–53.

———: 1991, "Teaching About the Nature of Science in the British National Curriculum," *Science Education* 75(1), 95–104.

Solomon, J.: 1993, *Teaching Science, Technology and Society,* Open University Press, Buckingham, UK.

Sorensen, R. A.: 1992, *Thought Experiments*, Oxford University Press, Oxford.

Souque, J-P.: 1988, "The Historical Epistemology of Gaston Bachelard and its Relevance to Science Education," *Thinking* 6(4), 8–13.

Stake, R. E. & Easley, J. A.: 1978, *Case Studies in Science Education* (vols.1, 2), US Government Printing Office, Washington, DC.

Stebbing, L. S.: 1937/1958, *Philosophy and the Physicists*, Dover Publications, New York.

Steen, W. J. van der: 1993, *A Practical Philosophy for the Life Sciences*, State University of New York Press, Albany, NY.

Stein, F.: 1989, "Project 2061: Education for a Changing Future." In D. E. Herget (ed.), *The History and Philosophy of Science in Science Teaching*, Florida State University, Tallahassee, FL, pp. 339–343.

Stein, H.: 1990, "On Locke, 'the Great Huygenius, and the Incomparable Mr. Newton'." In P. Bricker & R. I. G. Hughes (eds.), *Philosophical Perspectives on Newtonian Science*, MIT Press, Cambridge, MA, pp. 17–47.

Steinberg, M. S., Brown, D. E., & Clement, J.: 1990, "Genius is not Immune to Persistent Misconceptions: Conceptual Difficulties Impeding Isaac Newton and Contemporary Physics Students," *International Journal of Science Education* 12(3), 265–273.

Stenhouse, D.: 1985, *Active Philosophy in Education and Science*, Allen & Unwin, London.

———: 1986, "Conceptual Change in Science Education: Paradigms and Language Games," *Science Education* 70(4), 413–425.

Stevens, P: 1978, "On the Nuffield Philosophy of Science," *Journal of Philosophy of Education* 12, 99–111.

Stevenson, H. W., Lee, S. & Stigler, J. W.: 1986, "Mathematics Achievement of Chinese, Japanese and American Children," *Science* 231, 693–699.

———: 1992, "Learning from Asian Schools," *Scientific American* December, 32–38.

Stinner, A.: 1990, "Philosophy, Thought Experiments and Large Context Problems in the Secondary School Physics Course," *International Journal of Science* 12(3), 244–257.

——— & Williams, H.: 1993, "Conceptual Change, History, and Science Stories," *Interchange* 24(1–2), 87–104.

Strauss, S.(ed.): 1988, *Ontogeny, Phylogeny and Historical Development*, Ablex, Norwood.

Strike, K. A.: 1975, "The Logic of Learning by Discovery," *Review of Educational Research* 45, 461–483.

——— & Posner, G. J.: 1992, "A Revisionist Theory of Conceptual Change." In R. Duschl & R. Hamilton (eds.), *Philosophy of Science, Cognitive Psychology, and Educational Theory and Practice*, State University of New York Press, Albany, NY, pp. 147–176.

Suchting, W. A.: 1986, "Marx and the Problem of Knowledge." In his *Marx and Philosophy*, Macmillan, London, pp. 1–56.

———: 1992, "Constructivism Deconstructed," *Science & Education* 1(3), 223–254.

———: 1994, "Notes on the Cultural Significance of the Sciences," *Science & Education* 3(1) 1–56.

Summers, M. K.: 1982, "Philosophy of Science in the Science Teacher Education Curriculum," *European Journal of Science Education* 4, 19–28.

Sund, R. B. & Trowbridge, L. W.: 1967, *Teaching Science by Inquiry*, Charles Merrill, Columbus, OH.

Suppe, F. (ed.): 1977, *The Structure of Scientific Theories*, University of Illinois Press, Urbana, IL.

Sutton, C.: 1992, *Words, Science and Learning*, Open University Press, Buckingham, UK.

Swift, J. N.: 1988, "The Tyranny of Terminology: Biology," *The Science Teachers Bulletin* 60(2), 24–26.

Taub, L. C.: 1993, *Ptolemy's Universe: The Natural Philosophical and Ethical Foundations of Ptolemy's Astronomy*, Open Court, Chicago.

Taylor, L. W.: 1941, *Physics, the Pioneer Science*, Houghton and Mifflin, Boston. (Reprinted Dover, New York, 1959.)

Teichmann, J.: 1986a, "History of Physics and Physics Education in West Germany." In P. V. Thomsen (ed.), *Science Education and the History of Physics*, University of Aarhus, Denmark, pp. 252–255.

———: 1986b, "The Historical Experiment in Physics Education: Theoretical Observations and Practical Examples." In P. V. Thomsen (ed.), *Science Education and the History of Physics*, University of Aarhus, Denmark, pp. 189–221.

Terhart, E.: 1988, "Philosophy of Science and School Science Teaching," *International Journal of Science Education* 10, 11–16.

Thayer, H. S. (ed.): 1953, *Newton's Philosophy of Nature*, Macmillan, New York.

Thompson, J. J. (ed.): 1918, *Natural Science in Education*, HMSO, London. (Known as the *Thompson Report*.)

Thomsen, P. V. (ed.): 1986, *Science Education and the History of Physics*, University of Aarhus, Denmark.

Tobin, K. (ed.): 1993, *The Practice of Constructivism in Science and Mathematics Education*, AAAS Press, Washington, DC.

———: 1991, "Constructivist Perspectives on Research in Science Education," paper presented at the annual meeting of the National Association for Research in Science Teaching, Lake Geneva, WI.

Toulmin, S. E.: 1953, *The Philosophy of Science: An Introduction*, Hutchinson, London.

——— (ed.): 1970, *Physical Reality: Philosophical Essays on Twentieth-Century Physics*, Harper & Row, New York.

Tozer, S., Anderson, T. H., & Armbruster, B. B. (eds.): 1990, *Foundational Studies in Teacher Education: A Reexamination*, Teachers College Press, New York.

Urevbu, A. O.: 1987, "School Science in South Africa: An Assessment of the Pedagogic Impact of Third World Investment," *International Journal of Science Education* 9(1), 3–12.

Veblen, T.: 1969, *The Higher Learning in America*, Hill & Wang, New York.

Vedin, L-G.: 1986, "National Summary and Recommendations (Sweden)." In P. V. Thomsen (ed.), *Science Education and the History of Physics*, University of Aarhus, Denmark.

Vygotsky, L. S.: 1962, *Thought and Language*, MIT Press, Cambridge, MA.

———: 1978, *Mind in Society: The Development of Higher Psychological Processes*, Harvard University Press, Cambridge, MA.

Wagenschein, M.: 1962, *Die Pädagogische Dimension der Physik*, Westermann, Braunschweig.

Waks, L. J.: 1968, "Knowledge and Understanding as Educational Aims," *The Monist* 52, 104–119.

Wandersee, J. H.: 1985, "Can the History of Science Help Science Educators Anticipate Students' Misconceptions?" *Journal of Research in Science Teaching* 23(7), 581–597.

———: 1990, "On the Value and Use of the History of Science in Teaching Today's Science: Constructing Historical Vignettes." In D. E. Herget (ed.),

More History and Philosophy of Science in Science Teaching, Florida State University, Tallahassee, FL, pp. 278–283.

Waring, M.: 1979, *Social Pressures and Curriculum Innovation: A Study of the Nuffield Foundation Science Teaching Project*, Methuen, London.

Wartofsky, M. W.: 1968, "Metaphysics as a Heuristic for Science." In R. S. Cohen & M. W. Wartofsky (eds.), *Boston Studies in the Philosophy of Science 3*, 123–172. Republished in his *Models*, Reidel, Dordrecht, The Netherlands, 1979, pp. 40–89.

———: 1976, "The Relation Between Philosophy of Science and History of Science." In R. S. Cohen, P. K. Feyerabend & M. W. Wartofsky (eds.), *Essays in Memory of Imre Lakatos*, Reidel, Dordrecht, The Netherlands. Republished in his *Models*, Reidel, Dordrecht, The Netherlands, 1979, pp. 119–139.

———: 1979, "The Model Muddle: Proposals for an Immodest Realism." In his *Models: Representation and Scientific Understanding*, Reidel, Dordrecht, The Netherlands, pp. 1–11.

Weiher, C. F.: 1967, "To Define Motion," *New Scholasticism* 41, 58–78.

Weiss, I. R.: 1978, *Report of the 1977 National Survey of Science Mathematics and Social Studies Education*, US Government Printing Office, Washington, DC.

Welch, W. W.: 1973, "Review of the Research and Evaluation Program of Harvard Project Physics," *Journal of Research in Science Teaching* 10, 365–378.

———: 1979, "Twenty Years of Science Education Development: A Look Back," *Review of Research in Education* 7, 282–306.

———: 1981 "Inquiry in School Science." In N. C. Harms & R. E. Yager (eds.), *What Research Says to the Science Teacher*, vol. 3, NSTA, Washington, DC, pp. 53–72.

——— & Walberg, H. W. A.: 1972, "A National Experiment in Curriculum Evaluation," *American Educational Research Journal* 9, 373–383.

Wellington, J. J.: 1981, "What's Supposed to Happen, Sir?—Some Problems with Discovery Learning," *School Science Review* 63(222), 167–173.

Wenham, E. J., et al.: 1972, *Physics Concepts and Models*, Addison-Wesley, London.

Wenham, M.: 1987, "Singular Problems in Science and Science Education," *Journal of Philosophy of Education* 21(1), 47–58.

Westaway, F. W.: 1929, *Science Teaching*, Blackie and Son, London.

Westbury, I. & Wilkof, N. J. (eds.): 1978, *Joseph J. Schwab: Science, Curriculum, and Liberal Education*, University of Chicago Press, Chicago.

Westfall, R. S.: 1980, *Never at Rest: A Biography of Isaac Newton*, Cambridge University Press, Cambridge, UK.

Wheatley, G. H.: 1991, "Constructivist Perspectives on Science and Mathematics Learning," *Science Education* 75(1), 9–22.

Whewell, W.: 1840/1947, *Philosophy of the Inductive Sciences*, London.

———: 1855, "On the Influence of the History of Science upon Intellectual Education." In *Lectures on Education Delivered at the Royal Institution of Great Britain, 1854*, J. W. Parker & Son, London.

Whitaker, M. A. B.: 1979, "History & Quasi-history in Physics Education Parts I, II," *Physics Education* 14, 108–112, 239–242.

Whitaker, R. J.: 1983, "Aristotle is Not Dead: Student Understanding of Trajectory Motion," *American Journal Physics* 51(4), 352–357.

White, L.: 1962, *Medieval Technology and Social Change*, Oxford University Press, Oxford.

————: 1966, "Pumps and Pendula: Galileo and Technology." In C. L. Golino (ed.), *Galileo Reappraised*, University of California Press, Berkeley, CA, pp. 96–110.

White, R. T. & Gunstone, R. F.: 1989, "Metalearning and Conceptual Change," *International Journal of Science Education* 11, 577–586.

Whitehead, A. N.: 1947, "Technical Education and Its Relation to Science and Literature." In his *The Aims of Education and Other Essays*, Williams & Norgate, London.

Wicken, J. S.: 1976, "The Value of Historical Concepts in Science Education," *Journal of Chemical Education* 53, 96–97.

Wilson, E. O.: 1978, *On Human Nature*, Bantam Books, New York.

Winchester, I.: 1990, "Thought Experiments and Conceptual Revision in Science," *Studies in Philosophy and Education* 10(1), 73–80. Reprinted in M. R. Matthews (ed.), *History, Philosophy, and Science Teaching: Selected Readings*, OISE Press, Toronto and Teachers College Press, New York 1991.

Wiser, M. & Carey, S.: 1983, "When Heat and Temperature were One." In D. Gentner and A. L. Stevens (eds.), *Mental Models*, Lawrence Erlbaum, Hillsdale, NJ, pp. 271–297.

Wolf, F. A.: 1981, *Taking the Quantum Leap*, Harper & Row, New York.

Wolpert, L.: 1992, *The Unnatural Nature of Science*, Faber & Faber, London.

Woodhouse, H. & Ndognko, T.M.: 1993, "Women, Science Education, and Development in Cameroon: A Critical Study," *Interchange* 24(1–2), 131–158.

Woodhull, J. F.: 1910, "The Teaching of Physical Science," *Teachers College Record* 11(1), 1–82.

Woolgar, S.: 1986, "On the Alleged Distinction Between Discourse and *Praxis*," *Social Studies of Science* 16, 309–317.

Woolnough, B. E. (ed.): 1987, "Special Issue: Physics and Faith," *Physics Education* 22.

Yager, R. E.: 1984, "The Major Crisis in Science Education," *School Science and Mathematics* 84(3), 189–198.

———— (ed.): 1993, *The Science, Technology, Society Movement*, National Science Teachers Association, Washington, DC.

———— & Bonstetter, R. J.: 1984, "Student Perceptions of Science Teachers, Classes, and Course Content," *School Science and Mathematics* 84(5), 406–414.

———— & Penick, J. E.: 1985, "Taking New Goals for School Science Seriously," *Educational Leadership* 42(8), 86–87.

———— & Penick, J. E.: 1987, "Resolving the Crisis in Science Education: Understanding Before Resolution," *Science Education* 71(1), 49–55.

———— & Penick, J. E.: 1990, "Science Teacher Education." In W. R. Houston (ed.), *Handbook of Research on Teacher Education*, Macmillan, New York, pp. 657–673.

Yeany, R. H.: 1991, "A Unifying Theme in Science Education?" *NARST News* 33(2), 1–3.

Young, M. F. D.: 1976, "The Schooling of Science." In G. Whitty & M. F. D. Young (eds.), *Explorations in the Politics of School Knowledge*, Nafferton Books, Driffield, UK, pp. 47–61.

———— (ed.): 1971, *Knowledge and Control*, Collier Macmillan, London.

Ziman, J.: 1978, *Reliable Knowledge: An Exploration of the Grounds for Belief in Science,* Cambridge University Press, Cambridge.

Ziman, J.: 1980, *Teaching and Learning about Science and Society*, Cambridge University Press, Cambridge, UK.

Zukav, G.: 1979, *The Dancing Wu Li Masters*, Fontana, London.

Further Reading

The following works could be useful for those wanting an introduction to the themes of this book: science education, history and philosophy of science, and philosophy of education.

Amsterdamski, S.: 1975, *Between Experience and Metaphysics*, Reidel, Dordrecht, The Netherlands.

Bantock, G. H.: 1981, *The Parochialism of the Present*, Routledge & Kegan Paul, London.

Barrow, R. & Woods, R.: 1988, *An Introduction to Philosophy of Education*, Routledge, London, 3rd ed.

Brown, H. I.: 1979, *Perception, Theory and Commitment: The New Philosophy of Science*, University of Chicago Press, Chicago.

Bybee, R. W. et al. (eds.): 1992, *Teaching About the History and Nature of Science and Technology: Background Papers*, BSCS/SSEC, Colorado Springs, CO.

Bybee, R. W.: 1993, *Reforming Science Education: Social Perspectives and Personal Reflections,* Teachers College Press, New York.

Chalmers, A. F.: 1976, *What Is This Thing Called Science?* University of Queensland Press, St Lucia, Queensland, Australia.

————: 1990, *Science and its Fabrication*, Open University Press, Milton Keynes,

Cromer, A.: 1993, *Uncommon Sense: The Heretical Nature of Science,* Oxford University Press, New York.

DeBoer, G. E.: 1991, *A History of Ideas in Science Education*, Teachers College Press, New York.

Duschl, R. A.: 1990, *Restructuring Science Education: The Importance of Theories and Their Development*, Teachers College Press, New York.

———— & Hamilton, R. J. (eds.): 1992, *Philosophy of Science, Cognitive Psychology, and Educational Theory and Practice*, State University of New York Press, Albany, NY.

Fensham, P. (ed.): 1988, *Development and Dilemmas in Science Education*, Falmer Press, London.

Giere, R. N.: 1984, *Understanding Scientific Reasoning*, Holt, Rinehart and Winston, New York.

Gjertsen, D.: 1989, *Science and Philosophy: Past and Present*, Penguin, Harmondsworth, UK.

Goodman, D. & Russell, C. A.: 1991, *The Rise of Scientific Europe*, Hodder & Stoughton, London.

Martin, J. R.: 1994, *Changing the Educational Landscape*, Routledge, New York.

Martin, M.: 1972, *Concepts of Science Education*, Scott, Foresman & Co., New York (Reprinted, University Press of America, 1985).

Matthews, M. R.: 1980, *A Marxist Theory of Schooling: A Study in Epistemology and Education*, Harvester Press, Brighton, UK.

—— (ed.): 1989, *The Scientific Background to Modern Philosophy*, Hackett Publishing Company, Indianapolis, IN.

—— (ed.): 1991, *History, Philosophy and Science Teaching: Selected Readings*, OISE Press, Toronto.

Ronan, C. A.: 1982, *Science: Its History and Development Among the World's Cultures*, Facts on File Publications, New York.

Siegel, H.: 1988, *Educating Reason: Rationality, Critical Thinking, and Education*, Routledge, London.

Steen, W. J. van der: 1993, *A Practical Philosophy for the Life Sciences*, State University of New York Press, Albany, NY.

Wolpert, L.: 1992, *The Unnatural Nature of Science*, Faber & Faber, London.

Yager, R. E. (ed.): 1993, *The Science, Technology, Society Movement*, National Science Teachers Association, Washington, DC.

Ziman, J.: 1980, *Teaching and Learning about Science and Society*, Cambridge University Press, Cambridge, UK.

Addresses

The following organizations and associations have been mentioned in the text. Inquiries can be made to the addresses given for materials, publications, newsletters, membership and so on.

National Science Foundation
NSF
1800 G Street NW
Washington, DC 20550
USA

National Science Teachers Association
NSTA
1742 Connecticut Ave, NW
Washington, DC 20009
USA

US History of Science Society
The Executive Secretary
History of Science Society
University of Washington
Seattle, WA 98195
USA

US History of Science Society,
Education Committee
Dr David Rhees
The Bakken Museum
3537 Zenith Ave., South
Minneapolis, MN 55416
USA

US Philosophy of Science Association
The Executive Secretary
Philosophy of Science Association

Department of Philosophy
Michigan State University
East Lansing, MI 48824–1032
USA

Biological Sciences Curriculum Study
(BSCS)
BSCS
830 North Tejon Street 405
Colorado Springs, CO 80903
USA

American Association for the Advance-
ment of Science, Project 2061
Project 2061
AAAS
1333 H Street, N.W.
Washington DC 20005
USA

National Association for Research in
Science Teaching (NARST)
Dr John R. Staver
219 Bluemont Hall
Kansas State University
Manhattan, KS 66506
USA

Philosophy of Education Society (USA)

Professor Paul A. Wagner
School of Education, 269
University of Houston—Clear Lake
Houston, TX 77058–1098
USA

British Society for the History of Science

The Secretary, BSHS
31 High Street
Stanford in the Vale
Faringdon
Oxon. SN7 8LH
UK

British Society for the History of Science, Education Committee

Dr Isobel Falconer
Lumbo Farmhouse
St Andrews
Fife, KY16 8NS
UK

Association for Science Education (ASE)

ASE
College Lane
Hatfield
Hertfordshire, AL10 9AA
UK

European Physical Society, History of Physics and Physics Teaching Group.

Professor Fabio Bevilacqua
Dipartimento di Fisica, "A.Volta"
Universita di Pavia
Via A.Bassi 6
27100 Pavia
ITALY

International Organisation for Science and Technology Education (IOSTE)

Prof Glen S. Aikenhead
College of Education
University of Saskatchewan
Saskatoon, Sas. S7N OWO
CANADA

International Network of Philosophers of Education

Professor Dr Paul Smeyers
Faculty of Psychology and Pedagogy
in Education
Catholic University
Tiensestraat 102
3000 Leuven
BELGIUM

International Network for Information in Science and Technology Education

INISTE Secretariat
ED/STE
Unesco
7, place de Fontenoy
75700 Paris
FRANCE

International Society for the History, Philosophy, and Social Studies of Biology

The Secretary, IS/HPSSB
Science Studies Center
VPI & SU
Blacksburg, VA 24061–0247
USA

International History, Philosophy, and Science Teaching Group

Dr Michael R. Matthews
School of Education Studies
UNSW
Kensington
NSW 2033
AUSTRALIA

Index